D1233377

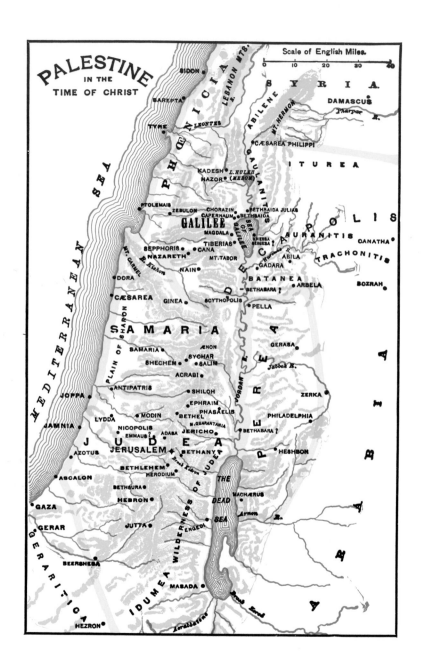

PALESTINE
IN THE
TIME OF CHRIST

Scale of English Miles.
0   10   20   30   40

A Harmony of the Gospels

for

HISTORICAL STUDY

AN ANALYTICAL SYNOPSIS
OF THE FOUR GOSPELS

by

WILLIAM ARNOLD STEVENS
Professor of New Testament Interpretation
ROCHESTER THEOLOGICAL SEMINARY

ERNEST DE WITT BURTON
Professor of New Testament Interpretation
UNIVERSITY OF CHICAGO

CHARLES SCRIBNER'S SONS *New York*

PREFACE TO THE FIRST EDITION.

THIS Harmony, like the small Outline Handbook of the Life of Christ which preceded it, is intended to promote and facilitate the historical study of the gospels. The Life of Christ is now engaging the attention of Biblical scholars to a remarkable degree. In the decades that followed the publication of Strauss's Life of Jesus in 1835 the literature of the subject was chiefly controversial. An apologetic motive was manifestly dominant in the powerful works of Neander, Ebrard, and Lange. At present it is the subject itself that commands attention. There is a deepening conviction that in Biblical science, and indeed in Christian theology as a whole, the study of the Life of Christ should be made primary and central. Books upon the subject are increasing in number. But it is to be remembered that the principal textbook is the fourfold gospel. The study of the Life of Christ is primarily the historical study of the four gospels, which implies the tracing of the events they narrate in their chronological sequence and in their organic connection. For this purpose a constant comparison of the four narratives is necessary, and a synopsis or harmony becomes in the very nature of the case indispensable.

In accordance with current usage we have used the title "Harmony," although, as frequently happens with technical terms, it is likely to convey to the general reader a sense not intended. To some it may perhaps require explanation that the proper object of a harmony of the gospels is not to harmonize them, if by that is meant bringing them into agreement. It is simply an arrangement by which the corresponding parts of different documents may be brought together before the eye and compared—a method not peculiar to Biblical study, but familiar to all students of literary and historical documents.

Accordingly we have made no attempt to harmonize what is not harmonious, but simply to exhibit the facts. Whatever discrepancies the four narratives contain, we have preferred to let the printed page display them equally with the agreements, rather than adopt an arrangement or a dissection which should withdraw them from view. Wherein the four writers differ, and how they differ, is precisely what the intelligent reader wishes to know; eventually he comes to value their writings even more for their differences than for their verbally exact agreements.

Still it is not to be forgotten that thus far every effort to accentuate their disagreement has only strengthened the impression of their concord as historical documents. The most powerful of all arguments for the substantial truthfulness of the witnessing evangelists is to be found in the self-consistency and verisimilitude of the history, when exhibited in a harmony constructed according to the principles indicated in this preface. If, after a century of modern criticism of the gospels, it is found that, despite all differences, the four mutually supplement and mutually interpret one another, so that from their complex combination there emerges *one* narrative, outlining a distinct historical figure, and producing upon the mind an irresistible impression of reality, it is difficult to imagine a more convincing attestation of the records on which the Christian church bases its faith in the person and work of its Founder than is furnished by this very fact.

If it be asked what distinctive features the present Harmony possesses to justify the adding of another to the already long list of books of this general class, the answer must be found, if at all, in the following three characteristics, which have been partly indicated above: (1) It is planned with special reference to the historical study of the gospels, rather than to the minute verbal comparison of parallel sections. (2) It endeavors, while exhibiting the parallelism of the gospels, paragraph by paragraph, at the same time to preserve, as far as is consistent with this endeavor, the structure and peculiarities of the several gospels; aiming not to indicate the solution of all harmonistic problems, but, as far as is possible consistently with the construction of a harmony at all, to leave all these problems where the gospels themselves leave them. (3) It is designed to render special assistance in the study of Christ's discourses and sayings, and this both in respect to the individual unity of the reports of them, and in respect to the parallelism of these reports one with another.

We have spoken of certain new features of the book as marking its individuality, and in a measure justifying its appearance. We do not, however, forget that in every true book it is the old that is best. If a correct historical combination of the gospels is approximately possible today, it is because Christian scholarship, from Tatian's Diatessaron down, has contributed toward its production. We have sought to use all accessible helps, ancient and modern. Our greatest debt to contemporary works of similar purpose with our own is, first, to the Harmony of Edward Robinson, and, next, to the Life of Our Lord by Samuel J. Andrews, a work into which has gone a lifetime of scholarly research, and to which all students of the Life of Christ are under large obligation. Equally great is our debt, though of a different kind, to the two volumes of Westcott and Hort's Greek New Testament, particularly for the light they have thrown on the textual character and structural peculiarities of the gospel histories. Nor can we fail to acknowledge, though without singling out individual names, our indebtedness to those scholars who have labored in the solution of the intricate question known as the synoptic problem. So intimate is the relation between this problem and that of the harmony that the two must almost of necessity be carried toward their final solution together. To Rev. Erastus Blakeslee of Boston is due the acknowledgment that but for his suggestion and urgency we should scarcely have undertaken the publication of this result of our study of the gospel history at this time, and that in the perfecting of the nomenclature of the Analytical Outline, particularly of the chapter-divisions, we are indebted to him for valuable suggestions.

In so far as the present work shall contribute to the right understanding of the relations of the gospels to one another, and more especially to a right apprehension of the life and teachings of our Lord Jesus Christ, the object in view in its preparation will have been attained.

WM. ARNOLD STEVENS.
ERNEST D. BURTON.

CHRISTMAS, ANNO DOMINI 1893.

PREFACE TO THE THIRD EDITION.

THE present edition represents a thorough revision, and is printed from new plates. The book has, however, undergone no radical change in form or character. The alterations are chiefly due to a more thorough application of the principles in accordance with which the first edition was constructed. We have from the beginning regarded it as our fundamental task to exhibit the testimony of the evangelists themselves. Our object has been, not by ingenuity to devise an order of events seemingly more probable than that of the evangelists, but with the utmost possible fidelity, consistently with the construction of a harmony at all, to present the history as they narrate it, both in matter and order. Without assuming that this order is for Biblical science a finality, we yet recognize that it must be the basis of any effort to reproduce the chronological order of the events in the life of Jesus, holding as we do that the gospel narratives are not mere collections of detached reminiscences, but are rather material from which the sequences of history are approximately recoverable.

While seeking to apply the principle above stated even more consistently and thoroughly than in the first edition, we have also endeavored to avoid unnecessary changes, having regard to those studies in the Life of Christ which have been based on the first edition of the Harmony.

The number and order of sections remain unchanged.

A change affecting the content of sections 29, 30 was made in the revised edition of 1902. Changes of a similar character have in this edition been made in sections 52, 55, 87, 94.

Changes of title have been made in sections 94, 95, 127.

A slight rearrangement of paragraphs has been made in section 133, the Last Supper.

In three instances, affecting six sections (27, 36, 55, 62, 87, 121), narratives similar to those constituting the proper content of the section, but assigned to a different position by the evangelist recording them, have been printed in parallel columns, being set in smaller type and inclosed in brackets to indicate that they are presented at this point for purposes of comparison only.

The list of the Repeated Sayings of Christ has been still further enlarged. In a few cases we have availed ourselves of a blank space in one of the columns of the page to print certain of the longer of these sayings in a form more convenient for their detailed comparison.

A third margin has been added to the page, showing the renderings adopted in the text of the American Revised Version of 1901.

In the interest of simplicity, a slight change has been made in the use of brackets.

Fuller explanation of all these matters will be found in Appendix I in connection with the detailed statement of the principles and methods followed in the construction of the Harmony, which in the first edition was included in the Preface.

The material which, originally appearing in the "Handbook of the Life of Christ," no longer in print, was transferred to this book in the revised edition of 1902, is retained in the present edition, constituting Appendices IV, V, VI.

CONTENTS.

	PAGE
Principal Divisions of the Harmony	1
Analytical Outline of the Four Gospels	3
Index to the Analytical Outline and Harmony	15
Text of the Harmony	19

Appendices

Appendix I. Principles and Methods of Construction 249

Appendix II. Sayings of Christ Assigned by the Evangelists to More than One Occasion 260

Appendix III. Old Testament Quotations in the Gospels 272

Appendix IV. Method of Study 278

Appendix V. Principal Divisions of the Life of Christ, with Calendar Dates 280

Appendix VI. Leading Events of Jewish History 281

PRINCIPAL DIVISIONS OF THE HARMONY.

PART I.—**THE THIRTY YEARS OF PRIVATE LIFE**: From the Birth of Jesus until the Coming of John the Baptist.

PART II.—**THE OPENING EVENTS OF CHRIST'S MINISTRY**: From the Coming of John the Baptist until the Public Appearance of Jesus in Jerusalem.

PART III.—**THE EARLY JUDEAN MINISTRY**: From the Public Appearance of Jesus in Jerusalem until his Return to Galilee.

PART IV.—**FIRST PERIOD OF THE GALILEAN MINISTRY**: From the Return to Galilee until the Choosing of the Twelve.

PART V.—**SECOND PERIOD OF THE GALILEAN MINISTRY**: From the Choosing of the Twelve until the Withdrawal into Northern Galilee.

PART VI.—**THIRD PERIOD OF THE GALILEAN MINISTRY**: From the Withdrawal into Northern Galilee until the Final Departure for Jerusalem.

PART VII.—**THE PEREAN MINISTRY**: From the Final Departure from Galilee until the Final Arrival in Jerusalem.

PART VIII.—**THE PASSION WEEK**: From the Final Arrival in Jerusalem until the Resurrection.

PART IX.—**THE FORTY DAYS**: From the Resurrection to the Ascension.

ANALYTICAL OUTLINE OF THE FOUR GOSPELS.

ARRANGED IN PARTS, CHAPTERS, AND SECTIONS.*

PART I.

THE THIRTY YEARS OF PRIVATE LIFE.

FROM THE BIRTH OF JESUS UNTIL THE COMING OF JOHN THE BAPTIST.

Chapter I. Introductory.

SECTION.

1. Prologue of John's gospel.
Jo. 1:1–18.

2. Preface of Luke's gospel.
Lu. 1:1–4.

3. The two genealogies.
Mt. 1:1–17.
Lu. 3:23–38.

Chapter II. The Annunciations.

4. Birth of John the Baptist promised.
Lu. 1:5–25.

5. The annunciation to Mary.
Lu. 1:26–38.

6. The annunciation to Joseph.
Mt. 1:18–25.

7. Mary's visit to Elisabeth.
Lu. 1:39–56.

Chapter III. Birth of John the Baptist and of Jesus.

8. Birth of John the Baptist.
Lu. 1:57–80.

9. Birth of Jesus the Christ.
⌐Mt. 1:18–25.⌐
Lu. 2:1–7.

10. The angels and the shepherds.
Lu. 2:8–20.

* For the use of brackets and half brackets see Appendix I.

Chapter IV.   The Infancy of Jesus.

SECTION.

11. The circumcision.

Lu. 2:21.

12. The presentation in the temple.

Lu. 2:22–39.

13. The Wise-men from the East.
      Mt. 2:1–12.

14. The flight into Egypt and return to Nazareth.
      Mt. 2:13–23.

Chapter V.   Jesus' Life in Nazareth.

15. Childhood at Nazareth.
      ⌐Mt. 2:23.¬   Lu. 2: ⌐39¬ 40.

16. Visit to Jerusalem when twelve years old.

Lu. 2:41–50.

17. Eighteen years at Nazareth.

Lu. 2:51, 52.

PART II.

THE OPENING EVENTS OF CHRIST'S MINISTRY.

FROM THE COMING OF JOHN THE BAPTIST UNTIL THE PUBLIC APPEARANCE OF JESUS IN JERUSALEM.

Chapter VI.   The Beginnings of the Gospel.

18. The ministry of John the Baptist.
      Mt. 3:1–12.   Mk. 1:1–8.   Lu. 3:1–20.

19. The baptism of Jesus.
      Mt. 3:13–17.   Mk. 1:9–11.   Lu. 3:21, 22 ⌐23a¬

20. The temptation in the wilderness.
      Mt. 4:1–11.   Mk. 1:12, 13.   Lu. 4:1–13.

Chapter VII.   The Beginnings of Faith.

21. John's testimony before the priests and Levites.

Jo. 1:19–28.

22. Jesus the Lamb of God.

Jo. 1:29–34.

SECTION.

23. The first three disciples.

                                            Jo. 1:35–42.

24. Philip and Nathanael.

                                            Jo. 1:43–51.

25. The first miracle: water made wine

                                            Jo. 2:1–11.

26. Sojourn in Capernaum.

                                            Jo. 2:12.

PART III.

THE EARLY JUDEAN MINISTRY.

FROM THE PUBLIC APPEARANCE OF JESUS IN JERUSALEM UNTIL HIS RETURN TO GALILEE.

Chapter VIII. The Beginnings of Christ's Work in Jerusalem.

27. First cleansing of the temple.

                                            Jo. 2:13–22.

28. Discourse with Nicodemus.

                                            Jo. 2:23—3:21.

Chapter IX. Period of Preaching and Baptizing in Judea.

29. Christ baptizing in Judea.

                                            Jo. 3:22–24.

30. John's testimony to Christ at Ænon.

                                            Jo. 3:25–36.

Chapter X. The Two Days' Ministry in Samaria.

31. The departure from Judea.
  ⌈Mt. 4:12.⌉   ⌈Mk. 1:14.⌉   Jo. 4:1–3.

32. Discourse with the woman of Samaria.

                                            Jo. 4:4–26.

33. The gospel in Sychar.

                                            Jo. 4:27–42.

PART IV.

FIRST PERIOD OF THE GALILEAN MINISTRY.

From the Return to Galilee until the Choosing of the Twelve.

Chapter XI.   The Beginnings of Christ's Public Work in Galilee.

SECTION.

34. The beginning of Christ's Galilean ministry.
   Mt. 4:12 [13–16] 17.   Mk. 1:14, 15.   Lu. 4:14, 15.   Jo. 4:43–45.

35. The nobleman's son.
   Jo. 4:46–54.

36. First rejection at Nazareth.
   Lu. 4:16–30.

37. Removal to Capernaum.
   ⌈Mt. 4:13–16.⌉   ⌈Lu. 4:31a.⌉

Chapter XII.   Call of the Four, and the First Preaching Tour.

38. The call of the Four.
   Mt. 4:18–22.   Mk. 1:16–20.   Lu. 5:1–11.

39. A day of miracles in Capernaum.
   Mt. 8:14–17.   Mk. 1:21–34.   Lu. 4:31–41.

40. First preaching tour in Galilee.
   ⌈Mt. 4:23.⌉   Mk. 1:35–45.   Lu. 4:42–44.
   Mt. 8:[1] 2–4   Lu. 5:12–16.

Chapter XIII.   Growing Hostility of the Scribes and Pharisees.

41. The paralytic borne of four.
   Mt. 9:[1] 2–8.   Mk. 2:1–12.   Lu. 5:17–26.

42. The call of Matthew.
   Mt. 9:9–13.   Mk. 2:13–17.   Lu. 5:27–32.

43. The question about fasting.
   Mt. 9:14–17.   Mk. 2:18–22.   Lu. 5:33–39.

44. The infirm man at the pool of Bethesda.
   Jo., chap. 5.

45. The disciples plucking grain.
   Mt. 12:1–8.   Mk. 2:23–28.   Lu. 6:1–5.

46. The man with the withered hand.
   Mt. 12:9–14.   Mk. 3:1–6.   Lu. 6:6–11.

PART V.

SECOND PERIOD OF THE GALILEAN MINISTRY.

From the Choosing of the Twelve until the Withdrawal into Northern Galilee.

Chapter XIV.   Organization of the Kingdom.

SECTION.

47. The wide-spread fame of Christ.
    Mt. 4:23–25.   Mk. 3:7–12.   ⌜Lu. 6:17–19.⌝
    Mt. 12:15–21.

48. The choosing of the Twelve.
    ⌜Mt. 10:2–4.⌝   Mk. 3:13–19a.   Lu. 6:12–19.

49. The sermon on the mount.
    Mt., chaps. 5, 6, 7, ⌜8:1⌝.   Lu. 6:20–49.

Chapter XV.   The Second Preaching Tour.

50. The centurion's servant.
    Mt. 8:5–13.   Lu. 7:1–10.

51. The raising of the widow's son at Nain.
    Lu. 7:11–17.

52. John the Baptist's last message.
    Mt. 11:2–30.   Lu. 7:18–35.

53. Anointing of Jesus in the house of Simon the Pharisee.
    Lu. 7:36–50.

54. Christ's companions on his second preaching tour.
    Lu. 8:1–3.

Chapter XVI.   A Day of Teaching by the Sea of Galilee.

55. Warnings to the scribes and Pharisees: "an eternal sin."
    Mt. 12:22–45.   Mk. 3:19b–30.

56. The true kindred of Christ.
    Mt. 12:46–50.   Mk. 3:31–35.   Lu. 8:19–21.

57. The parables by the sea.
    Mt. 13:1–53.   Mk. 4:1–34.   Lu. 8:4–18.

Chapter XVII.   A Day of Miracles by the Sea of Galilee.

58. The stilling of the tempest.
    Mt. 8:⌜18⌝23–27.   Mk. 4:35–41.   Lu. 8:22–25.

7

SECTION.

59. The Gadarene demoniacs.
    Mt. 8:28–34.   Mk. 5:1–20.   Lu. 8:26–39.
60. The raising of Jaïrus's daughter.
    Mt. 9:ᴛ1ᴚ18–26.   Mk. 5:21–43.   Lu. 8:40–56.
61. The two blind men, and the dumb demoniac.
    Mt. 9:27–34.

Chapter XVIII.   The Third Preaching Tour.

62. Second rejection at Nazareth.
    Mt. 13:54–58.   Mk. 6:1–6*a*.
63. Third preaching tour continued.
    Mt. 9:35.   Mk. 6:6*b*.
64. The mission of the Twelve.
    Mt. 9:36—11:1.   Mk. 6:7–13.   Lu. 9:1–6.
65. Death of John the Baptist.
    Mt. 14:1–12.   Mk. 6:14–29.   Lu. 9:7–9.

Chapter XIX.   The Crisis at Capernaum.

66. The feeding of the five thousand.
    Mt. 14:13–23.   Mk. 6:30–46.   Lu. 9:10–17.   Jo. 6:1–15.
67. Jesus walking on the water.
    Mt. 14:24–36.   Mk. 6:47–56.   Jo. 6:16–21.
68. Discourse on the Bread of Life.
                                                  Jo. 6:22–71.
69. Discourse on eating with unwashen hands.
    Mt. 15:1–20.   Mk. 7:1–23.

PART VI.

THIRD PERIOD OF THE GALILEAN MINISTRY.

FROM THE WITHDRAWAL INTO NORTHERN GALILEE UNTIL THE FINAL DEPARTURE
FOR JERUSALEM.

Chapter XX.   The First Northern Journey for Retirement.

70. Journey toward Tyre and Sidon; the Syrophœnician woman's daughter.
    Mt. 15:21–28.   Mk. 7:24–30.
71. Return through Decapolis; many miracles of healing.
    Mt. 15:29–31.   Mk. 7:31–37.

Chapter XXI.   A Brief Return to the Sea of Galilee.

SECTION.

72. The feeding of the four thousand.
Mt. 15:32–38.   Mk. 8:1–9.

73. The Pharisees and Sadducees demanding a sign from heaven.
Mt. 15:39—16:12.   Mk. 8:10–21.

74. The blind man near Bethsaida.
Mk. 8:22–26.

Chapter XXII.   The Second Northern Journey for Retirement.

75. Peter's confession.
Mt. 16:13–20.   Mk. 8:27–30.   Lu. 9:18–21.

76. Christ foretells his death and resurrection.
Mt. 16:21–28.   Mk. 8:31—9:1.   Lu. 9:22–27.

77. The transfiguration.
Mt. 17:1–13.   Mk. 9:2–13.   Lu. 9:28–36.

78. The demoniac boy.
Mt. 17:14–20.   Mk. 9:14–29.   Lu. 9:37–43a.

79. Christ again foretells his death and resurrection.
Mt. 17:22, 23.   Mk. 9:30–32.   Lu. 9:43b–45.

Chapter XXIII.   In Capernaum again.

80. The shekel in the fish's mouth.
Mt. 17:24–27.   ⌜Mk. 9:33a.⌝

81. Discourse on humility and forgiveness.
Mt., chap. 18.   Mk. 9:33–50.   Lu. 9:46–50.

Chapter XXIV.   An Autumn Visit to Jerusalem.

82. Christ at the feast of tabernacles.
Jo. 7:1–52.

83. The woman taken in adultery.
Jo. 7:53–8:11.

84. Discourse on the Light of the World.
Jo. 8:12–30.

85. Discourse on spiritual freedom.
Jo. 8:31–59.

PART VII.

THE PEREAN MINISTRY.

From the Final Departure from Galilee until the Final Arrival at Jerusalem.

Chapter XXV. From the Departure from Galilee until after the Feast of Dedication.

SECTION.

86. The final departure from Galilee.
    Mt. 19:1, 2.   Mk. 10:1.   Lu. 9:51-62.
    Mt. 8: [18] 19-22.

87. The mission of the Seventy.
                         Lu. 10:1-24.

88. The good Samaritan.
                         Lu. 10:25-37.

89. The visit to Martha and Mary.
                         Lu. 10:38-42.

90. Healing of the man born blind.
                                        Jo., chap. 9.

91. The Good Shepherd.
                                        Jo. 10:1-21.

92. Christ at the feast of dedication.
                                        Jo. 10:22-42.

Chapter XXVI. From the Feast of Dedication until after the Withdrawal to Ephraim.

93. Discourse on prayer.
                         Lu. 11:1-13.

94. Discourses against the Pharisees.
                         Lu. 11:14-54.

95. Teachings concerning trust in God and coming judgment.
                         Lu., chap. 12.

96. The Galileans slain by Pilate.
                         Lu. 13:1-9.

97. The woman healed on a sabbath.
                         Lu. 13:10-21.

98. The question whether few are saved.
                         Lu. 13:22-30.

99. Reply to the warning against Herod.
                         Lu. 13:31-35.

100. Discourse at a chief Pharisee's table.
                         Lu. 14:1-24.

101. Discourse on counting the cost.
                         Lu. 14:25-35.

SECTION.

102. Three parables of grace.

Lu., chap. 15.

103. Two parables of warning.

Lu., chap. 16.

104. Concerning forgiveness and faith.

Lu. 17:1-10.

105. The raising of Lazarus.

Jo. 11:1-46.

106. The withdrawal to Ephraim.

Jo. 11:47-54.

Chapter XXVII. From the Withdrawal to Ephraim until the Final Arrival in Jerusalem.

107. The ten lepers.

Lu. 17:11-19.

108. The coming of the kingdom.

Lu. 17:20—18:8.

109. The Pharisee and the publican.

Lu. 18:9-14.

110. Concerning divorce.
Mt. 19:3-12.   Mk. 10:2-12.

111. Christ blessing little children.
Mt. 19:13-15.   Mk. 10:13-16.   Lu. 18:15-17.

112. The rich young ruler.
Mt. 19:16—20:16.   Mk. 10:17-31.   Lu. 18:18-30.

113. Christ foretells his crucifixion.
Mt. 20:17-19.   Mk. 10:32-34.   Lu. 18:31-34.

114. Ambition of James and John.
Mt. 20:20-28.   Mk. 10:35-45.

115. The blind men near Jericho.
Mt. 20:29-34.   Mk. 10:46-52.   Lu. 18:35-43.

116. Visit to Zacchæus.

Lu. 19:1-10.

117. Parable of the minæ.

Lu. 19:11-28.

118. Anointing of Jesus by Mary of Bethany.
Mt. 26:6-13.   Mk. 14:3-9.   Jo. 11:55—12:11.

PART VIII.

THE PASSION WEEK.

FROM THE FINAL ARRIVAL IN JERUSALEM UNTIL THE RESURRECTION.

Chapter XXVIII.   Sunday.—A Day of Triumph.

SECTION.

119. The triumphal entry.
    MT. 21:1-11.   MK. 11:1-11.   LU. 19:29-44.   JO. 12:12-19.

Chapter XXIX.   Monday.—A Day of Authority.

120. The cursing of the fig tree.
    MT. 21:18, 19 [20-22].   MK. 11:12-14.

121. Second cleansing of the temple.
    MT. 21:12-17.   MK. 11:15-19.   LU. 19:45-48.

Chapter XXX.   Tuesday.—A Day of Conflict.

122. The fig tree withered away.
    ⌜MT. 21:20-22.⌝   MK. 11:20-25.

123. Christ's authority challenged.
    MT. 21:23-27.   MK. 11:27-33.   LU. 20:1-8.

124. Three parables of warning.
    MT. 21:28—22:14.   MK. 12:1-12.   LU. 20:9-19.

125. Three questions by the Jewish rulers.
    MT. 22:15-40.   MK. 12:13-34.   LU. 20:20-40.

126. Christ's unanswerable question.
    MT. 22:41-46.   MK. 12:35-37.   LU. 20:41-44.

127. Woes against the scribes and Pharisees.
    MT., chap. 23.   MK. 12:38-40.   LU. 20:45-47.

128. The widow's two mites.
                           MK. 12:41-44.   LU. 21:1-4.

129. Gentiles seeking Jesus.
                                                                        JO. 12:20-36.

130. The Jews' rejection of Christ.
                                                                        JO. 12:37-50.

12

SECTION.

131. Discourse concerning the destruction of Jerusalem and the end of the world.
    Mt., chaps. 24, 25.　　　Mk., chap. 13.　　　Lu. 21:5-38.
    ⌐Mt. 26:1, 2.⌐

132. Conspiracy between the chief priests and Judas.
    Mt. 26:1-5.　　　Mk. 14:1, 2.　　　Lu. 22:1-6.
    Mt. 26:14-16.　　　Mk. 14:10, 11.

Wednesday.—Without Record.

Chapter XXXI.　　Thursday.—The Last Day with the Disciples.

133. The Last Supper.
    Mt. 26:17-30.　　　Mk. 14:12-26.　　　Lu. 22:7-30.　　　Jo. 13:1-30.

134. Christ's farewell discourses.
    Mt. 26:31-35.　　　Mk. 14:27-31.　　　Lu. 22:31-38.　　　Jo. 13:31—16:33.

135. The intercessory prayer.
    　　　　　　　　　　　　　　　　　　　　　　　　　　　　Jo., chap. 17.

Chapter XXXII.　　Friday.—The Day of Suffering.

136. The agony in Gethsemane.
    ⌐Mt. 26:30.⌐　　　⌐Mk. 14:26.⌐
    Mt. 26:36-46.　　　Mk. 14:32-42.　　　Lu. 22:39-46.　　　⌐Jo. 18:1.⌐

137. The betrayal and arrest.
    Mt. 26:47-56.　　　Mk. 14:43-52.　　　Lu. 22:47-53.　　　Jo. 18:1-11 ⌐12⌐.

138. The trial before the Jewish authorities.
    Mt. 26:57—27:10.　　Mk. 14:53-72.　　　Lu. 22:54-71.　　　Jo. 18:12-27.
    　　　　　　　　　　⌐Mk. 15:1a.⌐

139. The trial before Pilate.
    Mt. 27:⌐2⌐ 11-31.　　Mk. 15:1-20.　　　Lu. 23:1-25.　　　Jo.18:28—19:16a

140. The crucifixion.
    Mt. 27:32-56.　　　Mk. 15:21-41.　　　Lu. 23:26-49.　　　Jo. 19:16b-37.

141. The burial.
    Mt. 27:57-61.　　　Mk. 15:42-47.　　　Lu. 23:50-56a.　　　Jo. 19:38-42.

Chapter XXXIII.　　Saturday.—The Day in the Tomb.

142. The watch at the sepulchre.
    Mt. 27:62-66.

PART IX.

THE FORTY DAYS.

FROM THE RESURRECTION UNTIL THE ASCENSION.

Chapter XXXIV.   The Day of Resurrection.   Christ's First Appearances.

SECTION.

143. The resurrection morning.
      MT. 28:1–10.   MK. 16:1–11.   LU. 23:56*b*—24:12.   JO. 20:1–18.

144. The report of the watch.
      MT. 28:11–15.

145. The walk to Emmaus.
                              MK. 16:12, 13.   LU. 24:13–35.

146. The appearance to the disciples in Jerusalem, Thomas being absent.
                              MK. 16:14.   LU. 24:36–43.   JO. 20:19–25.

Chapter XXXV.   Subsequent Appearances and the Ascension.

147. The appearance to Thomas with the other disciples.
                                                                             JO. 20:26–29.

148. The appearance to seven disciples by the Sea of Galilee.
                                                                             JO. 21:1–24.

149. The appearance to the eleven on a mountain in Galilee.
      MT. 28:16–20.   MK. 16:15–18.

150. Christ's final appearance and his ascension.
                              MK. 16:19, 20.   LU. 24:44–53.

151. The conclusion of John's gospel.
                                                                             JO. 20:30, 31.
                                                                             JO. 21:25.

INDEX

FOR FINDING ANY PASSAGE IN THE HARMONY.*

	SECTION.	PAGE.		SECTION.	PAGE.
Matt. **1**:1–17	3	20	Matt. **10**: ⌐2–4⌐	48	57
18–25	6	23	Matt. **11**:1	64	101
⌐18–25⌐	9	25	2–30	52	72
Matt. **2**:1–12	13	27	Matt. **12**:1–8	45	54
13–23	14	28	9–14	46	55
⌐23⌐	15	28	15–21	47	56
Matt. **3**:1–12	18	30	22–45	55	77
13–17	19	32	46–50	56	80
Matt. **4**:1 11	20	33	Matt. **13**:1–53	57	81
12	34	42	54–58	62	93
⌐12⌐	31	40	Matt. **14**:1–12	65	101
[13–16]	34	42	13–23	66	103
⌐13–16⌐	37	45	24–36	67	105
17	34	43	Matt. **15**:1 20	69	109
18–22	38	46	21–28	70	112
⌐23⌐	40	49	29–31	71	113
23–25	47	56	32–38	72	114
Matt. **5**:1–48	49	58	39	73	114
Matt. **6**:1–34	49	63	Matt. **16**:1–12	73	115
Matt. **7**:1–29	49	67	13–20	75	116
Matt. **8**:⌐1⌐	49	71	21–28	76	117
[1]	40	49	Matt. **17**:1–13	77	119
2–4	40	49	14–20	78	120
5–13	50	71	22, 23	79	122
14–17	39	48	24–27	80	122
⌐18⌐	58	88	Matt. **18**:1 35	81	123
[18]	86	132	Matt. **19**:1, 2	86	132
19–22	86	132	3–12	110	157
23–27	58	88	13–15	111	159
28–34	59	89	16–30	112	159
Matt. **9**:⌐1⌐	60	91	Matt. **20**:1–16	112	161
⌊1⌋	41	49	17–19	113	162
2–8	41	49	20–28	114	163
9–13	42	51	29–34	115	164
14–17	43	51	Matt. **21**:1–11	119	169
18–26	60	91	12–17	121	172
27–34	61	93	18, 19	120	171
35	63	95	[20–22]	120	171
Matt. **9**:36–38	64	95	⌐20–22⌐	122	173
Matt. **10**:1–42	64	96	23–27	123	174

*The page figure indicates the page on which the passage referred to begins. This index does not refer to "Repeated Sayings" or to passages from non-parallel sections printed in parallelism for the purpose of comparison. Concerning the former see Appendix II; concerning the latter see Appendix I, § iv. 1.

		SECTION.	PAGE.
Matt. **21**:28–46	. . . .	124	175
Matt. **22**:1–14	. . . .	124	177
15–40	. . . .	125	178
41–46	. . . .	126	181
Matt. **23**:1–39	. . . .	127	182
Matt. **24**:1–51	. . . .	131	186
Matt. **25**:1–46	. . . .	131	192
Matt. **26**:⌜1, 2⌝	. . . .	131	195
1–5	. . . .	132	195
6–13	. . . .	118	167
14–16	. . . .	132	196
17–30	. . . .	133	196
⌜30⌝	. . . .	136	210
31–35	. . . .	134	204
36–46	. . . .	136	210
47–56	. . . .	137	211
57–75	. . . .	138	215
Matt. **27**:1–10	. . . .	138	218
⌜2⌝	. . . .	139	220
11–31	. . . .	139	220
32–56	. . . .	140	227
57–61	. . . .	141	233
62–66	. . . .	142	234
Matt. **28**:1–10	. . . .	143	235
11–15	. . . .	144	238
16–20	. . . .	149	243
Mark **1**:1–8	. . . .	18	30
9–11	. . . .	19	32
12, 13	. . . .	20	33
⌜14⌝	. . . .	31	40
14, 15	. . . .	34	42
16–20	. . . .	38	46
21–34	. . . .	39	47
35–45	. . . .	40	48
Mark **2**:1–12	. . . .	41	49
13–17	. . . .	42	51
18–22	. . . .	43	51
23–28	. . . .	45	54
Mark **3**:1–6	. . . .	46	55
7–12	. . . .	47	56
13–19	. . . .	48	57
20–30	. . . .	55	77
31–35	. . . .	56	80
Mark **4**:1–34	. . . .	57	81
35–41	. . . .	58	88
Mark **5**:1–20	. . . .	59	89
21–43	. . . .	60	91
Mark **6**:1–6*a*	. . . .	62	93
6*b*	. . . .	63	95
7–13	. . . .	64	96
14–29	. . . .	65	101
30–46	. . . .	66	103
47–56	. . . .	67	105
Mark **7**:1–23	. . . .	69	109
24–30	. . . .	70	112
31–37	. . . .	71	113
Mark **8**:1–9	. . . .	72	114
10–21	. . . .	73	114
22–26	. . . .	74	116
27–30	. . . .	75	116
31–38	. . . .	76	117
Mark **9**:1	. . . .	76	118
2–13	. . . .	77	119
14–29	. . . .	78	120
30–32	. . . .	79	122
⌜33*a*⌝	. . . .	80	122
33–50	. . . .	81	123
Mark **10**:1	. . . .	86	132
2–12	. . . .	110	157
13–16	. . . .	111	159
17–31	. . . .	112	159
32–34	. . . .	113	162
35–45	. . . .	114	163
46–52	. . . .	115	164
Mark **11**:1–11	. . . .	119	169
12–14	. . . .	120	171
15–19	. . . .	121	172
20–25	. . . .	122	173
27–33	. . . .	123	174
Mark **12**:1–12	. . . .	124	175
13–34	. . . .	125	178
35–37	. . . .	126	181
38–40	. . . .	127	182
41–44	. . . .	128	184
Mark **13**:1–37	. . . .	131	186
Mark **14**:1, 2	. . . .	132	195
3–9	. . . .	118	167
10, 11	. . . .	132	196
12–26	. . . .	133	196
27–31	. . . .	134	204
⌜26⌝	. . . .	136	210
32–42	. . . .	136	210
43–52	. . . .	137	211
53–72	. . . .	138	215
Mark **15**:⌜1*a*⌝	. . . .	138	218
1–20	. . . .	139	220
21–41	. . . .	140	227
42–47	. . . .	141	233
Mark **16**:1–11	. . . .	143	235
12, 13	. . . .	145	239
14	. . . .	146	241
15–18	. . . .	149	243
19, 20	. . . .	150	245
Luke **1**:1–4	. . . .	2	19
5–25	. . . .	4	21
26–38	. . . .	5	22

		SECTION.	PAGE.			SECTION.	PAGE.
Luke	1 : 39–56	7	23	Luke 11 : 14–54		94	139
	57–80	8	24	Luke 12 : 1–59		95	143
Luke	2 : 1–7	9	25	Luke 13 : 1–9		96	146
	8–20	10	26		10–21	97	146
	21	11	26		22–30	98	147
	22–39	12	26		31–35	99	148
	⌐39⌐	15	28	Luke 14 : 1–24		100	148
	40	15	29		25–35	101	149
	41–50	16	29	Luke 15 : 1–32		102	150
	51, 52	17	29	Luke 16 : 1–31		103	151
Luke	3 : 1–18	18	30	Luke 17 : 1–10		104	153
	21, 22	19	32		11–19	107	155
	⌐23a⌐	19	33		20–37	108	156
	23–38	3	20	Luke 18 : 1–8		108	157
Luke	4 : 1–13	20	33		9–14	109	157
	14, 15	34	42		15–17	111	159
	16–30	36	43		18–30	112	159
	⌐31a⌐	37	45		31–34	113	162
	31–41	39	47		35–43	115	164
	42–44	40	48	Luke 19 : 1–10		116	165
Luke	5 : 1–11	38	46		11–28	117	165
	12–16	40	49		29–44	119	169
	17–26	41	49		45–48	121	172
	27–32	42	51	Luke 20 : 1–8		123	174
	33–39	43	51		9–19	124	175
Luke	6 : 1–5	45	54		20–40	125	178
	6–11	46	55		41–44	126	181
	12–19	48	57		45–47	127	182
	⌐17–19⌐	47	56	Luke 21 : 1–4		128	184
	20–49	49	58		5–38	131	186
Luke	7 : 1–10	50	71	Luke 22 : 1–6		132	195
	11–17	51	72		7–30	133	196
	18–35	52	72		31–38	134	204
	36–50	53	76		39–46	136	210
Luke	8 : 1–3	54	77		47–53	137	211
	4–18	57	81		54–71	138	215
	19–21	56	80	Luke 23 : 1–25		139	220
	22–25	58	88		26–49	140	227
	26–39	59	89		50–56a	141	233
	40–56	60	91		56b	143	235
Luke	9 : 1–6	64	96	Luke 24 : 1–12		143	235
	7–9	65	101		13–35	145	239
	10–17	66	103		36–43	146	241
	18–21	75	116		44–53	150	244
	22–27	76	117				
	28–36	77	119				
	37–43a	78	120	John 1 : 1–18		1	19
	43b–45	79	122		19–28	21	34
	46–50	81	123		29–34	22	34
	51–62	86	132		35–42	23	35
Luke 10 : 1–24		87	133		43–51	24	35
	25–37	88	135	John 2 : 1–11		25	35
	38–42	89	135		12	26	36
Luke 11 : 1–13		93	138		13–22	27	37

		SECTION.	PAGE.				SECTION.	PAGE.
John	2 : 23–25	28	38	John	12 : 1–11		118	167
John	3 : 1–21	28	38		12–19		119	169
	22–24	29	39		20–36		129	185
	25–36	30	39		37–50		130	186
John	4 : 1–3	31	40	John	13 : 1–30		133	198
	4–26	32	40		31–38		134	203
	27–42	33	41	John	14 : 1–31		134	205
	43–45	34	42	John	15 : 1–27		134	206
	46–54	35	43	John	16 : 1–33		134	207
John	5 : 1–47	44	52	John	17 : 1–26		135	209
John	6 : 1–15	66	103	John	18 : ⌐1¬		136	210
	16–21	67	105		1–11		137	211
	22–71	68	107		⌐12¬		137	213
John	7 : 1–52	82	128		12–27		138	213
	53	83	130		28–40		139	220
John	8 : 1–11	83	130	John	19 : 1–16a		139	224
	12–30	84	130		16b–37		140	228
	31–59	85	131		38–42		141	233
John	9 : 1–41	90	135	John	20 : 1–18		143	235
John	10 : 1–21	91	137		19–25		146	241
	22–42	92	137		26–29		147	242
John	11 : 1–46	105	154		30, 31		151	245
	47–54	106	155	John	21 : 1–24		148	242
	55–57	118	166		25		151	245

NOTE.—The following verses of the Version of 1611, being omitted from the Revised Version of 1881, are not contained in the Harmony: Matt. 17:21; 18:11; 23:14; Mark 7:16; 9:44, 46; 11:26; 15:28; Luke 17:36; 23:17; John 5:4.

PART I.

THE THIRTY YEARS OF PRIVATE LIFE.

FROM THE BIRTH OF JESUS UNTIL THE COMING OF JOHN THE BAPTIST.

---

§1. PROLOGUE OF JOHN'S GOSPEL.

JOHN 1:1-18.

1 In the beginning was the Word, and the Word was with God, and the Word was God. 2 The same was in the beginning with God. 3 All things were made [1]by[1] him; and without him [2]was not anything made that hath been made. 4 In him was life; and the life was the light of men. 5 And the light shineth in the darkness; and the darkness [3]apprehended it not. 6 There came a man, sent from God, whose name was John. 7 The same came for witness, that he might bear witness of the light, that all might believe through him. 8 He was not the light, but *came* that he might bear witness of the light. 9 [4]There was the true light, *even the light* which lighteth [5]every man, coming into the world. 10 He was in the world, and the world was made [1]by[1] him, and the world knew him not. 11 He came unto [6]his own, and they that were his own received him not. 12 But as many as received him, to them gave he the right to become children of God, *even* to them that believe on his name: 13 which[2] were [7]born, not of [8]blood, nor of the will of the flesh, nor of the will of man, but of God. 14 And the Word became flesh, and [9]dwelt among us (and we beheld his glory, glory as of [10]the only begotten from the Father), full of grace and truth. 15 John beareth witness of him, and crieth, saying, [11]This was he of whom I said, He that cometh after me is become before me: for he was [12]before me. 16 For of his fulness we all received, and grace for grace. 17 For the law was given [1]by[1] Moses; grace and truth came [1]by[1] Jesus Christ. 18 No man hath seen God at any time; [13]the only begotten Son, which[2] is in the bosom of the Father, he hath declared *him*.

§2. PREFACE OF LUKE'S GOSPEL.

LUKE 1:1-4.

1 Forasmuch as many have taken in hand to draw up a narrative concerning those matters which have been [14]fulfilled among us, 2 even as they delivered them unto us, which[2] from the beginning were eyewitnesses and ministers of the word, 3 it seemed good to me also, having traced the course of all things accurately from the first, to write unto thee in order, most excellent Theophilus; 4 that thou mightest know the certainty concerning the [15]things [16]wherein thou wast instructed. (+ §4)

ERV. mg.: [1] Or, *through*   [2] Or, *was not anything made. That which hath been made was life in him; and the life &c.*   [3] Or, *overcame.* See ch. xii. 35 (Gr.).   [4] Or, *The true light, which lighteth every man, was coming*   [5] Or, *every man as he cometh*   [6] Gr. *his own things.*   [7] Or, *begotten*   [8] Gr. *bloods.*   [9] Gr. *tabernacled.*   [10] Or, *an only begotten from a father*   [11] Some ancient authorities read (*this was he that said*).   [12] Gr. *first in regard of me.*   [13] Many very ancient authorities read *God only begotten.*   [14] Or, *fully established*   [15] Gr. *words.*   [16] Or, *which thou wast taught by word of mouth*

ARV. txt.: [1] through   [2] who

19

§ 3. THE TWO GENEALOGIES.

MATT. 1 : 1–17.

1 [1]The book of the [2]generation of Jesus Christ, the son of David, the son of Abraham.

2 Abraham begat Isaac;
and Isaac begat Jacob;
and Jacob begat Judah and his brethren;
3 and Judah begat Perez and Zerah of Tamar;
and Perez begat Hezron;
and Hezron begat [3]Ram;
4 and [3]Ram begat Amminadab;
and Amminadab begat Nahshon;
and Nahshon begat Salmon;
5 and Salmon begat Boaz of Rahab;
and Boaz begat Obed of Ruth;
and Obed begat Jesse;
6 and Jesse begat David the king.

And David begat Solomon of her *that had been the wife* of Uriah;
7 and Solomon begat Rehoboam;
and Rehoboam begat Abijah;
and Abijah begat [4]Asa;
8 and [4]Asa begat Jehoshaphat;
and Jehoshaphat begat Joram;
and Joram begat Uzziah;
9 And Uzziah begat Jotham;
and Jotham begat Ahaz;
and Ahaz begat Hezekiah;
10 and Hezekiah begat Manasseh;
and Manasseh begat [5]Amon;
and [5]Amon begat Josiah;

LUKE 3 : 23–38.

23 And Jesus himself, when he began *to teach*, was about thirty years of age, being the son (as was supposed) of Joseph, the *son* of Heli,
24 the *son* of Matthat,
the *son* of Levi,
the *son* of Melchi,
the *son* of Jannai,
the *son* of Joseph,
25 the *son* of Mattathias,
the *son* of Amos,
the *son* of Nahum,
the *son* of Esli,
the *son* of Naggai,
26 the *son* of Maath,
the *son* of Mattathias,
the *son* of Semein,
the *son* of Josech,
the *son* of Joda,
27 the *son* of Joanan,
the *son* of Rhesa,
the *son* of Zerubbabel,
the *son* of [6]Shealtiel,
the *son* of Neri,
28 the *son* of Melchi,
the *son* of Addi,
the *son* of Cosam,
the *son* of Elmadam,
the *son* of Er,
29 the *son* of Jesus,
the *son* of Eliezer,
the *son* of Jorim,
the *son* of Matthat,
the *son* of Levi,
30 the *son* of Symeon,
the *son* of Judas,
the *son* of Joseph,
the *son* of Jonam,
the *son* of Eliakim,
31 the *son* of Melea,
the *son* of Menna,
the *son* of Mattatha,

ERV. mg.: [1] Or, *The genealogy of Jesus Christ*   [2]Or, *birth*: as in ver. 18.   [3] Gr. *Aram.*   [4] Gr. *Asaph.*   [5] Gr. *Amos.*   [6] Gr. *Salathiel.*

MATT. 1.		LUKE 3.
11 and Josiah begat Jecho-niah and his brethren, at the time of the ¹carrying away to Babylon.		the *son* of Nathan,
		the *son* of David,
12 And after the ¹carry-ing away to Babylon, Jech-oniah begat ²Shealtiel;		32 the *son* of Jesse,
		the *son* of Obed,
and ²Shealtiel begat Zerub-babel;		the *son* of Boaz,
		the *son* of ³Salmon,
13 and Zerubbabel begat Abiud;		the *son* of Nahshon,
		33 the *son* of Amminadab,
and Abiud begat Eliakim;		⁴the *son* of ⁵Arni,
and Eliakim begat Azor;		the *son* of Hezron,
14 and Azor begat Sadoc;		the *son* of Perez,
and Sadoc begat Achim;		the *son* of Judah,
and Achim begat Eliud;		34 the *son* of Jacob,
15 and Eliud begat Eleazar;		the *son* of Isaac,
and Eleazar begat Matthan;		the *son* of Abraham,
and Matthan begat Jacob;		the *son* of Terah,
16 and Jacob begat Joseph the husband of Mary, of whom was born Jesus, who is called Christ.		the *son* of Nahor,
		35 the *son* of Serug,
		the *son* of Reu,
17 So all the generations from Abraham unto David are fourteen generations; and from David unto the ¹carry-ing away to Babylon fourteen generations; and from the ¹carrying away to Babylon unto the Christ fourteen generations.		the *son* of Peleg,
		the *son* of Eber,
		the *son* of Shelah,
		36 the *son* of Cainan,
		the *son* of Arphaxad,
		the *son* of Shem,
		the *son* of Noah,
		the *son* of Lamech,
		37 the *son* of Methuselah,
		the *son* of Enoch,
		the *son* of Jared,
		the *son* of Mahalaleel,
		the *son* of Cainan,
		38 the *son* of Enos,
		the *son* of Seth,
		the *son* of Adam,
		the *son* of God. (+ §20)

§4. BIRTH OF JOHN THE BAPTIST PROMISED.

LUKE 1:5–25.

5 There was in the days of Herod, king of Judæa, a certain priest named Zacharias, of the course of Abijah: and he had a wife of the daughters of Aaron, and her name was Elisabeth. 6 And they were both righteous before God, walking in all the commandments and ordinances of the Lord blameless. 7 And they had no child, because that Elisabeth was barren, and they both were *now* ⁶ well stricken in years.

ERV. mg.: ¹ Or, *removal to Babylon* ² Gr. *Salathiel.* ³ Some ancient authorities write *Sala.* ⁴ Many ancient authorities insert *the son of Admin*: and one writes *Admin* for *Amminadab.* ⁵ Some ancient authorities write *Aram.* ⁶ Gr. *advanced in their days.*

LUKE 1.

8 Now it came to pass, while he executed the priest's office before God in the order of his course, 9 according to the custom of the priest's office, his lot was to enter into the [1]temple of the Lord and burn incense. 10 And the whole multitude of the people were praying without at the hour of incense. 11 And there appeared unto him an angel of the Lord standing on the right side of the altar of incense. 12 And Zacharias was troubled when he saw *him*, and fear fell upon him. 13 But the angel said unto him, Fear not, Zacharias : because thy supplication is heard, and thy wife Elisabeth shall bear thee a son, and thou shalt call his name John. 14 And thou shalt have joy and gladness ; and many shall rejoice at his birth. 15 For he shall be great in the sight of the Lord, and he shall drink no wine nor [2]strong drink ; and he shall be filled with the [3]Holy Ghost[1], even from his mother's womb. 16 And many of the children of Israel shall he turn unto the Lord their God. 17 And he shall [4]go before his face in the spirit and power of Elijah, to turn the hearts of the fathers to the children, and the disobedient *to walk* in the wisdom of the just ; to make ready for the Lord a people prepared *for him*. 18 And Zacharias said unto the angel, Whereby shall I know this? For I am an old man, and my wife [5]well stricken in years. 19 And the angel answering said unto him, I am Gabriel, that stand in the presence of God ; and I was sent to speak unto thee, and to bring thee these good tidings. 20 And behold, thou shalt be silent and not able to speak, until the day that these things shall come to pass, because thou believedst not my words, which shall be fulfilled in their season. 21 And the people were waiting for Zacharias, and they marvelled [6]while he tarried in the [1]temple. 22 And when he came out, he could not speak unto them : and they perceived that he had seen a vision in the [1]temple : and he continued making signs unto them, and remained dumb. 23 And it came to pass, when the days of his ministration were fulfilled, he departed unto his house.

24 And after these days Elisabeth his wife conceived ; and she hid herself five months, saying, 25 Thus hath the Lord done unto me in the days wherein he looked upon *me*, to take away my reproach among men.

§ 5. THE ANNUNCIATION TO MARY.

LUKE 1 : 26–38.

26 Now in the sixth month the angel Gabriel was sent from God unto a city of Galilee, named Nazareth, 27 to a virgin betrothed to a man whose name was Joseph, of the house of David ; and the virgin's name was Mary. 28 And he came in unto her, and said, Hail, thou that art [7]highly favoured, the Lord *is* with [8]thee. 29 But she was greatly troubled at the saying, and cast in her mind what manner of salutation this might be. 30 And the angel said unto her, Fear not, Mary : for thou hast found [9]favour with God. 31 And behold, thou shalt conceive in thy womb, and bring forth a son, and shalt call his name JESUS. 32 He shall be great, and shall be called the Son of the Most High : and the Lord God shall give unto him the throne of his father David : 33 and he shall reign over the house of Jacob [10]for ever ; and of his kingdom there shall be no end. 34 And Mary said unto the angel, How shall this be, seeing I know not a man? 35 And the angel answered and said unto her, The Holy Ghost[1] shall come upon thee, and the power of the Most High shall overshadow thee : wherefore also [11]that which [12]is to be [13]born shall be called holy, the Son of God[2]. 36 And

---

ERV. mg.: [1] Or, *sanctuary.* [2] Gr. *sikera.* [3] Or, *Holy Spirit*: and so throughout this book. [4] Some ancient authorities read *come nigh before his face.* [5] Gr. *advanced in her days.* [6] Or, *at his tarrying* [7] Or, *endued with grace* [8] Many ancient authorities add *blessed* art *thou among women.* See ver. 42. [9] Or, *grace* [10] Gr. *unto the ages.* [11] Or, *the holy thing which is to be born shall be called the Son of God.* [12] Or, *is begotten* [13] Some ancient authorities add *of thee.*

ARV. txt.: [1] Holy Spirit [2] the holy thing which is begotten shall be called the Son of God

LUKE 1.

behold, Elisabeth thy kinswoman, she also hath conceived a son in her old age: and this is the sixth month with her that [1]was called barren. 37 For no word from God shall be void of power. 38 And Mary said, Behold, the [2]handmaid of the Lord; be it unto me according to thy word. And the angel departed from her.

§6. THE ANNUNCIATION TO JOSEPH.

MATT. 1:18–25.

18 Now the [3]birth [4]of Jesus Christ was on this wise: When his mother Mary had been betrothed to Joseph, before they came together she was found with child of the [5]Holy Ghost[1]. 19 And Joseph her husband, being a righteous man, and not willing to make her a public example, was minded to put her away privily. 20 But when he thought on these things, behold, an angel of the Lord appeared unto him in a dream, saying, Joseph, thou son of David, fear not to take unto thee Mary thy wife: for that which is [6]conceived in her is of the Holy Ghost[1]. 21 And she shall bring forth a son; and thou shalt call his name JESUS; for it is he that shall save his people from their sins. 22 Now all this is come to pass, that it might be fulfilled which was spoken by the Lord through the prophet, saying,

23 Behold, the virgin shall be with child, and shall bring forth a son,
And they shall call his name [7]Immanuel;

which is, being interpreted, God with us. 24 And Joseph arose from his sleep, and did as the angel of the Lord commanded him, and took unto him his wife; 25 and knew her not till she had brought forth a son: and he called his name JESUS.

§7. MARY'S VISIT TO ELISABETH.

LUKE 1:39–56.

39 And Mary arose in these days and went into the hill country with haste, into a city of Judah; 40 and entered into the house of Zacharias and saluted Elisabeth. 41 And it came to pass, when Elisabeth heard the salutation of Mary, the babe leaped in her womb; and Elisabeth was filled with the Holy Ghost[1]; 42 and she lifted up her voice with a loud cry, and said, Blessed *art* thou among women, and blessed *is* the fruit of thy womb. 43 And whence is this to me, that the mother of my Lord should come unto me? 44 For behold, when the voice of thy salutation came into mine ears, the babe leaped in my womb for joy. 45 And blessed *is* she that [8]believed; for there shall be a fulfilment of the things which have been spoken to her from the Lord. 46 And Mary said,

My soul doth magnify the Lord,
47 And my spirit hath rejoiced in God my Saviour.
48 For he hath looked upon the low estate of his [9]handmaiden[2]:
For behold, from henceforth all generations shall call me blessed.
49 For he that is mighty hath done to me great things;
And holy is his name.
50 And his mercy is unto generations and generations
On them that fear him.

ERV. mg.: [1] Or, *is* [2] Gr. *bondmaid.* [3] Or. *generation* as in ver. 1. [4] Some ancient authorities read *of the Christ.* [5] Or, *Holy Spirit*: and so throughout this book. [6] Gr. *begotten.* [7] Gr. *Emmanuel.* [8] Or, *believed that there shall be* [9] Gr. *bondmaiden.*

ARV. txt.: [1] Holy Spirit [2] handmaid

LUKE 1.

51 He hath shewed strength with his arm;
    He hath scattered the proud [1] in the imagination of their heart.
52 He hath put down princes from *their* thrones,
    And hath exalted them of low degree.
53 The hungry he hath filled with good things;
    And the rich he hath sent empty away.
54 He hath holpen [1] Israel his servant,
    That he might remember mercy
55 (As he spake unto our fathers)
    Toward Abraham and his seed for ever.
56 And Mary abode with her about three months, and returned unto her house.

§ 8. BIRTH OF JOHN THE BAPTIST.

LUKE 1 : 57–80.

57 Now Elisabeth's time was fulfilled that she should be delivered; and she brought forth a son. 58 And her neighbours and her kinsfolk heard that the Lord had magnified his mercy towards her; and they rejoiced with her. 59 And it came to pass on the eighth day, that they came to circumcise the child; and they would have called him Zacharias, after the name of his father. 60 And his mother answered and said, Not so; but he shall be called John. 61 And they said unto her, There is none of thy kindred that is called by this name. 62 And they made signs to his father, what he would have him called. 63 And he asked for a writing tablet, and wrote, saying, His name is John. And they marvelled all. 64 And his mouth was opened immediately, and his tongue *loosed*, and he spake, blessing God. 65 And fear came on all that dwelt round about them: and all these sayings were noised abroad throughout all the hill country of Judæa. 66 And all that heard them laid them up in their heart, saying, What then shall this child be? For the hand of the Lord was with him.

67 And his father Zacharias was filled with the Holy Ghost [2], and prophesied, saying,
68 Blessed *be* the Lord, the God of Israel;
    For he hath visited and wrought redemption for his people,
69 And hath raised up a horn of salvation for us
    In the house of his servant David
70 (As he spake by the mouth of his holy prophets which [3] have been since the world
    began [4]),
71 Salvation from our enemies, and from the hand of all that hate us;
72 To shew mercy towards our fathers,
    And to remember his holy covenant;
73 The oath which he sware unto Abraham our father,
74 To grant unto us that we being delivered out of the hand of our enemies
    Should serve him without fear,
75 In holiness and righteousness before him all our days.
76 Yea and thou, child, shalt be called the prophet of the Most High:
    For thou shalt go before the face of the Lord to make ready his ways;

ERV. mg.: [1] Or, *by*

ARV. txt.: [1] given help to   [2] Holy Spirit   [3] that   [4] from of old

LUKE 1.

77 To give knowledge of salvation unto his people
In the remission of their sins,
78 Because of the [1] tender mercy of our God,
[2] Whereby the dayspring from on high [3] shall visit us,
79 To shine upon them that sit in darkness and the shadow of death;
To guide our feet into the way of peace.

80 And the child grew, and waxed strong in spirit, and was in the deserts till the day of his shewing unto Israel.

§9. BIRTH OF JESUS THE CHRIST.

⌈MATT. 1:18–25.⌉

⌈18 Now the [4]birth [5]of Jesus Christ was on this wise: When his mother Mary had been betrothed to Joseph, before they came together she was found with child of the [6]Holy Ghost[1]. 19 And Joseph her husband, being a righteous man, and not willing to make her a public example, was minded to put her away privily. 20 But when he thought on these things, behold, an angel of the Lord appeared unto him in a dream, saying, Joseph, thou son of David, fear not to take unto thee Mary thy wife: for that which is [7]conceived in her is of the Holy Ghost[1]. 21 And she shall bring forth a son; and thou shalt call his name JESUS; for it is he that shall save his people from their sins. 22 Now all this is come to pass, that it might be fulfilled which was spoken by the Lord through the prophet, saying, 23 Behold, the virgin shall be
with child, and shall
bring forth a son,
And they shall call his
name [8]Immanuel;

LUKE 2:1–7.

1 Now it came to pass in those days, there went out a decree from Cæsar Augustus, that all [9]the world should be enrolled. 2 This was the first enrolment made when Quirinius was governor of Syria. 3 And all went to enrol themselves, every one to his own city. 4 And Joseph also went up from Galilee, out of the city of Nazareth, into Judæa, to the city of David, which is called Bethlehem, because he was of the house and family of David; 5 to enrol himself with Mary, who was betrothed to him, being great with child. 6 And it came to pass, while they were there, the days were fulfilled that she should be delivered. 7 And she brought forth her firstborn son; and she wrapped him in swaddling clothes, and laid him in a manger, because there was no room for them in the inn.

ERV. mg.: [1] Or, *heart of mercy* [2] Or, *Wherein* [3] Many ancient authorities read *hath visited us.* [4] Or, *generation*: as in ver. 1. [5] Some ancient authorities read *of the Christ.* [6] Or, *Holy Spirit*: and so throughout this book. [7] Gr. *begotten.* [8] Gr. *Emmanuel.* [9] Gr. *the inhabited earth.*

ARV. txt.: [1] Holy Spirit

⌐Matt. 1.⌐

which is, being interpreted,
God with us. 24 And Joseph
arose from his sleep, and did
as the angel of the Lord commanded him, and took unto
him his wife; 25 and knew her
not till she had brought forth
a son : and he called his name
Jesus.¹ (§ 6)

§ 10. THE ANGELS AND THE SHEPHERDS.

Luke 2 : 8–20.

8 And there were shepherds in the same country abiding in the field, and keeping ¹ watch
by night over their flock. 9 And an angel of the Lord stood by them, and the glory of the Lord
shone round about them : and they were sore afraid. 10 And the angel said unto them, Be
not afraid ; for behold, I bring you good tidings of great joy which shall be to all the people :
11 for there is born to you this day in the city of David a Saviour, which¹ is ²Christ the Lord.
12 And this *is* the sign unto you : Ye shall find a babe wrapped in swaddling clothes, and lying
in a manger. 13 And suddenly there was with the angel a multitude of the heavenly host
praising God, and saying,
  14 Glory to God in the highest,
  And on earth ³ peace among ⁴ men in whom he is well pleased.
15 And it came to pass, when the angels went away from them into heaven, the shepherds
said one to another, Let us now go even unto Bethlehem, and see this ⁵ thing that is come to
pass, which the Lord hath made known unto us. 16 And they came with haste, and found
both Mary and Joseph, and the babe lying in the manger. 17 And when they saw it they
made known concerning the saying which was spoken to them about this child. 18 And all
that heard it wondered at the things which were spoken unto them by the shepherds. 19 But
Mary kept all these ⁶ sayings, pondering them in her heart. 20 And the shepherds returned,
glorifying and praising God for all the things they had heard and seen, even as it was spoken
unto them.

§ 11. THE CIRCUMCISION.

Luke 2 : 21.

21 And when eight days were fulfilled for circumcising him, his name was called Jesus,
which was so called by the angel before he was conceived in the womb.

§ 12. THE PRESENTATION IN THE TEMPLE.

Luke 2 : 22–39.

22 And when the days of their purification according to the law of Moses were fulfilled,
they brought him up to Jerusalem, to present him to the Lord 23 (as it is written in the law
of the Lord, Every male that openeth the womb shall be called holy to the Lord), 24 and to

---

ERV. mg.: ¹ Or, *night-watches*   ² Or, *Anointed Lord*   ³ Many ancient authorities read *peace, good pleasure among men.*   ⁴ Gr.
men of good pleasure.   ⁵ Or, *saying*   ⁶ Or, *things*

ARV. txt.: ¹ **who**

LUKE 2.

offer a sacrifice according to that which is said in the law of the Lord, A pair of turtledoves, or two young pigeons. 25 And behold, there was a man in Jerusalem, whose name was Simeon; and this man was righteous and devout, looking for the consolation of Israel: and the Holy Spirit was upon him. 26 And it had been revealed unto him by the Holy Spirit, that he should not see death, before he had seen the Lord's Christ. 27 And he came in the Spirit into the temple: and when the parents brought in the child Jesus, that they might do concerning him after the custom of the law, 28 then he received him into his arms, and blessed God, and said,

29 Now lettest thou thy ¹servant depart, O¹ ²Lord,
  According to thy word, in peace ;
30 For mine eyes have seen thy salvation,
31 Which thou hast prepared before the face of all peoples ;
32 A light for ³revelation to the Gentiles,
  And the glory of thy people Israel.

33 And his father and his mother were marvelling at the things which were spoken concerning him; 34 and Simeon blessed them, and said unto Mary his mother, Behold, this *child* is set for the falling and rising up of many² in Israel; and for a sign which is spoken against; 35 yea and a sword shall pierce through thine own soul; that thoughts out of many hearts may be revealed. 36 And there was one Anna, a prophetess, the daughter of Phanuel, of the tribe of Asher (she was ⁴of a great age, having lived with a husband seven years from her virginity, 37 and she had been a widow even for³ fourscore and four years), which ⁴ departed not from the temple, worshipping with fastings and supplications night and day. 38 And coming up at that very hour she gave thanks unto God, and spake of him to all them that were looking for the redemption of Jerusalem. 39 And when they had accomplished all things that were according to the law of the Lord, they returned into Galilee, to their own city Nazareth.

§13. THE WISE-MEN FROM THE EAST.

MATT. 2:1-12.

1 Now when Jesus was born in Bethlehem of Judæa in the days of Herod the king, behold, ⁵wise men⁵ from the east came to Jerusalem, 2 saying, ⁶Where is he that is born King of the Jews? for we saw his star in the east, and are come to worship him. 3 And when Herod the king heard it, he was troubled, and all Jerusalem with him. 4 And gathering together all the chief priests and scribes of the people, he inquired of them where the Christ should be born. 5 And they said unto him, In Bethlehem of Judæa: for thus it is written ⁷by⁶ the prophet,

6 And thou Bethlehem, land of Judah,
  Art in no wise least among the princes of Judah :
  For out of thee shall come forth a governor,
  Which ⁷ shall be shepherd of my people Israel.

7 Then Herod privily called the ⁵wise men⁵, and learned of them carefully⁸ ⁸what time the star appeared. 8 And he sent them to Bethlehem, and said, Go and search out carefully⁸ concerning the young child; and when ye have found *him*, bring me word, that I also may

---

ERV. mg.: ¹ Gr. *bondservant.*   ² Gr. *Master.*   ³ Or, *the unveiling of the Gentiles*   ⁴ Gr. *advanced in many days.*   ⁵ Gr. *Magi*   Compare Esther i. 13; Dan. ii. 12.   ⁶ Or, *Where is the King of the Jews that is born?*   ⁷ Or, *through.*   ⁸ Or, *the time of the star that appeared*

ARV. txt.: ¹ Omit O   ² the rising of many   ³ unto   ⁴ who   ⁵ Wise-men   ⁶ through   ⁷ Who   ⁸ exactly

MATT. 2.

come and worship him. 9 And they, having heard the king, went their way; and lo, the star, which they saw in the east, went before them, till it came and stood over where the young child was. 10 And when they saw the star, they rejoiced with exceeding great joy. 11 And they came into the house and saw the young child with Mary his mother; and they fell down and worshipped him; and opening their treasures they offered unto him gifts, gold and frankincense and myrrh. 12 And being warned *of God* in a dream that they should not return to Herod, they departed into their own country another way.

§ 14. THE FLIGHT INTO EGYPT AND RETURN TO NAZARETH.

MATT. 2:13-23.

13 Now when they were departed, behold, an angel of the Lord appeareth to Joseph in a dream, saying, Arise and take the young child and his mother, and flee into Egypt, and be thou there until I tell thee: for Herod will seek the young child to destroy him. 14 And he arose and took the young child and his mother by night, and departed into Egypt; 15 and was there until the death of Herod: that it might be fulfilled which was spoken by the Lord through the prophet, saying, Out of Egypt did I call my son. 16 Then Herod, when he saw that he was mocked of the [1] wise men [1], was exceeding wroth, and sent forth, and slew all the male children that were in Bethlehem, and in all the borders thereof, from two years old and under, according to the time which he had carefully [2] learned of the [1] wise men [1]. 17 Then was fulfilled that which was spoken [2] by [3] Jeremiah the prophet, saying,

18 A voice was heard in Ramah,
    Weeping and great mourning,
    Rachel weeping for her children;
    And she would not be comforted, because they are not.

19 But when Herod was dead, behold, an angel of the Lord appeareth in a dream to Joseph in Egypt, 20 saying, Arise and take the young child and his mother, and go into the land of Israel: for they are dead that sought the young child's life. 21 And he arose and took the young child and his mother, and came into the land of Israel. 22 But when he heard that Archelaus was reigning over Judæa in the room of his father Herod, he was afraid to go thither; and being warned *of God* in a dream, he withdrew into the parts of Galilee, 23 and came and dwelt in a city called Nazareth: that it might be fulfilled which was spoken [2] by [3] the prophets, that he should be called a Nazarene.

§ 15. CHILDHOOD AT NAZARETH.*

⌜MATT. 2:23.⌝		LUKE 2:⌜39⌝ 40.
⌜23 and came and dwelt in a city called Nazareth: that it might be fulfilled which was		⌜39 And when they had accomplished all things that were according to the law of

---

ERV. mg.: [1] Gr. *Magi*   [2] Or, *through*

ARV. txt.: [1] Wise-men   [2] exactly   [3] through

---

*Some hints as to the circumstances of Jesus' life in Nazareth are found in the following passages:

Matt. 13:54-58. And coming into his own country he taught them in their synagogue, insomuch that they were astonished, and said, Whence hath this man this wisdom, and these mighty works? 55 Is not this the carpenter's son? is not his mother called Mary? and his brethren, James, and Joseph, and Simon, and Judas? 56 And his sisters, are they not all with us? Whence then hath this man all these things? 57 And they were

MATT. 2.		LUKE 2.
spoken ¹by¹ the prophets, that he should be called a Nazarene.¹ (§ 12)		the Lord, they returned into Galilee, to their own city Nazareth.¹ (§ 12) 40 And the child grew, and waxed strong, ²filled with wisdom: and the grace of God was upon him.

§ 16. VISIT TO JERUSALEM WHEN TWELVE YEARS OLD.

LUKE 2 : 41–50.

41 And his parents went every year to Jerusalem at the feast of the passover. 42 And when he was twelve years old, they went up after the custom of the feast; 43 and when they had fulfilled the days, as they were returning, the boy Jesus tarried behind in Jerusalem; and his parents knew it not; 44 but supposing him to be in the company, they went a day's journey; and they sought for him among their kinsfolk and acquaintance: 45 and when they found him not, they returned to Jerusalem, seeking for him. 46 And it came to pass, after three days they found him in the temple, sitting in the midst of the ³doctors², both hearing them, and asking them questions: 47 and all that heard him were amazed at his understanding and his answers. 48 And when they saw him, they were astonished: and his mother said unto him, ⁴Son, why hast thou thus dealt with us? behold, thy father and I sought thee sorrowing. 49 And he said unto them, How is it that ye sought me? wist³ ye not that I must be ⁵in my Father's house? 50 And they understood not the saying which he spake unto them.

§ 17. EIGHTEEN YEARS AT NAZARETH.

LUKE 2 : 51, 52.

51 And he went down with them, and came to Nazareth; and he was subject unto them: and his mother kept all *these* ⁶sayings in her heart.
52 And Jesus advanced in wisdom and ⁷stature, and in ⁸favour with God and men.

ERV. mg.: ¹ Or, *through* ² Gr. *becoming full of wisdom.* ³ Or, *teachers* ⁴ Gr.*Child.* ⁵ Or, *about my Father's business* Gr. *in the things of my Father.* ⁶ Or, *things* ⁷ Or, *age* ⁸ Or, *grace*

ARV. txt.: ¹ through ² teachers ³ knew

---

offended in him. But Jesus said unto them, A prophet is not without honour, save in his own country, and in his own house. 58 And he did not many mighty works there because of their unbelief. (§ 62)

Mark 6:1–5. And he went out from thence; and he cometh into his own country; and his disciples follow him. 2 And when the sabbath was come, he began to teach in the synagogue: and many hearing him were astonished, saying, Whence hath this man these things? and, What is the wisdom that is given unto this man, and *what mean* such mighty works wrought by his hands? 3 Is not this the carpenter, the son of Mary, and brother of James, and Joses, and Judas, and Simon? and are not his sisters here with us? And they were offended in him. 4 And Jesus said unto them, A prophet is not without honour, save in his own country, and among his own kin, and in his own house. 5 And he could there do no mighty work, save that he laid his hands upon a few sick folk, and healed them. (§ 62)

John 1:46. And Nathanael said unto him, Can any good thing come out of Nazareth? Philip saith unto him, Come and see. (§ 24)

John 7:5. For even his brethren did not believe on him. (§ 82)

PART II.

THE OPENING EVENTS OF CHRIST'S MINISTRY.

FROM THE COMING OF JOHN THE BAPTIST UNTIL THE PUBLIC APPEARANCE OF JESUS IN JERUSALEM.

---

§ 18. THE MINISTRY OF JOHN THE BAPTIST.

MATT. 3 : 1–12.	MARK 1 : 1–8.	LUKE 3 : 1–20.

1 And in those days cometh John the Baptist, preaching in the wilderness of Judæa, 2 saying, Repent ye; for the kingdom of heaven is at hand. 3 For this is he that was spoken of [1]by[1] Isaiah the prophet, saying,
  The voice of one crying in the wilderness,
  Make ye ready the way of the Lord,
  Make his paths straight.
4 Now John himself had his raiment of camel's hair, and a leathern girdle about his loins; and his food was locusts and wild honey. 5 Then went out unto him Jerusalem, and all Judæa, and all the region round about Jordan[2]; 6 and they were baptized of him in the river Jordan, confessing their sins.

[Paragraph continued on p. 31.]

1 The beginning of the gospel of Jesus Christ, [2]the Son of God.
2 Even as it is written [3]in Isaiah the prophet,
  Behold, I send my messenger before thy face,
  Who shall prepare thy way;
3 The voice of one crying in the wilderness,
  Make ye ready the way of the Lord,
  Make his paths straight;
4 John came, who baptized in the wilderness and preached the baptism of repentance unto remission of sins. 5 And there went out unto him all the country of Judæa, and all they of Jerusalem; and they were baptized of him in the river Jordan, confessing their sins. 6 And John was clothed with camel's hair, and *had* a leathern girdle about his loins, and did eat locusts and wild honey.

[Paragraph continued on p. 31.]

1 Now in the fifteenth year of the reign of Tiberius Cæsar, Pontius Pilate being governor of Judæa, and Herod being tetrarch of Galilee, and his brother Philip tetrarch of the region of Ituræa and Trachonitis, and Lysanias tetrarch of Abilene, 2 in the high-priesthood of Annas and Caiaphas, the word of God came unto John the son of Zacharias in the wilderness. 3 And he came into all the region round about Jordan[2], preaching the baptism of repentance unto remission of sins; 4 as it is written in the book of the words of Isaiah the prophet,
  The voice of one crying in the wilderness,
  Make ye ready the way of the Lord,
  Make his paths straight.
5 Every valley shall be filled, And every mountain and hill shall be brought low; And the crooked shall become straight, And the rough ways smooth;

ERV. mg.: [1] Or, *through*   [2] Some ancient authorities omit *the Son of God*.   [3] Some ancient authorities read *in the prophets*.

ARV. txt.: [1] through   [2] the Jordan

MATT. **3.**	MARK **1.**	LUKE **3.**
		6 And all flesh shall see the salvation of God.
7 But when he saw many of the Pharisees and Sadducees coming to his baptism, he said unto them, Ye offspring of vipers, who warned you to flee from the wrath to come ? 8 Bring forth therefore fruit worthy of [1]repentance : 9 and think not to say within yourselves, We have Abraham to our father : for I say unto you, that God is able of these stones to raise up children unto Abraham. 10 And even now is the axe laid unto[1] the root of the trees : every tree therefore that bringeth not forth good fruit is hewn down, and cast into the fire.		7 He said therefore to the multitudes that went out to be baptized of him, Ye offspring of vipers, who warned you to flee from the wrath to come? 8 Bring forth therefore fruits worthy of [1]repentance, and begin not to say within yourselves, We have Abraham to our father : for I say unto you, that God is able of these stones to raise up children unto Abraham. 9 And even now is the axe also laid unto[1] the root of the trees : every tree therefore that bringeth not forth good fruit is hewn down, and cast into the fire. 10 And the multitudes asked him, saying, What then must we do? 11 And he answered and said unto them, He that hath two coats, let him impart to him that hath none ; and he that hath food, let him do likewise. 12 And there came also [3]publicans to be baptized, and they said unto him, [4]Master[3], what must we do? 13 And he said unto them, Extort no more than that which is appointed you. 14 And [5]soldiers also asked him, saying, And we, what must we do? And he said unto them, Do violence to no man[4], neither [6]exact *anything*[5] wrongfully ; and be content with your wages.
11 I indeed baptize you [2]with[2] water unto repentance : but he that cometh after me is mightier	7 And he preached, saying, There cometh after me he that is mightier than I, the latchet of whose shoes I	15 And as the people were in expectation, and all men reasoned in their hearts concerning John, whether haply

ERV. mg. : [1] Or, *your repentance*   [2] Or, *in*   [3] See marginal note on Matt. v. 46.   [4] Or, *Teacher*   [5] Gr. *soldiers on service.*   [6] Or, *accuse* any one

ARV. txt. : [1] the axe lieth at   [2] in   [3] Teacher   [4] Extort from no man by violence   [5] accuse *any one*

MATT. 3.	MARK 1.	LUKE 3.
than I, whose shoes I am not [1]worthy to bear: he shall baptize you [2]with[1] the Holy Ghost[2] and *with*[3] fire: 12 whose fan is in his hand, and he will throughly[4] cleanse his threshing-floor; and he will gather his wheat into the garner, but the chaff he will burn up with unquenchable fire.	am not [1]worthy to stoop down and unloose. 8 I baptized you [2]with[1] water; but he shall baptize you [2]with[1] the Holy Ghost[2].	he were the Christ; 16 John answered, saying unto them all, I indeed baptize you with water; but there cometh he that is mightier than I, the latchet of whose shoes I am not [1]worthy to unloose: he shall baptize you [2]with[1] the Holy Ghost[2] and *with*[3] fire: 17 whose fan is in his hand, throughly[4] to cleanse his threshing-floor, and to gather the wheat into his garner; but the chaff he will burn up with unquenchable fire. 18 With many other exhortations therefore preached he [3]good tidings unto the people; 19 but Herod the tetrarch, being reproved by him for Herodias his brother's wife, and for all the evil things which Herod had done, 20 added yet this above all[5], that he shut up John in prison.

§ 19. THE BAPTISM OF JESUS.

MATT. 3:13–17.	MARK 1:9–11.	LUKE 3:21, 22, ⌜23a⌝.
13 Then cometh Jesus from Galilee to the Jordan unto John, to be baptized of him. 14 But John would have hindered him, saying, I have need to be baptized of thee, and comest thou to me? 15 But Jesus answering said unto him, Suffer [4]*it* now: for thus it becometh us to fulfil all righteousness. Then he suffereth him. 16 And Jesus, when he was baptized, went up straightway from the water: and lo, the heavens were opened [5]unto him, and	9 And it came to pass in those days, that Jesus came from Nazareth of Galilee, and was baptized of John [6]in the Jordan. 10 And straightway coming up out of the water, he saw the heavens rent asunder, and the Spirit as a dove descending upon him: 11 and a voice came out of the heavens, Thou art my beloved Son, in thee I am well pleased.	21 Now it came to pass, when all the people were baptized, that, Jesus also having been baptized, and praying, the heaven was opened, 22 and the Holy Ghost[2] descended in a bodily form, as a dove, upon him, and a voice came out of heaven, Thou art my beloved Son; in thee I am well pleased.

ERV. mg.:   [1] Gr. *sufficient*.   [2] Or, *in*   [3] Or, *the gospel*   [4] Or, *me*   [5] Some ancient authorities omit *unto him*.   [6] Gr. *into*

ARV. txt.:   [1] in   [2] Holy Spirit   [3] *in*   [4] thoroughly   [5] added this also to them all

Matt. 3.		Luke 3.
he saw the Spirit of God descending as a dove, and coming upon him ; 17 and lo, a voice out of the heavens, saying, ¹ This is my beloved Son, in whom I am well pleased.		
		⌐23 And Jesus himself, when he began *to teach*, was about thirty years of age,¹ (§ 3)

§ 20. THE TEMPTATION IN THE WILDERNESS.

Matt. 4:1–11.	Mark 1:12, 13.	Luke 4:1–13.
1 Then was Jesus led up of the Spirit into the wilderness to be tempted of the devil. 2 And when he had fasted forty days and forty nights, he afterward hungered. 3 And the tempter came and said unto him, If thou art the Son of God, command that these stones become ² bread. 4 But he answered and said, It is written, Man shall not live by bread alone, but by every word that proceedeth out of the mouth of God. 5 Then the devil taketh him into the holy city ; and he set him on the ³ pinnacle of the temple, 6 and saith unto him, If thou art the Son of God, cast thyself down : for it is written, He shall give his angels charge concerning thee : And on¹ their hands they shall bear thee up, Lest haply thou dash thy foot against a stone. 7 Jesus said unto him, Again it is written, Thou shalt not tempt² the Lord thy God. 8 Again, the devil taketh him unto an exceeding high moun-	12 And straightway the Spirit driveth him forth into the wilderness. 13 And he was in the wilderness forty days tempted of Satan ; and he was with the wild beasts ; and the angels ministered unto him.	1 And Jesus, full of the Holy Spirit, returned from the Jordan, and was led ⁴ by ³ the Spirit in the wilderness 2 during forty days, being tempted of the devil. And he did eat nothing in those days : and when they were completed, he hungered. 3 And the devil said unto him, If thou art the Son of God, command this stone that it become ⁵ bread. 4 And Jesus answered unto him, It is written, Man shall not live by bread alone. 5 And he led him up, and shewed him all the kingdoms of ⁶ the world in a moment of time. 6 And the devil said unto him, To thee will I give all this authority, and the glory of them : for it hath been delivered unto me ; and to whomsoever I will I give it. 7 If thou therefore wilt worship before me, it shall all be thine. 8 And Jesus answered and said unto him, It is written, Thou shalt worship the Lord thy God, and him only shalt thou serve. 9 And he led him to Jerusalem, and set him on

ERV. mg.: ¹ Or, *This is my Son; my beloved in whom I am well pleased.* See ch. xii. 18.   ² Gr. *loaves.*   ³ Gr. *wing.*   ⁴ Or, *in*
⁵ Or, *a loaf*   ⁶ Gr. *the inhabited earth.*

ARV. txt.: ¹ and, On   ² make trial of   ³ in

MATT. 4.

tain, and sheweth him all the kingdoms of the world, and the glory of them; 9 and he said unto him, All these things will I give thee, if thou wilt fall down and worship me. 10 Then saith Jesus unto him, Get thee hence, Satan: for it is written, Thou shalt worship the Lord thy God, and him only shalt thou serve. 11 Then the devil leaveth him; and behold, angels came and ministered unto him.

LUKE 4.

the [1]pinnacle of the temple, and said unto him, If thou art the Son of God, cast thyself down from hence: 10 for it is written,

He shall give his angels charge concerning thee,
to guard thee:

11 and,

On their hands they shall bear thee up,
Lest haply thou dash thy foot against a stone.

12 And Jesus answering said unto him, It is said, Thou shalt not tempt[1] the Lord thy God. 13 And when the devil had completed every temptation, he departed from him [2]for a season.

§ 21. JOHN'S TESTIMONY BEFORE THE PRIESTS AND LEVITES.

JOHN 1: 19–28.

19 And this is the witness of John, when the Jews sent unto him from Jerusalem priests and Levites to ask him, Who art thou? 20 And he confessed, and denied not; and he confessed, I am not the Christ. 21 And they asked him, What then? Art thou Elijah? And he saith, I am not. Art thou the prophet? And he answered, No. 22 They said therefore unto him, Who art thou? that we may give an answer to them that sent us. What sayest thou of thyself? 23 He said, I am the voice of one crying in the wilderness, Make straight the way of the Lord, as said Isaiah the prophet. 24 [3]And they had been sent from the Pharisees. 25 And they asked him, and said unto him, Why then baptizest thou, if thou art not the Christ, neither Elijah, neither the prophet? 26 John answered them, saying, I baptize [4]with[2] water: in the midst of you standeth one whom ye know not, 27 *even* he that cometh after me, the latchet of whose shoe I am not worthy to unloose. 28 These things were done in [5]Bethany beyond Jordan[3], where John was baptizing.

§ 22. JESUS THE LAMB OF GOD.

JOHN 1: 29–34.

29 On the morrow he seeth Jesus coming unto him, and saith, Behold, the Lamb of God, which[4] [6]taketh away the sin of the world! 30 This is he of whom I said, After me cometh a man which[4] is become before me: for he was [7]before me. 31 And I knew him not; but that he should be made manifest to Israel, for this cause came I baptizing [4]with[2] water.

ERV. mg.:   [1] Gr. *wing.*   [2] Or, *until*   [3] Or, *And* certain *had been sent from among the Pharisees.*   [4] Or, *in*   [5] Many ancient authorities read *Bethabarah,* some, *Betharabah.*   [6] Or, *beareth the sin*   [7] Gr. *first in regard of me.*

ARV. txt.:   [1] make trial of   [2] in   [3] the Jordan   [4] who

JOHN 1.

32 And John bare witness, saying, I have beheld the Spirit descending as a dove out of heaven; and it abode upon him. 33 And I knew him not: but he that sent me to baptize [1]with[1] water, he said unto me, Upon whomsoever thou shalt see the Spirit descending, and abiding upon him, the same is he that baptizeth [1]with[1] the Holy Spirit. 34 And I have seen, and have borne witness that this is the Son of God.

§ 23. THE FIRST THREE DISCIPLES.

JOHN 1: 35–42.

35 Again on the morrow John was standing, and two of his disciples; 36 and he looked upon Jesus as he walked, and saith, Behold, the Lamb of God! 37 And the two disciples heard him speak, and they followed Jesus. 38 And Jesus turned, and beheld them following, and saith unto them, What seek ye? And they said unto him, Rabbi (which is to say, being interpreted, [2]Master[2]), where abidest thou? 39 He saith unto them, Come, and ye shall see. They came therefore and saw where he abode; and they abode with him that day: it was about the tenth hour. 40 One of the two that heard John *speak*, and followed him, was Andrew, Simon Peter's brother. 41 He findeth first his own brother Simon, and saith unto him, We have found the Messiah (which is, being interpreted, [3]Christ). 42 He brought him unto Jesus. Jesus looked upon him, and said, Thou art Simon the son of [4]John: thou shalt be called Cephas (which is by interpretation, [5]Peter).

§ 24. PHILIP AND NATHANAEL.

JOHN 1: 43–51.

43 On the morrow he was minded to go forth into Galilee, and he findeth Philip: and Jesus saith unto him, Follow me. 44 Now Philip was from Bethsaida, of the city of Andrew and Peter. 45 Philip findeth Nathanael, and saith unto him, We have found him, of whom Moses in the law, and the prophets, did write[3], Jesus of Nazareth, the son of Joseph. 46 And Nathanael said unto him, Can any good thing come out of Nazareth? Philip saith unto him, Come and see. 47 Jesus saw Nathanael coming to him, and saith of him, Behold, an Israelite indeed, in whom is no guile! 48 Nathanael saith unto him, Whence knowest thou me? Jesus answered and said unto him, Before Philip called thee, when thou wast under the fig tree, I saw thee. 49 Nathanael answered him, Rabbi, thou art the Son of God; thou art King of Israel. 50 Jesus answered and said unto him, Because I said unto thee, I saw thee underneath the fig tree, believest thou? thou shalt see greater things than these. 51 And he saith unto him, Verily, verily, I say unto you, Ye shall see the heaven opened, and the angels of God ascending and descending upon the Son of man.

§ 25. THE FIRST MIRACLE: WATER MADE WINE.

JOHN 2: 1–11.

1 And the third day there was a marriage in Cana of Galilee; and the mother of Jesus was there: 2 and Jesus also was bidden, and his disciples, to the marriage. 3 And when the wine failed, the mother of Jesus saith unto him, They have no wine. 4 And Jesus saith

---

ERV. mg.: [1] Or, *in* [2] Or, *Teacher* [3] That is, *Anointed*. [4] Gr. *Joanes:* called in Matt. xvi. 17, *Jonah*. [5] That is, *Rock or Stone*.

ARV. txt.: [1] in [2] Teacher [3] wrote

unto her, Woman, what have I to do with thee? mine hour is not yet come. 5 His mother saith unto the servants, Whatsoever he saith unto you, do it. 6 Now there were six water-pots of stone set there after the Jews' manner of purifying, containing two or three firkins apiece. 7 Jesus saith unto them, Fill the waterpots with water. And they filled them up to the brim. 8 And he saith unto them, Draw out now, and bear unto the [1]ruler of the feast. And they bare it. 9 And when the ruler of the feast tasted the water [2]now become wine, and knew not whence it was (but the servants which[1] had drawn the water knew), the ruler of the feast calleth the bridegroom, 10 and saith unto him, Every man setteth on first the good wine ; and when *men* have drunk freely, *then* that which is worse : thou hast kept the good wine until now. 11 This beginning of his signs did Jesus in Cana of Galilee, and mani-fested his glory ; and his disciples believed on him.

§ 26. SOJOURN IN CAPERNAUM.

J OHN **2** : 12.

12 After this he went down to Capernaum, he, and his mother, and *his* brethren, and his disciples : and there they abode not many days.

ERV. mg.: [1] Or, *steward*   [2] Or, *that it had become*

ARV. txt.: [1] that

PART III.

THE EARLY JUDEAN MINISTRY.

FROM THE PUBLIC APPEARANCE OF JESUS IN JERUSALEM UNTIL HIS RETURN TO GALILEE.

§ 27. FIRST CLEANSING OF THE TEMPLE.

[MATT. 21 : 12–17. And Jesus entered into the temple [1] of God, and cast out all them that sold and bought in the temple, and overthrew the tables of the money-changers, and the seats of them that sold the doves; 13 and he saith unto them, It is written, My house shall be called a house of prayer : but ye make it a den of robbers. 14 And the blind and the lame came to him in the temple: and he healed them. 15 But when the chief priests and the scribes saw the wonderful things that he did, and the children that were crying in the temple and saying, Hosanna to the son of David; they were moved with indignation, 16 and said unto him, Hearest thou what these are saying? And Jesus saith unto them, Yea: did ye never read, Out

[MARK 11 : 15–18. And they come to Jerusalem : and he entered into the temple, and began to cast out them that sold and them that bought in the temple, and overthrew the tables of the money-changers, and the seats of them that sold the doves; 16 and he would not suffer that any man should carry a vessel through the temple. 17 And he taught, and said unto them, Is it not written, My house shall be called a house of prayer for all the nations? but ye have made it a den of robbers. 18 And the chief priests and the scribes heard it, and sought how they might destroy him : for they feared him, for all the multitude was astonished at his teaching.] (§ 121)

[LUKE 19 : 45–48. And he entered into the temple, and began to cast out them that sold, 46 saying unto them, It is written, And my house shall be a house of prayer : but ye have made it a den of robbers. 47 And he was teaching daily in the temple. But the chief priests and the scribes and the principal men of the people sought to destroy him : 48 and they could not find what they might do ; for the people all hung upon him, listening.] (§ 121)

JOHN 2 : 13–22.

13 And the passover of the Jews was at hand, and Jesus went up to Jerusalem. 14 And he found in the temple those that sold oxen and sheep and doves, and the changers of money sitting : 15 and he made a scourge of cords, and cast all out of the temple, both the sheep and the oxen; and he poured out the changers' money, and overthrew their tables; 16 and to them that sold the doves he said, Take these things hence ; make not my Father's house a house of merchandise. 17 His disciples remembered that it was written, The zeal of thine [1] house shall eat me up. 18 The Jews therefore answered and said unto him, What sign shewest thou unto us,

ERV. mg.: [1] Many ancient authorities omit *of God*.

ARV. txt.: [1] Zeal for thy

[MATT. 21.]

of the mouth of babes
and sucklings thou hast
perfected praise? 17 And
he left them, and went
forth out of the city to
Bethany, and lodged
there.]   (§ 121)

JOHN 2.

seeing that thou doest
these things? 19 Jesus
answered and said
unto them, Destroy
this [1] temple, and in
three days I will raise
it up. 20 The Jews
therefore said, Forty
and six years was
this [1] temple in build-
ing, and wilt thou
raise it up in three
days? 21 But he
spake of the [1] temple
of his body. 22 When
therefore he was
raised from the dead,
his disciples remem-
bered that he spake
this; and they be-
lieved the scripture,
and the word which
Jesus had said.

§ 28. DISCOURSE WITH NICODEMUS.

JOHN 2 : 23—3 : 21

2 : 23 Now when he was in Jerusalem at the passover, during the feast, many believed on his name, beholding his signs which he did. 24 But Jesus did not trust himself unto them, for that he knew all men, 25 and because he needed not that any one should bear witness concerning [2] man; for he himself knew what was in man.

3 : 1 Now there was a man of the Pharisees, named Nicodemus, a ruler of the Jews: 2 the same came unto him by night, and said to him, Rabbi, we know that thou art a teacher come from God : for no man [1] can do these signs that thou doest, except God be with him. 3 Jesus answered and said unto him, Verily, verily, I say unto thee, Except a man [2] be born [3] anew, he cannot see the kingdom of God. 4 Nicodemus saith unto him, How can a man be born when he is old? can he enter a second time into his mother's womb, and be born? 5 Jesus answered, Verily, verily, I say unto thee, Except a man [2] be born of water and the Spirit, he cannot enter into the kingdom of God. 6 That which is born of the flesh is flesh; and that which is born of the Spirit is spirit. 7 Marvel not that I said unto thee, Ye must be born [3] anew. 8 [4] The wind bloweth where it listeth [3], and thou hearest the voice thereof, but knowest not whence it cometh, and whither it goeth : so is every one that is born of the Spirit. 9 Nicodemus answered and said unto him, How can these things be? 10 Jesus answered and said unto him, Art thou the teacher of Israel, and understandest not these things? 11 Verily, verily, I say unto thee, We speak that [4] we do [5] know, and bear witness

ERV. mg.:   [1] Or, *sanctuary*   [2] Or, *a man; for . . . the man*   [3] Or, *from above*   [4] Or, *The Spirit breatheth*

ARV. txt.:   [1] no one   [2] Except one   [3] will   [4] that which   [5] *Omit* do

JOHN **3.**

of that[1] we have seen; and ye receive not our witness. 12 If I told you earthly things, and ye believe not, how shall ye believe, if I tell you heavenly things? 13 And no man[2] hath ascended into heaven, but he that descended out of heaven, *even* the Son of man, [1]which[3] is in heaven. 14 And as Moses lifted up the serpent in the wilderness, even so must the Son of man be lifted up: 15 that whosoever [2]believeth may in him have eternal life.

16 For God so loved the world, that he gave his only begotten Son, that whosoever believeth on him should not perish, but have eternal life. 17 For God sent not the Son into the world to judge the world; but that the world should be saved through him. 18 [a]He that believeth on him is not judged: he that believeth not hath been judged already, because he hath not believed on the name of the only begotten Son of God. 19 And this is the judgement, that the light is come into the world, and men loved the darkness rather than the light; for their works were evil. 20 For every one that [3]doeth ill[4] hateth the light, and cometh not to the light, lest his works should be [4]reproved. 21 But he that doeth the truth cometh to the light, that his works may be made manifest, [5]that they have been wrought in God.

§ 29. CHRIST BAPTIZING IN JUDEA.
JOHN **3**: 22–24.

22 After these things came Jesus and his disciples into the land of Judæa; and there he tarried with them, and baptized.* 23 And John also was baptizing in Ænon near to Salim, because there [6]was much water there: and they came, and were baptized. 24 For John was not yet cast into prison.

§ 30. JOHN'S TESTIMONY TO CHRIST AT ÆNON.
JOHN **3**: 25–36.

25 There arose therefore a questioning on the part of John's disciples with a Jew about purifying. 26 And they came unto John, and said to him, Rabbi, he that was with thee beyond Jordan[5], to whom thou hast borne witness, behold, the same baptizeth, and all men come to him. 27 John answered and said, A man can receive nothing, except it have been given him from heaven. 28 Ye yourselves bear me witness, that I said, I am not the Christ, but, that I am sent before him. 29 He that hath the bride is the bridegroom: but the friend of the bridegroom, which[6] standeth and heareth him, rejoiceth greatly because of the bridegroom's voice: this my joy therefore is fulfilled[7]. 30 He must increase, but I must decrease.

31 He that cometh from above is above all: he that is of the earth is of the earth, and of the earth he speaketh: [7]he that cometh. from heaven is above all. 32 What he hath seen and heard, of that he beareth witness; and no man receiveth his witness. 33 He that hath received his witness hath set his seal to *this*, that God is true. 34 For he whom God hath sent speaketh the words of God: for he giveth not the Spirit by measure. 35 The Father loveth the Son, and hath given all things into his hand. 36 He that believeth on the Son hath eternal life; but he that [8]obeyeth not the Son shall not see life, but the wrath of God abideth on him.

ERV. mg.: **1** Many ancient authorities omit *which is in heaven.* **2** Or, *believeth in him may have* **3** Or, *practiseth* **4** Or, *convicted* **5** Or, *because* **6** Gr. *were many waters.* **7** Some ancient authorities read *he that cometh from heaven beareth witness of what he hath seen and heard.* **8** Or, *believeth not*

ARV. txt.: **1** that which **2** no one **3** who **4** evil **5** the Jordan **6** that **7** made full

[a] Mark 16:16. He that believeth and is baptized shall be saved; but he that disbelieveth shall be condemned. (§ 149)
* Cf. John 4: 1, 2. (§ 31)

§ 31. THE DEPARTURE FROM JUDEA.

⌐MATT. 4:12.┐	⌐MARK 1:14.┐		JOHN 4:1-3.
⌐12 Now when he heard that John was delivered up, he withdrew into Galilee;┐ (§ 34)	⌐14 Now after that[1] John was delivered up, Jesus came into Galilee, preaching the gospel of God,┐ (§ 34)		1 When therefore the Lord knew how[2] that the Pharisees had heard that Jesus was making and baptizing more disciples than John 2 (although Jesus himself baptized not, but his disciples), 3 he left Judæa, and departed again into Galilee.

§ 32. DISCOURSE WITH THE WOMAN OF SAMARIA.

JOHN 4:4-26.

4 And he must needs pass through Samaria. 5 So he cometh to a city of Samaria, called Sychar, near to the parcel of ground that Jacob gave to his son Joseph: 6 and Jacob's [1] well was there. Jesus therefore, being wearied with his journey, sat [2] thus by the [1] well. It was about the sixth hour. 7 There cometh a woman of Samaria to draw water: Jesus saith unto her, Give me to drink. 8 For his disciples were gone away into the city to buy food. 9 The Samaritan woman therefore saith unto him, How is it that thou, being a Jew, askest drink of me, which [3] am a Samaritan woman? ([3] For Jews have no dealings with Samaritans.) 10 Jesus answered and said unto her, If thou knewest the gift of God, and who it is that saith to thee, Give me to drink; thou wouldest have asked of him, and he would have given thee living water. 11 The woman saith unto him, [4] Sir, thou hast nothing to draw with, and the well is deep: from [4] whence then hast thou that living water? 12 Art thou greater than our father Jacob, which [3] gave us the well, and drank thereof himself, and his sons, and his cattle? 13 Jesus answered and said unto her, Every one that drinketh of this water shall thirst again: 14 but whosoever drinketh of the water that I shall give him shall never thirst; but the water that I shall give him shall become in him a well of water springing up unto eternal life. 15 The woman saith unto him, [4] Sir, give me this water, that I thirst not, neither come all the way hither to draw. 16 Jesus saith unto her, Go, call thy husband, and come hither. 17 The woman answered and said unto him, I have no husband. Jesus saith unto her, Thou saidst well, I have no husband: 18 for thou hast had five husbands; and he whom thou now hast is not thy husband: this hast thou said truly. 19 The woman saith unto him, [4] Sir, I perceive that thou art a prophet. 20 Our fathers worshipped in this mountain; and ye say, that in Jerusalem is the place where men ought to worship. 21 Jesus saith unto her, Woman, believe me, the hour cometh, when neither in this mountain, nor in Jerusalem, shall ye worship the Father. 22 Ye worship that which ye know not: we worship that which we know: for salvation is from the Jews. 23 But the hour cometh, and now is,

---

ERV. mg.:   [1] Gr. *spring:* and so in ver. 14; but not in ver. 11, 12.   [2] Or, *as he was*   [3] Some ancient authorities omit *For Jews have no dealings with Samaritans.*   [4] Or, *Lord*

ARV. txt.:   [1] *Omit* that   [2] *Omit* how   [3] *who*   [4] *Omit* from

JOHN 4.

when the true worshippers shall worship the Father in spirit and truth : [1] for such doth the Father seek to be his worshippers. 24 [2] God is a Spirit: and they that worship him must worship in spirit and truth. 25 The woman saith unto him, I know that Messiah cometh (which [1] is called Christ): when he is come, he will declare unto us all things. 26 Jesus saith unto her, I that speak unto thee am *he*.

§33. THE GOSPEL IN SYCHAR.

JOHN 4: 27–42.

27 And upon this came his disciples; and they marvelled that he was speaking with a woman; yet no man said, What seekest thou? or, Why speakest thou with her? 28 So the woman left her waterpot, and went away into the city, and saith to the men [2], 29 Come, see a man, which [3] told me all things that *ever* I did: can this be the Christ? 30 They went out of the city, and were coming to him. 31 In the mean while the disciples prayed him, saying, Rabbi, eat. 32 But he said unto them, I have meat to eat that ye know not. 33 The disciples therefore said one to another, Hath any man brought him *aught* to eat? 34 Jesus saith unto them, My meat is to do the will of him that sent me, and to accomplish his work. 35 Say not ye, There are yet four months, and *then* cometh the harvest? behold, I say unto you, Lift up your eyes, and look on the fields, that they are [3] white already unto harvest. 36 He that reapeth receiveth wages, and gathereth fruit unto life eternal; that he that soweth and he that reapeth may rejoice together. 37 For herein is the saying true, One soweth, and another reapeth. 38 I sent you to reap that whereon ye have not laboured: others have laboured, and ye are entered into their labour.

39 And from that city many of the Samaritans believed on him because of the word of the woman, who testified, He told me all things that *ever* I did. 40 So when the Samaritans came unto him, they besought him to abide with them: and he abode there two days. 41 And many more believed because of his word; 42 and they said to the woman, Now we believe, not because of thy speaking: for we have heard for ourselves, and know that this is indeed the Saviour of the world.

ERV. mg.: [1] Or, *for such the Father also seeketh* [2] Or, *God is spirit* [3] Or, *while unto harvest. Already he that reapeth &c.*

ARV. txt.: [1] he that [2] people [3] who

PART IV.

FIRST PERIOD OF THE GALILEAN MINISTRY.

FROM THE RETURN TO GALILEE UNTIL THE CHOOSING OF THE TWELVE.

---

§ 34. THE BEGINNING OF CHRIST'S GALILEAN MINISTRY.

MATT. 4 : 12 [13–16] 17.	MARK 1 : 14, 15.	LUKE 4 : 14, 15.	JOHN 4 : 43–45.
12 Now when he heard that John was delivered up,* he withdrew into Galilee; [13 and leaving Nazareth, he came and dwelt in Capernaum, which is by the sea, in the borders of Zebulun and Naphtali: 14 that it might be fulfilled which was spoken ¹by¹ Isaiah the prophet, saying, 15 The land of Zebulun and the land of Naphtali, ²Toward the sea, beyond Jordan², Galilee of the ³Gentiles, 16 The people which³ sat in darkness Saw a great light,	14 Now after that⁴ John was delivered up,* Jesus came into Galilee, preaching the gospel of God, 15 and saying, The time is fulfilled, and the kingdom of God is at hand: repent ye, and believe in the gospel.	14 And Jesus returned in the power of the Spirit into Galilee: and a fame went out concerning him through all the region round about. 15 And he taught in their synagogues, being glorified of all.	43 And after the two days he went forth from thence into Galilee. 44 For Jesus himself testified, that a prophet hath no honour in his own country. 45 So when he came into Galilee, the Galilæans received him, having seen all things⁵ that he did in Jerusalem at the feast: for they also went unto the feast.

---

*The facts concerning the imprisonment of John are more fully stated in the following passages:
Matt. 14: 3–5. For Herod had laid hold on John, and bound him, and put him in prison for the sake of Herodias, his brother Philip's wife. 4 For John said unto him, It is not lawful for thee to have her. 5 And when he would have put him to death, he feared the multitude, because they counted him as a prophet. (§ 65)
Mark 6: 17, 18. For Herod himself had sent forth and laid hold upon John, and bound him in prison for the sake of Herodias, his brother Philip's wife: for he had married her. 18 For John said unto Herod, It is not lawful for thee to have thy brother's wife. (§ 65)
Luke 3: 19, 20. But Herod the tetrarch, being reproved by him for Herodias his brother's wife, and for all the evil things which Herod had done, 20 added yet this above all, that he shut up John in prison. (§ 18)

ERV. mg.: ¹ Or, *through*   ² Gr. *The way of the sea.*   ³ Gr. *nations*: and so elsewhere.

ARV. txt.: ¹ through   ² the Jordan   ³ that   ⁴ *Omit* that   ⁵ all the things

MATT. **4.**		
And to them which[1] sat in the region and shadow of death, To them did light spring up.] (§ 37) 17 From that time began Jesus to preach, and to say, Repent ye; for the kingdom of heaven is at hand. (+ § 38)		

§ 35. THE NOBLEMAN'S SON.

JOHN 4: 46–54.

46 .He came therefore again unto Cana of Galilee, where he made the water wine. And there was a certain [1]nobleman, whose son was sick at Capernaum. 47 When he heard that Jesus was come out of Judæa into Galilee, he went unto him, and besought *him* that he would come down, and heal his son; for he was at the point of death. 48 Jesus therefore said unto him, Except ye see signs and wonders, ye will in no wise believe. 49 The [1]nobleman saith unto him, [2]Sir, come down ere my child die. 50 Jesus saith unto him, Go thy way; thy son liveth. The man believed the word that Jesus spake unto him, and he went his way. 51 And as he was now going down, his [3]servants met him, saying, that his son lived. 52 So he inquired of them the hour when he began to amend. They said therefore unto him, Yesterday at the seventh hour the fever left him. 53 So the father knew that *it was* at that hour in which Jesus said unto him, Thy son liveth: and himself believed, and his whole house. 54 This is again the second sign that Jesus did, having come out of Judæa into Galilee.

§ 36. FIRST REJECTION AT NAZARETH.

		LUKE **4**: 16–30.
[MATT. 13 : 54–58. And coming into his own country he taught them in their synagogue, insomuch that they were astonished, and said, Whence hath this man this wisdom, and these [4]mighty works? 55 Is not this the carpenter's son? is not his mother called Mary? and his brethren, James, and Joseph, and Simon, and Judas? 56 And	[MARK 6: 1–6a. And he went out from thence; and he cometh into his own country; and his disciples follow him. 2 And when the sabbath was come, he began to teach in the synagogue: and [5]many hearing him were astonished, saying, Whence hath this man these things? and, What is the wisdom that is given unto this man, and *what mean*	16 And he came to Nazareth, where he had been brought up: and he entered, as his custom was, into the synagogue on the sabbath day, and stood up to read. 17 And there was delivered unto him [6]the book of the prophet Isaiah. And he opened the [7]book, and found the place where it was written,

ERV. mg.: [1] Or, *king's officer* [2] Or, *Lord* [3] Gr. *bondservants.* [4] Gr. *powers.* [5] Some ancient authorities insert *the.* [6] Or, *a roll* [7] Or, *roll*

ARV. txt.: [1] that

[MATT. **13**.]

his sisters, are they not all with us? Whence then hath this man all these things? 57 And they were [1]offended in him. [a]But Jesus said unto them, A prophet is not without honour, save in his own country, and in his own house. 58 And he did not many [2]mighty works there because of their unbelief.]   (§ 62)

[MARK **6**.]

such [2]mighty works wrought by his hands? 3 Is not this the carpenter, the son of Mary, and brother of James, and Joses, and Judas, and Simon? and are not his sisters here with us? And they were [1]offended in him. 4 [a]And Jesus said unto them, A prophet is not without honour, save in his own country, and among his own kin, and in his own house. 5 And he could there do no [3]mighty work, save that he laid his hands upon a few sick folk, and healed them. 6 And he marvelled because of their unbelief.]   (§ 62)

LUKE **4**.

18 The Spirit of the Lord is upon me,
    [4]Because he anointed me to preach [5]good tidings to the poor:
He hath sent me to proclaim release to the captives,
And recovering of sight to the blind,
To set at liberty them that are bruised,
19 To proclaim the acceptable year of the Lord.
20 And he closed the [6]book, and gave it back to the attendant, and sat down: and the eyes of all in the synagogue were fastened on him. 21 And he began to say unto them, Today hath this scripture been fulfilled in your ears. 22 And all bare him witness, and wondered at the words of grace which proceeded out of his mouth: and they said, Is not this Joseph's son? 23 And he said unto them, Doubtless ye will say unto me this parable, Physician, heal thyself: whatsoever we have heard done at Capernaum, do also here in thine own country. 24 And he said, [a]Verily I say unto you, No prophet is acceptable in his own country. 25 But of a truth I say unto you, There were many widows in Israel in the days of Elijah, when the heaven was shut up three years and six months, when there came a great famine over all the land; 26 and unto none of them was Elijah sent,

---

ERV. mg.:   [1] Gr. *caused to stumble.*   [2] Gr. *powers.*   [3] Gr. *power.*   [4] Or, *Wherefore*   [5] Or, *the gospel*   [6] Or, *roll*

[a] Matt. 13:57 (§ 62); Mark 6:4 (§ 62). See above. Cf. also John 4:44 (§ 34).

LUKE 4.

but only to [1]Zarephath, in the land of Sidon, unto a woman that was a widow. 27 And there were many lepers in Israel in the time of Elisha the prophet; and none of them was cleansed, but only Naaman the Syrian. 28 And they were all filled with wrath in the synagogue, as they heard these things; 29 and they rose up, and cast him forth out of the city, and led him unto the brow of the hill whereon their city was built, that they might throw him down headlong. 30 But he passing through the midst of them went his way. (+ §39)

§37. REMOVAL TO CAPERNAUM.

⌈MATT. 4:13–16.⌉

⌈13 and leaving Nazareth, he came and dwelt in Capernaum, which is by the sea, in the borders of Zebulun and Naphtali: 14 that it might be fulfilled which was spoken [2]by[1] Isaiah the prophet, saying,
15 The land of Zebulun and the land of Naphtali,
[3]Toward the sea, beyond Jordan[2],
Galilee of the [4]Gentiles,
16 The people which[3] sat in darkness
Saw a great light,
And to them which[3] sat in the region and shadow of death,
To them did light spring up.⌉ (§34)

⌈LUKE 4:31a.⌉

⌈31 And he came down to Capernaum, a city of Galilee.⌉ (§39)

ERV. mg.: [1] Gr. *Sarepta.* [2] Or, *through* [3] Gr. *The way of the sea.* [4] Gr. *nations*: and so elsewhere.

ARV. txt.: [1] through [2] the Jordan [3] that

§ 38. THE CALL OF THE FOUR.

MATT. 4:18–22.	MARK 1:16–20.	LUKE 5:1–11.

18 And walking by the sea of Galilee, he saw two brethren, Simon who is called Peter, and Andrew his brother, casting a net into the sea; for they were fishers. 19 And he saith unto them, Come ye after me, and I will make you fishers of men. 20 And they straightway left the nets, and followed him. 21 And going on from thence he saw other two brethren, [1]James the *son* of Zebedee, and John his brother, in the boat with Zebedee their father, mending their nets; and he called them. 22 And they straightway left the boat and their father, and followed him. (+ § 47)

16 And passing along by the sea of Galilee, he saw Simon and Andrew the brother of Simon casting a net in the sea: for they were fishers. 17 And Jesus said unto them, Come ye after me, and I will make you to become fishers of men. 18 And straightway they left the nets, and followed him. 19 And going on a little further, he saw James the *son* of Zebedee, and John his brother, who also were in the boat mending the nets. 20 And straightway he called them: and they left their father Zebedee in the boat with the hired servants, and went after him.

1 Now it came to pass, while the multitude pressed upon him and heard the word of God, that he was standing by the lake of Gennesaret; 2 and he saw two boats standing by the lake: but the fishermen had gone out of them, and were washing their nets. 3 And he entered into one of the boats, which was Simon's, and asked him to put out a little from the land. And he sat down and taught the multitudes out of the boat. 4 And when he had left speaking, he said unto Simon, Put out into the deep, and let down your nets for a draught. 5 And Simon answered and said, Master, we toiled all night, and took nothing: but at thy word I will let down the nets. 6 And when they had this done[1], they inclosed a great multitude of fishes; and their nets were breaking; 7 and they beckoned unto their partners in the other boat, that they should come and help them. And they came, and filled both the boats, so that they began to sink. 8 But Simon Peter, when he saw it, fell down at Jesus' knees, saying, Depart from me; for I am a sinful man, O Lord 9 For he was amazed, and all that were with him, at the draught of the fishes which they had taken; 10 and so were also James and John, sons of

ERV. mg.: [1] Or, *Jacob*: and so elsewhere

ARV. txt.: [1] done this

LUKE 5.

Zebedee, which[1] were partners with Simon. And Jesus said unto Simon, Fear not; from henceforth thou shalt [1]catch men. 11 And when they had brought their boats to land, they left all, and followed him. (+ § 40)

§ 39. A DAY OF MIRACLES IN CAPERNAUM.

MATT. 8 : 14–17.

MARK 1 : 21–34.

21 And they go into Capernaum; and straightway on the sabbath day he entered into the synagogue and taught. 22 And they were astonished at his teaching: for he taught them as having authority, and not as the scribes. 23 And straightway there was in their synagogue a man with an unclean spirit; and he cried out, 24 saying, What have we to do with thee, thou Jesus of Nazareth[2]? art thou come to destroy us? I know thee who thou art, the Holy One of God. 25 And Jesus rebuked [2]him, saying, Hold thy peace, and come out of him. 26 And the unclean spirit, [3]tearing him and crying with a loud voice, came out of him. 27 And they were all amazed, insomuch that they questioned among themselves, saying, What is this? a new teaching! with authority he commandeth even the unclean spirits, and they obey him. 28 And the report of him went out straightway everywhere into all the region of Galilee round about.

LUKE 4 : 31–41.

31 And he came down to Capernaum, a city of Galilee. And he was teaching them on the sabbath day: 32 and they were astonished at his teaching; for his word was with authority. 33 And in the synagogue there was a man, which[3] had a spirit of an unclean [4]devil[4]; and he cried out with a loud voice, 34 [5]Ah! what have we to do with thee, thou Jesus of Nazareth[2]? art thou come to destroy us? I know thee who thou art, the Holy One of God. 35 And Jesus rebuked him, saying, Hold thy peace, and come out of him. And when the [4]devil[4] had thrown him down in the midst he came out of him, having done him no hurt. 36 And amazement came upon all, and they spake together, one with another, saying, What is [6]this word? for with authority and power he commandeth the unclean spirits, and they come out. 37 And there went forth a rumour concerning him into every place of the region round about.

ERV. mg.: [1] Gr. *take alive.* [2] Or, *it* [3] Or, *convulsing* [4] Gr. *demon.* [5] Or, *Let alone* [6] Or, *this word, that with authority* . . . . *come out?*

ARV. txt.: [1] who [2] Jesus thou Nazarene [3] that [4] demon

MATT. 8.	MARK 1.	LUKE 4.
14 And when Jesus was come into Peter's house, he saw his wife's mother lying sick of a fever. 15 And he touched her hand, and the fever left her; and she arose, and ministered unto him.	29 And straightway, [3] when they were come out of the synagogue, they came into the house of Simon and Andrew, with James and John. 30 Now Simon's wife's mother lay sick of a fever; and straightway they tell him of her: 31 and he came and took her by the hand, and raised her up; and the fever left her, and she ministered unto them.	38 And he rose up from the synagogue, and entered into the house of Simon. And Simon's wife's mother was holden with a great fever; and they besought him for her. 39 And he stood over her, and rebuked the fever; and it left her: and immediately she rose up and ministered unto them.
16 And when even was come, they brought unto him many [1] possessed with devils [1]: and he cast out the spirits with a word, and healed all that were sick: 17 that it might be fulfilled which was spoken [2] by [2] Isaiah the prophet, saying, Himself took our infirmities, and bare our diseases. (+ § 86)	32 And at even, when the sun did set, they brought unto him all that were sick, and them that were [1] possessed with devils [1]. 33 And all the city was gathered together at the door. 34 And he healed many that were sick with divers diseases, and cast out many [4] devils [1]; and he suffered not the [4] devils [1] to speak, because they knew [5] him.	40 And when the sun was setting, all they that had any sick with divers diseases brought them unto him; and he laid his hands on every one of them, and healed them. 41 And [4] devils [1] also came out from many, crying out, and saying, Thou art the Son of God. And rebuking them, he suffered them not to speak, because they knew that he was the Christ.

§ 40.   FIRST PREACHING TOUR IN GALILEE.

⌐MATT. 4:23.⌐ MATT. 8: [1] 2–4.	MARK 1: 35–45.	LUKE 4: 42–44. LUKE 5: 12–16.
	35 And in the morning, a great while before day, he rose up and went out, and departed into a desert place, and there prayed. 36 And Simon and they that were with him followed after him; 37 and they found him and say unto him, All are seeking thee. 38 And he saith unto them, Let us go elsewhere into the next towns, that I may preach there also; for to this end came I forth.	4:42 And when it was day, he came out and went into a desert place: and the multitudes sought after him, and came unto him, and would have stayed him, that he should not go from them. 43 But he said unto them, I must preach the [6] good tidings of the kingdom of God to the other cities also: for therefore was I sent.

ERV. mg.:   [1] Or, *demoniacs*   [2] Or, *through*   [3] Some ancient authorities read *when he was come out of the synagogue, he came &c.*
[4] Gr. *demons*.   [5] Many ancient authorities add *to be Christ*. See Luke iv. 41.   [6] Or, *gospel*

ARV. txt.:   [1] demons   [2] through

⌜MATT. 4.⌝	MARK 1.	LUKE 4.
⌜4 : 23 And ¹ Jesus went about in all Galilee, teaching in their synagogues, and preaching the ² gospel of the kingdom, and healing all manner of disease and all manner of sickness among the people.⌉ (§ 47)	39 And he went into their synagogues throughout all Galilee, preaching and casting out ³ devils ².	44 And he was preaching in the synagogues of ⁹ Galilee. (+ § 38)
[8 : 1 And when he was come down from the mountain, great multitudes followed him.] 2 And behold, there came to him a leper and worshipped him, saying, Lord, if thou wilt, thou canst make me clean. 3 And he stretched forth his hand, and touched him, saying, I will; be thou made clean. And straightway his leprosy was cleansed. 4 And Jesus saith unto him, See thou tell no man; but go thy way ¹, shew thyself to the priest, and offer the gift that Moses commanded, for a testimony unto them. (+ § 50)	40 And there cometh to him a leper, beseeching him, ⁴ and kneeling down to him, and saying unto him, If thou wilt, thou canst make me clean. 41 And being moved with compassion, he stretched forth his hand, and touched him, and saith unto him, I will; be thou made clean. 42 And straightway the leprosy departed from him, and he was made clean. 43 And he ⁵ strictly charged him, and straightway sent him out, 44 and saith unto him, See thou say nothing to any man: but go thy way ¹, shew thyself to the priest, and offer for thy cleansing the things which Moses commanded, for a testimony unto them. 45 But he went out, and began to publish it much, and to spread abroad the ⁶ matter, insomuch that ⁷ Jesus could no more openly enter into ⁸ a city, but was without in desert places: and they came to him from every quarter.	5 : 12 And it came to pass, while he was in one of the cities, behold, a man full of leprosy: and when he saw Jesus, he fell on his face, and besought him, saying, Lord, if thou wilt, thou canst make me clean. 13 And he stretched forth his hand, and touched him, saying, I will; be thou made clean. And straightway the leprosy departed from him. 14 And he charged him to tell no man: but go thy way, and shew thyself to the priest, and offer for thy cleansing, according as Moses commanded, for a testimony unto them. 15 But so much the more went abroad the report concerning him: and great multitudes came together to hear, and to be healed of their infirmities. 16 But he withdrew himself in the deserts, and prayed.

§ 41. THE PARALYTIC BORNE OF FOUR.

MATT. 9 : [1] 2–8.	MARK 2 : 1–12.	LUKE 5 : 17–26.
[1 And he entered into a boat, and crossed over, and came into his own city.] 2 And	1 And when he entered again into Capernaum after some days, it was noised that	17 And it came to pass on one of those days, that he was teaching; and there were

ERV. mg.: ¹ Some ancient authorities read *he.* ² Or, *good tidings:* and so elsewhere. ³ Gr. *demons.* ⁴ Some ancient authorities omit *and kneeling down to him.* ⁵ Or, *sternly* ⁶ Gr. *word.* ⁷ Gr. *he.* ⁸ Or, *the city* ⁹ Very many ancient authorities read *Judæa.*

ARV. txt.: ¹ *Omit* thy way ² demons

MATT. 9.	MARK 2.	LUKE 5.
behold, they brought to him a man sick of the palsy, lying on a bed: and Jesus seeing their faith said unto the sick of the palsy, [1] Son, be of good cheer; thy sins are forgiven. 3 And behold, certain of the scribes said within themselves, This man blasphemeth. 4 And Jesus [2] knowing their thoughts, said, Wherefore think ye evil in your hearts? 5 For whether [1] is easier, to say, Thy sins are forgiven; or to say, Arise, and walk? 6 But that ye may know that the Son of man hath [3] power [2] on earth to forgive sins (then saith he to the sick of the palsy), Arise, and take up thy bed, and go unto thy house. 7 And he arose, and departed to his house. 8 But when the multitudes saw it, they were afraid, and glorified God, which [3] had given such [3] power [2] unto men.	he was [4] in the house. 2 And many were gathered together, so that there was no longer room *for them*, no, not even about the door: and he spake the word unto them. 3 And they come, bringing unto him a man sick of the palsy, borne of four. 4 And when they could not [5] come nigh unto him for the crowd, they uncovered the roof where he was: and when they had broken it up, they let down the bed whereon the sick of the palsy lay. 5 And Jesus seeing their faith saith unto the sick of the palsy, [1] Son, thy sins are forgiven. 6 But there were certain of the scribes sitting there, and reasoning in their hearts, 7 Why doth this man thus speak? he blasphemeth: who can forgive sins but one, *even* God? 8 And straightway Jesus, perceiving in his spirit that they so reasoned within themselves, saith unto them, Why reason ye these things in your hearts? 9 Whether [1] is easier, to say to the sick of the palsy, Thy sins are forgiven; or to say, Arise, and take up thy bed, and walk? 10 But that ye may know that the Son of man hath [3] power [2] on earth to forgive sins (he saith to the sick of the palsy), 11 I say unto thee, Arise, take up thy bed, and go unto thy house. 12 And he arose, and straightway took up the bed, and went forth before them	Pharisees and doctors of the law sitting by, which [3] were come out of every village of Galilee and Judæa and Jerusalem: and the power of the Lord was with him [6] to heal. 18 And behold, men bring on a bed a man that was palsied: and they sought to bring him in, and to lay him before him. 19 And not finding by what *way* they might bring him in because of the multitude, they went up to the housetop, and let him down through the tiles with his couch into the midst before Jesus. 20 And seeing their faith, he said, Man, thy sins are forgiven thee. 21 And the scribes and the Pharisees began to reason, saying, Who is this that speaketh blasphemies? Who can forgive sins, but God alone? 22 But Jesus perceiving their reasonings, answered and said unto them, [7] What [4] reason ye in your hearts? 23 Whether [5] is easier to say, Thy sins are forgiven thee; or to say, Arise and walk? 24 But that ye may know that the Son of man hath [3] power [2] on earth to forgive sins (he said unto him that was palsied), I say unto thee, Arise, and take up thy couch, and go unto thy house. 25 And immediately he rose up before them, and took up that whereon he lay, and departed to his house, glorifying God. 26 And amazement took hold on all, and they glorified God; and they were

ERV. mg.:   [1] Gr. *Child.*   [2] Many ancient authorities read *seeing.*   [3] Or, *authority*   [4] Or. *at home*   [5] Many ancient authorities read *bring him unto him.*   [6] Gr. *that he should heal.*   Many ancient authorities read *that* he *should heal them.*   [7] Or, *Why*

ARV. txt.:   [1] which   [2] authority   [3] who   [4] Why   [5] Which

MARK 2.	LUKE 5.
all; insomuch that they were all amazed, and glorified God, saying, We never saw it on this fashion.	filled with fear, saying, We have seen strange things to-day.

§ 42. THE CALL OF MATTHEW.

MATT. 9 : 9–13.	MARK 2 : 13–17.	LUKE 5 : 27–32.
9 And as Jesus passed by from thence, he saw a man, called Matthew, sitting at the place of toll: and he saith unto him, Follow me. And he arose, and followed him. 10 And it came to pass, as he [1]sat at meat in the house, behold, many publicans and sinners came and sat down with Jesus and his disciples. 11 And when the Pharisees saw it, they said unto his disciples, Why eateth your [2]Master[1] with the publicans and sinners? 12 But when he heard it, he said, They that are [3]whole have no need of a physician, but they that are sick. 13 But go ye and learn what *this* meaneth, I desire mercy, and not sacrifice: for I came not to call the righteous, but sinners.	13 And he went forth again by the sea side; and all the multitude resorted unto him, and he taught them. 14 And as he passed by, he saw Levi the *son* of Alphæus sitting at the place of toll, and he saith unto him, Follow me. And he arose and followed him. 15 And it came to pass, that he was sitting at meat in his house, and many [4]publicans and sinners sat down with Jesus and his disciples: for there were many, and they followed him. 16 And the scribes [5]of the Pharisees, when they saw that he was eating with the sinners and publicans, said unto his disciples, [6]He eateth [7]and drinketh with publicans and sinners[2]. 17 And when Jesus heard it, he saith unto them, They that are [3]whole have no need of a physician, but they that are sick: I came not to call the righteous, but sinners.	27 And after these things he went forth, and beheld a publican, named Levi, sitting at the place of toll, and said unto him, Follow me. 28 And he forsook all, and rose up and followed him. 29 And Levi made him a great feast in his house: and there was a great multitude of publicans and of others that were sitting at meat with them. 30 And [8]the Pharisees and their scribes murmured against his disciples, saying, Why do ye eat and drink with the publicans and sinners? 31 And Jesus answering said unto them, They that are whole[3] have no need of a physician; but they that are sick. 32 I am not come to call the righteous but sinners to repentance.

§ 43. THE QUESTION ABOUT FASTING.

MATT. 9 : 14–17.	MARK 2 : 18–22.	LUKE 5 : 33–39.
14 Then come to him the disciples of John, saying, Why do we and the Pharisees	18 And John's disciples and the Pharisees were fasting: and they come and say unto	33 And they said unto him, The disciples of John fast often, and make supplica-

ERV. mg.: [1] Gr. *reclined*: and so always.　　[2] Or, *Teacher*　　[3] Gr. *strong*.　　[4] See marginal note on Matt. v. 46.　　[5] Some ancient authorities read *and the Pharisees*.　　[6] Or, How is it *that he eateth . . . sinners?*　　[7] Some ancient authorities omit *and drinketh*.　　[8] Or, *the Pharisees and the scribes among them*

ARV. txt.: [1] Teacher　　[2] *How is it* that he . . . sinners?　　[3] in health

MATT. 9.	MARK 2.	LUKE 5.
fast ¹oft, but thy disciples fast not? 15 And Jesus said unto them, Can the sons of the bride-chamber mourn, as long as the bridegroom is with them? but the days will come, when the bridegroom shall be taken away from them, and then will they fast. 16 And no man putteth a piece of undressed cloth upon an old garment; for that which should fill it up taketh from the garment, and a worse rent is made. 17 Neither do *men* put new wine into old ²wine-skins: else the skins burst, and the wine is spilled, and the skins perish: but they put new wine into fresh wine-skins, and both are preserved. (+ § 60)	him, Why do John's disciples and the disciples of the Pharisees fast, but thy disciples fast not? 19 And Jesus said unto them, Can the sons of the bride-chamber fast, while the bridegroom is with them? as long as they have the bridegroom with them, they cannot fast. 20 But the days will come, when the bridegroom shall be taken away from them, and then will they fast in that day. 21 No man seweth a piece of undressed cloth on an old garment: else that which should fill it up taketh from it, the new from the old, and a worse rent is made. 22 And no man putteth new wine into old ²wine-skins: else the wine will burst the skins, and the wine perisheth, and the skins: but *they put* new wine into fresh wine-skins.	tions; likewise also the *disciples* of the Pharisees; but thine eat and drink. 34 And Jesus said unto them, Can ye make the sons of the bride-chamber fast, while the bridegroom is with then.? 35 But the days will come; and when the bridegroom shall be taken away from them, then will they fast in those days. 36 And he spake also a parable unto them; No man rendeth a piece from a new garment and putteth it upon an old garment; else he will rend the new, and also the piece from the new will not agree with the old. 37 And no man putteth new wine into old ²wine-skins; else the new wine will burst the skins, and itself will be spilled, and the skins will perish. 38 But new wine must be put into fresh wine-skins. 39 And no man having drunk old *wine* desireth new: for he saith, The old is ³good.

§ 44. THE INFIRM MAN AT THE POOL OF BETHESDA.

JOHN, CHAP. 5.

1 After these things there was ⁴a feast of the Jews; and Jesus went up to Jerusalem.

2 Now there is in Jerusalem by the sheep *gate* a pool, which is called in Hebrew ⁵Bethesda, having five porches. 3 In these lay a multitude of them that were sick, blind, halt, ⁶withered. 5 And a certain man was there, which¹ had been thirty and eight years in his infirmity. 6 When Jesus saw him lying, and knew that he had been now a long time *in that case*, he saith unto him, Wouldest thou be made whole? 7 The sick man answered him, ⁷Sir, I have no man, when the water is troubled, to put me into the pool: but while I am coming, another steppeth down before me. 8 Jesus saith unto him, Arise, take up thy bed, and walk. 9 And straightway the man was made whole, and took up his bed and walked.

ERV. mg.: ¹ Some ancient authorities omit *oft*. ² That is, *skins used as bottles*. ³ Many ancient authorities read *better*. ⁴ Many ancient authorities read *the feast*. ⁵ Some ancient authorities read *Bethsaida*, others, *Bethzatha*. ⁶ Many ancient authorities add *wholly or in part, waiting for the moving of the water*: 4 *for an angel of the Lord went down at certain seasons into the pool, and troubled the water: whosoever then first after the troubling of the water stepped in was made whole, with whatsoever disease he was holden.* ⁷ Or, *Lord*

ARV. txt.: ¹ who

JOHN 5.

Now it was the sabbath on that day. 10 So the Jews said unto him that was cured, It is the sabbath, and it is not lawful for thee to take up thy bed. 11 But he answered them, He that made me whole, the same said unto me, Take up thy bed, and walk. 12 They asked him, Who is the man that said unto thee, Take up *thy bed*, and walk? 13 But he that was healed wist[1] not who it was: for Jesus had conveyed himself away, a multitude being in the place. 14 Afterward Jesus findeth him in the temple, and said unto him, Behold, thou art made whole: sin no more, lest a worse thing befall thee. 15 The man went away, and told the Jews that it was Jesus which[2] had made him whole. 16 And for this cause did the Jews persecute[3] Jesus, because he did these things on the sabbath. 17 But Jesus answered them, My Father worketh even until now, and I work. 18 For this cause therefore the Jews sought the more to kill him, because he not only brake the sabbath, but also called God his own Father, making himself equal with God.

19 Jesus therefore answered and said unto them,

Verily, verily, I say unto you, The Son can do nothing of himself, but what he seeth the Father doing: for what things soever he doeth, these the Son also doeth in like manner. 20 For the Father loveth the Son, and sheweth him all things that himself doeth: and greater works than these will he shew him, that ye may marvel. 21 For as the Father raiseth the dead and quickeneth them[4], even so the Son also quickeneth[5] whom he will. 22 For neither doth the Father judge any man, but he hath given all judgement unto the Son; 23 that all may honour the Son, even as they honour the Father. He that honoureth not the Son honoureth not the Father which[6] sent him. 24 Verily, verily, I say unto you, He that heareth my word, and believeth him that sent me, hath eternal life, and cometh not into judgement, but hath passed out of death into life. 25 Verily, verily, I say unto you, The hour cometh, and now is, when the dead shall hear the voice of the Son of God; and they that hear shall live. 26 For as the Father hath life in himself, even so gave he to the Son also to have life in himself: 27 and he gave him authority to execute judgement, because he is [1]the Son[7] of man. 28 Marvel not at this: for the hour cometh, in which all that are in the tombs shall hear his voice, 29 and shall come forth; they that have done good, unto the resurrection of life; and they that have [2]done ill[8] unto the resurrection of judgement.

30 I can of myself do nothing: as I hear, I judge: and my judgement is righteous; because I seek not mine own will, but the will of him that sent me. 31 If I bear witness of myself, my witness is not true. 32 It is another that beareth witness of me; and I know that the witness which he witnesseth of me is true. 33 Ye have sent unto John, and he hath borne witness unto the truth. 34 But the witness which I receive is not from man: howbeit I say these things, that ye may be saved. 35 He was the lamp that burneth and shineth: and ye were willing to rejoice for a season in his light. 36 But the witness which I have is greater than *that of* John: for the works which the Father hath given me to accomplish, the very works that I do, bear witness of me, that the Father hath sent me. 37 And the Father which[6] sent me, he hath borne witness of me. Ye have neither heard his voice at any time, nor seen his form. 38 And ye have not his word abiding in you: for whom he sent, him ye believe not. 39 [3]Ye search the scriptures, because ye think that in them ye have eternal life; and these are they which bear witness of me; 40 and ye will not come to me, that ye may have life. 41 I receive not glory from men. 42 But I know you, that ye have not the love of God in yourselves. 43 I am come in my Father's name, and ye receive me not: if another shall come in his own name, him ye will receive. 44 How can ye believe,

---

RV. mg.: [1] Or, *a son of man* [2] Or, *practised* [3] Or, *Search the scriptures*

ARV. txt : [1] knew [2] who [3] the Jews persecuted [4] giveth them life [5] giveth life to [6] that [7] a son [8] evil

JOHN 5.

which[1] receive glory one of another, and the glory that *cometh* from [1] the only God ye seek not? 45 Think not that I will accuse you to the Father: there is one that accuseth you, *even* Moses, on whom ye have set your hope. 46 For if ye believed Moses, ye would believe me; for he wrote of me. 47 But if ye believe not his writings, how shall ye believe my words?

§ 45. THE DISCIPLES PLUCKING GRAIN.

MATT. 12:1–8.	MARK 2:23–28.	LUKE 6:1–5.
1 At that season Jesus went on the sabbath day through the cornfields[2]; and his disciples were an hungred[3], and began to pluck ears of corn[4], and to eat. 2 But the Pharisees, when they saw it, said unto him, Behold, thy disciples do that which is not lawful to do upon the sabbath. 3 But he said unto them, Have ye not read what David did, when he was an hungred[3], and they that were with him; 4 how he entered into the house of God, and [2]did eat[5] the shewbread, which it was not lawful for him to eat, neither for them that were with him, but only for the priests? 5 Or have ye not read in the law, how[6] that on the sabbath day the priests in the temple profane the sabbath, and are guiltless? 6 But I say unto you that [3]one greater than the temple is here. 7 But if ye had known what this meaneth, I desire mercy, and not sacrifice, ye would not have condemned the guiltless. 8 For the Son of man is lord of the sabbath.	23 And it came to pass, that he was going on the sabbath day through the cornfields[2]; and his disciples [4]began, as they went, to pluck the ears of corn[4]. 24 And the Pharisees said unto him, Behold, why do they on the sabbath day that which is not lawful? 25 And he said unto them, Did ye never read what David did, when he had need, and was an hungred[3], he, and they that were with him? 26 How he entered into the house of God [5]when Abiathar was high priest, and did eat[5] the shewbread, which it is not lawful to eat save for the priests, and gave also to them that were with him? 27 And he said unto them, The sabbath was made for man, and not man for the sabbath: 28 so that the Son of man is lord even of the sabbath.	1 Now it came to pass on a [6]sabbath, that he was going through the cornfields[2]; and his disciples plucked the ears of corn[4], and did eat, rubbing them in their hands. 2 But certain of the Pharisees said, Why do ye that which it is not lawful to do on the sabbath day? 3 And Jesus answering them said, Have ye not read even this, what David did, when he was an hungred[3], he, and they that were with him; 4 how he entered into the house of God, and did take[7] and eat[5] the shewbread, and gave also to them that were with him; which it is not lawful to eat save for the priests alone? 5 And he said unto them, The Son of man is lord of the sabbath.

ERV. mg.: [1] Some ancient authorities read *the only* one. [2] Some ancient authorities read *they did eat.* [3] Gr. *a greater thing.* [4] Gr. *began to make* their *way plucking.* [5] Some ancient authorities read *in the days of Abiathar the high priest.* [6] Many ancient authorities insert *second-first.*

ARV. txt.: [1] who [2] grainfields [3] hungry [4] *Omit* of corn [5] ate [6] *Omit* how [7] took

§46. THE MAN WITH THE WITHERED HAND.

MATT. **12**:9–14.

9 And he departed thence, and went into their synagogue: 10 and behold, a man having a withered hand. And they asked him, saying, Is it lawful to heal on the sabbath day? that they might accuse him. 11 And he said unto them, ᵃ What man shall there be of you, that shall have one sheep, and if this fall into a pit on the sabbath day, will he not lay hold on it, and lift it out? 12 How much then is a man of more value than a sheep! Wherefore it is lawful to do good on the sabbath day. 13 Then saith he to the man, Stretch forth thy hand. And he stretched it forth; and it was restored whole, as the other. 14 But the Pharisees went out, and took counsel against him, how they might destroy him. (+ § 47)

MARK **3**:1–6.

1 And he entered again into the synagogue; and there was a man there which¹ had his hand withered. 2 And they watched him, whether he would heal him on the sabbath day; that they might accuse him. 3 And he saith unto the man that had his hand withered, ¹ Stand forth. 4 And he saith unto them, Is it lawful on the sabbath day to do good, or to do harm? to save a life, or to kill? But they held their peace. 5 And when he had looked round about on them with anger, being grieved at the hardening of their heart, he saith unto the man, Stretch forth thy hand. And he stretched it forth: and his hand was restored. 6 And the Pharisees went out, and straightway with the Herodians took counsel against him, how they might destroy him.

LUKE **6**:6–11.

6 And it came to pass on another sabbath, that he entered into the synagogue and taught: and there was a man there, and his right hand was withered. 7 And the scribes and the Pharisees watched him, whether he would heal on the sabbath; that they might find how to accuse him. 8 But he knew their thoughts; and he said to the man that had his hand withered, Rise up, and stand forth in the midst. And he arose and stood forth. 9 And Jesus said unto them, I ask you, Is it lawful on the sabbath to do good, or to do harm? to save a life, or to destroy it? 10 And he looked round about on them all, and said unto him, Stretch forth thy hand. And he did *so*: and his hand was restored. 11 But they were filled with ² madness; and communed one with another what they might do to Jesus.

ERV. mg.: ¹ Gr. *Arise into the midst.* ² Or, *foolishness*

ARV. txt.: ¹ who

ᵃ Luke 14:5. Which of you shall have an ass or an ox fallen into a well, and will not straightway draw him up on a sabbath day? (§ 100)

PART V.

SECOND PERIOD OF THE GALILEAN MINISTRY.

From the Choosing of the Twelve until the Withdrawal into Northern Galilee

---

§ 47. THE WIDE-SPREAD FAME OF CHRIST.

Matt. 4:23–25. Matt. 12:15–21.	Mark 3:7–12.	⌜Luke 6:17 ·19.⌝
4:23 And [1]Jesus went about in all Galilee, teaching in their synagogues, and preaching the [2]gospel of the kingdom, and healing all manner of disease and all manner of sickness among the people. 24 And the report of him went forth into all Syria: and they brought unto him all that were sick, holden with divers diseases and torments, [3]possessed with devils[1], and epileptic, and palsied; and he healed them. 25 And there followed him great multitudes from Galilee and Decapolis and Jerusalem and Judæa and *from* beyond Jordan[2]. (+ § 49)		
12:15 And Jesus perceiving *it* withdrew from thence: and many followed him; and he healed them all, 16 and charged them that they should not make him known: 17 that it might be fulfilled which was spoken [4]by [3] Isaiah the prophet, saying, 18 Behold, my servant whom I have chosen;	7 And Jesus with his disciples withdrew to the sea: and a great multitude from Galilee followed: and from Judæa, 8 and from Jerusalem, and from Idumæa, and beyond Jordan[2], and about Tyre and Sidon, a great multitude, hearing [5]what great things he did, came unto him. 9 And he spake to his disciples, that a	⌜17 and he came down with them, and stood on a level place, and a great multitude of his disciples, and a great number of the people from all Judæa and Jerusalem, and the sea coast of Tyre and Sidon, which[4] came to hear him, and to be healed of their diseases; 18 and they that were troubled with un-

---

ERV. mg.: [1] Some ancient authorities read *he*. [2] Or, *good tidings*: and so elsewhere. [3] Or, *demoniacs* [4] Or, *through* [5] Or, *all the things that he did.*

ARV. txt.: [1] demons [2] the Jordan [3] through [4] who

MATT. 12.	MARK 3.	LUKE 6.
My beloved in whom my soul is well pleased: I will put my Spirit upon him, And he shall declare judgement to the Gentiles. 19 He shall not strive, nor cry aloud; Neither shall any one hear his voice in the streets. 20 A bruised reed shall he not break, And smoking flax shall he not quench, Till he send forth judgement unto victory. 21 And in his name shall the Gentiles hope. (+ § 55)	little boat should wait on him because of the crowd, lest they should throng him: 10 ror he had healed many; insomuch that as many as had ¹ plagues ² pressed upon him that they might touch him. 11 And the unclean spirits, whensoever they beheld him, fell down before him, and cried, saying, Thou art the Son of God. 12 And he charged them much that they should not make him known.	clean spirits were healed. 19 And all the multitude sought to touch him: for power came forth from him, and healed *them* all.¹ (§ 48)

§ 48. THE CHOOSING OF THE TWELVE.

⌈MATT. 10 : 2-4.⌉	MARK 3 : 13-19.	LUKE 6 : 12-19.
	13 And he goeth up into the mountain, and calleth unto him whom he himself would: and they went unto him. 14 And he appointed ⁴ twelve, that they might be with him, and that he might send them forth to preach, 15 and to have authority to cast out ⁵ devils¹: 16 ⁶ and Simon he surnamed Peter; 17 and James the *son* of Zebedee, and John the brother of James; and them he surnamed Boanerges, which is, Sons of thunder: 18 and Andrew, and Philip, and Bartholomew, and Matthew, and Thomas, and James the *son* of Alphæus, and Thaddæus, and Simon the ³ Cana-	12 And it came to pass in these days, that he went out into the mountain to pray; and he continued all night in prayer to God. 13 And when it was day, he called his disciples: and he chose from them twelve, whom also he named apostles; 14 Simon, whom he also named Peter, and Andrew his brother, and James and John, and Philip and Bartholomew, 15 and Matthew and Thomas, and James *the son* of Alphæus, and Simon which ² was called the Zealot, 16 and Judas *the* ⁷ son of James, and Judas Iscariot, which ² was the ³ traitor; 17 and he came down with them, and stood
⌈2 Now the names of the twelve apostles are these: The first, Simon, who is called Peter, and Andrew his brother; James the *son* of Zebedee, and John his brother; 3 Philip, and Bartholomew; Thomas, and Matthew the publican; James the *son* of Alphæus, and Thaddæus; 4 Simon the ³ Cananæan, and Judas Iscar-		

ERV. mg.: ¹ Gr. *scourges*. ² Gr. *fell*. ³ Or, *Zealot*. See Luke vi. 15: Acts i. 13. ⁴ Some ancient authorities add *whom also he named apostles*. See Luke vi. 13. ⁵ Gr. *demons*. ⁶ Some ancient authorities insert *and he appointed twelve*. ⁷ Or, *brother*. See Jude 1.

ARV. txt.: ¹ demons ² who ³ who became a

MATT. 10.	MARK 3.	LUKE 6.
iot, who also [1] betrayed him.[1] (§ 64)	næan, 19 and Judas Iscariot, which[1] also betrayed him.	on a level place, and a great multitude of his disciples, and a great number of the people from all Judæa and Jerusalem, and the sea coast of Tyre and Sidon, which[1] came to hear him, and to be healed of their diseases; 18 and they that were troubled with unclean spirits were healed. 19 And all the multitude sought to touch him: for power came forth from him, and healed *them* all.

§ 49. THE SERMON ON THE MOUNT.

MATT., chs. 5, 6, 7, ⌐8:1¬.		LUKE 6: 20–49.
1 And seeing the multitudes, he went up into the mountain: and when he had sat down, his disciples came unto him: 2 and he opened his mouth and taught them, saying,		20 And he lifted up his eyes on his disciples, and said,
3 Blessed are the poor in spirit: for theirs is the kingdom of heaven.		Blessed *are* ye poor: for yours is the kingdom of God.
4 [2] Blessed are they that mourn: for they shall be comforted.		21 Blessed *are* ye that hunger now: for ye shall be filled.
5 Blessed are the meek: for they shall inherit the earth.		Blessed *are* ye that weep now: for ye shall laugh.
6 Blessed are they that hunger and thirst after righteousness: for they shall be filled.		
7 Blessed are the merciful: for they shall obtain mercy.		
8 Blessed are the pure in heart: for they shall see God.		
9 Blessed are the peacemakers: for they shall be called sons of God.		

ERV. mg.: [1] Or, *delivered him up*: and so always.   [2] Some ancient authorities transpose ver. 4 and 5.

ARV. txt.: [1] who

MATT. 5.		LUKE 6

MATT. 5.

10 Blessed are they that have been persecuted for righteousness' sake: for theirs is the kingdom of heaven. 11 Blessed are ye when *men* shall reproach you, and persecute you, and say all manner of evil against you falsely, for my sake. 12 Rejoice, and be exceeding glad: for great is your reward in heaven: for so persecuted they the prophets which[1] were before you.

13 ªYe are the salt of the earth: but if the salt have lost its savour, wherewith shall it be salted? it is thenceforth good for nothing, but to be cast out and trodden under foot of men. 14 Ye are the light of the world. A city set on a hill cannot be hid. 15 ᵇNeither do *men* light a

LUKE 6

22 Blessed are ye, when men shall hate you, and when they shall separate you *from their company*, and reproach you, and cast out your name as evil, for the Son of man's sake. 23 Rejoice in that day, and leap *for joy*: for behold, your reward is great in heaven: for in the same manner did their fathers unto the prophets.

24 But woe unto you that are rich! for ye have received your consolation.
25 Woe unto you, ye that are full now! for ye shall hunger.
Woe *unto you*, ye that laugh now! for ye shall mourn and weep.
26 Woe *unto you*, when all men shall speak well of you! for in the same manner did their fathers to the false prophets.

ARV. txt.: ¹ that

ª Mark 9:50. Salt is good: but if the salt have lost its saltness, wherewith will ye season it? Have salt in yourselves, and be at peace one with another. (§81)

ª Luke 14:34, 35. Salt therefore is good: but if even the salt have lost its savour, wherewith shall it be seasoned? 35 It is fit neither for the land nor for the dunghill: *men* cast it out. (§101)

ᵇ Mark 4:21. Is the lamp brought to be put under the bushel, or under the bed, *and* not to be put on the stand? (§57)

ᵇ Luke 8:16. And no man, when he hath lighted a lamp, covereth it with a vessel, or putteth it under a bed; but putteth it on a stand, that they which enter in may see the light. (§57)

ᵇ Luke 11:33. No man, when he hath lighted a lamp, putteth it in a cellar, neither under the bushel, but on the stand, that they which enter in may see the light. (§94)

MATT. **5.**

LUKE **6.**

lamp, and put it under the bushel, but on the stand ; and it shineth unto all that are in the house. 16 Even so let your light shine before men, that they may see your good works, and glorify your Father which[1] is in heaven.

17 Think not that I came to destroy the law or the prophets : I came not to destroy, but to fulfil. 18 For verily I say unto you, [a] Till heaven and earth pass away, one jot or one tittle shall in no wise pass away from the law, till all things be accomplished. 19 Whosoever therefore shall break one of these least commandments, and shall teach men so, shall be called least in the kingdom of heaven : but whosoever shall do and teach them, he shall be called great in the kingdom of heaven. 20 For I say unto you, that except your righteousness shall exceed *the righteousness* of the scribes and Pharisees, ye shall in no wise enter into the kingdom of heaven.

21 Ye have heard that it was said to them of old time, Thou shalt not kill ; and whosoever shall kill shall be in danger of the judgement : 22 but I say unto you, that every one who is angry with his [1]brother shall be in danger of the judgement ; and whosoever shall say to his brother, [2] Raca, shall be in danger of the council ; and whosoever

---

ERV. mg.:   [1] Many ancient authorities insert [after *brother*] *without cause.*   [2] An expression of contempt.

ARV. txt.:   [1] who

[a] Luke 16: 17 But it is easier for heaven and earth to pass away, than for one tittle of the law to fall. (§ 103)

MATT. 5.		LUKE 6.

shall say, [1] Thou fool, shall be in danger [2] of the [3] hell of fire. 23 If therefore thou art offering thy gift at the altar, and there rememberest that thy brother hath aught against thee, 24 leave there thy gift before the altar, and go thy way, first be reconciled to thy brother, and then come and offer thy gift. 25 [a] Agree with thine adversary quickly, whiles [1] thou art with him in the way; lest haply the adversary deliver thee to the judge, and the judge [4] deliver thee to the officer, and thou be cast into prison. 26 Verily I say unto thee, Thou shalt by no means come out thence, till thou have paid the last farthing.

27 Ye have heard that it was said, Thou shalt not commit adultery: 28 but I say unto you, that every one that looketh on a woman to lust after her hath committed adultery with her already in his heart. 29 [b] And if thy right eye causeth thee to stumble, pluck it out, and cast it from thee: for it is profitable for thee that one of thy members should perish, and

ERV. mg.: [1] Or, *Moreh*, a Hebrew expression of condemnation. [2] Gr. *unto* or *into*. [3] Gr. *Gehenna of fire*. Some ancient authorities omit *deliver thee*.

ARV. txt.: [1] while

[a] Luke 12:58, 59. For as thou art going with thine adversary before the magistrate, on the way give diligence to be quit of him; lest haply he hale thee unto the judge, and the judge shall deliver thee to the officer, and the officer shall cast thee into prison. 59 I say unto thee, Thou shalt by no means come out thence, till thou have paid the very last mite. (§ 95)

[b] Matt. 18:8, 9. And if thy hand or thy foot causeth thee to stumble, cut it off, and cast it from thee: it is good for thee to enter into life maimed or halt, rather than having two hands or two feet to be cast into the eternal fire. 9 And if thine eye causeth thee to stumble, pluck it out, and cast it from thee: it is good for thee to enter into life with one eye, rather than having two eyes to be cast into the hell of fire. (§ 81)

[b] Mark 9:43, 47. And if thy hand cause thee to stumble, cut it off: it is good for thee to enter into life maimed, rather than having thy two hands to go into hell, into the unquenchable fire ... 47 And if thine eye cause thee to stumble, cast it out: it is good for thee to enter into the kingdom of God with one eye, rather than having two eyes to be cast into hell; (§ 81)

MATT. 5.

not thy whole body be cast into [1] hell. 30 And if thy right hand causeth thee to stumble, cut it off, and cast it from thee : for it is profitable for thee that one of thy members should perish, and not thy whole body go into [1] hell. 31 It was said also, Whosoever shall put away his wife, let him give her a writing of divorcement : 32 [a] but I say unto you, that every one that putteth away his wife, saving for the cause of fornication, maketh her an adulteress : and whosoever shall marry her when she is put away committeth adultery.

33 Again, ye have heard that it was said to them of old time, Thou shalt not forswear thyself, but shalt perform unto the Lord thine oaths : 34 but I say unto you, Swear not at all ; neither by the heaven, for it is the throne of God ; 35 nor by the earth, for it is the footstool of his feet ; nor [2] by Jerusalem, for it is the city of the great King. 36 Neither shalt thou swear by thy head, for thou canst not make one hair white or black. 37 [3] But let your speech be, Yea, yea ; Nay, nay : and whatsoever is more than these is of [4] the evil one.

38 Ye have heard that it was said, An eye for an eye,

LUKE 6.

27 But I say unto you which [1] hear, Love your ene-

ERV. mg.: [1] Gr. Gehenna.   [2] Or, toward   [3] Some ancient authorities read But your speech shall be.   [4] Or, evil: as in ver. 39; vi. 13.

ARV. txt.: [1] that

[a] Matt. 19:9. And I say unto you, Whosoever shall put away his wife, except for fornication, and shall marry another committeth adultery : and he that marrieth her when she is put away committeth adultery. (§ 110)

[a] Mark 10:11. And he saith unto them, Whosoever shall put away his wife, and marry another, committeth adultery against her: (§ 110)

[a] Luke 16:18. Every one that putteth away his wife, and marrieth another, committeth adultery : and he that marrieth one that is put away from a husband committeth adultery. (§ 103)

MATT. 5.	LUKE 6.
and a tooth for a tooth : 39 but I say unto you, Resist not [1] him that is evil : but whosoever smiteth thee on thy right cheek, turn to him the other also. 40 And if any man would go to law with thee, and take away thy coat, let him have thy cloke also. 41 And whosoever shall [2] compel thee to go one mile, go with him twain[1]. 42 Give to him that asketh thee, and from him that would borrow of thee turn not thou away. 43 Ye have heard that it was said, Thou shalt love thy neighbour, and hate thine enemy : 44 but I say unto you, Love your enemies, and pray for them that persecute you ; 45 that ye may be sons of your Father which [2] is in heaven : for he maketh his sun to rise on the evil and the good, and sendeth rain on the just and the unjust. 46 For if ye love them that love you, what reward have ye ? do not even the [3] publicans the same ? 47 And if ye salute your brethren only, what do ye more *than others?* do not even the Gentiles the same? 48 Ye therefore shall be perfect, as your heavenly Father is perfect. 6:1 Take heed that ye do not your righteousness before men, to be seen of them : else ye have no reward with your Father which [2] is in heaven. 2 When therefore thou doest alms, sound not a	mies, do good to them that hate you, 28 bless them that curse you, pray for them that despitefully use you. 29 To him that smiteth thee on the *one* cheek offer also the other ; and from him that taketh away thy cloke withhold not thy coat also. 30 Give to every one that asketh thee ; and of him that taketh away thy goods ask them not again. 31 [a] And as ye would that men should do to you, do ye also to them likewise. 32 And if ye love them that love you, what thank have ye? for even sinners love those that love them. 33 And if ye do good to them that do good to you, what thank have ye? for even sinners do the same. 34 And if ye lend to them of whom ye hope to receive, what thank have ye? even sinners lend to sinners, to receive again as much. 35 But love your enemies, and do *them* good, and lend, [4] never despairing ; and your reward shall be great, and ye shall be sons of the Most High : for he is kind toward the unthankful and evil. 36 Be ye merciful, even as your Father is merciful. [Paragraph continued on page 67.]

ERV. mg.: [1] Or, *evil* [2] Gr. *impress.* [3] That is, *collectors or renters of Roman taxes;* and so elsewhere. [4] Some ancient authorities read *despairing of no man.*

ARV. txt.: [1] *two* [2] *who*

[a] Cf. Matt. 7 : 12, p. 69.

MATT. **6.**

LUKE **6.**

trumpet before thee, as the hypocrites do in the synagogues and in the streets, that they may have glory of men. Verily I say unto you, They have received their reward. 3 But when thou doest alms, let not thy left hand know what thy right hand doeth: 4 that thine alms may be in secret: and thy Father which[1] seeth in secret shall recompense thee.

5 And when ye pray, ye shall not be as the hypocrites: for they love to stand and pray in the synagogues and in the corners of the streets, that they may be seen of men. Verily I say unto you, They have received their reward. 6 But thou, when thou prayest, enter into thine inner chamber, and having shut thy door, pray to thy Father which[1] is in secret, and thy Father which[1] seeth in secret shall recompense thee. 7 And in praying use not vain repetitions, as the Gentiles do: for they think that they shall be heard for their much speaking. 8 [a]Be not therefore like unto them: for [1]your Father knoweth what things ye have need of, before ye ask him. 9 [b]After this manner therefore pray ye: Our Father which[1] art in heaven, Hallowed be thy

ERV. mg.:   [1] Some ancient authorities read *God your Father.*

ARV. txt.:   [1] who

[a]Cf. Matt. 6: 32, p. 67.

[a] Luke 12: 30. For all these things do the nations of the world seek after: but your Father knoweth that ye have need of these things. (§ 95)

[b] Luke 11: 2–4. When ye pray, say, Father, Hallowed be thy name. Thy kingdom come. 3 Give us day by day our daily bread. 4 And forgive us our sins; for we ourselves also forgive every one that is indebted to us. And bring us not into temptation. (§ 93)

MATT. 6.		LUKE 6.

name. 10 Thy kingdom come. Thy will be done, as in heaven, so on earth. 11 Give us this day ¹ our daily bread. 12 And forgive us our debts, as we also have forgiven our debtors. 13 And bring us not into temptation, but deliver us from ² the evil ³ *one.* 14 ªFor if ye forgive men their trespasses, your heavenly Father will also forgive you. 15 ᵇBut if ye forgive not men their trespasses, neither will your Father forgive your trespasses.

16 Moreover when ye fast, be not, as the hypocrites, of a sad countenance: for they disfigure their faces, that they may be seen of men to fast. Verily I say unto you, They have received their reward. 17 But thou, when thou fastest, anoint thy head, and wash thy face; 18 that thou be not seen of men to fast, but of thy Father which¹ is in secret: and thy Father, which¹ seeth in secret, shall recompense thee.

19 ᶜLay not up for yourselves treasures upon the earth, where moth and rust doth² consume, and where thieves ⁴break through and steal: 20 but lay up for yourselves treasures in

---

ERV. mg.: ¹ Gr. *our bread for the coming day.* ² Or, *evil* ³ Many authorities, some ancient, but with variations, add *For thine is the kingdom, and the power, and the glory, for ever. Amen.* ⁴ Gr. *dig through.*

ARV. txt.: ¹ who ² *Omit* doth

ªMark 11:25. And whensoever ye stand praying, forgive, if ye have aught against any one; that your Father also which is in heaven may forgive you your trespasses. (§ 122)

ᵇMatt. 18:35. So shall also my heavenly Father do unto you, if ye forgive not every one his brother from your hearts. (§ 81)

ᶜLuke 12:33, 34. Sell that ye have, and give alms; make for yourselves purses which wax not old, a treasure in the heavens that faileth not, where no thief draweth near, neither moth destroyeth. 34 For where your treasure is, there will your heart be also. (§ 95)

MATT. **6.**

heaven, where neither moth nor rust doth consume, and where thieves do not [1]break through nor steal: 21 for where thy treasure is, there will thy heart be also. 22 [a]The lamp of the body is the eye : if therefore thine eye be single, thy whole body shall be full of light. 23 But if thine eye be evil, thy whole body shall be full of darkness. If therefore the light that is in thee be darkness, how great is the darkness! 24 [b]No man can serve two masters: for either he will hate the one, and love the other ; or else he will hold to one, and despise the other. Ye cannot serve God and mammon. 25 [c]Therefore I say unto you, Be not anxious for your life, what ye shall eat, or what ye shall drink ; nor yet for your body, what ye shall put on. Is not the life more than the food, and the body than the raiment? 26 Behold the birds of the heaven, that they sow not, neither do they reap, nor gather into barns ; and your heavenly Father feedeth them. Are not ye of much more value than they? 27 And which of you by being anxious can add one cubit unto his [2]stature[1]? 28 And why are ye anxious concern-

LUKE **[12]**.

[[c]Luke 12:22–31. And he said unto his disciples, Therefore I say unto you, Be not anxious for *your* [3]life, what ye shall eat; nor yet for your body, what ye shall put on. 23 For the [3]life is more than the food, and the body than the raiment. 24 Consider the ravens, that they sow not, neither reap; which have no store-chamber nor barn; and God feedeth them : of how much more value are ye than the birds! 25 And which of you by being anxious can add a cubit unto his [2]stature[1]? 26 If then ye are not able to do even that which is least, why are ye anxious concerning the rest? 27 Consider the lilies,

---

ERV. mg.: [1] Gr. *dig through.*   [2] Or, *age*   [3] Or, *soul*

ARV. txt.: [1] the measure of his life

---

[a]Luke 11:34–36. The lamp of thy body is thine eye: when thine eye is single, thy whole body also is full of light; but when it is evil, thy body also is full of darkness. 35 Look therefore whether the light that is in thee be not darkness. 36 If therefore thy whole body be full of light, having no part dark, it shall be wholly full of light, as when the lamp with its bright shining doth give thee light. (§ 55)

[b]Luke 16:13. No servant can serve two masters: for either he will hate the one, and love the other; or else he will hold to one, and despise the other. Ye cannot serve God and mammon. (§ 103)

[c]Luke 12:22–31. (§ 95) See above.

MATT. 6.

ing raiment? Consider the lilies of the field, how they grow; they toil not, neither do they spin: 29 yet I say unto you, that even Solomon in all his glory was not arrayed like one of these. 30 But if God doth so clothe the grass of the field, which to-day is, and to-morrow is cast into the oven, *shall he* not much more *clothe* you, O ye of little faith? 31 Be not therefore anxious, saying, What shall we eat? or, What shall we drink? or, Wherewithal shall we be clothed? 32 [a] For after all these things the Gentiles seek; for your heavenly Father knoweth that ye have need of all these things. 33 But seek ye first his kingdom, and his righteousness; and all these things shall be added unto you. 34 Be not therefore anxious for the morrow: for the morrow will be anxious for itself. Sufficient unto the day is the evil thereof.

7:1 Judge not, that ye be not judged. 2 For with what judgement ye judge, ye shall be judged: [b] and with what measure ye mete, it shall be measured unto you.

[Paragraph continued on next page.]

LUKE [12].

how they grow: they toil not, neither do they spin; yet I say unto you, Even Solomon in all his glory was not arrayed like one of these. 28 But if God doth so clothe the grass in the field, which to-day is, and to-morrow is cast into the oven; how much more *shall he clothe* you, O ye of little faith? 29 And seek not ye what ye shall eat, and what ye shall drink, neither be ye of doubtful mind. 30 For all these things do the nations of the world seek after: but your Father knoweth that ye have need of these things. 31 Howbeit[1] seek ye [1] his kingdom, and these things shall be added unto you.] (§ 95)

6:37 And judge not, and ye shall not be judged: and condemn not, and ye shall not be condemned: release, and ye shall be released: 38 give, and it shall be given unto you; good measure, pressed down, shaken together, running over, shall they give into your bosom. [b] For with what measure ye mete it shall be measured to you again.

ERV. mg.: [1] Many ancient authorities read *the kingdom of God.*

ARV. txt.: [1] Yet

[a] Cf. Matt. 6:8, p. 64, and Luke 12:30 (§ 95) above.

[b] Mark 4:24. With what measure ye mete it shall be measured unto you: and more shall be given unto you. (§ 57)

MATT. 7.

3 And why beholdest thou the mote that is in thy brother's eye, but considerest not the beam that is in thine own eye? 4 Or how wilt thou say to thy brother, Let me cast out the mote out of thine eye; and lo, the beam is in thine own eye? 5 Thou hypocrite, cast out first the beam out of thine own eye; and then shalt thou see clearly to cast out the mote out of thy brother's eye.

6 Give not that which is holy unto the dogs, neither cast your pearls before the swine, lest haply they trample them under their feet, and turn and rend you.

7 [a]Ask, and it shall be given you; seek, and ye shall find; knock, and it shall be opened unto you: 8 for every one that asketh receiveth; and he that seeketh findeth; and to him that knocketh it shall be opened. 9 Or what man is there of you, who, if his son shall ask him for a loaf, will

LUKE 6.

39 And he spake also a parable unto them, [b]Can the blind guide the blind? shall they not both fall into a pit? 40 [c]The disciple is not above his [1]master[1]: but every one when he is perfected shall be as his [1]master[1]. 41 And why beholdest thou the mote that is in thy brother's eye, but considerest not the beam that is in thine own eye? 42 Or how canst thou say to thy brother, Brother, let me cast out the mote that is in thine eye, when thou thyself beholdest not the beam that is in thine own eye? Thou hypocrite, cast out first the beam out of thine own eye, and then shalt thou see clearly to cast out the mote that is in thy brother's eye.

[Paragraph continued on next page.]

[[a]Luke 11: 9-13. And I say unto you, Ask, and it shall be given you; seek, and ye shall find; knock, and it shall be opened unto you. 10 For every one that asketh receiveth; and he that seeketh findeth; and to him that knocketh it shall be opened. 11 And of which of you that is a father shall his son ask [2]a loaf, and he give him a stone? or a

ERV. mg.: [1]Or, *teacher*   [2]Some ancient authorities omit *a loaf, and he give him a stone?* or.

ARV. txt.: [1]teacher

[a]Luke 11: 9-13. (§ 93) See above.
[b]Matt. 15: 14. And if the blind guide the blind, both shall fall into the pit. (§ 69)
[c]Matt. 10: 24, 25. A disciple is not above his master, nor a servant above his lord. 25 It is enough for the disciple that he be as his master, and the servant as his lord. (§ 64)
[c]John 13: 16. A servant is not greater than his lord; neither one that is sent greater than he that sent him. (§ 133)
[c]John 15: 20. Remember the word that I said unto you, A servant is not greater than his lord. (§ 134)

MATT. 7.

give him a stone; 10 or if he shall ask for a fish, will give him a serpent? 11 If ye then, being evil, know how to give good gifts unto your children, how much more shall your Father which[1] is in heaven give good things to them that ask him? 12 [a]All things therefore whatsoever ye would that men should do unto you, even so do ye also unto them: [b]for this is the law and the prophets.

13 [c]Enter ye in by the narrow gate: for wide [1]is the gate, and broad is the way, that leadeth to destruction, and many be[2] they that enter in thereby. 14 [2]For narrow is the gate, and straitened the way, that leadeth unto life, and few be[2] they that find it.

15 Beware of false prophets, which[1] come to you in sheep's clothing, but inwardly are ravening wolves. 16[d]By their fruits ye shall know them. Do *men* gather grapes of thorns, or figs of thistles? 17 Even so every good tree bringeth forth good fruit; but the corrupt tree bringeth forth evil fruit. 18 A good tree cannot bring forth evil fruit, neither can a corrupt tree bring forth good fruit. 19 Every tree that bringeth

LUKE [11].

fish, and he for a fish give him a serpent? 12 Or *if* he shall ask an egg, will he give him a scorpion? 13 If ye then, being evil, know how to give good gifts unto your children, how much more shall *your* heavenly Father give the Holy Spirit to them that ask him?] (§ 93)

6 : 43 [d]For there is no good tree that bringeth forth corrupt fruit; nor again a corrupt tree that bringeth forth good fruit. 44 For each tree is known by its own fruit. For of thorns men do not gather figs, nor of a bramble bush gather they grapes. 45 The good man out of the good treasure of his heart bringeth forth that which is

---

ERV. mg.: [1] Some ancient authorities omit *is the gate*. [2] Many ancient authorities read *How narrow is the gate, &c.*

ARV. txt.: [1] who [2] are

---

[a] Cf. Luke 6 : 31 (p. 63).

[b] Matt. 22 : 40. On these two commandments hangeth the whole law, and the prophets. (§ 125)

[c] Luke 13 : 24. Strive to enter in by the narrow door: for many, I say unto you, shall seek to enter in, and shall not be able. (§ 98)

[d] Matt. 12 : 33–35. Either make the tree good, and its fruit good; or make the tree corrupt, and its fruit corrupt: for the tree is known by its fruit. 34 Ye offspring of vipers, how can ye, being evil, speak good things? for out of the abundance of the heart the mouth speaketh. 35 The good man out of his good treasure bringeth forth good things: and the evil man out of his evil treasure bringeth forth evil things. (§ 55)

MATT. 7.

not forth good fruit is hewn down, and cast into the fire. 20 Therefore by their fruits ye shall know them. 21 Not every one that saith unto me, Lord, Lord, shall enter into the kingdom of heaven; but he that doeth the will of my Father which[1] is in heaven. 22 Many will say to me in that day, Lord, Lord, did we not prophesy by thy name, and by thy name cast out [1]devils[2], and by thy name do many [2]mighty works? 23 [a]And then will I profess unto them, I never knew you: depart from me, ye that work iniquity. 24 Every one therefore which[3] heareth these words of mine, and doeth them, shall be likened unto a wise man, which[1] built his house upon the rock: 25 and the rain descended, and the floods came, and the winds blew, and beat upon that house: and it fell not: for it was founded upon the rock. 26 And every one that heareth these words of mine, and doeth them not, shall be likened unto a foolish man, which[1] built his house upon the sand: 27 and the rain descended, and the floods came, and the winds blew, and smote upon that house; and it fell: and great was the fall thereof. 28 And it came to pass, when Jesus ended[4] these words, the multitudes were

LUKE 6.

good; and the evil *man* out of the evil *treasure* bringeth forth that which is evil: for out of the abundance of the heart his mouth speaketh. 46 And why call ye me, Lord, Lord, and do not the things which I say? 47 Every one that cometh unto me, and heareth my words, and doeth them, I will shew you to whom he is like: 48 he is like a man building a house, who digged and went deep, and laid a foundation upon the rock: and when a flood arose, the stream brake against that house, and could not shake it: [3]because it had been well builded. 49 But he that heareth, and doeth not, is like a man that built a house upon the earth without a foundation; against which the stream brake, and straightway it fell in; and the ruin of that house was great.

ERV. mg.: [1] Gr. *demons.* [2] Gr. *powers.* [3] Many ancient authorities read *for it had been founded upon the rock*: as in Matt. vii. 25.

ARV. txt.: [1] who [2] demons [3] that [4] had finished

[a] Luke 13:27. And he shall say, I tell you, I know not whence ye are; depart from me, all ye workers of iniquity. (§ 98)

MATT. 7.

astonished at his teaching:
29 for he taught them as *one*
having authority, and not as
their scribes.

⌐8:1 And when he was
come down from the moun-
tain, great multitudes followed him.⌐ (§ 40)

§ 50. THE CENTURION'S SERVANT.

MATT. 8:5-13.

5 And when he was en-
tered into Capernaum, there
came unto him a centurion,
beseeching him, 6 and saying,
Lord, my ¹servant lieth in the
house sick of the palsy, grievously tormented. 7 And he
saith unto him, I will come
and heal him. 8 And the
centurion answered and said,
Lord, I am not ²worthy that
thou shouldest come under
my roof: but only say ³the
word, and my ¹servant shall
be healed. 9 For I also am a
man ⁴under authority, having under myself soldiers: and
I say to this one, Go, and he
goeth; and to another, Come,
and he cometh; and to my
⁵servant, Do this, and he
doeth it. 10 And when Jesus
heard it, he marvelled, and
said to them that followed,
Verily I say unto you, ⁶I have
not found so great faith, no,
not in Israel. 11 ᵃAnd I say
unto you, that many shall
come from the east and the
west, and shall ⁷sit down with

LUKE 7:1-10.

1 After he had ended all his
sayings in the ears of the people, he entered into Capernaum.
2 And a certain centurion's
⁵servant, who was ⁸dear unto
him, was sick and at the
point of death. 3 And when
he heard concerning Jesus,
he sent unto him elders of
the Jews, asking him that he
would come and save his ⁵servant. 4 And they, when they
came to Jesus, besought him
earnestly, saying, He is
worthy that thou shouldest
do this for him: 5 for he
loveth our nation, and himself built us our synagogue.
6 And Jesus went with them.
And when he was now not far
from the house, the centurion
sent friends to him, saying
unto him, Lord, trouble not
thyself: for I am not ²worthy
that thou shouldest come
under my roof: 7 wherefore
neither thought I myself
worthy to come unto thee;
but ⁹say the word, and my

ERV. mg.: ¹ Or, *boy* ² Gr. *sufficient.* ³ Gr. *with a word.* ⁴ Some ancient authorities insert *set*: as in Luke vii. 8. ⁵ Gr. *bond-servant.* ⁶ Many ancient authorities read *With no man in Israel have I found so great faith.* ⁷ Gr. *recline.* ⁸ Or, *precious to him* Or, *honourable with him* ⁹ Gr. *say with a word.*

ᵃ Luke 13:28, 29. There shall be the weeping and gnashing of teeth, when ye shall see Abraham, and Isaac
and Jacob, and all the prophets, in the kingdom of God, and yourselves cast forth without. 29 And they shall
come from the east and west, and from the north and south, and shall sit down in the kingdom of God. (§ 98)

MATT. 8.		LUKE 7.
Abraham, and Isaac, and Jacob, in the kingdom of heaven: 12 ᵃbut the sons of the kingdom shall be cast forth into the outer darkness: there shall be the weeping and gnashing[1] of teeth. 13 And Jesus said unto the centurion, Go thy way; as thou hast believed, *so* be it done unto thee. And the [1]servant was healed in that hour. (+ § 39)		[1]servant shall be healed. 8 For I also am a man set under authority, having under myself soldiers: and I say to this one, Go, and he goeth; and to another, Come, and he cometh; and to my [2]servant, Do this, and he doeth it. 9 And when Jesus heard these things, he marvelled at him, and turned and said unto the multitude that followed him, I say unto you, I have not found so great faith, no, not in Israel. 10 And they that were sent, returning to the house, found the [2]servant whole.

§ 51. THE RAISING OF THE WIDOW'S SON AT NAIN.

LUKE 7:11–17.

11 And it came to pass [3]soon afterwards, that he went to a city called Nain; and his disciples went with him, and a great multitude. 12 Now when he drew near to the gate of the city, behold, there was carried out one that was dead, the only son of his mother, and she was a widow: and much people of the city was with her. 13 And when the Lord saw her, he had compassion on her, and said unto her, Weep not. 14 And he came nigh and touched the bier: and the bearers stood still. And he said, Young man, I say unto thee, Arise. 15 And he that was dead sat up, and began to speak. And he gave him to his mother. 16 And fear took hold on all: and they glorified God, saying, A great prophet is arisen among us: and, God hath visited his people. 17 And this report went forth concerning him in the whole of Judæa, and all the region round about.

§ 52. JOHN THE BAPTIST'S LAST MESSAGE.

MATT. 11:2–30.		LUKE 7:18–35.
2 Now when John heard in the prison the works of the Christ, he sent by his dis-		18 And the disciples of John told him of all these things. 19 And John calling

---

ERV. mg.:   [1]Or, *boy*   [2]Gr. *bondservant.*   [3]Many ancient authorities read *on the next day.*

ARV. txt.:   [1]the gnashing

ᵃMatt. 13:42. And shall cast them into the furnace of fire: there shall be the weeping and gnashing of teeth. (§ 57)
ᵃMatt. 13:50. And shall cast them into the furnace of fire: there shall be the weeping and gnashing of teeth. (§ 57)
ᵃMatt. 22:13. And cast him out into the outer darkness; there shall be the weeping and gnashing of teeth. (§ 124)
ᵃMatt. 24:51. And shall cut him asunder, and appoint his portion with the hypocrites: there shall be the weeping and gnashing of teeth. (§ 131)
ᵃMatt. 25:30. And cast ye out the unprofitable servant into the outer darkness: there shall be the weeping and gnashing of teeth. (§ 131)

MATT. 11.		LUKE 7.

MATT. 11.

ciples, 3 and said unto him, Art thou he that cometh, or look we for another? 4 And Jesus answered and said unto them, Go your way[1] and tell John the things which ye do[2] hear and see : 5 the blind receive their sight, and the lame walk, the lepers are cleansed, and the deaf hear, and the dead are raised up, and the poor have [1]good tidings preached to them. 6 And blessed is he, whosoever shall find none[3] occasion of stumbling in me.

7 And as these went their way, Jesus began to say unto the multitudes concerning John, What went ye out into the wilderness to behold? a reed shaken with the wind? 8 But what went ye out for[4] to see? a man clothed in soft *raiment*? Behold, they that wear soft *raiment* are in kings' houses. 9 [2]But wherefore went ye out? to see a prophet? Yea, I say unto you, and much more than a prophet. 10 This is he, of whom it is written,

LUKE 7.

unto him [3]two of his disciples sent them to the Lord, saying, Art thou he that cometh, or look we for another? 20 And when the men were come unto him, they said, John the Baptist hath sent us unto thee, saying, Art thou he that cometh, or look we for another? 21 In that hour he cured many of diseases and [4]plagues and evil spirits ; and on many that were blind he bestowed sight. 22 And he answered and said unto them, Go your way[1], and tell John what things[5] ye have seen and heard ; the blind receive their sight, the lame walk, the lepers are cleansed, and the deaf hear, the dead are raised up, the poor have [1]good tidings preached to them. 23 And blessed is he, whosoever shall find none[3] occasion of stumbling in me.

24 And when the messengers of John were departed, he began to say unto the multitudes concerning John, What went ye out into the wilderness to behold? a reed shaken with the wind? 25 But what went ye out to see? a man clothed in soft raiment? Behold, they which[6] are gorgeously apparelled, and live delicately, are in kings' courts. 26 But what went ye out to see? a prophet? Yea, I say unto you, and much more than a prophet. 27 This is he of whom it is written,

---

ERV. mg.: [1] Or, *the gospel* [2] Many ancient authorities read *But what went ye out to see? a prophet?* [3] Gr. *certain two.* [4] Gr. *scourges.*

ARV. txt.: [1] *Omit* your way. [2] *Omit* do [3] ne [4] *Omit* for [5] the things which [6] that

MATT. 11.		LUKE 7.
Behold, I send my messenger before thy face, Who shall prepare thy way before thee.		Behold, I send my messenger before thy face, Who shall prepare thy way before thee.

MATT. 11.

Behold, I send my messenger before thy face,
Who shall prepare thy way before thee.
11 Verily I say unto you, Among them that are born of women there hath not arisen a greater than John the Baptist: yet he that is [1]but little in the kingdom of heaven is greater than he. 12 [a]And from the days of John the Baptist until now the kingdom of heaven suffereth violence, and men of violence take it by force. 13 For all the prophets and the law prophesied until John. 14 And if ye are willing to receive [2]*it*, this is Elijah, which [1] is to come. 15 [b]He that hath ears [3]to hear, let him hear.
16 But whereunto shall I liken this generation? It is like unto children sitting in the marketplaces, which [2] call unto their fellows, 17 and say, We piped unto you, and ye did not dance; we wailed, and ye did not [4]mourn. 18 For John came neither eating nor drinking, and they say, He hath a [5]devil [3]. 19 The Son of man came eating and drinking, and they say, Behold, a gluttonous man, and a winebibber, a friend of publicans

LUKE 7.

Behold, I send my messenger before thy face,
Who shall prepare thy way before thee.
28 I say unto you, Among them that are born of women there is none greater than John: yet he that is [1]but little in the kingdom of God is greater than he. 29 And all the people when they heard, and the publicans, justified God, [6]being baptized with the baptism of John. 30 But the Pharisees and the lawyers rejected for themselves the counsel of God, [7]being not baptized of him.

31 Whereunto then shall I liken the men of this generation, and to what are they like? 32 They are like unto children that sit in the marketplace, and call one to another; which [2] say, We piped unto you, and ye did not dance; we wailed, and ye did not weep. 33 For John the Baptist is come eating no bread nor drinking wine; and ye say, He hath a [5]devil [3]. 34 The Son of man is come eating and drinking; and ye say, Behold, a gluttonous man, and a wine-

---

ERV. mg.   [1] Gr. *lesser*.   [2] Or, him   [3] Some ancient authorities omit *to hear*.   [4] Gr. *beat the breast*.   [5] Gr. *demon*.   [6] Or, *having been*   [7] Or, *not having been*

ARV. txt.:   [1] that   [2] who   [3] demon

---

[a] Luke 16:16. The law and the prophets *were* until John: from that time the gospel of the kingdom of God is preached, and every man entereth violently into it. (§ 103)
　[b] Matt. 13:9. He that hath ears, let him hear. (§ 57)
　[b] Matt. 13:43. He that hath ears, let him hear. (§ 57)
　[b] Mark 4:9. Who hath ears to hear, let him hear. (§ 57)
　[b] Mark 4:23. If any man hath ears to hear, let him hear. (§ 57)
　[b] Luke 8:8. He that hath ears to hear, let him hear. (§ 57)
　[b] Luke 14:35. He that hath ears to hear, let him hear. (§ 101)

MATT. 11.

and sinners! And wisdom [1] is justified by her [2] works.

20 Then began he to upbraid the cities wherein most of his [3] mighty works were done, because they repented not. 21 [a] Woe unto thee, Chorazin! woe unto thee, Bethsaida! for if the [3] mighty works had been done in Tyre and Sidon which were done in you, they would have repented long ago in sackcloth and ashes. 22 Howbeit[1] I say unto you, it shall be more tolerable for Tyre and Sidon in the day of judgement, than for you. 23 And thou, Capernaum, shalt thou be exalted unto heaven? thou shalt [4] go down unto Hades: for if the [3] mighty works had been done in Sodom which were done in thee, it would have remained until this day. 24 Howbeit[1] I say unto you, that it shall be more tolerable for the land of Sodom in the day of judgement, than for thee.

25 [b] At that season Jesus answered and said, I [5] thank thee, O Father, Lord of heaven and earth, that thou didst hide these things from the wise and understanding, and didst reveal them unto babes: 26 yea, Father, [6] for so it was well-pleasing in thy sight. 27 [c] All things have been delivered unto me of my

LUKE 7.

bibber, a friend of publicans and sinners! 35 And wisdom [1] is justified of all her children.

[[a] Luke 10:12–15. I say unto you, It shall be more tolerable in that day for Sodom, than for that city. 13 Woe unto thee, Chorazin! woe unto thee, Bethsaida! for if the [3] mighty works had been done in Tyre and Sidon, which were done in you, they would have repented long ago, sitting in sackcloth and ashes. 14 Howbeit[1] it shall be more tolerable for Tyre and Sidon in the judgement, than for you. 15 And thou, Capernaum, shalt thou be exalted unto heaven? thou shalt be brought down unto Hades.] (§ 87)

[[b] Luke 10:21, 22. In that same hour he rejoiced [7] in the Holy Spirit, and said, I [5] thank thee, O Father, Lord of heaven and earth, that thou didst hide these things from the wise and understanding, and didst reveal them unto babes: yea, Father; [6] for so it was well-pleasing in thy sight. 22 All things have been delivered unto me of my

ERV. mg.: [1] Or, *was* [2] Many ancient authorities read *children*: as in Luke vii. 35. [3] Gr. *powers*. [4] Many ancient authorities read *be brought down*. [5] Or, *praise* [6] Or, *that* [7] Or, *by*

ARV. txt.: [1] But

[a] Luke 10:12–15. (§ 87) See above.
[b] Luke 10:21, 22. (§ 87) See above.
[c] Matt. 28:18. All authority hath been given unto me in heaven and on earth. (§ 149)
[c] Luke 10:22. (§ 87) See above.

MATT. 11.		[LUKE 10.]
Father : ª and no one knoweth the Son, save the Father ; neither doth any know the Father, save the Son, and he to whomsoever the Son willeth to reveal *him*.		Father: and no one knoweth who the Son is, save the Father; and who the Father is, save the Son, and he to whomsoever the Son willeth to reveal *him*.] (§ 87)
28 Come unto me, all ye that labour and are heavy laden, and I will give you rest. 29 Take my yoke upon you, and learn of me ; for I am meek and lowly in heart : and ye shall find rest unto your souls. 30 For my yoke is easy, and my burden is light.		

§ 53. ANOINTING OF JESUS IN THE HOUSE OF SIMON THE PHARISEE.

LUKE 7 : 36–50.

36 And one of the Pharisees desired him that he would eat with him. And he entered into the Pharisee's house, and sat down to meat. 37 And behold, a woman which[1] was in the city, a sinner ; and when she knew that he was sitting at meat in the Pharisee's house, she brought [1] an alabaster cruse of ointment, 38 and standing behind at his feet, weeping, she began to wet his feet with her tears, and wiped them with the hair of her head, and [2] kissed his feet, and anointed them with the ointment. 39 Now when the Pharisee which[2] had bidden him saw it, he spake within himself, saying, This man, if he were [3] a prophet, would have perceived who and what manner of woman this is which[2] toucheth him, that she is a sinner. 40 And Jesus answering said unto him, Simon, I have somewhat to say unto thee. And he saith, [4] Master[3], say on. 41 A certain lender had two debtors : the one owed five hundred [5] pence[4], and the other fifty. 42 When they had not *wherewith* to pay, he forgave them both. Which of them therefore will love him most? 43 Simon answered and said, He, I suppose, to whom he forgave the most. And he said unto him, Thou hast rightly judged. 44 And turning to the woman, he said unto Simon, Seest thou this woman? I entered into thine[5] house, thou gavest me no water for my feet : but she hath wetted my feet with her tears, and wiped them with her hair. 45 Thou gavest me no kiss : but she, since the time I came in, hath not ceased to [6] kiss my feet. 46 My head with oil thou didst not anoint : but she hath anointed my feet with ointment. 47 Wherefore I say unto thee, Her sins, which are many, are forgiven ; for she loved much : but to whom little is forgiven, *the same* loveth little. 48 And he said unto her, Thy sins are forgiven. 49 And they that sat at meat with him began to say [7] within themselves, Who is this that even forgiveth sins? 50 And he said unto the woman, Thy faith hath saved thee ; go in peace.

ERV. mg.: ¹ Or, *a flask* ² Gr. *kissed much.* ³ Some ancient authorities read *the prophet.* See John i. 21, 25. ⁴ Or, *Teacher* ⁵ See marginal note on Matt. xviii. 28. ⁶ Gr. *kiss much.* ⁷ Or, *among*

ARV. txt.: ¹ who ² that ³ Teacher ⁴ shillings ⁵ thy

ª Luke 10 : 22. See above.
ª John 6 : 46. Not that any man hath seen the Father, save he which is from God, he hath seen the Father (§ 68)

§ 54. CHRIST'S COMPANIONS ON HIS SECOND PREACHING TOUR.

LUKE 8 : 1–3.

1 And it came to pass soon afterwards, that he went about through cities and villages, preaching and bringing the ¹good tidings of the kingdom of God, and with him the twelve, 2 and certain women which¹ had been healed of evil spirits and infirmities, Mary that was called Magdalene, from whom seven ²devils² had gone out, 3 and Joanna the wife of Chuza³ Herod's steward, and Susanna, and many others, which⁴ ministered unto ³them of their substance. (+ § 57)

§ 55. WARNINGS TO THE SCRIBES AND PHARISEES: "AN ETERNAL SIN."

MATT. 12 : 22–45.	MARK 3 : 20–30.	[LUKE 11 : 14–23.]
	20 And he cometh ⁶into a house.* And the multitude cometh together again, so that they could not so much as eat bread. 21 And when his friends heard it, they went out to lay hold on him: for they said, He is beside himself.	
22 Then was brought unto him ⁴one possessed with a devil⁵, blind and dumb: and he healed him, insomuch that the dumb man spake and saw. 23 And all the multitudes were amazed, and said, Is this⁶ the son of David? 24 But when the Pharisees heard it, they said, This man doth not cast out ²devils² but ⁵by Beelzebub the prince of the ²devils². And knowing their thoughts he said unto them, Every kingdom divided against itself is brought to desolation; and every city or house divided against itself shall not stand: 26 and if Satan casteth out Satan, he is divided against himself; how then shall his kingdom stand? 27 And if I ⁵by Beelzebub cast out ²devils², ⁵by whom	22 And the scribes which⁴ came down from Jerusalem said, He hath Beelzebub, and, ⁷By the prince of the ²devils² casteth he out the ²devils². 23 And he called them unto him, and said unto them in parables, How can Satan cast out Satan? 24 And if a kingdom be divided against itself, that kingdom cannot stand. 25 And if a house be divided against itself, that house will not be able to stand. 26 And if Satan hath risen up against himself, and is divided, he cannot stand, but hath an end. 27 But no one can enter into the house of the strong *man*, and spoil his goods, except he first bind the strong *man*; and then he will spoil his house. [Paragraph continued on page 78.]	[Luke 11:14 23. And he was casting out a ⁸devil⁵ which⁷ was dumb. And it came to pass, when the ⁸devil⁵ was gone out, the dumb man spake; and the multitudes marvelled. 15 But some of them said, ⁷By Beelzebub the prince of the ²devils² casteth he out ²devils². 16 And others, tempting⁸ *him*, sought of him a sign from heaven. 17 But he, knowing their thoughts, said unto them, Every kingdom divided against itself is brought to desolation; ⁹and a house *divided* against a house falleth. 18 And if Satan also is divided against himself, how shall his kingdom stand? because ye say that I cast out ²devils² ⁵by Beelzebub. 19 And if I ⁵by Beelzebub cast out ²devils², by whom do your sons cast them out? therefore shall they be your judges. 20 But if I by the finger

ERV. mg.: ¹ Or, *gospel* ² Gr. *demons.* ³ Many ancient authorities read *him.* ⁴ Or, *a demoniac* ⁵ Or, *in* ⁶ Or, *home* ⁷ Or, *In* ⁸ Gr. *demon.* ⁹ Or, *and house falleth upon house*

ARV. txt.: ¹ who ² demons ³ Chuzas ⁴ that ⁵ demon ⁶ Can this be ⁷ that ⁸ trying *ARV. and AV. include this sentence in vs. 19.

MATT. 12.	MARK 3.	[LUKE 11.]
do your sons cast them out? therefore shall they be your judges. 28 But if I [1] by the Spirit of God cast out [2]devils[1], then is the kingdom of God come upon you. 29 Or how can one enter into the house of the strong *man*, and spoil his goods, except he first bind the strong *man*? and then he will spoil his house. 30 He that is not with me is against me; and he that gathereth not with me scattereth. 31 [a]Therefore I say unto you, Every sin and blasphemy shall be forgiven [3]unto men; but the blasphemy against the Spirit shall not be forgiven. 32 And whosoever shall speak a word against the Son of man, it shall be forgiven him; but whosoever shall speak against the Holy Spirit, it shall not be forgiven him, neither in this [4]world, nor in that which is to come.	28 [a]Verily I say unto you, All their sins shall be forgiven unto the sons of men, and their blasphemies wherewith soever they shall blaspheme: 29 but whosoever shall blaspheme against the Holy Spirit hath never forgiveness, but is guilty of an eternal sin: 30 because they said, He hath an unclean spirit.	of God cast out [2]devils[1], then is the kingdom of God come upon you. 21 When the strong *man* fully armed guardeth his own court, his goods are in peace: 22 but when a stronger than he shall come upon him, and overcome him, he taketh from him his whole armour wherein he trusted, and divideth his spoils. 23 He that is not with me is against me; and he that gathereth not with me scattereth.] (§ 94)
33 [b]Either make the tree good, and its fruit good; or make the tree corrupt, and its fruit corrupt: for the tree is known by its fruit. 34 Ye offspring of vipers, how can ye, being evil, speak good things? for out of the abundance of the heart the mouth speaketh. 35 The good man out of his good treasure bringeth forth good things: and		[b Luke 6: 43–45. For there is no good tree that bringeth forth corrupt fruit; nor again a corrupt tree that bringeth forth good fruit. 44 For each tree is known by its own fruit. For of thorns men do not gather figs, nor of a bramble bush gather they grapes. 45 The good man out of the good treasure of his heart bringeth forth that which is good; and the evil *man* out of

ERV. mg.: [1] Or, *in* [2] Gr. *demons.* [3] Some ancient authorities read *unto you men.* [4] Or, *age*

ARV. txt.: [1] demons

[a] Luke 12: 10. And every one who shall speak a word against the Son of man, it shall be forgiven him: but unto him that blasphemeth against the Holy Spirit it shall not be forgiven. (§ 95)

[b] Matt. 7: 16–18, 20. By their fruits ye shall know them. Do *men* gather grapes of thorns, or figs of thistles? 17 Even so every good tree bringeth forth good fruit; but the corrupt tree bringeth forth evil fruit. 18 A good tree cannot bring forth evil fruit, neither can a corrupt tree bring forth good fruit. . . . . 20 Therefore by their fruits ye shall know them. (§ 49)

[b] Luke 6: 43–45. (§ 49) See above.

78

MATT. 12.

the evil man out of his evil treasure bringeth forth evil things. 36 And I say unto you, that every idle word that men shall speak, they shall give account thereof in the day of judgement. 37 For by thy words thou shalt be justified, and by thy words thou shalt be condemned.

38 [a]Then certain of the scribes and Pharisees answered him, saying, [1]Master[1], we would see a sign from thee. 39 But he answered and said unto them, [b]An evil and adulterous generation seeketh after a sign; and there shall no sign be given to it but the sign of Jonah the prophet: 40 for as Jonah was three days and three nights in the belly of the [2]whale; so shall the Son of man be three days and three nights in the heart of the earth. 41 The men of Nineveh shall stand up in the judgement with this generation, and shall condemn it: for they repented at the preaching of Jonah; and behold, [3]a greater than Jonah is here. 42 The queen of the south shall rise up in the judgement with this generation, and shall condemn it: for she came from the ends of the earth to hear the wisdom of Solomon; and behold, [3]a greater than Solomon is here.

[LUKE 6.]

the evil *treasure* bringeth forth that which is evil: for out of the abundance of the heart his mouth speaketh.] (§49)

[[a]Luke 11:29–32. And when the multitudes were gathering together unto him, he began to say, This generation is an evil generation: it seeketh after a sign; and there shall no sign be given to it but the sign of Jonah. 30 For even as Jonah became a sign unto the Ninevites, so shall also the Son of man be to this generation. 31 The queen of the south shall rise up in the judgement with the men of this generation, and shall condemn them: for she came from the ends of the earth to hear the wisdom of Solomon; and behold, [3]a greater than Solomon is here. 32 The men of Nineveh shall stand up in the judgement with this generation, and shall condemn it: for they repented at the preaching of Jonah; and behold, [3]a greater than Jonah is here.] (§94)

ERV. mg.: [1]Or, *Teacher* [2]Gr. *sea-monster*. [3]Gr. *more than*.

ARV. txt.: [1]Teacher

[a]Luke 11:29–32. (§94) See above.
[b]Matt. 16:4. An evil and adulterous generation seeketh after a sign; and there shall no sign be given unto it, but the sign of Jonah. (§73)
[b]Mark 8:12. Why doth this generation seek a sign? verily I say unto you, There shall no sign be given unto this generation. (§73)
[b]Luke 11:29. (§94) See above.

MATT. 12.

43 [a] But the unclean spirit, when [1] he is gone out of the man, passeth through waterless places, seeking rest, and findeth it not. 44 Then [1] he saith, I will return into my house whence I came out; and when [1] he is come, [1] he findeth it empty, swept, and garnished. 45 Then goeth [1] he, and taketh with [2] himself seven other spirits more evil than [2] himself, and they enter in and dwell there: and the last state of that man becometh worse than the first. Even so shall it be also unto this evil generation.

[LUKE 11.]

[[a] Luke 11:24-26. The unclean spirit when [1] he is gone out of the man, passeth through waterless places, seeking rest; and finding none, [1] he saith, I will turn back unto my house whence I came out. 25 And when [1] he is come, [1] he findeth it swept and garnished. 26 Then goeth [1] he, and taketh to him seven other spirits more evil than [2] himself; and they enter in and dwell there: and the last state of that man becometh worse than the first.] (§ 94)

§ 56. THE TRUE KINDRED OF CHRIST.

MATT. 12:46-50.

46 While he was yet speaking to the multitudes, behold, his mother and his brethren stood without, seeking to speak to him. 47 [3] And one said unto him, Behold, thy mother and thy brethren stand without, seeking to speak o thee. 48 But he answered and said unto him that told him, Who is my mother? and who are my brethren? 49 And he stretched forth his hand towards his disciples, and said, Behold, my mother and my brethren! 50 For whosoever shall do the will of my Father which [1] is in heaven, he is my brother, and sister, and mother.

MARK 3:31-35.

31 And there come his mother and his brethren; and, standing without, they sent unto him, calling him. 32 And a multitude was sitting about him; and they say unto him, Behold, thy mother and thy brethren without seek for thee. 33 And he answereth them, and saith, Who is my mother and my brethren? 34 And looking round on them which [2] sat round about him, he saith, Behold, my mother and my brethren! 35 For whosoever shall do the will of God, the same is my brother, and sister, and mother.

LUKE 8:19-21.

19 And there came to him his mother and brethren, and they could not come at him for the crowd. 20 And it was told him, Thy mother and thy brethren stand without, desiring to see thee. 21 But he answered and said unto them, My mother and my brethren are these which [2] hear the word of God, and do it. (+ § 58)

ERV. mg.: [1] Or, it [2] Or, itself [3] Some ancient authorities omit ver. 47.

ARV. txt.: [1] who [2] that

[a] Luke 11:24-26. (§ 94) See above.

§ 57. THE PARABLES BY THE SEA.

MATT. 13:1–53.	MARK 4:1–34.	LUKE 8:4–18.

1 On that day went Jesus out of the house, and sat by the sea side. 2 And there were gathered unto him great multitudes, so that he entered into a boat, and sat; and all the multitude stood on the beach. 3 And he spake to them many things in parables, saying, Behold, the sower went forth to sow; 4 and as he sowed, some *seeds* fell by the way side, and the birds came and devoured them: 5 and others fell upon the rocky places, where they had not much earth: and straightway they sprang up, because they had no deepness of earth: 6 and when the sun was risen, they were scorched; and because they had no root, they withered away. 7 And others fell upon the thorns; and the thorns grew up, and choked them: 8 and others fell upon the good ground, and yielded fruit, some a hundredfold, some sixty, some thirty. 9 ᵃHe that hath ¹ears, let him hear.

1 And again he began to teach by the sea side. And there is gathered unto him a very great multitude, so that he entered into a boat, and sat in the sea; and all the multitude were by the sea on the land. 2 And he taught them many things in parables, and said unto them in his teaching, 3 Hearken: Behold, the sower went forth to sow: 4 and it came to pass, as he sowed, some *seed* fell by the way side, and the birds came and devoured it. 5 And other fell on the rocky *ground*, where it had not much earth; and straightway it sprang up, because it had no deepness of earth: 6 and when the sun was risen, it was scorched; and because it had no root, it withered away. 7 And other fell among the thorns, and the thorns grew up, and choked it, and it yielded no fruit. 8 And others fell into the good ground, and yielded fruit, growing up and increasing; and brought forth, thirtyfold, and sixtyfold, and a hundredfold. 9 And he said, ᵃWho hath ears to hear, let him hear.

4 And when a great multitude came together, and they of every city resorted unto him, he spake by a parable: 5 The sower went forth to sow his seed: and as he sowed, some fell by the way side; and it was trodden under foot, and the birds of the heaven devoured it. 6 And other fell on the rock; and as soon as it grew, it withered away, because it had no moisture. 7 And other fell amidst the thorns; and the thorns grew with it, and choked it. 8 And other fell into the good ground, and grew, and brought forth fruit a hundredfold. As he said these things, he cried, ᵃHe that hath ears to hear, let him hear.

10 And the disciples came, and said unto him, Why speakest thou unto them in parables? 11 And he answered and said unto them, Unto you it is given to know

10 And when he was alone, they that were about him with the twelve asked of him the parables. 11 And he said unto them, Unto you is given the mystery of the kingdom

9 And his disciples asked him what this parable might be. 10 And he said, Unto you it is given to know the mysteries of the kingdom of God: but to the rest in parables;

ERV. mg.: ¹ Some ancient authorities add here, and in ver. 43, [after *ears*] *to hear*: as in Mark iv. 9; Luke viii. 8.

ᵃCf. Matt. 13:43 (p. 87); Mark 4:23 (p. 84).
ᵃMatt. 11:15. He that hath ears to hear, let him hear. (§ 52)
ᵃLuke 14:35. He that hath ears to hear, let him hear. (§ 101)

MATT. 13.	MARK 4.	LUKE 8.
the mysteries of the kingdom of heaven, but to them it is not given. 12 ªFor whosoever hath, to him shall be given, and he shall have abundance: but whosoever hath not, from him shall be taken away even that which he hath. 13 Therefore speak I to them in parables; because seeing they see not, and hearing they hear not, neither do they understand. 14 And unto them is fulfilled the prophecy of Isaiah, which saith,	of God: but unto them that are without, all things are done in parables: 12 that seeing they may see, and not perceive; and hearing they may hear, and not understand; lest haply they should turn again, and it should be forgiven them.	that seeing they may not see, and hearing they may not understand.

Matt. (continued):

> By hearing ye shall hear,
>   and shall in no wise understand;
> And seeing ye shall see,
>   and shall in no wise perceive:

15 For this people's heart is
      waxed gross,
And their ears are dull of
      hearing,
And their eyes they have
      closed;
Lest haply they should
      perceive with their eyes,
And hear with their ears,
And understand with their
      heart,
And should turn again,
And I should heal them.

16 ᵇBut blessed are your eyes, for they see; and your ears, for they hear. 17 For verily I say unto you, that many prophets and righteous men desired to see the things which ye see, and saw them not; and to hear the things which ye hear, and heard them not.

ª Cf. Mark 4:25; Luke 8:18 (p. 84), and references there.

ᵇ Luke 10:23, 24. And turning to the disciples, he said privately, Blessed are the eyes which see the things which ye see: 24 for I say unto you, that many prophets and kings desired to see the things which ye see, and saw them not; and to hear the things which ye hear, and heard them not. (§ 87)

MATT. 13.

18 Hear then ye the parable of the sower. 19 When any one heareth the word of the kingdom, and understandeth it not, *then* cometh the evil *one*, and snatcheth away that which hath been sown in his heart. This is he that was sown by the way side. 20 And he that was sown upon the rocky places, this is he that heareth the word, and straightway with joy receiveth it; 21 yet hath he not root in himself, but endureth for a while; and when tribulation or persecution ariseth because of the word, straightway he stumbleth. 22 And he that was sown among the thorns, this is he that heareth the word; and the care of the [1] world, and the deceitfulness of riches, choke the word, and he becometh unfruitful. 23 And he that was sown upon the good ground, this is he that heareth the word, and understandeth it; who verily heareth fruit, and bringeth forth, some a hundredfold, some sixty, some thirty.

MARK 4.

13 And he saith unto them, Know ye not this parable? and how shall ye know all the parables? 14 The sower soweth the word. 15 And these are they by the way side, where the word is sown; and when they have heard, straightway cometh Satan, and taketh away the word which hath been sown in them. 16 And these in like manner are they that are sown upon the rocky *places*, who, when they have heard the word, straightway receive it with joy; 17 and they have no root in themselves, but endure for a while; then, when tribulation or persecution ariseth because of the word, straightway they stumble. 18 And others are they that are sown among the thorns; these are they that have heard the word, 19 and the cares of the [1] world, and the deceitfulness of riches, and the lusts of other things entering in, choke the word, and it becometh unfruitful. 20 And those are they that were sown upon the good ground; such as hear the word, and accept it, and bear fruit, thirtyfold, and sixtyfold, and a hundredfold.

21 And he said unto them, [a] Is the lamp brought to be put under the bushel, or under the bed, *and* not to be

LUKE 8.

11 Now the parable is this: The seed is the word of God. 12 And those by the way side are they that have heard; then cometh the devil, and taketh away the word from their heart, that they may not believe and be saved. 13 And those on the rock *are* they which [1], when they have heard, receive the word with joy; and these have no root, which [1] for a while believe, and in time of temptation fall away. 14 And that which fell among the thorns, these are they that have heard, and as they go on their way they are choked with cares and riches and pleasures of *this* life, and bring no fruit to perfection. 15 And that in the good ground, these are such as in an honest and good heart, having heard the word, hold it fast, and bring forth fruit with patience.

16 [a] And no man, when he hath lighted a lamp, covereth it with a vessel, or putteth it under a bed; but putteth it

---

ERV. mg.: [1] Or, *age*

ARV. txt.: [1] who

---

[a] Matt. 5:15. Neither do *men* light a lamp, and put it under the bushel, but on the stand; and it shineth unto all that are in the house. (§49)

[a] Luke 11:33. No man when he hath lighted a lamp, putteth it in a cellar, neither under the bushel, but on the stand, that they which enter in may see the light. (§55)

MATT. 13.	MARK 4.	LUKE 8.
	put on the stand? 22 [a]For there is nothing hid, save that it should be manifested; neither was *anything* made secret, but that it should come to light. 23 [b]If any man hath ears to hear, let him hear. 24 And he said unto them, Take heed what ye hear: [c]with what measure ye mete it shall be measured unto you: and more shall be given unto you. 25 [d]For he that hath, to him shall be given: and he that hath not, from him shall be taken away even that which he hath.	on a stand, that they which[1] enter in may see the light. 17 [a]For nothing is hid, that shall not be made manifest; nor *anything* secret, that shall not be known and come to light. 18 Take heed therefore how ye hear: [d]for whosoever hath, to him shall be given; and whosoever hath not, from him shall be taken away even that which he [4]thinketh he hath. (+ § 56)
24 Another parable set he before them, saying, The kingdom of heaven is likened unto a man that sowed good seed in his field: 25 but while men slept, his enemy came and sowed [1]tares also among the wheat, and went away. 26 But when the blade sprang up, and brought forth fruit, then appeared the tares also. 27 And the [2]servants of the householder came and said unto him, Sir, didst thou not sow good seed in thy field? whence then hath it tares? 28 And he said unto them, [3]An enemy hath done this.		

ERV. mg.: [1] Or, *darnel* [2] Gr. *bondservants.* [3] Gr. *A man that is an enemy.* [4] Or, *seemeth to have*

ARV. txt.: [1] that

[a] Matt. 10:26. For there is nothing covered, that shall not be revealed; and hid, that shall not be known. (§ 64)

[a] Luke 12:2. But there is nothing covered up, that shall not be revealed: and hid, that shall not be known. (§ 95)

[b] Cf. Matt. 13:9; Mark 4:9; Luke 8:8 (p. 81), and references there; also Matt. 13:43 (p. 87).

[c] Matt. 7:2. And with what measure ye mete, it shall be measured unto you. (§ 49)

[c] Luke 6:38. For with what measure ye mete it shall be measured to you again. (§ 49)

[d] Matt. 25:29. For unto every one that hath shall be given, and he shall have abundance: but from him that hath not, even that which he hath shall be taken away. (§ 131)

[d] Cf. Matt. 13:12 (p. 82).

[d] Luke 19:26. I say unto you, that unto every one that hath shall be given; but from him that hath not, even that which he hath shall be taken away from him. (§ 117)

MATT. 13.	MARK 4.	[LUKE 13.]
And the [1]servants say unto him, Wilt thou then that we go and gather them up? 29 But he saith, Nay; lest haply while ye gather up the tares, ye root up the wheat with them. 30 Let both grow together until the harvest: and in the time of the harvest I will say to the reapers, gather up first the tares, and bind them in bundles to burn them: but gather the wheat into my barn.		
	26 And he said, So is the kingdom of God, as if a man should cast seed upon the earth; 27 and should sleep and rise night and day, and the seed should spring up and grow, he knoweth not how. 28 The earth [2]beareth fruit of herself; first the blade, then the ear, then the full corn[1] in the ear. 29 But when the fruit [3]is ripe, straightway he [4]putteth forth the sickle, because the harvest is come.	
31 [a]Another parable set he before them, saying, The kingdom of heaven is like unto a grain of mustard seed, which a man took, and sowed in his field: 32 which indeed is less than all seeds; but when it is grown, it is greater than the herbs, and becometh a tree, so that the birds of the heaven come and lodge in the branches thereof.	30 [a]And he said, How shall we liken the kingdom of God? or in what parable shall we set it forth? 31 [5]It is like a grain of mustard seed, which, when it is sown upon the earth, though it be less than all the seeds that are upon the earth, 32 yet when it is sown, groweth up, and becometh greater than all the herbs, and putteth out great branches; so that the birds of the heaven can lodge under the shadow thereof.	[[a]Luke 13:18, 19. He said therefore, Unto what is the kingdom of God like? and whereunto shall I liken it? 19 It is like unto a grain of mustard seed, which a man took, and cast into his own garden; and it grew, and became a tree; and the birds of the heaven lodged in the branches thereof.] (§97)

ERV. mg.: [1] Gr. *bondservants*   [2] Or, *yieldeth*   [3] Or, *alloweth*   [4] Or, *sendeth forth*   [5] Gr. *As unto*

ARV. txt.: [1] *grain*

[a] Luke 13:18, 19. (§97) See above.

MATT. **13.**

33 ^aAnother parable spake he unto them: The kingdom of heaven is like unto leaven, which a woman took, and hid in three ¹measures of meal, till it was all leavened.

34 All these things spake Jesus in parables unto the multitudes; and without a parable spake he nothing unto them: 35 that it might be fulfilled which was spoken ²by¹ the prophet, saying,

I will open my mouth in parables;

I will utter things hidden from the foundation ³of the world.

36 Then he left the multitudes, and went into the house : and his disciples came unto him, saying, Explain unto us the parable of the tares of the field. 37 And he answered and said, He that soweth the good seed is the Son of man; 38 and the field is the world; and the good seed, these are the sons of the kingdom; and the tares are the sons of the evil *one*; 39 and the enemy that sowed them is the devil: and the harvest is ⁴the end of the world; and the reapers are angels. 40 As therefore the tares are gathered up and burned with fire; so shall it be in ⁴the end of the world. 41 The Son of man shall send forth his angels, and they shall gather out of his king-

MARK **4.**

33 And with many such parables spake he the word unto them, as they were able to hear it: 34 and without a parable spake he not unto them: but privately to his own disciples he expounded all things.

[LUKE **13.**]

[ᵃLuke 13:20, 21. And again he said, Whereunto shall I liken the kingdom of God? 21 It is like unto leaven, which a woman took and hid in three ¹measures of meal, till it was all leavened.]
(§ 97)

ERV. mg.: ¹ The word in the Greek denotes the Hebrew seah, a measure containing nearly a peck and a half. ² Or, *through* ³ **Many** ancient authorities omit *of the world.* ⁴ Or, *the consummation of the age*

ARV. txt.: ¹ through

ᵃ Luke 13:20, 21. (§ 97) See above.

MATT. **13.**

dom all things that cause stumbling, and them that do iniquity, 42 [a]and shall cast them into the furnace of fire : there shall be the weeping and gnashing[1] of teeth. 43 Then shall the righteous shine forth as the sun in the kingdom of their Father. [b]He that hath ears, let him hear.

44 The kingdom of heaven is like unto a treasure hidden in the field; which a man found, and hid; and [1]in his joy he goeth and selleth all that he hath, and buyeth that field.

45 Again, the kingdom of heaven is like unto a man that is a merchant seeking goodly pearls : 46 and having found one pearl of great price, he went and sold all that he had, and bought it.

47 Again, the kingdom of heaven is like unto a [2]net, that was cast into the sea, and gathered of every kind : 48 which, when it was filled, they drew up on the beach; and they sat down, and gathered the good into vessels, but the bad they cast away. 49 So shall it be in [3]the end of the world: the angels

---

ERV. mg.: [1] Or, *for joy thereof* [2] Gr. *drag-net.* [3] Or, *the consummation of the age*

ARV. txt.: [1] the gnashing

[a] Matt. 8:12. But the sons of the kingdom shall be cast forth into the outer darkness: there shall be the weeping and gnashing of teeth. (§ 50)

[a] Cf. Matt. 13:50. (p. 88)

[a] Matt. 22:13. And cast him out into the outer darkness: there shall be the weeping and gnashing of teeth. (§ 124)

[a] Matt. 24:51. And shall cut him asunder, and appoint his portion with the hypocrites: there shall be the weeping and gnashing of teeth. (§ 131)

[a] Matt. 25:30. And cast ye out the unprofitable servant into the outer darkness: there shall be the weeping and gnashing of teeth. (§ 131)

[a] Luke 13:28. There shall be the weeping and gnashing of teeth, when ye shall see Abraham, and Isaac, and Jacob, and all the prophets, in the kingdom of God, and yourselves cast forth without. (§ 98)

[b] Cf. Matt. 13:9; Mark 4:9; Luke 8:8 (p. 81), and references there; also Mark 4:23 (p. 84).

MATT. 13.

shall come forth, and sever the wicked from among the righteous, 50 ᵃand shall cast them into the furnace of fire : there shall be the weeping and gnashing[1] of teeth.

51 Have ye understood all these things? They say unto him Yea. 52 And he said unto them, Therefore every scribe who hath been made a disciple to the kingdom of heaven is like unto a man that is a householder, which[2] bringeth forth out of his treasure things new and old.

53 And it came to pass, when Jesus had finished these parables, he departed thence. (+ § 62)

§ 58. THE STILLING OF THE TEMPEST.

MATT. 8: ⌜18⌝ 23–27.

⌜18 Now when Jesus saw great multitudes about him, he gave commandment to depart unto the other side.⌝ (§ 86)

23 And when he was entered into a boat, his disciples followed him. 24 And behold, there arose a great tempest in the sea, insomuch that the boat was covered with the waves : but he was asleep. 25 And they came to him, and awoke him, saying, Save, Lord ; we perish. 26 And he saith unto them, Why are ye fearful, O ye of little faith? Then he arose, and rebuked the winds and the sea ; and there was a great calm. 27

MARK 4: 35–41.

35 And on that day, when even was come, he saith unto them, Let us go over unto the other side. 36 And leaving the multitude, they take him with them, even as he was, in the boat. And other boats were with him. 37 And there ariseth a great storm of wind, and the waves beat into the boat, insomuch that the boat was now filling. 38 And he himself was in the stern, asleep on the cushion : and they awake him, and say unto him, [1]Master[3], carest thou not that we perish? 39 And he awoke, and rebuked the wind, and said unto the sea, Peace, be still. And the wind

LUKE 8: 22–25.

22 Now it came to pass on one of those days, that he entered into a boat, himself and his disciples ; and he said unto them, Let us go over unto the other side of the lake : and they launched forth. 23 But as they sailed he fell asleep : and there came down a storm of wind on the lake ; and they were filling *with water*, and were in jeopardy. 24 And they came to him, and awoke him, saying, Master, master, we perish. And he awoke, and rebuked the wind and the raging of the water : and they ceased, and there was a calm. 25 And he said unto them, Where is your

---

ERV. mg..   1 Or, *Teacher*

ARV. txt.:   1 the gnashing   2 who   3 Teacher

ᵃ Cf. Matt. 13 : 42 (p. 87), and references there.

MATT. 8.

And the men marvelled, saying, What manner of man is this, that even the winds and the sea obey him?

MARK 4.

ceased, and there was a great calm. 40 And he said unto them, Why are ye fearful? have ye not yet faith? 41 And they feared exceedingly, and said one to another, Who then is this, that even the wind and the sea obey him?

LUKE 8.

faith? And being afraid they marvelled, saying one to another, Who then is this, that he commandeth even the winds and the water, and they obey him.

§ 59. THE GADARENE DEMONIACS.

MATT. 8:28–34.

28 And when he was come to the other side into the country of the Gadarenes, there met him two [1]possessed with devils[1], coming forth out of the tombs, exceeding fierce, so that no man could pass by that way. 29 And behold, they cried out, saying, What have we to do with thee, thou Son of God? art thou come hither to torment us before the time? 30 Now there was afar off from them a herd of many swine feeding. 31 And the [2]devils[1] besought him, saying, If thou cast us out, send us away into the herd of swine. 32 And he said unto them, Go. And they came out, and went into the swine: and behold, the whole herd rushed down the steep into the sea, and perished in the waters.

[Paragraph continued on page 90.]

MARK 5:1–20.

1 And they came to the other side of the sea, into the country of the Gerasenes. 2 And when he was come out of the boat, straightway there met him out of the tombs a man with an unclean spirit, 3 who had his dwelling in the tombs: and no man could any more bind him, no, not with a chain; 4 because that he had been often bound with fetters and chains, and the chains had been rent asunder by him, and the fetters broken in pieces: and no man had strength to tame him. 5 And always, night and day, in the tombs and in the mountains, he was crying out, and cutting himself with stones. 6 And when he saw Jesus from afar, he ran and worshipped him; 7 and crying out with a loud voice, he saith, What have I to do with thee, Jesus, thou Son of the Most High God? I adjure thee by God, torment me not. 8 For he said unto him, Come forth, thou unclean spirit, out of the man. 9 And he asked him, What is

LUKE 8:26–39.

26 And they arrived at the country of the [3]Gerasenes, which is over against Galilee. 27 And when he was come forth upon the land, there met him a certain man out of the city, who had [2]devils[1]; and for a long time he had worn no clothes, and abode not in *any* house, but in the tombs. 28 And when he saw Jesus, he cried out, and fell down before him, and with a loud voice said, What have I to do with thee, Jesus, thou Son of the Most High God? I beseech thee, torment me not. 29 For he commanded[2] the unclean spirit to come out from the man. For [4]oftentimes it had seized him: and he was kept under guard, and bound with chains and fetters; and breaking the bands asunder, he was driven of the [5]devil[3] into the deserts. 30 And Jesus asked him, What is thy name? And he said, Legion; for many [2]devils[1] were entered into him. 31 And they intreated him that he would not command them

ERV. mg.: [1] Or, *demoniacs* [2] Gr. *demons.* [3] Many ancient authorities read *Gergesenes*; others, *Gadarenes*: and so in ver. 37. [4] Or, *of a long time* [5] Gr. *demon.*

ARV. txt.: [1] demons [2] was commanding [3] demon

MATT. 8.	MARK 5.	LUKE 8.
	thy name? And he saith unto him, My name is Legion; for we are many. 10 And he besought him much that he would not send them away out of the country. 11 Now there was there on the mountain side a great herd of swine feeding. 12 And they besought him, saying, Send us into the swine, that we may enter into them. 13 And he gave them leave. And the unclean spirits came out, and entered into the swine: and the herd rushed down the steep into the sea, *in number* about two thousand; and they were choked [2] in the sea.	to depart into the abyss. 32 Now there was there a herd of many swine feeding on the mountain: and they intreated him that he would give them leave to enter into them. And he gave them leave. 33 And the [3]devils[1] came out from the man, and entered into the swine: and the herd rushed down the steep into the lake, and were choked[2].
33 And they that fed them fled, and went away into the city, and told everything, and what was befallen to them that were [1]possessed with devils[1]. 34 And behold, all the city came out to meet Jesus: and when they saw him, they besought *him* that he would depart from their borders. (+ § 41)	14 And they that fed them fled, and told it in the city, and in the country. And they came to see what it was that had come to pass. 15 And they come to Jesus, and behold [2]him that was possessed with devils[1] sitting, clothed and in his right mind, *even* him that had the legion: and they were afraid. 16 And they that saw it declared unto them how it befell [2]him that was possessed with devils[1], and concerning the swine. 17 And they began to beseech him to depart from their borders. 18 And as he was entering into the boat, he that had been possessed with [3]devils[1] besought him that he might be with him. 19 And he suffered him not, but saith unto him, Go to thy house unto thy friends, and tell them how great things	34 And when they that fed them saw what had come to pass, they fled, and told it in the city and in the country. 35 And they went out to see what had come to pass; and they came to Jesus, and found the man, from whom the [3]devils[1] were gone out, sitting, clothed and in his right mind, at the feet of Jesus: and they were afraid. 36 And they that saw it told them how he that was possessed with [3]devils[1] was [4]made whole. 37 And all the people of the country of the Gerasenes round about asked him to depart from them; for they were holden with great fear: and he entered into a boat, and returned. 38 But the man from whom the [3]devils[1] were gone out prayed him that he might be with him: but he sent him away,

---

RV. mg.: [1] Or, *demoniacs*   [2] Or, *the demoniac*   [3] Gr. *demons.*   [4] Or, *saved*

ARV. txt.: [3] demons   [2] drowned

MARK 5.	LUKE 8.
the Lord hath done for thee, and *how* he had mercy on thee. 20 And he went his way, and began to publish in Decapolis how great things Jesus had done for him : and all men did marvel [1].	saying, 39 Return to thy house and declare how great things God hath done for thee. And he went his way, publishing throughout the whole city how great things Jesus had done for him.

§60. THE RAISING OF JAÏRUS'S DAUGHTER.

MATT. 9 : ⌐1⌐ 18–26.	MARK 5 : 21–43.	LUKE 8 : 40–56.
⌐1 And he entered into a boat, and crossed over, and came into his own city.⌐ (§ 41)		
18 While he spake these things unto them, behold, there came [1] a ruler, and worshipped him, saying, My daughter is even now dead : but come and lay thy hand upon her, and she shall live. 19 And Jesus arose, and followed him, and *so did* his disciples.	21 And when Jesus had crossed over again in the boat unto the other side, a great multitude was gathered unto him : and he was by the sea. 22 And there cometh one of the rulers of the synagogue, Jaïrus by name ; and seeing him, he falleth at his feet, 23 and beseecheth him much, saying, My little daughter is at the point of death : *I pray thee,* that thou come and lay thy hands on her, that she may be [2] made whole, and live. 24 And he went with him ; and a great multitude followed him, and they thronged him.	40 And as Jesus returned, the multitude welcomed him ; for they were all waiting for him. 41 And behold, there came a man named Jaïrus, and he was a ruler of the synagogue : and he fell down at Jesus' feet, and besought him to come into his house ; 42 for he had an only daughter, about twelve years of age, and she lay a dying [3]. But as he went the multitudes thronged him.
20 And behold, a woman, who had an issue of blood twelve years, came behind him, and touched the border of his garment : 21 for she said within herself, If I do but touch his garment, I shall be [2] made whole. 22 But Jesus turning and seeing her said, Daughter, be of good cheer ; thy faith hath [3] made thee whole. And the woman was [2] made whole from that hour.	25 And a woman, which [2] had an issue of blood twelve years, 26 and had suffered many things of many physicians, and had spent all that she had, and was nothing bettered, but rather grew worse, 27 having heard the things concerning Jesus, came in the crowd behind, and touched his garment. 28 For she said, If I touch but his garments, I shall be [2] made whole. 29 And straightway the fountain	43 And a woman having an issue of blood twelve years, which [2] [4] had spent all her living upon physicians, and could not be healed of any, 44 came behind him, and touched the border of his garment : and immediately the issue of her blood stanched. 45 And Jesus said, Who is it that touched me ? And when all denied, Peter said, [5] and they that were with him, Master, the multitudes press thee and

---

ERV. mg.: [1] Gr. *one ruler.* [2] Or, *saved* [3] Or, *saved thee* [4] Some ancient authorities omit *had spent all her living upon physicians, and.* [5] Some ancient authorities omit *and they that were with him.*

ARV. txt.: [1] marvelled [2] who [3] was dying

MATT. 9.	MARK 5.	LUKE 8.

MARK 5.

of her blood was dried up; and she felt in her body that she was healed of her [1] plague. 30 And straightway Jesus, perceiving in himself that the power *proceeding* from him had gone forth, turned him about in the crowd, and said, Who touched my garments? 31 And his disciples said unto him, Thou seest the multitude thronging thee, and sayest thou, Who touched me? 32 And he looked round about to see her that had done this thing. 33 But the woman fearing and trembling, knowing what had been done to her, came and fell down before him, and told him all the truth. 34 And he said unto her, Daughter, thy faith hath [2] made thee whole; go in peace, and be whole of thy [1] plague.

35 While he yet spake, they come from the ruler of the synagogue's *house*, saying, Thy daughter is dead: why troublest thou the [3] Master [1] any further? 36 But Jesus, [4] not heeding the word spoken, saith unto the ruler of the synagogue, Fear not, only believe. 37 And he suffered no man to follow with him, save Peter, and James, and John the brother of James. 38 And they come to the house of the ruler of the synagogue; and he beholdeth a tumult, and *many* weeping and wailing greatly. 39 And when he was entered in, he saith unto them, Why make ye a tumult, and weep? the

LUKE 8.

crush *thee*. 46 But Jesus said, Some one did touch me: for I perceived that power had gone forth from me. 47 And when the woman saw that she was not hid, she came trembling, and falling down before him declared in the presence of all the people for what cause she touched him, and how she was healed immediately. 48 And he said unto her, Daughter, thy faith hath [2] made thee whole; go in peace.

49 While he yet spake, there cometh one from the ruler of the synagogue's *house*, saying, Thy daughter is dead; trouble not the [3] Master [1]. 50 But Jesus hearing it, answered him, Fear not: only believe, and she shall be [5] made whole. 51 And when he came to the house, he suffered not any man to enter in with him, save Peter, and John, and James, and the father of the maiden and her mother. 52 And all were weeping, and bewailing her: but he said, Weep not; for she is not dead, but sleepeth. 53 And they laughed him to scorn, knowing that she was dead. 54 But he, taking her by the hand,

MATT. 9.

23 And when Jesus came into the ruler's house, and saw the flute-players, and the crowd making a tumult,

ERV. mg.: [1] Gr. *scourge*: [2] Or, *saved thee* [3] Or, *Teacher* [4] Or, *overhearing* [5] Or, *saved*

ARV. txt.: [1] Teacher

MATT. 9.	MARK 5.	LUKE 8.
24 he said, Give place: for the damsel is not dead, but sleepeth. And they laughed him to scorn. 25 But when the crowd was put forth, he entered in, and took her by the hand; and the damsel arose. 26 And [1] the fame hereof went forth into all that land.	child is not dead, but sleepeth. 40 And they laughed him to scorn. But he, having put them all forth, taketh the father of the child and her mother and them that were with him, and goeth in where the child was. 41 And taking the child by the hand, he saith unto her, Talitha cumi; which is, being interpreted, Damsel, I say unto thee, Arise. 42 And straightway the damsel rose up, and walked; for she was twelve years old. And they were amazed straightway with a great amazement. 43 And he charged them much that no man should know this: and he commanded that *something* should be given her to eat.	called, saying, Maiden, arise. 55 And her spirit returned, and she rose up immediately: and he commanded that *something* be given her to eat. 56 And her parents were amazed: but he charged them to tell no man what had been done.

§61. THE TWO BLIND MEN, AND THE DUMB DEMONIAC.

MATT. 9:27-34.

27 And as Jesus passed by from thence, two blind men followed him, crying out, and saying, Have mercy on us, thou son of David. 28 And when he was come into the house, the blind men came to him: and Jesus saith unto them, Believe ye that I am able to do this? They say unto him, Yea, Lord. 29 Then touched he their eyes, saying, According to your faith be it done unto you. 30 And their eyes were opened. And Jesus [2] strictly charged them, saying, See that no man know it. 31 But they went forth, and spread abroad his fame in all that land.

32 And as they went forth, behold, there was brought to him a dumb man possessed with a [3] devil [1]. 33 And when the [3] devil [1] was cast out, the dumb man spake: and the multitudes marvelled, saying, It was never so seen in Israel. 34 But the Pharisees said, [4] By the prince of the [5] devils [2] casteth he out [5] devils [2]. (+ §63)

§62. SECOND REJECTION AT NAZARETH.

MATT. 13:54-58.	MARK 6:1-6a.	
54 And coming into his own country he taught them in their synagogue, insomuch that they were astonished,	1 And he went out from thence; and he cometh into his own country; and his disciples follow him. 2 And	[Luke 4:16-30. And he came to Nazareth, where he had been brought up: and he entered, as his custom was, into the syna-

ERV. mg.: [1] Gr. *this fame.*   [2] Or, *sternly*   [3] Gr. *demon.*   [4] Or, *In*   [5] Gr. *demons.*

ARV. txt.: [1] demon   [2] demons

MATT. 13.	MARK 6.	[LUKE 4.]

MATT. 13.

and said, Whence hath this man this wisdom, and these [1]mighty works? 55 Is not this the carpenter's son? is not his mother called Mary? and his brethren, James, and Joseph, and Simon, and Judas? 56 And his sisters, are they not all with us? Whence then hath this man all these things? 57 And they were [2]offended in him. But Jesus said unto them, [a]A prophet is not without honour, save in his own country, and in his own house. 58 And he did not many [1]mighty works there because of their unbelief. (+ § 65)

MARK 6.

when the sabbath was come, he began to teach in the synagogue: and [3]many hearing him were astonished, saying, Whence hath this man these things? and, What is the wisdom that is given unto this man, and *what mean* such [1]mighty works wrought by his hands? 3 Is not this the carpenter, the son of Mary, and brother of James, and Joses, and Judas, and Simon? and are not his sisters here with us? And they were [2]offended in him. 4 And Jesus said unto them, [a]A prophet is not without honour, save in his own country, and among his own kin, and in his own house. 5 And he could there do no [4]mighty work, save that he laid his hands upon a few sick folk, and healed them. 6 And he marvelled because of their unbelief.

[LUKE 4.]

gogue on the sabbath day, and stood up to read. 17 And there was delivered unto him [5]the book of the prophet Isaiah. And he opened the [6]book, and found the place where it was written,

18 The Spirit of the Lord is upon me,

    [7]Because he anointed me to preach [8]good tidings to the poor:

He hath sent me to proclaim release to the captives,

And recovering of sight to the blind,

To set at liberty them that are bruised,

19 To proclaim the acceptable year of the Lord.

20 And he closed the [6]book, and gave it back to the attendant, and sat down: and the eyes of all in the synagogue were fastened on him. 21 And he began to say unto them, To-day hath this scripture been fulfilled in your ears. 22 And all bare him witness, and wondered at the words of grace which proceeded out of his mouth: and they said, Is not this Joseph's son? 23 And he said unto them, Doubtless ye will say unto me this parable, Physician, heal thyself: whatsoever we have heard done at Capernaum, do also here in thine own country. 24 And he said, Verily I say unto you, No prophet is acceptable in his own country. 25 But of a truth I say unto you, There were many widows in Israel in the days of Elijah, when the heaven was shut up three years and six months, when there

---

ERV. mg.: [1] Gr. *powers*. [2] Gr. *caused to stumble*. [3] Some ancient authorities insert *the*. [4] Gr. *power*. [5] Or, *a roll* [6] Or, *roll* [7] Or, *wherefore* [8] Or, *the gospel*

[a] Luke 4:24　(§ 36)　See above.　Cf. also John 4:44.　(§ 34)

[LUKE 4.]
came a great famine over all the land; 26 and unto none of them was Elijah sent, but only to [1]Zarephath, in the land of Sidon, unto a woman that was a widow. 27 And there were many lepers in Israel in the time of Elisha the prophet; and none of them was cleansed, but only Naaman the Syrian. 28 And they were all filled with wrath in the synagogue, as they heard these things; 29 and they rose up, and cast him forth out of the city, and led him unto the brow of the hill whereon their city was built, that they might throw him down headlong. 30 But he passing through the midst of them went his way.] (§ 36)

§ 63.   THIRD PREACHING TOUR CONTINUED.

MATT. 9 : 35.

35 And Jesus went about all the cities and the villages, teaching in their synagogues, and preaching the gospel of the kingdom, and healing all manner of disease and all manner of sickness.

MARK 6 : 6b.

And he went round about the villages teaching.

§ 64.   THE MISSION OF THE TWELVE.

MATT. 9 : 36—11 : 1.

36 But when he saw the multitudes, he was moved with compassion for them, because they were distressed and scattered, as sheep not having a shepherd. 37 Then saith he unto his disciples, [a]The harvest truly[1] is plenteous, but the labourers are

MARK 6 : 7-13.

LUKE 9 : 1-6.

ERV. mg.: [1]Gr. *Sarepta.*

ARV. txt.: [1]indeed

[a]Luke 10:2. The harvest is plenteous, but the labourers are few: pray ye therefore the Lord of the harvest, that he send forth labourers into his harvest. (§ 87)

MATT. 9.	MARK 6.	LUKE 9.
few. 38 Pray ye therefore the Lord of the harvest, that he send forth labourers into his harvest. 10:1 And he called unto him his twelve disciples, and gave them authority over unclean spirits, to cast them out, and to heal all manner of disease and all manner of sickness. 2 Now the *names of the twelve apostles are these: The first, Simon, who is called Peter, and Andrew his brother; James the *son* of Zebedee, and John his brother; 3 Philip, and Bartholomew; Thomas, and Matthew the publican; James the *son* of Alphæus, and Thaddæus; 4 Simon the ¹Cananæan, and Judas Iscariot, who also ²betrayed him. 5 These twelve Jesus sent forth, and charged them, saying, Go not into *any* way of the Gentiles, and enter not into any city of the Samaritans: 6 but go rather to the lost sheep of the house of Israel. 7 ªAnd as ye go, preach, saying, The kingdom of heaven is at hand. 8 Heal the sick, raise the dead, cleanse the lepers, cast out ³devils¹: freely ye received, freely give. 9 Get you no gold, nor silver, nor brass in your ⁴purses; 10 no wallet for *your* journey,	7 And he called² unto him the twelve, and began to send them forth by two and two; and he gave them authority over the unclean spirits;	1 And he called the twelve together, and gave them power and authority over all ³devils¹, and to cure diseases.
	8 ªand he charged them that they should take nothing for *their*	2 And he sent them forth to preach the kingdom of God, and to heal ⁵the sick. 3 ªAnd he said unto them, Take nothing for your journey, neither staff, nor

ERV. mg.: ¹ Or, *Zealot.* See Luke vi. 15; Acts i. 13.   ² Or, *delivered him up*: and so always.   ³ Gr. *demons.*   ⁴ Gr. *girdles.*   ⁵ Some ancient authorities omit *the sick.*

ARV. txt.: ¹ demons   ² calleth

* Cf. § 48.
ª Luke 10: 3–12. Go your ways: behold, I send you forth as lambs in the midst of wolves. 4 Carry no purse, no wallet, no shoes: and salute no man on the way. 5 And into whatsoever house ye shall enter, first say, Peace *be* to this house. 6 And if a son of peace be there, your peace shall rest upon him: but if not, it shall turn to you again. 7 And in that same house remain, eating and drinking such things as they give: for the labourer is worthy of his hire. Go not from house to house. 8 And into whatsoever city ye enter, and they

MATT. 10.	MARK 6.	LUKE 9.
neither two coats, nor shoes, nor staff: for the labourer is worthy of his food. 11 And into whatsoever city or village ye shall enter, search out who in it is worthy; and there abide till ye go forth. 12 And as ye enter into the house, salute it. 13 And if the house be worthy, let your peace come upon it: but if it be not worthy, let your peace return to you. 14 And whosoever shall not receive you, nor hear your words, as ye go forth out of that house or that city, shake off the dust of your feet. 15 Verily I say unto you, It shall be more tolerable for the land of Sodom and Gomorrah in the day of judgement, than for that city. 16 Behold, I send you forth as sheep in the midst of wolves: be ye therefore wise as serpents, and ¹harmless as doves. 17 ªBut beware of men: for they will deliver you up to councils, and in their synagogues they will scourge you; 18 yea and before governors and kings shall ye be brought for my sake, for a testimony to them and to the Gentiles. 19 ᵇBut when they	journey, save a staff only; no bread, no wallet, no ²money in their ³purse; 9 but *to go* shod with sandals: and, *said he*, put not on two coats. 10 And he said unto them, Wheresoever ye enter into a house, there abide till ye depart thence. 11 And whatsoever place shall not receive you, and they hear you not, as you go forth thence, shake off the dust that is under your feet for a testimony unto them. [ª Mark 13:9, 11–13. But take ye heed to yourselves: for they shall deliver you up to councils; and in synagogues shall ye be beaten; and before governors and kings shall ye stand for my sake, for a testimony unto them. .... 11 And when they lead you *to judgement*, and deliver you	wallet, nor bread, nor money; neither have two coats. 4 And into whatsoever house ye enter, there abide, and thence depart. 5 And as many as receive you not, when ye depart from that city, shake off the dust from your feet for a testimony against them. [ª Luke 21:12-19. But before all these things, they shall lay their hands on you, and shall persecute you, delivering you up to the synagogues and prisons, ⁴bringing you before kings and governors for my name's sake. 13 It shall turn¹ unto you for a testimony. 14 Settle it therefore

ERV. mg.: ¹ Or, *simple* ² Gr. *brass.* ³ Gr. *girdle.* ⁴ Gr. you *being brought.*

ARV. txt.: ¹ turn out

receive you, eat such things as are set before you: 9 and heal the sick that are therein, and say unto them, The kingdom of God is come nigh unto you. 10 But into whatsoever city ye shall enter, and they receive you not, go out into the streets thereof and say, 11 Even the dust from your city, that cleaveth to our feet, we do wipe off against you: howbeit know this, that the kingdom of God is come nigh. 12 I say unto you, It shall be more tolerable in that day for Sodom, than for that city. (§ 87)

ª Matt. 24:9. Then shall they deliver you up unto tribulation, and shall kill you. (§ 131)

ª Mark 13:9, 11–13. (§ 131) See above.

ª Luke 21:12-19. (§ 131) See above.

ᵇ Luke 12:11, 12. And when they bring you before the synagogues, and the rulers, and the authorities, be not anxious how or what ye shall answer, or what ye shall say: 12 for the Holy Spirit shall teach you in that very hour what ye ought to say. (§ 95)

MATT. 10.	MARK [13].	LUKE [21].
deliver you up, be not anxious how or what ye shall speak: for it shall be given you in that hour what ye shall speak. 20 For it is not ye that speak, but the Spirit of your Father that speaketh in you. 21 [a] And brother shall deliver up brother to death, and the father his child: and children shall rise up against parents, and [1] cause them to be put to death. 22 [b] And ye shall be hated of all men for my name's sake: but he that endureth to the end, the same shall be saved. 23 But when they persecute you in this city, flee into the next: for verily I say unto you, Ye shall not have gone through the cities of Israel, till the Son of man be come. 24 [c] A disciple is not above his [2] master[1], nor a [3] servant above his lord. 25 It is enough for the disciple that he be as his [2] master[1], and the [3] servant as his lord. If they have called the master of the house [4] Beelzebub, how much more *shall they call*[2] them of his household! 26 Fear them not therefore:	up, be not anxious beforehand what ye shall speak: but whatsoever shall be given you in that hour, that speak ye: for it is not ye that speak, but the Holy Ghost.[3] 12 And brother shall deliver up brother to death, and the father his child; and children shall rise up against parents, and [1] cause them to be put to death. 13 And ye shall be hated of all men for my name's sake: but he that endureth to the end, the same shall be saved.] (§ 131)	in your hearts, not to meditate beforehand how to answer: 15 for I will give you a mouth and wisdom, which all your adversaries shall not be able to withstand or to gainsay. 16 But ye shall be delivered up even by parents, and brethren, and kinsfolk, and friends; and *some* of you [5] shall they cause to be put to death. 17 And ye shall be hated of all men for my name's sake. 18 And not a hair of your head shall perish. 19 In your patience ye shall win your [6] souls.] (§ 131)

ERV. mg.:   [1] Or, *put them to death*   [2] Or, *teacher*   [3] Gr. *bondservant.*   [4] Gr. *Beelzebul*: and so elsewhere.   [5] Or, *shall they put to death*   [6] Or, *lives*

ARV. txt.:   [1] teacher   [2] *Omit: shall they call*   [3] Holy Spirit

[a] Mark 13:12; Luke 21:16. (§ 131) See above.

[a] John 16:2. They shall put you out of the synagogues: yea, the hour cometh, that whosoever killeth you shall think that he offereth service unto God. (§ 134)

[b] Mark 13:13; Luke 21:17, 19. (§ 131) See above.

[b] Matt. 24:9, 13. And ye shall be hated of all the nations for my name's sake. 13 But he that endureth to the end, the same shall be saved. (§ 131)

[b] John 15:21. But all these things will they do unto you for my name's sake, because they know not him that sent me. (§ 134)

[c] Luke 6:40. The disciple is not above his master: but every one when he is perfected shall be as his master. (§ 49)

[c] John 13:16. Verily, verily, I say unto you, A servant is not greater than his lord; neither one that is sent greater than he that sent him. (§ 133)

[c] John 15:20. Remember the word that I said unto you, A servant is not greater than his lord. (§ 134)

MATT. **10.**

ᵃfor there is nothing covered, that shall not be revealed; and hid, that shall not be known. 27 What I tell you in the darkness, speak ye in the light: and what ye hear in the ear, proclaim upon the housetops. 28 And be not afraid of them which¹ kill the body, but are not able to kill the soul: but rather fear him which² is able to destroy both soul and body in ¹hell. 29 Are not two sparrows sold for a farthing³? and not one of them shall fall on the ground without your Father: 30 ᵇbut the very hairs of your head are all numbered. 31 Fear not therefore; ye are of more value than many sparrows. 32 Every one therefore who shall confess ²me before men, ³him will I also confess before my Father which² is in heaven. 33 ᶜBut whosoever shall deny me before men, him will I also deny before my Father which² is in heaven.

34 ᵈThink not that I came

LUKE **[12].**

[ᵃLuke 12:2–9. But there is nothing covered up, that shall not be revealed: and hid, that shall not be known. 3 Wherefore whatsoever ye have said in the darkness shall be heard in the light: and what ye have spoken in the ear in the inner chambers shall be proclaimed upon the housetops. 4 And I say unto you my friends, Be not afraid of them which¹ kill the body, and after that have no more that they can do. 5 But I will warn you whom ye shall fear: Fear him, which² after he hath killed hath ⁴power to cast into ¹hell; yea, I say unto you, Fear him. 6 Are not five sparrows sold for two farthings⁴? and not one of them is forgotten in the sight of God. 7 But the very hairs of your head are all numbered. Fear not: ye are of more value than many sparrows. 8 And I say unto you, Every one who shall confess ²me before men, ³him shall the Son of man also confess before the angels of God: 9 but he that denieth me in the presence of men shall be denied in the presence of the angels of God.] (§95)

ERV. mg.: ¹ Gr. *Gehenna*. ² Gr. *in me*. ³ Gr. *in him*. ⁴ Or, *authority*

ARV. txt.: ¹ that ² who ³ penny ⁴ pence

ᵃMark 4:22. For there is nothing hid, save that it should be manifested; neither was *anything* made secret, but that it should come to light. (§57)

ᵃLuke 8:17. For nothing is hid, that shall not be made manifest; nor *anything* secret, that shall not be known and come to light. (§57)

ᵃLuke 12:2–9. (§95) See above.

ᵇLuke 21:18. And not a hair of your head shall perish (§131). See also Luke 12:7 (§95) above.

ᶜMark 8:38. For whosoever shall be ashamed of me and of my words in this adulterous and sinful generation, the Son of man also shall be ashamed of him, when he cometh in the glory of his Father with the holy angels. (§76)

ᶜLuke 9:26. For whosoever shall be ashamed of me and of my words, of him shall the Son of man be ashamed, when he cometh in his own glory, and *the glory* of the Father, and of the holy angels. (§76)

ᶜLuke 12:9. (§95) See above.

ᵈLuke 12:51–53. Think ye that I am come to give peace in the earth? I tell you, Nay; but rather division: 52 for there shall be from henceforth five in one house divided, three against two, and two against three. 53 They shall be divided, father against son, and son against father; mother against daughter, and daughter against her mother; mother in law against her daughter in law, and daughter in law against her mother in law. (§95)

MATT. 10.	MARK 6.	LUKE 9.
to ¹send peace on the earth : I came not to ¹send peace, but a sword. 35 For I came to set a man at variance against his father, and the daughter against her mother, and the daughter in law against her mother in law: 36 and a man's foes *shall be* they of his own household. 37 ᵃHe that loveth father or mother more than me is not worthy of me ; and he that loveth son or daughter more than me is not worthy of me. 38 ᵇAnd he that doth not take his cross and follow after me is not worthy of me. 39 ᶜHe that ²findeth his ³life shall lose it ; and he that ⁴loseth his ³life for my sake shall find it. 40 ᵈHe that receiveth you receiveth me, and he that receiveth me receiveth him that		

ERV. mg.:   ¹ Gr. *cast.*   ² Or, *found*   ³ Or, *soul*   ⁴ Or, *lost*

ᵃ Luke 14: 26. If any man cometh unto me, and hateth not his own father, and mother, and wife, and children, and brethren, and sisters, yea, and his own life also, he cannot be my disciple. (§ 101)

ᵇ Matt. 16: 24. If any man would come after me, let him deny himself, and take up his cross, and follow me. (§ 76)

ᵇ Mark 8: 34. If any man would come after me, let him deny himself, and take up his cross, and follow me. (§ 76)

ᵇ Luke 9: 23. If any man would come after me, let him deny himself, and take up his cross daily, and follow me. (§ 76)

ᵇ Luke 14: 27. Whosoever doth not bear his own cross, and come after me, cannot be my disciple. (§ 101)

ᶜ Matt. 16: 25. For whosoever would save his life shall lose it ; and whosoever shall lose his life for my sake shall find it. (§ 76)

ᶜ Mark 8: 35. For whosoever would save his life shall lose it: and whosoever shall lose his life for my sake and the gospel's shall save it. (§ 76)

ᶜ Luke 9: 24. For whosoever would save his life shall lose it; but whosoever shall lose his life for my sake, the same shall save it. (§ 76)

ᶜ Luke 17: 33. Whosoever shall seek to gain his life shall lose it: but whosoever shall lose *his life* shall preserve it. (§ 108)

ᶜ John 12: 25. He that loveth his life loseth it; and he that hateth his life in this world shall keep it unto life eternal. (§ 129)

ᵈ Matt. 18: 5. And whoso shall receive one such little child in my name receiveth me. (§ 81)

ᵈ Mark 9: 37. Whosoever shall receive one of such little children in my name, receiveth me: and whosoever receiveth me, receiveth him that sent me. (§ 81)

ᵈ Luke 9: 48. Whosoever shall receive this little child in my name, receiveth me: and whosoever shall receive me receiveth him that sent me: for he that is least among you all, the same is great. (§ 81)

ᵈ Luke 10: 16. He that heareth you heareth me; and he that rejecteth you rejecteth me; and he that rejecteth me rejecteth him that sent me. (§ 87)

ᵈ John 13: 20. Verily, verily, I say unto you, He that receiveth whomsoever I send receiveth me; and he that receiveth me receiveth him that sent me. (§ 133)

MATT. 10.	MARK 6.	LUKE 9.
sent me. 41 He that receiveth a prophet in the name of a prophet shall receive a prophet's reward; and he that receiveth a righteous man in the name of a righteous man shall receive a righteous man's reward. 42 ⁱAnd whosoever shall give to drink unto one of these little ones a cup of cold water only, in the name of a disciple, verily I say unto you, he shall in no wise lose his reward.		
11:1 And it came to pass, when Jesus had made an end of ¹ commanding his twelve disciples, he departed thence to teach and preach in their cities. (+ §52)	12 And they went out, and preached that *men* should repent. 13 And they cast out many ¹devils², and anointed with oil many that were sick, and healed them.	6 And they departed, and went throughout the villages, preaching the gospel and healing everywhere.

§65. DEATH OF JOHN THE BAPTIST.

MATT. 14:1–12.	MARK 6:14–29.	LUKE 9:7–9.
1 At that season Herod the tetrarch heard the report concerning Jesus, 2 and said unto his servants, This is John the Baptist; he is risen from the dead; and therefore do these powers work in him. 3 For Herod had laid hold on John, and bound him, and put him in prison for the sake of Herodias, his brother Philip's wife. 4 For John said unto him, It is not lawful for thee to have her. 5 And when he would have put him to death, he feared the multitude, because they counted him as a prophet. 6 But when Herod's birthday came, the daughter	14 And king Herod heard *thereof*; for his name had become known: and ²he said, John ³the Baptist³ is risen from the dead, and therefore do these powers work in him. 15 But others said, It is Elijah. And others said, *It is* a prophet, *even* as one of the prophets. 16 But Herod, when he heard *thereof*, said, John, whom I beheaded, he is risen. 17 For Herod himself had sent forth and laid hold upon John, and bound him in prison for the sake of Herodias, his brother Philip's wife: for he had married her. 18 For John said unto Herod, It is not	7 Now Herod the tetrarch heard of all that was done: and he was much perplexed, because that it was said by some, that John was risen from the dead; 8 and by some, that Elijah had appeared; and by others, that one of the old prophets was risen again. 9 And Herod said, John I beheaded: but who is this, about whom I hear such things? And he sought to see him. [See Luke 3:19, 20; page 32.]

ERV. mg.: ¹ Gr. *demons*. ² Some ancient authorities read *they*. ³ Gr. *the Baptizer*.

ARV. txt.: ¹ had finished ² demons. ³ Baptizer.

ⁱ **Mark 9:41.** For whosoever shall give you a cup of water to drink, because ye are Christ's, verily I say unto you, he shall in no wise lose his reward. (§81)

MATT. 14.

of Herodias danced in the midst, and pleased Herod. 7 Whereupon he promised with an oath to give her whatsoever she should ask. 8 And she, being put forward by her mother, saith, Give me here in a charger[1] the head of John the Baptist. 9 And the king was grieved; but for the sake of his oaths, and of them which sat at meat with him, he commanded it to be given; 10 and he sent, and beheaded John in the prison. 11 And his head was brought in a charger[1], and given to the damsel: and she brought it to her mother. 12 And his disciples came, and took up the corpse, and buried him; and they went and told Jesus.

MARK 6.

lawful for thee to have thy brother's wife. 19 And Herodias set herself against him, and desired to kill him; and she could not; 20 for Herod feared John, knowing that he was a righteous man and a holy[2], and kept him safe. And when he heard him, he [1]was much perplexed; and he heard him gladly. 21 And when a convenient day was come, that Herod on his birthday made a supper to his lords, and the [2]high captains, and the chief men of Galilee; 22 and when [3]the daughter of Herodias herself came in and danced, [4]she pleased Herod and them that sat at meat with him; and the king said unto the damsel, Ask of me whatsoever thou wilt, and I will give it thee. 23 And he sware unto her, Whatsoever thou shalt ask of me, I will give it thee, unto the half of my kingdom. 24 And she went out, and said unto her mother, What shall I ask? And she said, The head of John [5]the Baptist[3]. 25 And she came in straightway with haste unto the king, and asked, saying, I will that thou forthwith give me in a charger[1] the head of John [5]the Baptist. 26 And the king was exceeding sorry; but for the sake of his oaths, and of them that sat at meat, he would not reject her. 27 And straightway the king sent forth a soldier of his guard, and commanded to

---

ERV. mg.: [1] Many ancient authorities read *did many things.*　[2] Or, *military tribunes* Gr. *chiliarchs.*　[3] Some ancient authorities read *his daughter Herodias.*　[4] Or, *it*　[5] Gr. *the Baptizer.*

ARV. txt.: [1] On a platter　[2] a righteous and holy man　[3] Baptizer

MARK 6.

bring his head: and he went and beheaded him in the prison, 28 and brought his head in a charger[1], and gave it to the damsel; and the damsel gave it to her mother. 29 And when his disciples heard *thereof*, they came and took up his corpse, and laid it in a tomb.

§ 66. THE FEEDING OF THE FIVE THOUSAND.

MATT. 14:13–23.	MARK 6:30–46.	LUKE 9:10–17.	JOHN 6:1–15.
13 Now when Jesus heard *it*, he withdrew from thence in a boat, to a desert place apart: and when the multitudes heard *thereof*, they followed him [1]on foot from the cities. 14 And he came forth, and saw a great multitude, and he had compassion on them, and healed their sick. 15 And when even was come, the disciples came to him, saying, The place is desert, and the time is already past; send the multitudes away, that they may go into the villages, and buy themselves food. 16 But Jesus said unto them, They have no need to go away; give ye them to eat. 17 And they say unto him, We have here but five loaves, and two fishes. 18 And he said, Bring	30 And the apostles gather themselves together unto Jesus; and they told him all things, whatsoever they had done, and whatsoever they had taught. 31 And he saith unto them, Come ye yourselves apart into a desert place, and rest a while. For there were many coming and going, and they had no leisure so much as to eat. 32 And they went away in the boat to a desert place apart. 33 And *the people* saw them going, and many knew *them*, and they ran there together[2] [1]on foot from all the cities, and outwent them. 34 And he came forth and saw a great multitude, and he had compassion on them, because they were as sheep not having a	10 And the apostles, when they were returned, declared unto him what things they had done. And he took them, and withdrew apart to a city called Bethsaida. 11 But the multitudes perceiving it followed him: and he welcomed them, and spake to them of the kingdom of God, and them that had need of healing he healed[3]. 12 And the day began to wear away; and the twelve came, and said unto him, Send the multitude away, that they may go into the villages and country round about, and lodge, and get victuals[4]: for we are here in a desert place. 13 But he said unto them, Give ye them to eat. And they said, We have no more than	1 After these things Jesus went away to the other side of the sea of Galilee, which is *the sea* of Tiberias. 2 And a great multitude followed him, because they beheld the signs which he did on them that were sick. 3 And Jesus went up into the mountain, and there he sat with his disciples. 4 Now the passover, the feast of the Jews, was at hand. 5 Jesus therefore lifting up his eyes, and seeing that a great multitude cometh unto him, saith unto Philip, Whence are we to buy [2]bread, that these may eat? 6 And this he said to prove him: for he himself knew what he would do. 7 Philip answered him, Two hundred [3]pennyworth[5] of

ERV mg.: [1] Or, *by land* [2] Gr. *loaves.* [3] See marginal note on Matt. xviii. 28.

ARV. txt.: [1] on a platter [2] together there [3] cured [4] provisions [5] shillings' worth

MATT. 14.	MARK 6.	LUKE 9.	JOHN 6.
them hither to me. 19 And he commanded the multitudes to [1]sit down on the grass; and he took the five loaves, and the two fishes, and looking up to heaven, he blessed, and brake and gave the loaves to the disciples, and the disciples to the multitudes. 20 And they did all eat[1], and were filled: and they took up that which remained over of the broken pieces, twelve baskets full. 21 And they that did eat were about five thousand men, beside[2] women and children.	shepherd: and he began to teach them many things. 35 And when the day was now far spent, his disciples came unto him, and said, The place is desert, and the day is now far spent: 36 send them away, that they may go into the country and villages round about, and buy themselves somewhat to eat. 37 But he answered and said unto them, Give ye them to eat. And they say unto him, Shall we go and buy two hundred [2]pennyworth[3] of bread, and give them to eat? 38 And he saith unto them, How many loaves have ye? go *and* see. And when they knew, they say, Five, and two fishes. 39 And he commanded them that all should [1]sit down by companies upon the green grass. 40 And they sat down in ranks, by hundreds, and by fifties. 41 And he took the five loaves and the two fishes, and looking up to heaven, he blessed, and brake the loaves; and he gave to the disciples to set before them; and the two fishes divided he	five loaves and two fishes; except we should go and buy food for all this people. 14 For they were about five thousand men. And he said unto his disciples, Make them [1]sit down in companies, about fifty each. 15 And they did so, and made them all [1]sit down. 16 And he took the five loaves and the two fishes, and looking up to heaven, he blessed them, and brake; and gave to the disciples to set before the multitude. 17 And they did eat[4], and were all filled: and there was taken up that which remained over to them of broken pieces, twelve baskets.	[3]bread is not sufficient for them, that every one may take a little. 8 One of his disciples, Andrew, Simon Peter's brother, saith unto him, 9 There is a lad here, which[5] hath five barley loaves, and two fishes: but what are these among so many? 10 Jesus said, Make the people sit down. Now there was much grass in the place. So the men sat down, in number about five thousand. 11 Jesus therefore took the loaves; and having given thanks, he distributed to them that were set down; likewise also of the fishes as much as they would. 12 And when they were filled, he saith unto his disciples, Gather up the broken pieces which remain over, that nothing be lost. 13 So they gathered them up, and filled twelve baskets with broken pieces from the five barley loaves, which remained over unto them that had eaten.

ERV. mg.: [1] Gr. *recline*.　[2] See marginal note on Matt. xviii. 28.　[3] Gr. *loaves*.

ARV. txt.: [1] all ate　[2] besides　[3] shillings' worth　[4] ate　[5] who

MATT. 14.	MARK 6.		JOHN 6.
	among them all. 42 And they did all eat[1], and were filled. 43 And they took up broken pieces, twelve basketfuls, and also of the fishes. 44 And they that ate the loaves were five thousand men.		
22 And straightway he constrained the disciples to enter into the boat, and to go before him unto the other side, till he should send the multitudes away. 23 And after he had sent the multitudes away, he went up into the mountain apart to pray: and when even was come, he was there alone.	45 And straightway he constrained his disciples to enter into the boat, and to go before *him* unto the other side to Bethsaida, while he himself sendeth the multitude away. 46 And after he had taken leave of them, he departed into the mountain to pray.		14 When therefore the people saw the [1]sign which he did, they said, This is of a truth the prophet that cometh into the world. 15 Jesus therefore perceiving that they were about to come and take him by force, to make him king, withdrew again into the mountain himself alone.

§ 67. JESUS WALKING ON THE WATER.

MATT. 14:24-36.	MARK 6:47-56.		JOHN 6:16-21.
24 But the boat [2]was now in the midst of the sea, distressed by the waves; for the wind was contrary. 25 And in the fourth watch of the night he came unto them, walking upon the sea. 26 And when the disciples saw him walking on the sea, they were troubled, saying, It is an apparition[2]; and they cried out for fear. 27 But straightway Jesus spake unto	47 And when even was come, the boat was in the midst of the sea, and he alone on the land. 48 And seeing them distressed in rowing, for the wind was contrary unto them, about the fourth watch of the night he cometh unto them, walking on the sea; and he would have passed by them: 49 but they, when they saw him walking on the sea, supposed that		16 And when evening came, his disciples went down unto the sea; 17 and they entered into a boat, and were going over the sea unto Capernaum. And it was now dark, and Jesus had not yet come to them. 18 And the sea was rising by reason of a great wind that blew. 19 When therefore they had rowed about five and twenty or thirty furlongs, they behold

ERV. mg.: [1] Some ancient authorities read *signs*. [2] Some ancient authorities read *was many furlongs distant from the land.*

ARV. txt.: [1] all ate [2] a ghost

105

MATT. 14.	MARK 6.		JOHN 6.
them, saying, Be of good cheer; it is I; be not afraid. 28 And Peter answered him and said, Lord, if it be thou, bid me come unto thee upon the waters. 29 And he said, Come. And Peter went down from the boat, and walked upon the waters, [1] to come to Jesus. 30 But when he saw the [2] wind, he was afraid; and beginning to sink, he cried out, saying, Lord, save me. 31 And immediately Jesus stretched forth his hand, and took hold of him, and saith unto him, O thou of little faith, wherefore didst thou doubt? 32 And when they were gone up into the boat, the wind ceased. 33 And they that were in the boat worshipped him, saying, Of a truth thou art the Son of God.	it was an apparition [1], and cried out : 50 for they all saw him, and were troubled. But he straightway spake to them, and saith unto them, Be of good cheer: it is I; be not afraid.		Jesus walking on the sea, and drawing nigh unto the boat: and they were afraid. 20 But he saith unto them, It is I; be not afraid.
	51 And he went up unto them into the boat; and the wind ceased: and they were sore amazed in themselves; 52 for they understood not concerning the loaves, but their heart was hardened.		21 They were willing therefore to receive him into the boat: and straightway the boat was at the land whither they were going.
34 And when they had crossed over, they came to the land, unto Gennesaret. 35 And when the men of that place knew him, they sent into all that region round about, and brought unto him all that were sick; 36 and they besought	53 And when they had [3] crossed over, they came to the land unto Gennesaret, and moored to the shore. 54 And when they were come out of the boat, straightway *the people* knew him, 55 and ran round about that whole region, and		

ERV. mg.: [1] Some ancient authorities read *and came.*   [2] Many ancient authorities add [after *wind*] *strong.*   [3] Or, *crossed over to the land, they came unto Gennesaret.*

ARV. txt.: [1] a ghost

MATT. 14.	MARK 6.	
him that they might only touch the border of his garment: and as many as touched were made whole.	began to carry about on their beds those that were sick, where they heard he was. 56 And wheresoever he entered, into villages, or into cities, or into the country, they laid the sick in the market-places, and besought him that they might touch if it were but the border of his garment: and as many as touched [1] him were made whole.	

§68. DISCOURSE ON THE BREAD OF LIFE.

JOHN 6:22-71.

22 On the morrow the multitude which[1] stood on the other side of the sea saw that there was none[2] other [2]boat there, save one, and that Jesus entered not with his disciples into the boat, but *that* his disciples went away alone   23 (howbeit there came [3]boats from Tiberias nigh unto the place where they ate the bread after the Lord had given thanks): 24 when the multitude therefore saw that Jesus was not there, neither his disciples, they themselves got into the [3]boats, and came to Capernaum, seeking Jesus. 25 And when they found him on the other side of the sea, they said unto him, Rabbi, when camest thou hither? 26 Jesus answered them and said, Verily, verily, I say unto you, Ye seek me, not because ye saw signs, but because ye ate of the loaves, and were filled. 27 Work not for the meat[3] which perisheth, but for the meat[3] which abideth unto eternal life, which the Son of man shall give unto you: for him the Father, *even* God, hath sealed. 28 They said therefore unto him, What must we do, that we may work the works of God? 29 Jesus answered and said unto them, This is the work of God, that ye believe on him whom [4]he hath sent. 30 They said therefore unto him, What then doest thou for a sign, that we may see, and believe thee? what workest thou? 31 Our fathers ate the manna in the wilderness; as it is written, He gave them bread out of heaven to eat. 32 Jesus therefore said unto them, Verily, verily, I say unto you, It was not Moses that gave you the bread out of heaven; but my Father giveth you the true bread out of heaven. 33 For the bread of God is that which cometh down out of heaven, and giveth life unto the world. 34 They said therefore unto him, Lord, evermore give us this bread. 35 Jesus said unto them, I am the bread of life: he that cometh to me shall not hunger, and he that believeth on me shall never thirst. 36 But I said unto you, that ye have seen me, and yet believe not. 37 All that which the Father giveth me shall come unto me; and him that cometh to me I will in no wise cast out. 38 For I am come down from heaven, not to do mine own will, but the will of him that sent me. 39 And this is the will of him that sent me, that of all that which he hath given me I should lose nothing, but should raise it

ERV. mg.: ¹ Or, *it* ² Gr. *little boat*. ³ Gr. *little boats*. ⁴ Or, *he sent*

ARV. txt.: ¹ that ² no ³ food

JOHN 6.

up at the last day. 40 For this is the will of my Father, that every one that beholdeth the Son, and believeth on him, should have eternal life; and [1]I will raise him up at the last day.

41 The Jews therefore murmured concerning him, because he said, I am the bread which came down out of heaven. 42 And they said, Is not this Jesus, the son of Joseph, whose father and mother we know? how doth he now say, I am come down out of heaven? 43 Jesus answered and said unto them, Murmur not among yourselves. 44 No man can come to me, except the Father which[1] sent me draw him: and I will raise him up in the last day. 45 It is written in the prophets, And they shall all be taught of God. Every one that hath heard from the Father, and hath learned, cometh unto me. 46 [a]Not that any man hath seen the Father, save he which[1] is from God, he hath seen the Father. 47 Verily, verily, I say unto you, He that believeth hath eternal life. 48 I am the bread of life. 49 Your fathers did eat[2] the manna in the wilderness, and they died. 50 This is the bread which cometh down out of heaven, that a man may eat thereof, and not die. 51 I am the living bread which came down out of heaven : if any man eat of this bread, he shall live for ever : yea and the bread which I will give is my flesh, for the life of the world.

52 The Jews therefore strove one with another, saying, How can this man give us his flesh to eat? 53 Jesus therefore said unto them, Verily, verily, I say unto you, Except ye eat the flesh of the Son of man and drink his blood, ye have not life in yourselves. 54 He that eateth my flesh and drinketh my blood hath eternal life ; and I will raise him up at the last day. 55 For my flesh is [2]meat indeed, and my blood is [3]drink indeed. 56 He that eateth my flesh and drinketh my blood abideth in me, and I in him. 57 As the living Father sent me, and I live because of the Father; so he that eateth me, he also shall live because of me. 58 This is the bread which came down out of heaven: not as the fathers did eat[2], and died: he that eateth this bread shall live for ever. 59 These things said he in [4]the synagogue, as he taught in Capernaum.

60 Many therefore of his disciples, when they heard *this*, said, This is a hard saying; who can hear [5]it? 61 But Jesus knowing in himself that his disciples murmured at this, said unto them Doth this cause you to stumble? 62 *What* then if ye should behold the Son of man ascending where he was before? 63 It is the spirit that quickeneth[3]; the flesh profiteth nothing : the words that I have spoken unto you are spirit, and are life. 64 But there are some of you that believe not. For Jesus knew from the beginning who they were that believed not, and who it was that should betray him. 65 And he said, For this cause have I said unto you, that no man can come unto me, except it be given unto him of the Father.

66 Upon this many of his disciples went back, and walked no more with him. 67 Jesus said therefore unto the twelve, Would ye also go away? 68 Simon Peter answered him, Lord, to whom shall we go? thou [6]hast the words of eternal life. 69 And we have believed and know that thou art the Holy One of God. 70 Jesus answered them, Did not I choose you the twelve, and one of you is a devil? 71 Now he spake of Judas *the son* of Simon Iscariot, for he it was that should betray him, *being* one of the twelve.

ERV. mg.: [1] Or, *that I should raise him up*   [2] Gr. *true meat.*   [3] Gr. *true drink.*   [4] Or, *a synagogue*   [5] Or, *him*   [6] Or, *hast words*

ARV. txt. [1] that   [2] ate   [3] giveth life

---

[a] Matt. 11:27. And no one knoweth the Son, save the Father; neither doth any know the Son, and he to whomsoever the Son willeth to reveal *him*. (§52)

[a] Luke 10:22. And no one knoweth who the Son is, save the Father; and who the Father is, save the Son, and he to whomsoever the Son willeth to reveal *him*. (§87)

§69. DISCOURSE ON EATING WITH UNWASHEN HANDS.

MATT. 15:1-20.

1 Then there come to Jesus from Jerusalem Pharisees and scribes, saying, 2 Why do thy disciples transgress the tradition of the elders? for they wash not their hands when they eat bread. 3 And he answered and said unto them, Why do ye also transgress the commandment of God because of your tradition? 4 For God said, Honour thy father and thy mother: and, He that speaketh evil of father or mother, let him [1] die the death. 5 But ye say, Whosoever shall say to his father or his mother, That wherewith thou mightest have been profited by me is given *to God*; 6 he shall not honour his [2] father. And ye have made void the [3] word of God because of your tradition. 7 Ye hypocrites, well did Isaiah prophesy of you, saying,

8 This people honoureth me with their lips;
But their heart is far from me.
9 But in vain do they worship me,
Teaching *as their* doctrines the precepts of men.

MARK 7:1-23.

1 And there are gathered together unto him the Pharisees, and certain of the scribes, which [1] had come from Jerusalem, 2 and had seen that some of his disciples ate their bread with [4] defiled, that is, unwashen, hands. 3 For the Pharisees, and all the Jews, except they wash their hands [5] diligently, eat not, holding the tradition of the elders: 4 and *when they come* from the marketplace, except they [6] wash [2] themselves, they eat not: and many other things there be [3], which they have received to hold, [7] washings of cups, and pots, and brasen [8] vessels. 5 And the Pharisees and the scribes ask him, Why walk not thy disciples according to the tradition of the elders, but eat their bread with [4] defiled hands? 6 And he said unto them, Well did Isaiah prophesy of you hypocrites, as it is written,

This people honoureth me with their lips,
But their heart is far from me.
7 But in vain do they worship me,
Teaching *as their* doctrines the precepts of men.
8 Ye leave the commandment of God, and hold fast the tradition of men. 9 And he said unto them, Full well do ye reject the commandment of

---

ERV. mg.: [1] Or, *surely die*   [2] Some ancient authorities add *or his mother*.   [3] Some ancient authorities read *law*.   [4] Or, *common*   [5] Or, *up to the elbow* Gr. *with the fist.*   [6] Gr. *baptize.* Some ancient authorities read *sprinkle themselves.*   [7] Gr. *baptizings.*   [8] Many ancient authorities add *and couches.*

ARV. txt.: [1] who   [2] bathe   [3] are

MATT. 15.	MARK 7.	
	God, that ye may keep your tradition. 10 For Moses said, Honour thy father and thy mother; and, He that speaketh evil of father or mother, let him ³ die the death : 11 but ye say, If a man shall say to his father or his mother, That wherewith thou mightest have been profited by me is Corban, that is to say, Given *to God*; 12 ye no longer suffer him to do aught for his father or his mother; 13 making void the word of God by your tradition, which ye have delivered : and many such like things ye do.	
[Cf. vss. 4–6, p. 109.]		
10 And he called to him the multitude, and said unto them, Hear, and understand : 11 Not that which entereth into the mouth defileth the man; but that which proceedeth out of the mouth, this defileth the man. 12 Then came the disciples, and said unto him, Knowest thou that the Pharisees were ¹ offended, when they heard this saying? 13 But he answered and said, Every ² plant which my heavenly Father planted not, shall be rooted up. 14 Let them alone : they are blind guides. ᵃ And if the blind guide the blind, both shall fall into a pit.	14 And he called to him the multitude again, and said unto them, Hear me all of you, and understand : 15 There is nothing from without the man, that going into him can defile him : but the things which proceed out of the man are those that defile the ⁴ man.	
15 And Peter answered and and said unto him, Declare unto us the parable. 16 And he said, Are ye also even yet without understanding? 17 Perceive ye not, that whatso-	17 And when he was entered into the house from the multitude, his disciples asked of him the parable. 18 And he saith unto them, Are ye so without understanding	

ERV. mg.: ¹ Gr. *caused to stumble.* ² Gr. *planting.* ³ Or, *surely die* ⁴ Many ancient authorities insert [after *man*] ver. 16 *If any man hath ears to hear, let him hear.*

ᵃ Luke 6 : 39. Can the blind guide the blind? shall they not both fall into a pit? (§ 49)

MATT. 15.

ever goeth into the mouth passeth into the belly, and is cast out into the draught? 18 But the things which proceed out of the mouth come forth out of the heart; and they defile the man. 19 For out of the heart come forth evil thoughts, murders, adulteries, fornications, thefts, false witness, railings: 20 these are the things which defile the man: but to eat with unwashen hands defileth not the man.

MARK 7.

also? Perceive ye not, that whatsoever from without goeth into the man, *it* cannot defile him; 19 because it goeth not into his heart, but into his belly, and goeth out into the draught? *This he said*, making all meats clean. 20 And he said, That which proceedeth out of the man, that defileth the man. 21 For from within, out of the heart of men,[1] evil thoughts proceed, fornications, thefts, murders, adulteries, 22 covetings, wickednesses, deceit, lasciviousness, an evil eye, railing, pride, foolishness: 23 all these evil things proceed from within, and defile the man.

REV. mg.: [1] Gr. *thoughts that are evil.*

111

PART VI.

THIRD PERIOD OF THE GALILEAN MINISTRY.

FROM THE WITHDRAWAL INTO NORTHERN GALILEE UNTIL THE FINAL DEPARTURE
FOR JERUSALEM.

---

§ 70. JOURNEY TOWARD TYRE AND SIDON; THE SYROPHŒNICIAN WOMAN'S
DAUGHTER.

MATT. 15 : 21-28.

21 And Jesus went out thence, and withdrew into the parts of Tyre and Sidon. 22 And behold, a Canaanitish woman came out from those borders, and cried, saying, Have mercy on me, O Lord, thou son of David; my daughter is grievously vexed with a [1]devil[1]. 23 But he answered her not a word. And his disciples came and besought him, saying, Send her away; for she crieth after us. 24 But he answered and said, I was not sent but unto the lost sheep of the house of Israel. 25 But she came and worshipped him, saying, Lord, help me. 26 And he answered and said, It is not meet to take the children's [2]bread and cast it to the dogs. 27 But she said, Yea, Lord: for even the dogs eat of the crumbs which fall from their masters' table. 28 Then Jesus answered and said unto her, O woman, great is thy faith: be it done unto thee even as thou wilt. And her daughter was healed from that hour.

MARK 7 : 24-30.

24 And from thence he arose, and went away into the borders of Tyre [3]and Sidon. And he entered into a house, and would have no man know it: and he could not be hid. 25 But straightway a woman, whose little daughter had an unclean spirit, having heard of him, came and fell down at his feet. 26 Now the woman was a [4]Greek, a Syrophœnician by race. And she besought him that he would cast forth the [1]devil[1] out of her daughter. 27 And he said unto her, Let the children first be filled: for it is not meet to take the children's [2]bread and cast it to the dogs. 28 But she answered and saith unto him, Yea, Lord: even the dogs under the table eat of the children's crumbs. 29 And he said unto her, For this saying go thy way; the [1]devil[1] is gone out of thy daughter. 30 And she went away unto her house, and found the child laid upon the bed, and the [1]devil[1] gone out.

ERV. mg.: [1] Gr. *demon*. [2] Or, *loaf* [3] Some ancient authorities omit *and Sidon*. [4] Or, *Gentile*

ARV. txt.: [1] demon

§71. RETURN THROUGH DECAPOLIS; MANY MIRACLES OF HEALING.

MATT. 15 : 29–31.

29 And Jesus departed thence, and came nigh unto the sea of Galilee; and he went up into the mountain, and sat there. 30 And there came unto him great multitudes, having with them the lame, blind, dumb, maimed, and many others, and they cast them down at his feet; and he healed them: 31 insomuch that the multitude wondered, when they saw the dumb speaking, the maimed whole, and the lame walking, and the blind seeing: and they glorified the God of Israel.

MARK 7 : 31–37.

31 And again he went out from the borders of Tyre, and came through Sidon unto the sea of Galilee, through the midst of the borders of Decapolis.

32 And they bring unto him one that was deaf, and had an impediment in his speech; and they beseech him to lay his hand upon him. 33 And he took him aside from the multitude privately, and put his fingers into his ears, and he spat, and touched his tongue; 34 and looking up to heaven, he sighed, and saith unto him, Ephphatha, that is, Be opened. 35 And his ears were opened, and the bond of his tongue was loosed, and he spake plain. 36 And he charged them that they should tell no man: but the more he charged them, so much the more a great deal they published it. 37 And they were beyond measure astonished, saying, He hath done all things well: he maketh even the deaf to hear, and the dumb to speak.

§ 72. THE FEEDING OF THE FOUR THOUSAND.

MATT. 15 : 32–38.

32 And Jesus called unto him his disciples, and said, I have compassion on the multitude, because they continue with me now three days and have nothing to eat: and I would not send them away fasting, lest haply they faint in[1] the way. 33 And the disciples say unto him, Whence should we have so many loaves in a desert place, as to fill so great a multitude? 34 And Jesus saith unto them, How many loaves have ye? And they said, Seven, and a few small fishes. 35 And he commanded the multitude to sit down on the ground; 36 and he took the seven loaves and the fishes; and he gave thanks and brake, and gave to the disciples, and the disciples to the multitudes. 37 And they did all eat[2], and were filled: and they took up that which remained over of the broken pieces, seven baskets full. 38 And they that did eat were four thousand men, beside[3] women and children.

MARK 8 : 1–9.

1 In those days, when there was again a great multitude, and they had nothing to eat, he called unto him his disciples, and saith unto them, 2 I have compassion on the multitude, because they continue with me now three days, and have nothing to eat: 3 and if I send them away fasting to their home, they will faint in[1] the way; and some of them are come from far. 4 And his disciples answered him, Whence shall one be able to fill these men with [1]bread here in a desert place? 5 And he asked them, How many loaves have ye? And they said, Seven. 6 And he commandeth the multitude to sit down on the ground: and he took the seven loaves, and having given thanks, he brake, and gave to his disciples, to set before them; and they set them before the multitude. 7 And they had a few small fishes: and having blessed them, he commanded to set these also before them. 8 And they did eat[4], and were filled: and they took up, of broken pieces that remained over, seven baskets. 9 And they were about four thousand: and he sent them away.

§ 73. THE PHARISEES AND SADDUCEES DEMANDING A SIGN FROM HEAVEN.

MATT. 15 : 39—16 : 12.

39 And he sent away the multitudes, and entered into

MARK 8 : 10–21.

10 And straightway he entered into the boat with his

ERV. mg.: [1] Gr. *loaves.*

ARV. txt.: [1] on   [2] all ate   [3] besides   [4] ate

MATT. 15.

the boat, and came into the borders of Magadan.

16:1 And the Pharisees and Sadducees came, and tempting[1] him asked him to shew them a sign from heaven. 2 [a]But he answered and said unto them, [1]When it is evening, ye say, *It will be* fair weather: for the heaven is red. 3 And in the morning, *It will be* foul weather to-day: for the heaven is red and lowring[2]. Ye know how to discern the face of the heaven; but ye cannot *discern* the signs of the times. 4 [b]An evil and adulterous generation seeketh after a sign; and there shall no sign be given unto it, but the sign of Jonah. And he left them, and departed.

5 And the disciples came to the other side and forgot to take [2]bread. 6 And Jesus said unto them, [c]Take heed and beware of the leaven of the Pharisees and Sadducees. 7 And they reasoned among themselves, saying, [3]We took no [2]bread. 8 And Jesus perceiving it said, O ye of little faith, why reason ye among yourselves, because ye have

MARK 8.

disciples, and came into the parts of Dalmanutha.

11 And the Pharisees came forth, and began to question with him, seeking of him a sign from heaven, tempting[1] him. 12 And he sighed deeply in his spirit, and saith, [b]Why doth this generation seek a sign? verily I say unto you, There shall no sign be given unto this generation. 13 And he left them, and again entering into *the boat* departed to the other side.

14 And they forgot to take bread; and they had not in the boat with them more than one loaf. 15 And he charged them, saying, [c]Take heed, beware of the leaven of the Pharisees and the leaven of Herod. 16 And they reasoned one with another, [4]saying, [5]We have no bread. 17 And Jesus perceiving it saith unto them, Why reason ye, because

---

ERV. mg.: [1]The following words, to the end of ver. 3, are omitted by some of the most ancient and other important authorities. [2]Gr. *loaves.* [3]Or, It is *because we took no bread.* [4]Some ancient authorities read *because they had no bread.* [5]Or, It is *because we have no bread.*

ARV. txt.: [1]trying [2]lowering

---

[a]Luke 12:54-56. And he said to the multitudes also, When ye see a cloud rising in the west, straightway ye say, There cometh a shower; and so it cometh to pass. 55 And when *ye see* a south wind blowing, ye say, There will be a scorching heat; and it cometh to pass. 56 Ye hypocrites, ye know how to interpret the face of the earth and the heaven; but how is it that ye know not how to interpret this time? (§ 95)

[b]Matt. 12:39. An evil and adulterous generation seeketh after a sign; and there shall no sign be given to it but the sign of Jonah the prophet. (§ 55)

[b]Luke 11:29. This generation is an evil generation: it seeketh after a sign; and there shall no sign be given to it but the sign of Jonah. (§ 94)

[c]Luke 12:1. Beware ye of the leaven of the Pharisees, which is hypocrisy. (§ 95)

[c]Cf. Matt. 16:11, p. 116.

MATT. 16.	MARK 8.	
no ¹bread? 9 Do ye not yet perceive, neither remember the five loaves **of** the five thousand, and how many ²baskets ye took up? 10 Neither the seven loaves of the four thousand, and how many ²baskets ye took up? 11 How is it that ye do not perceive that I spake not to you concerning ¹bread? ªBut beware of the leaven of the Pharisees and Sadducees. 12 Then understood they how¹ that he bade them not beware of the leaven of ¹bread, but of the teaching of the Pharisees and Sadducees.	ye have no bread? do ye not yet perceive, neither understand? have ye your heart hardened? 18 Having eyes, see ye not? and having ears, hear ye not? and do ye not remember? 19 When I brake the five loaves among the five thousand, how many ³baskets full of broken pieces took ye up? They say unto him, Twelve. 20 And when the seven among the four thousand, how many ²basketfuls of broken pieces took ye up? And they say unto him, Seven. 21 And he said unto them, Do ye not yet understand?	

§74.   THE BLIND MAN NEAR BETHSAIDA.

MARK 8 : 22–26.

22 And they come unto Bethsaida. And they bring to him a blind man, and beseech him to touch him. 23 And he took hold of the blind man by the hand, and brought him out of the village; and when he had spit on his eyes, and laid his hands upon him, he asked him, Seest thou aught? 24 And he looked up, and said, I see men; for I behold *them* as trees, walking. 25 Then again he laid his hands upon his eyes; and he looked stedfastly, and was restored, and saw all things clearly. 26 And he sent him away to his home, saying, Do not even enter into the village.

§75.   PETER'S CONFESSION.

MATT. 16:13–20.	MARK 8:27–30.	LUKE 9:18–21.
13 Now when Jesus came into the parts of Cæsarea Philippi, he asked his disciples, saying, Who do men say ⁴that the Son of man is? 14 And they said, Some *say* John the Baptist; some, Elijah: and others, Jeremiah, or one of the prophets. 15 He saith unto them, But who say ye that I am? 16 And	27 And Jesus went forth, and his disciples, into the villages of Cæsarea Philippi: and in² the way he asked his disciples, saying unto them, Who do men say that I am? 28 And they told him, saying, John the Baptist: and others, Elijah; but others, One of the prophets. 29 And he asked them, But who say ye that I	18 And it came to pass, as he was praying alone³, the disciples were with him: and he asked them, saying, Who do the multitudes say that I am? 19 And they answering said, John the Baptist; but others *say*, Elijah; and others, that one of the old prophets is risen again. 20 And he said unto them, But

ERV. mg.: ¹ Gr. *loaves*.   ² *Basket* in ver. 9 and 10 represents different Greek words.   ³ *Basket* in ver. 19 and 20 represents different Greek words.   ⁴ Many ancient authorities read *that I the Son of man am*.   See Mark viii. 27; Luke ix. 18.

ARV. txt.: ¹*Omit* how   ²on   ³apart

ªSee Mark 8:15 and note ᶜ on page 115.

MATT. 16.	MARK 8.	LUKE 9.
Simon Peter answered and said, Thou art the Christ, the Son of the living God. 17 And Jesus answered and said unto him, Blessed art thou, Simon Bar-Jonah : for flesh and blood hath not revealed it unto thee, but my Father which[1] is in heaven. 18 And I also say unto thee, that thou art [1]Peter, and upon this [2]rock I will build my church ; and the gates of Hades shall not prevail against it. 19 I will give unto thee the keys of the kingdom of heaven : [a]and whatsoever thou shalt bind on earth shall be bound in heaven : and whatsoever thou shalt loose on earth shall be loosed in heaven. 20 Then charged he the disciples that they should tell no man that he was the Christ.	am? Peter answereth and saith unto him, Thou art the Christ. 30 And he charged them that they should tell no man of him.	who say ye that I am? And Peter answering said, The Christ of God. 21 But he charged them, and commanded *them* to tell this to no man ; [Paragraph continued in §76.]

§76. CHRIST FORETELLS HIS DEATH AND RESURRECTION.

MATT. 16: 21-28.	MARK 8:31—9:1.	LUKE 9: 22-27.
21 From that time began [3]Jesus to shew unto his disciples, how[2] that [b]he must go unto Jerusalem, and suffer many things of the elders and chief priests and scribes, and be killed, and the third day be raised up. 22 And Peter took him, and began to rebuke him, saying, [4]Be it far from	31 And he began to teach them, that [b]the Son of man must suffer many things, and be rejected by the elders, and the chief priests, and the scribes, and be killed, and after three days rise again. 32 And he spake the saying openly. And Peter took him, and began to rebuke him.	22 saying, [b] The Son of man must suffer many things, and be rejected of the elders and chief priests and scribes, and be killed, and the third day be raised up. [Paragraph continued on next page.]

ERV. mg.: [1] Gr. *Petros.* [2] Gr. *petra.* [3] Some ancient authorities read *Jesus Christ.* [4] Or, God *have mercy on thee.*

ARV. txt.: [1] who [2] *Omit* how

[a] Matt. 18:18. Verily I say unto you, What things soever ye shall bind on earth shall be bound in heaven: and what things soever ye shall loose on earth shall be loosed in heaven. (§81)
[a] John 20:23. Whose soever sins ye forgive, they are forgiven unto them ; whose soever *sins* ye retain, they are retained. (§146)
[b] Luke 17:25. But first must he suffer many things and be rejected of this generation. (§108) Cf. also Matt. 17:22; Mark 9:31; Luke 9:44; (§79) and Matt. 20:18; Mark 10:33; Luke 18:31. (§113)

MATT. 16.	MARK 8.	LUKE 9.
thee, Lord : this shall never be unto thee. 23 But he turned, and said unto Peter, Get thee behind me, Satan : thou art a stumblingblock unto me : for thou mindest not the things of God, but the things of men. 24 Then said Jesus unto his disciples, ᵃ If any man would come after me, let him deny himself, and take up his cross, and follow me. 25 ᵇ For whosoever would save his ¹ life shall lose it : and whosoever shall lose his ¹ life for my sake shall find it. 26 For what shall a man be profited, if he shall gain the whole world, and forfeit his ¹ life? or what shall a man give in exchange for his ¹ life? 27 For the Son of man shall come in the glory of his Father with his angels ; and then shall he render unto every man according to his ² deeds. 28 Verily I say unto you, There be ¹ some of them that stand here, which ² shall in no wise taste of death, till they see the Son of man coming in his kingdom.	33 But he turning about, and seeing his disciples, rebuked Peter, and saith, Get thee behind me, Satan : for thou mindest not the things of God, but the things of men. 34 And he called unto him the multitude with his disciples, and said unto them, ᵃ If any man would come after me, let him deny himself, and take up his cross, and follow me. 35 ᵇ For whosoever would save his ¹ life shall lose it ; and whosoever shall lose his ¹ life for my sake and the gospel's shall save it. 36 For what doth it profit a man, to gain the whole world, and forfeit his ¹ life? 37 For what should a man give in exchange for his ¹ life? 38 ᶜ For whosoever shall be ashamed of me and of my words in this adulterous and sinful generation, the Son of man also shall be ashamed of him, when he cometh in the glory of his Father with the holy angels. 9 : 1 And he said unto them, Verily I say unto you, There be ¹ some here of them that stand *by*, which ² shall in no wise taste of death, till they see the kingdom of God come with power.	23 And he said unto all, ᵃ If any man would come after me, let him deny himself, and take up his cross daily, and follow me 24 ᵇ For whosoever would save his ¹ life shall lose it ; but whosoever shall lose his ¹ life for my sake, the same shall save it. 25 For what is a man profited, if he gain the whole world, and lose or forfeit his own self? 26 ᶜ For whosoever shall be ashamed of me and of my words, of him shall the Son of man be ashamed, when he cometh in his own glory, and *the glory* of the Father, and of the holy angels. 27 But I tell you of a truth, There be ¹ some of them that stand here, which ² shall in no wise taste of death, till they see the kingdom of God.

ᵃ Matt. 10 : 38. And he that doth not take his cross and follow after me, is not worthy of me. (§ 64)

ᵃ Luke 14 : 27. Whosoever doth not bear his own cross, and come after me, cannot be my disciple. (§ 101)

ᵇ Matt. 10 : 39. He that findeth his life shall lose it ; and he that loseth his life for my sake shall find it. (§ 64)

ᵇ Luke 17 : 33. Whosoever shall seek to gain his life shall lose it : but whosoever shall lose *his life* shall preserve it. (§ 108)

ᵇ John 12 : 25. He that loveth his life loseth it ; and he that hateth his life in this world shall keep it unto life eternal. (§ 129)

ᶜ Matt. 10 : 33. But whosoever shall deny me before men, him will I also deny before my Father which is in heaven. (§ 64)

ᶜ Luke 12 : 9. But he that denieth me in the presence of men shall be denied in the presence of the angels of God. (§ 95)

§77. THE TRANSFIGURATION.

MATT. 17:1-13.	MARK 9:2-13.	LUKE 9:28-36.
1 And after six days Jesus taketh with him Peter, and James, and John his brother, and bringeth them up into a high mountain apart: 2 and he was transfigured before them: and his face did shine as the sun, and his garments became white as the light. 3 And behold, there appeared unto them Moses and Elijah talking with him. 4 And Peter answered, and said unto Jesus, Lord, it is good for us to be here: if thou wilt, I will make here three [1]tabernacles; one for thee, and one for Moses, and one for Elijah. 5 While he was yet speaking, behold, a bright cloud overshadowed them: and behold, a voice out of the cloud, saying, This is my beloved Son, in whom I am well pleased; hear ye him. 6 And when the disciples heard it, they fell on their face, and were sore afraid. 7 And Jesus came and touched them and said, Arise, and be not afraid. 8 And lifting up their eyes, they saw no one, save Jesus only.	2 And after six days Jesus taketh with him Peter, and James, and John, and bringeth them up into a high mountain apart by themselves: and he was transfigured before them: 3 and his garments became glistering, exceeding white; so as no fuller on earth can whiten them. 4 And there appeared unto them Elijah with Moses: and they were talking with Jesus. 5 And Peter answereth and saith to Jesus, Rabbi, it is good for us to be here: and let us make three [1]tabernacles; one for thee, and one for Moses, and one for Elijah. 6 For he wist[1] not what to answer; for they became sore afraid. 7 And there came a cloud overshadowing them: and there came a voice out of the cloud, This is my beloved Son: hear ye him. 8 And suddenly looking round about, they saw no one any more, save Jesus only with themselves.	28 And it came to pass about eight days after these sayings, he[2] took with him Peter and John and James, and went up into the mountain to pray. 29 And as he was praying, the fashion of his countenance was altered, and his raiment *became* white *and* dazzling. 30 And behold, there talked with him two men, which[3] were Moses and Elijah; 31 who appeared in glory, and spake of his [2]decease which he was about to accomplish at Jerusalem. 32 Now Peter and they that were with him were heavy with sleep: but [3]when they were fully awake, they saw his glory, and the two men that stood with him. 33 And it came to pass, as they were parting from him, Peter said unto Jesus, Master, it is good for us to be here: and let us make three [1]tabernacles; one for thee, and one for Moses, and one for Elijah: not knowing what he said. 34 And while he said these things, there came a cloud, and overshadowed them: and they feared as they entered into the cloud. 35 And a voice came out of the cloud, saying, This is [4]my Son, my chosen: hear ye him. 36 And when the voice [5]came, Jesus was found alone. And they held their peace, and told no man in those days any of the things which they had seen.

ERV. mg.: [1] Or, *booths* [2] Or, *departure* [3] Or, *having remained awake* [4] Many ancient authorities read *my beloved Son.* See Matt. xvii. 5; Mark ix. 7. [5] Or, *was past*

ARV. txt.: [1] knew [2] that he [3] who

MATT. 17	MARK 9.
9 And as they were coming down from the mountain, Jesus commanded them, saying, Tell the vision to no man, until the Son of man be risen from the dead. 10 And his disciples asked him, saying, Why then say the scribes that Elijah must first come? 11 And he answered and said, Elijah indeed cometh, and shall restore all things: 12 but I say unto you, that Elijah is come already, and they knew him not, but did unto him whatsoever they listed[1]. Even so shall the Son of man also suffer of them. 13 Then understood the disciples that he spake unto them of John the Baptist.	9 And as they were coming down from the mountain, he charged them that they should tell no man what things they had seen, save when the Son of man should have risen again from the dead. 10 And they kept the saying, questioning among themselves what the rising again from the dead should mean. 11 And they asked him, saying, [1]The scribes say that Elijah must first come[2]. 12 And he said unto them, Elijah indeed cometh first, and restoreth all things: and how is it written of the Son of man, that he should suffer many things and be set at nought? 13 But I say unto you, that Elijah is come, and they have also done unto him whatsoever they listed[1], even as it is written of him.

§ 78. THE DEMONIAC BOY.

MATT. 17:14-20.	MARK 9:14-29.	LUKE 9:37-43a.
14 And when they were come to the multitude, there came to him a man, kneeling to him, and saying, 15 Lord, have mercy on my son: for he is epileptic, and suffereth grievously: for oft-times he falleth into the fire, and oft-times into the water. 16 And I brought him to thy disciples, and they could not cure him. 17 And Jesus answered and said, O faithless and perverse generation, how long shall I be with you? how long shall I bear with you? bring him	14 And when they came to the disciples, they saw a great multitude about them, and scribes questioning with them. 15 And straightway all the multitude, when they saw him, were greatly amazed, and running to him saluted him. 16 And he asked them, What question ye with them? 17 And one of the multitude answered him, [2]Master[3], I brought unto thee my son, which[4] hath a dumb spirit; 18 and wheresoever it taketh him, it [3]dasheth him down:	37 And it came to pass, on the next day, when they were come down from the mountain, a great multitude met him. 38 And behold, a man from the multitude cried, saying, [2]Master[3], I beseech thee to look upon my son; for he is mine only child: 39 and behold, a spirit taketh him, and he suddenly crieth out; and it [4]teareth him that he foameth, and it hardly departeth from him, bruising him sorely. 40 And I besought thy disciples to cast it out; and they

ERV. mg.:   [1] Or, *How is it that the scribes say . . . come?*   [2] Or, *Teacher*   [3] Or, *rendeth him*   [4] Or, *convulseth*

ARV. txt.:   [1] would   [2] *How is it* that the scribes say . . . come?   [3] Teacher   [4] who

MATT. 17.	MARK 9.	LUKE 9.
hither to me. 18 And Jesus rebuked him; and the [1]devil[1] went out from[2] him: and the boy was cured from that hour. 19 Then came the disciples to Jesus apart, and said, Why could not we cast it out? 20 And he saith unto them, a Because of your little faith: for verily I say unto you, If ye have faith as a grain of mustard seed, ye shall say unto this mountain, Remove hence to yonder place; and it shall remove; and nothing shall be impossible unto [2]you.	and he foameth, and grindeth his teeth, and pineth away: and I spake to thy disciples that they should cast it out; and they were not able. 19 And he answereth them and saith, O faithless generation, how long shall I be with you? how long shall I bear with you? bring him unto me. 20 And they brought him unto him: and when he saw him, straightway the spirit [3]tare him grievously; and he fell on the ground, and wallowed foaming. 21 And he asked his father, How long time is it since this hath come unto him? And he said, From a child. 22 And oft-times it hath cast him both into the fire and into the waters, to destroy him: but if thou canst do anything, have compassion on us, and help us. 23 And Jesus said unto him, If thou canst! All things are possible to him that believeth. 24 Straightway the father of the child cried out, and [4]said, I believe; help thou mine unbelief. 25 And when Jesus saw that a multitude came running together, he rebuked the unclean spirit, saying unto him, Thou dumb and deaf spirit, I command thee, come	could not. 41 And Jesus answered and said, O faithless and perverse generation, how long shall I be with you, and bear with you? bring hither thy son. 42 And as he was yet a coming, the [1]devil[1] [5]dashed him down, and [3]tare *him* grievously. But Jesus rebuked the unclean spirit, and healed the boy, and gave him back to his father. 43 And they were all astonished at the majesty of God.

ERV. mg.: [1] Gr. *demon.*   [2] Many authorities, some ancient, insert [after *you.*] ver. 21 *But this kind goeth not out save by prayer and fasting.* See Mark ix. 29.   [3] Or, *convulsed*   [4] Many ancient authorities add *with tears.*   [5] Or, *rent him*

ARV. txt.: [1] demon   [2] of

---

a Matt. 21:21. Verily I say unto you, If ye have faith, and doubt not, ye shall not only do what is done to the fig tree, but even if ye shall say unto this mountain, Be thou taken up and cast into the sea, it shall be done. (§ 122)

a Mark 11:22, 23. Have faith in God. 23 Verily I say unto you, Whosoever shall say unto this mountain, Be thou taken up and cast into the sea; and shall not doubt in his heart, but shall believe that what he saith cometh to pass; he shall have it. (§ 122)

a Luke 17:6. If ye have faith as a grain of mustard seed, ye would say unto this sycamore tree, Be thou rooted up, and be thou planted in the sea; and it would have obeyed you. (§ 104)

MARK 9.

out of him, and enter no more into him. 26 And having cried out, and [1]torn him much, he came out: and *the child*[1] became as one dead; insomuch that the more part said, He is dead. 27 But Jesus took him by the hand, and raised him up; and he arose. 28 And when he was come into the house, his disciples asked him privately, [2]*saying*[2], We could not cast it out[3]. 29 And he said unto them, This kind can come out by nothing, save by [3]prayer.

§ 79. CHRIST AGAIN FORETELLS HIS DEATH AND RESURRECTION.

MATT. 17 : 22, 23.	MARK 9 : 30–32.	LUKE 9 : 43*b*–45.
22 And while they [4]abode in Galilee, Jesus said unto them, [a]The Son of man shall be delivered up into the hands of men; 23 and they shall kill him, and the third day he shall be raised up. And they were exceeding sorry.	30 And they went forth from thence, and passed through Galilee; and he would not that any man should know it. 31 For he taught his disciples, and said unto them, [a]The Son of man is delivered up into the hands of men, and they shall kill him; and when he is killed, after three days he shall rise again. 32 But they understood not the saying, and were afraid to ask him.	43*b* But while all were marvelling at all the things which he did, he said unto his disciples, 44 Let these words sink into your ears: [a]for the Son of man shall be delivered up into the hands of men. 45 But they understood not this saying, and it was concealed from them, that they should not perceive it: and they were afraid to ask him about this saying.

§ 80. THE SHEKEL IN THE FISH'S MOUTH.

MATT. 17 : 24–27.	⌜MARK 9 :33*a*.⌝
24 And when they were come to Capernaum, they that received the [5]half-shekel came to Peter, and said, Doth not your [6]master[4] pay the [5]half-shekel? 25 He saith, Yea.	⌜33 And they came to Capernaum:⌝ (§ 81)

ERV. mg.: [1] Or, *convulsed* [2] Or, How is it *that we could not cast it out?* [3] Many ancient authorities add *and fasting.* [4] Some ancient authorities read *were gathering themselves together.* [5] Gr. *didrachma.* [6] Or, *teacher.*

ARV. txt.: [1] *the boy* [2] *Omit saying* [3] *How is it* that we could not cast it out? [4] *teacher*

[a] Cf. Matt. 16: 21; Mark 8: 31; Luke 9: 22 (§ 76) and references there.

MATT. **17.**

And when he came into the house, Jesus spake first to him, saying, What thinkest thou, Simon? the kings of the earth, from whom do they receive toll or tribute? from their sons, or from strangers? 26 And when he said, From strangers, Jesus said unto him, Therefore the sons are free. 27 But, lest we cause them to stumble, go thou to the sea, and cast a hook, and take up the fish that first cometh up; and when thou hast opened his mouth, thou shalt find a [1]shekel: that take, and give unto them for me and thee.

§81. DISCOURSE ON HUMILITY AND FORGIVENESS.

MATT., CHAP. **18.**	MARK **9: 33-50.**	LUKE **9: 46-50.**
1 In that hour came the disciples unto Jesus, saying, Who then is [2]greatest in the kingdom of heaven? 2 And he called to him a little child, and set him in the midst of them, 3 and said, [a]Verily I say unto you, Except ye turn, and become as little children, ye shall in no wise enter into the kingdom of heaven. 4 Whosoever therefore shall	33 And they came to Capernaum: and when he was in the house he asked them, What were ye reasoning in[1] the way? 34 But they held their peace: for they had disputed one with another in[1] the way, who *was* the [2]greatest. 35 And he sat down, and called the twelve; and he saith unto them, [b]If any man would be first, he shall be last	46 And there arose a reasoning among them, which of them, should be [2]greatest[2]. 47 But when Jesus saw the reasoning of their heart, he took a little child, and set him by his side, 48 and said unto them, [Paragraph continued on p. 124.]

ERV. mg.: [1] Gr. *stater.* [2] Gr. *greater.*

ARV. txt.: [1] on [2] was the greatest

[a] Mark 10:15. Verily I say unto you, Whosoever shall not receive the kingdom of God as a little child, he shall in no wise enter therein. (§111)

[a] Luke 18:17. Verily I say unto you, Whosoever shall not receive the kingdom of God as a little child, he shall in no wise enter therein. (§111)

[b] Matt. 20:26, 27. But whosoever would become great among you shall be your minister; 27 and whosoever would be first among you shall be your servant. (§114)

[b] Matt. 23:11. But he that is greatest among you shall be your servant. (§127)

[b] Mark 10:43, 44. But whosoever would become great among you, shall be your minister: 44 and whosoever would be first among you, shall be servant of all. (§114)

[b] Luke 22:26. But he that is the greater among you, let him become as the younger; and he that is chief, as he that doth serve. (§133)

MATT. 18.	MARK 9.	LUKE 9.
humble himself as this little child, the same is the ¹greatest in the kingdom of heaven. 5ª And whoso shall receive one such little child in my name receiveth me : [Paragraph continued below.]	of all, and minister² of all. 36 And he took a little child, and set him in the midst of them : and taking him in his arms, he said unto them, 37 ªWhosoever shall receive one of such little children in my name, receiveth me: and whosoever receiveth me, receiveth not me, but him that sent me. 38 John said unto him, ³Master³, we saw one casting out ⁴devils⁴ in thy name: and we forbade him, because he followed not us. 39 But Jesus said, Forbid him not: for there is no man which⁵ shall do a ⁵mighty work in my name, and be able quickly to speak evil of me. 40 For he that is not against us is for us. 41 ᶜFor whosoever shall give you a cup of water to drink, ⁶because ye are Christ's, verily I say unto you, he shall in no wise lose his reward. 42 ᵇAnd whosoever shall cause one of these little ones that believe ⁷on me to stumble, it were better for him if ²a great millstone were hanged about his neck, and he were cast into the sea.	ªWhosoever shall receive this little child in my name receiveth me : and whosoever shall receive me receiveth him that sent me: ᵈfor he that is ⁸least among you all, the same is great. 49 And John answered and said, Master, we saw one casting out ⁴devils⁴ in thy name; and we forbade him, because he followeth not with us. 50 But Jesus said unto him, Forbid *him* not: for he that is not against you is for you.
6 ᵇbut whoso shall cause one of these little ones which¹ believe on me to stumble, it ¹s profitable for him that ²a great millstone should be hanged about his neck, and *that* he should be sunk		

ERV. mg.: ¹ Gr. *greater.* ² Gr. *a millstone turned by an ass.* ³ Or, *Teacher* ⁴ Gr. *demons.* ⁵ Gr. *power.* ⁶ Gr. *in name that ye are.* ⁷ Many ancient authorities omit *on me.* ⁸ Gr. *lesser.*

ARV. txt.: ¹ that ² servant ³ Teacher ⁴ demons ⁵ who

ª Matt. 10:40. He that receiveth you receiveth me, and he that receiveth me receiveth him that sent me. (§64)
ª Luke 10:16. He that heareth you heareth me; and he that rejecteth you rejecteth me; and he that rejecteth me rejecteth him that sent me. (§87)
ª John 13:20. Verily, verily, I say unto you, He that receiveth whomsoever I send receiveth me; and he that receiveth me receiveth him that sent me. (§133)
ᵇ Luke 17:2. It were well for him if a millstone were hanged about his neck, and he were thrown into the sea, rather than that he should cause one of these little ones to stumble. (§104)
ᶜ Matt. 10:42. And whosoever shall give to drink unto one of these little ones a cup of cold water only, in the name of a disciple, verily I say unto you, he shall in no wise lose his reward. (§64)
ᵈ See note ᵇ on page 123.

MATT. 18.	MARK 9.	[LUKE 15.]
in the depth of the sea. 7 ^aWoe unto the world because of occasions of stumbling! for it must needs be that the occasions come; but woe to that man through whom the occasion cometh! 8 ^bAnd if thy hand or thy foot causeth thee to stumble, cut it off, and cast it from thee: it is good for thee to enter into life maimed or halt, rather than having two hands or two feet to be cast into the eternal fire. 9 And if thine eye causeth thee to stumble, pluck it out, and cast it from thee: it is good for thee to enter into life with one eye, rather than having two eyes to be cast into the ¹hell of fire. 10 See that ye despise not one of these little ones; for I say unto you, that in heaven their angels do always behold the face of my Father which¹ is in ²heaven. 12 ^cHow think ye? if any man have a hundred sheep, and one of them be gone astray, doth he not leave the ninety and nine, and go unto the mountains, and seek that which goeth astray? 13 And if so be that	43 ^bAnd if thy hand cause thee to stumble, cut it off: it is good for thee to enter into life maimed, rather than having thy two hands to go into ³hell, into the unquenchable ⁴fire. 45 And if thy foot cause thee to stumble, cut it off: it is good for thee to enter into life halt, rather than having thy two feet to be cast into ³hell. 47 And if thine eye cause thee to stumble, cast it out: it is good for thee to enter into the kingdom of God with one eye, rather than having two eyes to be cast into ³hell; 48 where their worm dieth not, and the fire is not quenched. 49 For every one shall be salted with ⁵fire. 50 ^dSalt is good: but if the salt have lost its saltness, wherewith will ye season it? Have salt in yourselves, and be at peace one with another.	[^cLuke 15:4–7. What man of you, having a hundred sheep, and having lost one of them, doth not leave the ninety and nine in the wilderness, and go after that which is lost, until he find it? 5 And when he hath found it, he layeth it on his

---

ERV. mg.: ¹ Gr. *Gehenna of fire*. ² Many authorities, some ancient, insert [after *heaven*] ver. 11 *For the Son of man came to save that which was lost*. See Luke xix. 10. ³ Gr. *Gehenna*. ⁴ Ver. 44 and 46 (which are identical with ver. 48) are omitted by the best ancient authorities. ⁵ Many ancient authorities add *and every sacrifice shall be salted with salt*. See Lev. ii. 13.

ARV. txt.: ¹ who

---

^a Luke 17:1. It is impossible but that occasions of stumbling should come: but woe unto him, through whom they come! (§104)

^b Matt. 5:29, 30. And if thy right eye causeth thee to stumble, pluck it out, and cast it from thee: for it is profitable for thee that one of thy members should perish, and not thy whole body be cast into hell. 30 And if thy right hand causeth thee to stumble, cut it off, and cast it from thee: for it is profitable for thee that one of thy members should perish, and not thy whole body go into hell. (§49)

^c Luke 15:4–7. (§102) See above.

^d Matt. 5:13. Ye are the salt of the earth: but if the salt have lost its savour, wherewith shall it be salted? (§49)

^d Luke 14:34. Salt therefore is good: but if even the salt have lost its savour, wherewith shall it be seasoned? (§101)

MATT. 18.

he find it, verily I say unto you, he rejoiceth over it more than over the ninety and nine which have not gone astray. 14 Even so it is not [1] the will of [2] your Father which[1] is in heaven, that one of these little ones should perish.

15 [a] And if thy brother sin [3] against thee, go, shew him his fault between thee and him alone: if he hear thee, thou hast gained thy brother. 16 But if he hear *thee* not, take with thee one or two more, that at the mouth of two witnesses or three every word may be established. 17 And if he refuse to hear them, tell it unto the [4] church: and if he refuse to hear the [4] church also, let him be unto thee as the Gentile and the publican. 18 Verily I say unto you, [b] What things soever ye shall bind on earth shall be bound in heaven: and what things soever ye shall loose on earth shall be loosed in heaven. 19 Again I say unto you, that if two of you shall agree on earth as touching anything that they shall ask, it shall be done for them of my Father which[1] is in heaven. 20 For where two

[LUKE 15.]

shoulders, rejoicing. 6 And when he cometh home, he calleth together his friends and his neighbours, saying unto them, Rejoice with me, for I have found my sheep which was lost. 7 I say unto you, that even so there shall be joy in heaven over one sinner that repenteth, *more* than over ninety and nine righteous persons, which[1] need no repentance.] (§ 102)

ERV. mg.: [1] Gr. *a thing willed before your Father*.   [2] Some ancient authorities read *my*.   [3] Some ancient authorities omit *against thee*.   [4] Or, *congregation*

ARV. txt.: [1] who

[a] Luke 17: 3. If thy brother sin, rebuke him; and if he repent, forgive him. (§ 104)
[b] Matt. 16: 19. I will give unto thee the keys of the kingdom of heaven: and whatsoever thou shalt bind on earth shall be bound in heaven: and whatsoever thou shalt loose on earth shall be loosed in heaven. (§ 75)
[b] John 20: 23. Whose soever sins ye forgive, they are forgiven unto them; whose soever *sins* ye retain, they are retained. (§ 146)

Matt. **18.**

or three are gathered together in my name, there am I in the midst of them.

21 Then came Peter, and said to him, ᵃLord, how oft shall my brother sin against me, and I forgive him? until seven times? 22 Jesus saith unto him, I say not unto thee, Until seven times; but, Until ¹seventy times seven. 23 Therefore is the kingdom of heaven likened unto a certain king, which¹ would make a reckoning with his ²servants. 24 And when he had begun to reckon, one was brought unto him, which² owed him ten thousand ³talents. 25 But forasmuch as he had not *wherewith* to pay, his lord commanded him to be sold, and his wife, and children, and all that he had, and payment to be made. 26 The ⁴servant therefore fell down and worshipped him, saying, Lord, have patience with me, and I will pay thee all. 27 And the lord of that ⁴servant, being moved with compassion, released him, and forgave him the ⁵debt. 28 But that ⁴servant went out, and found one of his fellow-servants, which¹ owed him a hundred ⁶pence³: and he laid hold on him, and took *him* by the throat, saying, Pay what thou owest. 29 So his fellow-servant fell down and besought him, saying, Have patience with me,

---

ERV. mg.: ¹ Or, *seventy times and seven* ² Gr. *bondservants.* ³ This talent was probably worth about £240. ⁴ Gr. *bondservant.* ⁵ Gr. *loan.* ⁶ The word in the Greek denotes a coin worth about eight pence halfpenny.

ARV. txt.: ¹ who ² that ³ shillings

ᵃ Luke 17:4. And if he sin against thee seven times in the day, and seven times turn again to thee, saying, I repent; thou shalt forgive him. (§104)

MATT. **18.**

and I will pay thee. 30 And he would not: but went and cast him into prison, till he should pay that which was due. 31 So when his fellow-servants saw what was done, they were exceeding sorry, and came and told unto their lord all that was done. 32 Then his lord called him unto him, and saith to him, Thou wicked ¹servant, I forgave thee all that debt, because thou besoughtest me: 33 shouldest not thou also have had mercy on thy fellow-servant, even as I had mercy on thee? 34 And his lord was wroth, and delivered him to the tormentors, till he should pay all that was due. 35 ªSo shall also my heavenly Father do unto you, if ye forgive not every one his brother from your hearts.

§ 82. CHRIST AT THE FEAST OF TABERNACLES.

JOHN 7: 1-52.

1 And after these things Jesus walked in Galilee: for he would not walk in Judæa, because the Jews sought to kill him. 2 Now the feast of the Jews, the feast of tabernacles, was at hand. 3 His brethren therefore said unto him, Depart hence, and go into Judæa, that thy disciples also may behold thy works which thou doest. 4 For no man doeth anything in secret, ²and himself seeketh to be known openly. If thou doest these things, manifest thyself to the world. 5 For even his brethren did not believe on him. 6 Jesus therefore saith unto them, My time is not yet come; but your time is alway¹ ready. 7 The world cannot hate you; but me it hateth, because I testify of it, that its works are evil. 8 Go ye up unto the feast: I go not up ³yet² unto this feast; because my time is not yet fulfilled. 9 And having said these things unto them, he abode *still* in Galilee.

10 But when his brethren were gone up unto the feast, then went he also up, not publicly, but as it were in secret. 11 The Jews therefore sought him at the feast, and said, Where is he? 12 And there was much murmuring among the multitudes concerning him: some said, He is a good man; others said, Not so, but he leadeth the multitude astray. 13 Howbeit³ no man spake openly of him for fear of the Jews.

ERV. mg.: ¹ Gr. *bondservant* ² Some ancient authorities read *and seeketh it to be known openly.* ³ Many ancient authorities omit *yet.*

ARV. txt.: ¹ always ² *Omit* yet ³ Yet

ª Matt. 6:15. But if ye forgive not men their trespasses, neither will your Father forgive your trespasses. (§ 49)

JOHN 7.

14 But when it was now the midst of the feast Jesus went up into the temple, and taught. 15 The Jews therefore marvelled, saying, How knoweth this man letters, having never learned? 16 Jesus therefore answered them, and said, My teaching is not mine, but his that sent me. 17 If any man willeth to do his will, he shall know of the teaching, whether it be [1] of God, or *whether* I speak from myself. 18 He that speaketh from himself seeketh his own glory: but he that seeketh the glory of him that sent him, the same is true, and no unrighteousness is in him. 19 Did not Moses give you the law, and *yet* none of you doeth the law? Why seek ye to kill me? 20 The multitude answered, Thou hast a [1]devil[2]: who seeketh to kill thee? 21 Jesus answered and said unto them, I did one work, and ye all [2]marvel. 22 For this cause hath Moses given[3] you circumcision (not that it is of Moses, but of the fathers); and on the sabbath ye circumcise a man. 23 If a man receiveth circumcision on the sabbath, that the law of Moses may not be broken; are ye wroth with me, because I made a man every whit whole on the sabbath? 24 Judge not according to appearance, but judge righteous judgement.

25 Some therefore of them of Jerusalem said, Is not this he whom they seek to kill? 26 And lo, he speaketh openly, and they say nothing unto him. Can it be that the rulers indeed know that this is the Christ? 27 Howbeit we know this man whence he is: but when the Christ cometh, no one knoweth whence he is. 28 Jesus therefore cried in the temple, teaching and saying, Ye both know me, and know whence I am; and I am not come of myself, but he that sent me is true, whom ye know not. 29 I know him; because I am from him, and he sent me. 30 They sought therefore to take him: and no man laid his hand on him, because his hour was not yet come. 31 But of the multitude many believed on him; and they said, When the Christ shall come, will he do more signs than those which this man hath done? 32 The Pharisees heard the multitude murmuring these things concerning him; and the chief priests and the Pharisees sent officers to take him. 33 Jesus therefore said, Yet a little while am I with you, and I go unto him that sent me. 34 Ye shall seek me, and shall not find me: and where I am, ye cannot come. 35 The Jews therefore said among themselves, Whither will this man go that we shall not find him? will he go unto the Dispersion [3]among the Greeks, and teach the Greeks? 36 What is this word that he said, Ye shall seek me, and shall not find me: and where I am, ye cannot come?

37 Now on the last day, the great *day* of the feast, Jesus stood and cried, saying, If any man thirst, let him come unto me, and drink. 38 He that believeth on me, as the scripture hath said, out of his belly[4] shall flow rivers of living water. 39 But this spake he of the Spirit, which they that believed on him were to receive: [4]for the Spirit was not yet *given*; because Jesus was not yet glorified. 40 *Some* of the multitude therefore, when they heard these words, said, This is of a truth the prophet. 41 Others said, This is the Christ. But some said, What, doth the Christ come out of Galilee? 42 Hath not the scripture said that the Christ cometh of the seed of David, and from Bethlehem, the village where David was? 43 So there arose a division in the multitude because of him. 44 And some of them would have taken him; but no man laid hands on him.

45 The officers therefore came to the chief priests and Pharisees; and they said unto them, Why did ye not bring him? 46 The officers answered, Never man so spake. 47 The Pharisees therefore answered them, Are ye also led astray? 48 Hath any of the rulers believed on him, or of the Pharisees? 49 But this multitude which[5] knoweth not the law

---

ERV. mg.: [1] Gr. *demon* [2] Or, *marvel because of this. Moses hath given you circumcision* [3] Gr. *of.* [4] Some ancient authorities read *for the Holy Spirit was not yet given*.

ARV. txt.: [1] is [2] demon [3] ye all marvel because thereof. 22 Moses hath given [4] said, from within him [5] that

are accursed. 50 Nicodemus saith unto them (he that came to him before, being one of them), 51 Doth our law judge a man, except it first hear from himself and know what he doeth? 52 They answered and said unto him, Art thou also of Galilee? Search, and [1] see that out of Galilee ariseth no prophet.

§ 83. THE WOMAN TAKEN IN ADULTERY.

JOHN 7 : 53—8 : 11.

53 [2] And they went every man unto his own house: 8 : 1 but Jesus went unto the mount of Olives. 2 And early in the morning he came again into the temple, and all the people came unto him ; and he sat down, and taught them. 3 And the scribes and the Pharisees bring a woman taken in adultery; and having set her in the midst, 4 they say unto him, [3] Master [1], this woman hath been taken in adultery, in the very act. 5 Now in the law Moses commanded us to stone such: what then sayest thou of her? 6 And this they said, [4] tempting [2] him, that they might have *whereof* to accuse him. But Jesus stooped down, and with his finger wrote on the ground. 7 But when they continued asking him, he lifted up himself, and said unto them, He that is without sin among you, let him first cast a stone at her. 8 And again he stooped down, and with his finger wrote on the ground. 9 And they, when they heard it, went out one by one, beginning from the eldest, *even* unto the last: and Jesus was left alone, and the woman, where she was, in the midst. 10 And Jesus lifted up himself, and said unto her, Woman, where are they? did no man condemn thee? 11 And she said, No man, Lord. And Jesus said, Neither do I condemn thee: go thy way; from henceforth sin no more.

§ 84. DISCOURSE ON THE LIGHT OF THE WORLD.

JOHN 8 : 12–30.

12 Again therefore Jesus spake unto them, saying, I am the light of the world: he that followeth me shall not walk in the darkness, but shall have the light of life. 13 The Pharisees therefore said unto him, Thou bearest witness of thyself; thy witness is not true. 14 Jesus answered and said unto them, Even if I bear witness of myself, my witness is true ; for I know whence I came, and whither I go ; but ye know not whence I come, or whither I go. 15 Ye judge after the flesh ; I judge no man. 16 Yea and if I judge, my judgement is true ; for I am not alone, but I and the Father that sent me. 17 Yea and in your law it is written, that the witness of two men is true. 18 I am he that beareth witness of myself, and the Father that sent me beareth witness of me. 19 They said therefore unto him, Where is thy father [3]? Jesus answered, Ye know neither me, nor my Father: if ye knew me, ye would know my Father also. 20 These words spake he in the treasury, as he taught in the temple : and no man took him ; because his hour was not yet come.

21 He said therefore again unto them, I go away, and ye shall seek me, and shall die in your sin: whither I go, ye cannot come. 22 The Jews therefore said, Will he kill himself, that he saith, Whither I go, ye cannot come? 23 And he said unto them, Ye are from beneath ; I am from above: ye are of this world ; I am not of this world. 24 I said therefore unto you, that ye shall die in your sins: for except ye believe that [5] I am *he*, ye shall die in your sins. 25 They said therefore unto him, Who art thou? Jesus said unto them, [6] Even that which I have also spoken unto you from the beginning. 26 I have many things to speak and to judge concerning you: howbeit he that sent me is true ; and the things which I heard from him, these speak I [7] unto the world. 27 They perceived not that he spake to them of the Father. 28 Jesus therefore said, When ye have lifted up the Son of man, then shall ye

---

ERV. mg.: [1] Or, *see: for out of Galilee &c.*   [2] Most of the ancient authorities omit John vii. 53—viii. 11. Those which contain it vary much from each other. [3] Or, *Teacher* [4] Or, *trying* [5] Or, *I am* [6] Or, How is it *that I even speak to you at all?* [7] Gr. *into.*

ARV. txt.: [1] Teacher [2] trying [3] Father

JOHN 8.

know that [1]I am *he*, and *that* I do nothing of myself, but as the Father taught me, I speak these things. 29 And he that sent me is with me ; he hath not left me alone; for I do always the things that are pleasing to him. 30 As he spake these things, many believed on him.

§ 85. DISCOURSE ON SPIRITUAL FREEDOM.

JOHN 8 : 31-59.

31 Jesus therefore said to those Jews which[1] had believed him, If ye abide in my word, *then* are ye truly my disciples ; 32 and ye shall know the truth, and the truth shall make you free. 33 They answered unto him, We be[2] Abraham's seed, and have never yet been in bondage to any man : how sayest thou, Ye shall be made free? 34 Jesus answered them, Verily, verily, I say unto you, Every one that committeth sin is the bondservant of sin. 35 And the bondservant abideth not in the house for ever : the son abideth for ever. 36 If therefore the Son shall make you free, ye shall be free indeed. 37 I know that ye are Abraham's seed ; yet ye seek to kill me, because my word [2]hath not free course in you. 38 I speak the things which I have seen with [3]*my* Father : and ye also do the things which ye heard from *your* father. 39 They answered and said unto him, Our father is Abraham. Jesus saith unto them, If ye [4]were Abraham's children, [5]ye would do the works of Abraham. 40 But now ye seek to kill me, a man that hath told you the truth, which I heard from God : this did not Abraham. 41 Ye do the works of your father. They said unto him, We were not born of fornication ; we have one Father, *even* God. 42 Jesus said unto them, If God were your Father, ye would love me : for I came forth and am come from God ; for neither have I come of myself, but he sent me. 43 Why do ye not [6]understand my speech? *Even* because ye cannot hear my word. 44 Ye are of *your* father the devil, and the lusts of your father it is your will to do. He was a murderer from the beginning, and [7]stood[3] not in the truth, because there is no truth in him. [8]When he speaketh a lie, he speaketh of his own : for he is a liar, and the father thereof. 45 But because I say the truth, ye believe me not. 46 Which of you convicteth me of sin? If I say truth, why do ye not believe me? 47 He that is of God heareth the words of God : for this cause ye hear *them* not, because ye are not of God. 48 The Jews answered and said unto him, Say we not well that thou art a Samaritan, and hast a [9]devil[4]? 49 Jesus answered, I have not a [9]devil[4]; but I honour my Father, and ye dishonour me. 50 But I seek not mine own glory : there is one that seeketh and judgeth. 51 Verily, verily, I say unto you, If a man keep my word, he shall never see death. 52 The Jews said unto him, Now we know that thou hast a [9]devil[4]. Abraham is dead[5], and the prophets ; and thou sayest, If a man keep my word, he shall never taste of death. 53 Art thou greater than our father Abraham, which[6] is dead[5]? and the prophets are dead[5]: whom makest thou thyself? 54 Jesus answered, If I glorify myself, my glory is nothing : it is my Father that glorifieth me ; of whom ye say, that he is your God ; 55 and ye have not known him : but I know him ; and if I should say, I know him not, I shall be like unto you, a liar : but I know him, and keep his word. 56 Your father Abraham rejoiced [10]to see my day ; and he saw it, and was glad. 57 The Jews therefore said unto him, Thou art not yet fifty years old, and hast thou seen Abraham? 58 Jesus said unto them, Verily, verily, I say unto you, Before Abraham [11]was[7], I am. 59 They took up stones therefore to cast at him : but Jesus [12]hid himself, and went out of the [13]temple.

PART VII.

THE PEREAN MINISTRY.

FROM THE FINAL DEPARTURE FROM GALILEE UNTIL THE FINAL ARRIVAL AT JERUSALEM.

§ 86. THE FINAL DEPARTURE FROM GALILEE.

MATT. 19:1, 2.
MATT. 8: [18] 19–22.

1 And it came to pass when Jesus had finished these words, he departed from Galilee, and came into the borders of Judæa beyond Jordan[1]; 2 and great multitudes followed him; and he healed them there. (+ § 110)

[8:18 Now when Jesus saw great multitudes about him, he gave commandment to depart unto the other side.] 19 And there came [1] a scribe, and said unto him, [2]Master[2], I will follow thee whithersoever thou goest. 20 And Jesus saith unto him, The foxes have holes, and the birds of the heaven *have* [3]nests; but

MARK 10:1.

1 And he arose from thence, and cometh into the borders of Judæa and beyond Jordan[1]; and multitudes come together unto him again; and, as he was wont, he taught them again.

LUKE 9:51–62.

51 And it came to pass, when the days [4]were well-nigh come that he should be received up, he stedfastly set his face to go to Jerusalem, 52 and sent messengers before his face: and they went, and entered into a village of the Samaritans, to make ready for him. 53 And they did not receive him, because his face was *as though he were* going to Jerusalem. 54 And when his disciples James and John saw *this*, they said, Lord, wilt thou that we bid fire to come down from heaven, and consume [5]them? 55 But he turned, and rebuked [6]them. 56 And they went to another village.

57 And as they went in [3] the way, a certain man said unto him, I will follow thee whithersoever thou goest. 58 And Jesus said unto him, The foxes have holes, and the birds of the heaven *have* [3]nests; but the Son of man hath not where to lay his head. 59 And he said unto another, Follow me. But he

MATT. 8		LUKE 9
the Son of man hath not where to lay his head. 21 And another of the disciples said unto him, Lord, suffer me first to go and bury my father. 22 But Jesus saith unto him, Follow me; and leave the dead to bury their own dead. (+ §58)		said, Lord, suffer me first to go and bury my father. 60 But he said unto him, Leave the dead to bury their own dead; but go thou and publish abroad the kingdom of God. 61 And another also said, I will follow thee, Lord; but first suffer me to bid farewell to them that are at my house. 62 But Jesus said unto him, No man, having put his hand to the plough, and looking back, is fit for the kingdom of God.

§87. THE MISSION OF THE SEVENTY.

LUKE 10: 1-24.

1 Now after these things the Lord appointed seventy [1] others, and sent them two and two before his face into every city and place, whither he himself was about to come. 2 [a] And he said unto them, The harvest [1] is plenteous, but the labourers are few: pray ye therefore the Lord of the harvest, that he send forth labourers into his harvest. 3 [b] Go your ways: behold, I send you forth as lambs in the midst of wolves. 4 Carry no purse, no wallet, no shoes: and salute no man on the way. 5 And into whatsoever house ye shall [2] enter, first say, Peace be to this house. 6 And if a son of peace be there, your peace shall rest upon [3] him: but if not, it shall turn to you again. 7 And in that same house remain, eating and drinking such things

---

ERV. mg.: [1] Many ancient authorities add *and two*: and so in ver. 17. [2] Or, *enter first, say* [3] Or, *it*

ARV. txt.: [1] harvest indeed.

---

[a] Matt. 9:37, 38. Then saith he unto his disciples, The harvest truly is plenteous, but the labourers are few. 38 Pray ye therefore the Lord of the harvest, that he send forth labourers into his harvest. (§64)

[b] Matt. 10:7-16. And as ye go, preach, saying, The kingdom of heaven is at hand. 8 Heal the sick, raise the dead, cleanse the lepers, cast out devils: freely ye received, freely give. 9 Get you no gold, nor silver, nor brass in your purses; 10 no wallet for *your* journey, neither two coats, nor shoes, nor staff: for the labourer is worthy of his food. 11 And into whatsoever city or village ye shall enter, search out who in it is worthy; and there abide till ye go forth. 12 And as ye enter into the house, salute it. 13 And if the house be worthy, let your peace come upon it: but if it be not worthy, let your peace return to you. 14 And whosoever shall not receive you, nor hear your words, as ye go forth out of that house or that city, shake off the dust of your feet. 15 Verily I say unto you, It shall be more tolerable for the land of Sodom and Gomorrah in the day of judgement, than for that city.

16 Behold, I send you forth as sheep in the midst of wolves: be ye therefore wise as serpents, and harmless as doves. (§64)

[b] Mark 6:8-11. And he charged them that they should take nothing for *their* journey, save a staff only; no bread, no wallet, no money in their purse; 9 but *to go* shod with sandals: and, *said he*, put not on two coats. 10 And he said unto them, Wheresoever ye enter into a house, there abide till ye depart thence. 11 And whatsoever place shall not receive you, and they hear you not, as ye go forth thence, shake off the dust that is under your feet for a testimony unto them. (§64)

[b] Luke 9:3-5. And he said unto them, Take nothing for your journey, neither staff, nor wallet, nor bread, nor money; neither have two coats. 4 And into whatsoever house ye enter, there abide, and thence depart. 5 And as many as receive you not, when ye depart from that city, shake off the dust from your feet for a testimony against them. (§64)

LUKE 10.

as they give : for the labourer is worthy of his hire. Go not from house to house. 8 And into whatsoever city ye enter, and they receive you, eat such things as are set before you : 9 and heal the sick that are therein, and say unto them, The kingdom of God is come nigh unto you. 10 But into whatsoever city ye shall enter, and they receive you not, go out into the streets thereof and say, 11 Even the dust from your city, that cleaveth to our feet, we do[1] wipe off against you : howbeit[2] know this, that the kingdom of God is come nigh. 12 [a]I say unto you, It shall be more tolerable in that day for Sodom, than for that city. 13 Woe unto thee, Chorazin ! woe unto thee, Bethsaida ! for if the [1]mighty works had been done in Tyre and Sidon, which were done in you, they would have repented long ago, sitting in sackcloth and ashes. 14 Howbeit[3] it shall be more tolerable for Tyre and Sidon in the judgement, than for you. 15 And thou, Capernaum, shalt thou be exalted unto heaven ? thou shalt be brought down unto Hades. 16 [b]He that heareth you heareth me ; and he that rejecteth you rejecteth me ; and he that rejecteth me rejecteth him that sent me.

17 And the seventy returned with joy, saying, Lord, even the [2]devils[4] are subject unto us in thy name. 18 And he said unto them, I beheld Satan fallen as lightning from heaven. 19 [c]Behold, I have given you authority to tread upon serpents and scorpions, and over all the power of the enemy : and nothing shall in any wise hurt you. 20 Howbeit[5] in this rejoice not, that the spirits are subject unto you ; but rejoice that your names are written in heaven.

21 [d]In that same hour he rejoiced [3]in the Holy Spirit, and said, I [4]thank thee, O Father, Lord of heaven and earth, that thou didst hide these things from the wise and understanding, and didst reveal them unto babes : yea, Father ; [5]for so it was well-pleasing in thy sight. 22 [e]All things have been delivered unto me of my Father : [f]and no one knoweth who the Son is, save the Father ; and who the Father is, save the Son, and he to whomsoever the Son willeth

---

ERV. mg. : [1]Gr. *powers.* [2]Gr. *demons* [3]Or, *by* [4]Or, *praise* [5]Or, *that*

ARV. txt. : [1]*Omit* do [2]nevertheless [3]But [4]demons [5]Nevertheless

---

[a]Matt. 11 : 21–24. Woe unto thee, Chorazin ! woe unto thee, Bethsaida ! for if the mighty works had been done in Tyre and Sidon which were done in you, they would have repented long ago in sackcloth and ashes. 22 Howbeit I say unto you, it shall be more tolerable for Tyre and Sidon in the day of judgement, than for you. 23 And thou, Capernaum, shalt thou be exalted unto heaven ? thou shalt go down unto Hades : for if the mighty works had been done in Sodom which were done in thee, it would have remained until this day. 24 Howbeit I say unto you, that it shall be more tolerable for the land of Sodom in the day of judgement than for thee. (§ 52)

[b]Matt. 10 : 40. He that receiveth you receiveth me, and he that receiveth me receiveth him that sent me. (§ 64)

[b]Matt. 18 : 5. And whoso shall receive one such little child in my name, receiveth me. (§ 81)

[b]Mark 9 : 37. Whosoever shall receive one of such little children in my name receiveth me : and whosoever receiveth me, receiveth not me, but him that sent me. (§ 81)

[b]Luke 9 : 48. Whosoever shall receive this little child in my name receiveth me : and whosoever shall receive me receiveth him that sent me. (§ 81)

[b]John 13 : 20. Verily, verily, I say unto you, He that receiveth whomsoever I send receiveth me ; and he that receiveth me receiveth him that sent me. (§ 133)

[c]Mark 16 : 18. They shall take up serpents, and if they drink any deadly thing, it shall in no wise hurt them ; they shall lay hands on the sick, and they shall recover. (§ 149)

[d]Matt. 11 : 25–27. At that season Jesus answered and said, I thank thee, O Father, Lord of heaven and earth, that thou didst hide these things from the wise and understanding, and didst reveal them unto babes : 26 yea, Father, for so it was well-pleasing in thy sight. 27 All things have been delivered unto me of my Father : and no one knoweth the Son, save the Father ; neither doth any know the Father, save the Son, and he to whomsoever the Son willeth to reveal *him.* (§ 52)

[e]Matt. 28 : 18. All authority hath been given unto me in heaven and on earth. (§ 149)

[f]John 6 : 46. Not that any man hath seen the Father, save he which is from God, he hath seen the **Father.** (§ 68)

LUKE 10.

to reveal *him.* 23 And turning to the disciples, he said privately, ᵃBlessed *are* the eyes which see the things that ye see : 24 for I say unto you, that many prophets and kings desired to see the things which ye see, and saw them not ; and to hear the things which ye hear, and heard them not.

§88. THE GOOD SAMARITAN.

LUKE 10 : 25-37.

25 And behold, a certain lawyer stood up and tempted¹ him, saying, ¹Master², what shall I do to inherit eternal life ? 26 And he said unto him, What is written in the law ? how readest thou ? 27 And he answering said, Thou shalt love the Lord thy God ²with all thy heart, and with all thy soul, and with all thy strength, and with all thy mind ; and thy neighbour as thyself. 28 And he said unto him, Thou hast answered right : this do, and thou shalt live. 29 But he, desiring to justify himself, said unto Jesus, And who is my neighbour ? 30 Jesus made answer and said, A certain man was going down from Jerusalem to Jericho ; and he fell among robbers, which³ both stripped him and beat him, and departed, leaving him half dead. 31 And by chance a certain priest was going down that way : and when he saw him, he passed by on the other side. 32 And in like manner a Levite also, when he came to the place, and saw him, passed by on the other side. 33 But a certain Samaritan, as he journeyed, came where he was : and when he saw him, he was moved with compassion, 34 and came to him, and bound up his wounds, pouring on *them* oil and wine ; and he set him on his own beast, and brought him to an inn, and took care of him. 35 And on the morrow he took out two ³pence⁴, and gave them to the host, and said, Take care of him ; and whatsoever thou spendest more, I, when I come back again, will repay thee. 36 Which of these three, thinkest thou, proved neighbour unto him that fell among the robbers ? 37 And he said, He that shewed mercy on him. And Jesus said unto him, Go, and do thou likewise.

§89. THE VISIT TO MARTHA AND MARY.

LUKE 10 : 38-42.

38 Now as they went on their way, he entered into a certain village : and a certain woman named Martha received him into her house. 39 And she had a sister called Mary, which³ also sat at the Lord's feet, and heard his word. 40 But Martha was ⁴cumbered about much serving ; and she came up to him, and said, Lord, dost thou not care that my sister did leave me to serve alone ? bid her therefore that she help me. 41 But the Lord answered and said unto her, ⁵Martha, Martha, thou art anxious and troubled about many things : 42 ⁶but one thing is needful : for Mary hath chosen the good part, which shall not be taken away from her.

§90. HEALING OF THE MAN BORN BLIND.

JOHN, CHAP. 9.

1 And as he passed by, he saw a man blind from his birth. 2 And his disciples asked him, saying, Rabbi, who did sin⁵, this man, or his parents, that he should be born blind ?

ERV. mg.: ¹ Or, *Teacher* ² Gr. *from.* ³ See marginal note on Matt. xviii. 28. ⁴ Gr. *distracted.* ⁵ A few ancient authorities read *Martha, Martha, thou art troubled : Mary hath chosen &c.* ⁶ Many ancient authorities read *but few things are needful, or one.*

ARV. txt.: ¹ made trial of ² Teacher ³ who ⁴ shillings ⁵ sinned

---

ᵃ Matt. 13 : 16, 17. But blessed are your eyes, for they see ; and your ears, for they hear. 17 For verily I say unto you, that many prophets and righteous men desired to see the things which ye see, and saw them not ; and to hear the things which ye hear, and heard them not. (§57)

JOHN 9.

3 Jesus answered, Neither did this man sin, nor his parents: but that the works of God should be made manifest in him. 4 We must work the works of him that sent me, while it is day: the night cometh, when no man can work. 5 When I am in the world, I am the light of the world. 6 When he had thus spoken, he spat on the ground, and made clay of the spittle, [1]and anointed his eyes with the clay, 7 and said unto him, Go, wash in the pool of Siloam (which is by interpretation, Sent). He went away therefore, and washed, and came seeing. 8 The neighbours therefore, and they which[1] saw him aforetime, that he was a beggar, said, Is not this he that sat and begged? 9 Others said, It is he: others said, No, but he is like him. He said, I am *he*. 10 They said therefore unto him, How then were thine eyes opened? 11 He answered, The man that is called Jesus made clay, and anointed mine eyes, and said unto me, Go to Siloam, and wash: so I went away and washed, and I received sight. 12 And they said unto him, Where is he? He saith, I know not.

13 They bring to the Pharisees him that aforetime was blind. 14 Now it was the sabbath on the day when Jesus made the clay, and opened his eyes. 15 Again therefore the Pharisees also asked him how he received his sight. And he said unto them, He put clay upon mine eyes, and I washed, and do see[2]. 16 Some therefore of the Pharisees said, This man is not from God, because he keepeth not the sabbath. But others said, How can a man that is a sinner do such signs? And there was a division among them. 17 They say therefore unto the blind man again, What sayest thou of him, in that he opened thine eyes? And he said, He is a prophet. 18 The Jews therefore did not believe concerning him, that he had been blind, and had received his sight, until they called the parents of him that had received his sight, 19 and asked them, saying, Is this your son, who ye say was born blind? how then doth he now see? 20 His parents answered and said, We know that this is our son, and that he was born blind: 21 but how he now seeth, we know not; or who opened his eyes, we know not: ask him; he is of age; he shall speak for himself. 22 These things said his parents, because they feared the Jews: for the Jews had agreed already, that if any man should confess him *to be* Christ, he should be put out of the synagogue. 23 Therefore said his parents, He is of age; ask him. 24 So they called a second time the man that was blind, and said unto him, Give glory to God; we know that this man is a sinner. 25 He therefore answered, Whether he be[3] a sinner, I know not: one thing I know, that, whereas I was blind, now I see. 26 They said therefore unto him, What did he to thee? how opened he thine eyes? 27 He answered them, I told you even now, and ye did not hear: wherefore would ye hear it again? would ye also become his disciples? 28 And they reviled him, and said, Thou art his disciple, but we are disciples of Moses. 29 We know that God hath spoken unto Moses: but as for this man, we know not whence he is. 30 The man answered and said unto them, Why, herein is the marvel, that ye know not whence he is, and *yet* he opened mine eyes. 31 We know that God heareth not sinners: but if any man be a worshipper of God, and do his will, him he heareth. 32 Since the world began it was never heard that any one opened the eyes of a man born blind. 33 If this man were not from God, he could do nothing. 34 They answered and said unto him, Thou wast altogether born in sins, and dost thou teach us? And they cast him out.

35 Jesus heard that they had cast him out; and finding him, he said, Dost thou believe on [2]the Son of God? 36 He answered and said, And who is he, Lord, that I may believe on him? 37 Jesus said unto him, Thou hast both seen him, and he it is that speaketh with thee. 38 And he said, Lord, I believe. And he worshipped him. 39 And Jesus said, For

---

ERV. mg.:   [1] Or, *and with the clay thereof anointed* his *eyes*   [2] Many ancient authorities read *the Son of man.*

ARV. txt.:   [1] that   [2] and I see   [3] is

JOHN 9.

judgement came I into this world, that they which[1] see not may see; and that they which[1] see may become blind. 40 Those of the Pharisees which[2] were with him heard these things, and said unto him, Are we also blind? 41 Jesus said unto them, If ye were blind, ye would have no sin: but now ye say, We see: your sin remaineth.

§91 THE GOOD SHEPHERD.

JOHN 10:1-21.

1 Verily, verily, I say unto you, He that entereth not by the door into the fold of the sheep, but climbeth up some other way, the same is a thief and a robber. 2 But he that entereth in by the door is [1] the shepherd of the sheep. 3 To him the porter openeth; and the sheep hear his voice: and he calleth his own sheep by name, and leadeth them out. 4 When he hath put forth all his own, he goeth before them, and the sheep follow him: for they know his voice. 5 And a stranger will they not follow, but will flee from him: for they know not the voice of strangers. 6 This [2]parable spake Jesus unto them: but they understood not what things they were which he spake unto them.

7 Jesus therefore said unto them again, Verily, verily, I say unto you, I am the door of the sheep. 8 All that came before me are thieves and robbers: but the sheep did not hear them. 9 I am the door: by me if any man enter in, he shall be saved, and shall go in and go out, and shall find pasture. 10 The thief cometh not, but that he may steal, and kill, and destroy: I came that they may have life, and may [3]have *it* abundantly. 11 I am the good shepherd: the good shepherd layeth down his life for the sheep. 12 He that is a hireling, and not a shepherd, whose own the sheep are not, beholdeth the wolf coming, and leaveth the sheep, and fleeth, and the wolf snatcheth them, and scattereth *them*: 13 *he fleeth* because he is a hireling, and careth not for the sheep. 14 I am the good shepherd; and I know mine own, and mine own know me, 15 even as the Father knoweth me, and I know the Father; and I lay down my life for the sheep. 16 And other sheep I have, which are not of this fold: them also I must [4]bring, and they shall hear my voice; and [5]they shall become one flock, one shepherd. 17 Therefore doth the Father love me, because I lay down my life, that I may take it again. 18 No one [6]taketh it away from me, but I lay it down of myself. I have [7]power to lay it down, and I have [7]power to take it again. This commandment received I from my Father.

19 There arose a division again among the Jews because of these words. 20 And many of them said, He hath a [8]devil[3], and is mad; why hear ye him? 21 Others said, These are not the sayings of one possessed with a [8]devil[3]. Can a [8]devil[3] open the eyes of the blind?

§92. CHRIST AT THE FEAST OF DEDICATION.

JOHN 10:22-42.

22 [9]And it was the feast of the dedication at Jerusalem: it was winter; 23 and Jesus was walking in the temple in Solomon's porch. 24 The Jews therefore came round about him, and said unto him, How long dost thou hold us in suspense? If thou art the Christ, tell us plainly. 25 Jesus answered them, I told you, and ye believe not: the works that I do in my Father's name, these bear witness of me. 26 But ye believe not, because ye are not of

---

ERV. mg.: [1] Or, *a shepherd* [2] Or, *proverb* [3] Or, *have abundance* [4] Or, *lead* [5] Or, *there shall be one flock* [6] Some ancient authorities read *took it away.* [7] Or, *right* [8] Gr. *demon.* [9] Some ancient authorities read *At that time was the feast.*

ARV. txt.: [1] that [2] who [3] demon

JOHN 10.

my sheep. 27 My sheep hear my voice, and I know them, and they follow me: 28 and I give unto them eternal life; and they shall never perish, and no one shall snatch them out of my hand. 29 ¹My father, which¹ hath given *them* unto me, is greater than all; and no one is able to snatch ²*them* out of the Father's hand. 30 I and the Father are one. 31 The Jews took up stones again to stone him. 32 Jesus answered them, Many good works have I shewed you from the Father; for which of those works do ye stone me? 33 The Jews answered him, For a good work we stone thee not, but for blasphemy; and because that thou, being a man, makest thyself God. 34 Jesus answered them, Is it not written in your law, I said, Ye are gods? 35 If he called them gods, unto whom the word of God came (and the scripture cannot be broken), 36 say ye of him, whom the Father ³sanctified and sent into the world, Thou blasphemest; because I said, I am *the* Son of God? 37 If I do not the works of my Father, believe me not. 38 But if I do them, though ye believe not me, believe the works: that ye may know and understand that the Father is in me, and I in the Father. 39 They sought again to take him: and he went forth out of their hand.

40 And he went away again beyond Jordan² into the place where John was at the first baptizing; and there he abode. 41 And many came unto him; and they said, John indeed did no sign; but all things whatsoever John spake of this man were true. 42 And many believed on him there.

§ 93. DISCOURSE ON PRAYER.

LUKE 11:1-13.

1 And it came to pass, as he was praying in a certain place, that when he ceased, one of his disciples said unto him, Lord, teach us to pray, even as John also taught his disciples. 2 And he said unto them, ªWhen ye pray, say, ⁴Father, Hallowed be thy name. Thy kingdom ⁵come. 3 Give us day by day ⁶our daily bread. 4 And forgive us our sins; for we ourselves also forgive every one that is indebted to us. And bring us not into ⁷temptation.

5 And he said unto them, Which of you shall have a friend, and shall go unto him at midnight, and say to him, Friend, lend me three loaves; 6 for a friend of mine is come to me from a journey, and I have nothing to set before him; 7 and he from within shall answer and say, Trouble me not: the door is now shut and my children are with me in bed; I cannot rise and give thee? 8 I say unto you, Though he will not rise and give him, because he is his friend, yet because of his importunity he will arise and give him ⁸as many as he needeth. 9 And I say unto you, ᵇAsk, and it shall be given you; seek, and ye shall find; knock, and it shall be opened unto you. 10 For every one that asketh receiveth; and he that seeketh findeth; and to him that knocketh it shall be opened. 11 And of which of you

---

ERV. mg.: ¹ Some ancient authorities read *That which my Father hath given unto me.* ² Or, aught ³ Or, *consecrated* ⁴Many ancient authorities read *Our Father, which art in heaven.* See Matt. vi. 9. ⁵ Many ancient authorities add *Thy will be done, as in heaven, so on earth.* See Matt. vi. 10. ⁶ Gr. *Our bread for the coming day.* ⁷ Many ancient authorities add *but deliver us from the evil* one (or, *from evil*). See Matt. vi. 13. ⁸ Or, *whatsoever things*

ARV. txt.: ¹ who ² the Jordan

ªMatt. 6:9-13. After this manner therefore pray ye: Our Father which art in heaven, Hallowed be thy name. 10 Thy kingdom come. Thy will be done, as in heaven, so on earth. 11 Give us this day our daily bread. 12 And forgive us our debts, as we also have forgiven our debtors. 13 And bring us not into temptation, but deliver us from the evil *one.* (§ 49)

ᵇMatt. 7:7-11. Ask, and it shall be given you; seek, and ye shall find; knock, and it shall be opened unto you: 8 for every one that asketh receiveth; and he that seeketh findeth; and to him that knocketh it shall be opened. 9 Or what man is there of you, who, if his son shall ask him for a loaf, will give him a stone; 10 or if he shall ask for a fish, will give him a serpent? 11 If ye then, being evil, know how to give good gifts unto your children, how much more shall your Father which is in heaven give good things to them that ask him? (§ 49)

Luke 11.

that is a father shall his son ask [1] a loaf, and he will give him a stone? or a fish, and he for a fish give him a serpent? 12 Or *if* he shall ask an egg, will he give him a scorpion? 13 If ye then, being evil, know how to give good gifts unto your children, how much more shall *your* heavenly Father give the Holy Spirit to them that ask him?

§ 94. DISCOURSES AGAINST THE PHARISEES.

[MATT. 12:22-32. Then was brought unto him [2] one possessed with a devil[1], blind and dumb: and he healed him, insomuch that the dumb man spake and saw. 23 And all the multitudes were amazed, and said, Is this[2] the son of David? 24 But when the Pharisees heard it, they said, This man doth not cast out [3] devils[3], but [4] by Beelzebub the prince of the [3] devils[2]. 25 And knowing their thoughts he said unto them, Every kingdom divided against itself is brought to desolation; and every city or house divided against itself shall not stand: 26 and if Satan casteth out Satan, he is divided against himself; how then shall his kingdom stand? 27 And if I [4] by Beelzebub cast out [3] devils[3], [4] by whom do your sons cast them out? therefore shall they be your judges. 28 But if I [4] by the Spirit of God cast out [3] devils[3], then is the kingdom of God come upon you. 29 Or how can one enter into the house of the strong *man*, and spoil his goods, except he first bind the strong *man*? and then he will spoil his house. 30 He that is not with me is against me; and he that gathereth not with me scattereth. 31 Therefore I say unto you, Every sin

[MARK 3:22-30. And the scribes which[4] came down from Jerusalem said, He hath Beelzebub, and, [5] By the prince of the [3] devils[3] casteth he out the [3] devils[3]. 23 And he called them unto him, and said unto them in parables, How can Satan cast out Satan? 24 And if a kingdom be divided against itself, that kingdom cannot stand. 25 And if a house be divided against itself, that house will not be able to stand. 26 And if Satan hath risen up against himself, and is divided, he cannot stand, but hath an end. 27 But no one can enter into the house of the strong *man*, and spoil his goods, except he first bind the strong *man*; and then he will spoil his house. 28 Verily I say unto you, All their sins shall be forgiven unto the sons of men, and their blasphemies wherewith soever they shall blaspheme: 29 but whosoever shall blaspheme against the Holy Spirit hath never forgiveness, but is guilty of an eternal sin: 30 because they said, he hath an unclean spirit.] (§ 55)

LUKE 11:14-54.

14 And he was casting out a [6] devil[1] which[5] was dumb. And it came to pass, when the [6] devil[1] was gone out, the dumb man spake; and the multitudes marvelled. 15 But some of them said, [5] By Beelzebub the prince of the [3] devils[3] casteth he out [3] devils[3]. 16 And others, tempting[6] *him*, sought of him a sign from heaven. 17 But he, knowing their thoughts, said unto them, Every kingdom divided against itself is brought to desolation; [7] and a house *divided* against a house falleth. 18 And if Satan also is divided against himself, how shall his kingdom stand? because ye say that I cast out [3] devils[3] [4] by Beelzebub. 19 And if I [4] by Beelzebub cast out [3] devils[3], by whom do your sons cast them out? therefore shall they be your judges. 20 But if I by the finger of God cast out [3] devils[3], then is the kingdom of God come upon you. 21 When the strong *man* fully armed guardeth his own court, his goods are in peace: but when a stronger than he shall come upon him, and overcome him, he taketh from him his whole armour wherein he trusted,

ERV. mg.: [1] Some ancient authorities omit *a loaf, and he will give him a stone?* or.   [2] Or, *a demoniac*   [3] Gr. *demons.*   [4] Or, *in*
[5] Or, *In*   [6] Gr. *demon.*   [7] Or, *and house falleth upon house.*

ARV. txt.: [1] demon   [2] Can this be   [3] demons   [4] that   [5] *that*   [6] trying

[MATT. 12.]

and blasphemy shall be forgiven [1]unto men; but the blasphemy against the Spirit shall not be forgiven. 32 And whosoever shall speak a word against the Son of man, it shall be forgiven him; but whosoever shall speak against the Holy Spirit, it shall not be forgiven him, neither in this [2]world, nor in that which is to come.] (§ 55)

[[a]Matt. 12:43–45. But the unclean spirit, when [3]he is gone out of the man, passeth through waterless places, seeking rest, and findeth it not. 44 Then [3]he saith, I will return into my house whence I came out; and when [3]he is come, [3]he findeth it empty, swept and garnished. 45 Then goeth [3]he, and taketh with [4]himself seven other spirits more evil than [4]himself, and they enter in and dwell there: and the last state of that man becometh worse than the first. Even so shall it be also unto this evil generation.] (§ 55)

[[b]Matt. 12:38–42. Then certain of the scribes and Pharisees answered him, saying, [5]Master[1], we would see a sign from thee.

LUKE 11.

and divideth his spoils. 23 He that is not with me is against me; and he that gathereth not with me scattereth.

24 [a]The unclean spirit when [3]he is gone out of the man, passeth through waterless places, seeking rest; and finding none, [3]he saith, I will turn back unto my house whence I came out. 25 And when [3]he is come, [3]he findeth it swept and garnished. 26 Then goeth [3]he, and taketh *to him* seven other spirits more evil than [4]himself; and they enter in and dwell there: and the last state of that man becometh worse than the first.

27 And it came to pass, as he said these things, a certain woman out of the multitude lifted up her voice, and said unto him, Blessed is the womb that bare thee, and the breasts which thou didst suck. 28 But he said, Yea rather, blessed are they that hear the word of God, and keep it.

29 [b]And when the multitudes were gathering together unto him, he began to say, This generation is an evil gen-

---

ERV. mg.: [1] Some ancient authorities read *unto you men.*   [2] Or, *age*   [3] Or, *it*   [4] Or, *itself*   [5] Or, *Teacher*

ARV. txt.: [1] Teacher

[a] Matt. 12:43–45. (§ 55) See above.
[b] Matt. 12:38–42. (§ 55) See above.
[b] Matt. 16:4. An evil and adulterous generation seeketh after a sign; and there shall no sign be given unto it, but the sign of Jonah. (§ 73)
[b] Mark 8:12. Why doth this generation seek a sign? verily I say unto you, There shall no sign be given unto this generation. (§ 73)

[MATT. 12.]

39 But he answered and said unto them, An evil and adulterous generation seeketh after a sign; and there shall no sign be given to it but the sign of Jonah the prophet: 40 for as Jonah was three days and three nights in the belly of the [1] whale; so shall the Son of man be three days and three nights in the heart of the earth. 41 The men of Nineveh shall stand up in the judgement with this generation, and shall condemn it: for they repented at the preaching of Jonah; and behold, [2] a greater than Jonah is here. 42 The queen of the south shall rise up in the judgement with this generation, and shall condemn it: for she came from the ends of the earth to hear the wisdom of Solomon; and behold, [2] a greater than Solomon is here.]
(§ 55)

LUKE 11.

eration: it seeketh after a sign; and there shall no sign be given to it but the sign of Jonah. 30 For even as Jonah became a sign unto the Ninevites, so shall also the Son of man be to this generation. 31 The queen of the south shall rise up in the judgement with the men of this generation, and shall condemn them: for she came from the ends of the earth to hear the wisdom of Solomon; and behold, [2] a greater than Solomon is here. 32 The men of Nineveh shall stand up in the judgement with this generation, and shall condemn it: for they repented at the preaching of Jonah; and behold, [2] a greater than Jonah is here.

33 [a] No man, when he hath lighted a lamp, putteth it in a cellar, neither under the bushel, but on the stand, that they which enter in may see the light. 34 [b] The lamp of thy body is thine eye: when thine eye is single, thy whole body also is full of light; but when it is evil, thy body also is full of darkness. 35 Look therefore whether the light that is in thee be not darkness. 36 If therefore thy whole body be full of light, having no part dark, it shall be wholly full of light, as when the lamp with its bright shining doth give thee light.

RV. mg.: [1] Gr. *sea-monster*. [2] Gr. *more than*

[a] Matt. 5:15. Neither do *men* light a lamp, and put it under the bushel, but on the stand; and it shineth unto all that are in the house. (§ 49)

[a] Mark 4:21. Is the lamp brought to be put under the bushel, or under the bed, *and* not to be put on the stand? (§ 57)

[a] Luke 8:16. And no man, when he hath lighted a lamp, covereth it with a vessel, or putteth it under a bed; but putteth it on a stand, that they which enter in may see the light. (§ 57)

[b] Matt. 6:22, 23. The lamp of the body is the eye: if therefore thine eye be single, thy whole body shall be full of light. 23 But if thine eye be evil, thy whole body shall be full of darkness. If therefore the light that is in thee be darkness, how great is the darkness! (§ 49)

LUKE 11.

37 Now as he spake, a Pharisee asketh him to [1]dine with him: and he went in, and sat down to meat. 38 And when the Pharisee saw it, he marvelled that he had not first washed[1] before [1]dinner. 39 And the Lord said unto him, ᵃNow do ye Pharisees[2] cleanse the outside of the cup and of the platter; but your inward part is full of extortion and wickedness. 40 Ye foolish ones, did not he that made the outside make the inside also? 41 Howbeit[3] give for alms those things which [2]are within; and behold, all things are clean unto you.

42 ᵇBut woe unto you Pharisees! for ye tithe mint and rue and every herb, and pass over judgement[4] and the love of God: but these ought ye to have done, and not to leave the other undone. 43 ᶜWoe unto you Pharisees! for ye love the chief seats in the synagogues, and the salutations in the marketplaces. 44 ᵈWoe unto you! for ye are as the tombs which appear not, and the men that walk over *them* know it not.

45 And one of the lawyers answering saith unto him, [3]Master[5], in saying this thou reproachest us also. 46 And he said, Woe unto you lawyers also! ᵉfor ye lade[6] men with burdens grievous to be borne, and ye yourselves touch not the burdens with one of your fingers. 47 ᶠWoe unto you! for ye build the tombs of the prophets, and your fathers killed them. 48 So ye are witnesses and consent unto the works of your fathers: for they killed them, and ye build *their tombs*. 49 ᵍTherefore also said the wisdom of God, I will send unto them prophets and apostles; and *some* of them they shall kill and persecute; 50 that the blood of all the prophets, which was shed from the foundation of the world, may be required of this generation; 51 from the blood of Abel unto the blood of Zachariah, who perished between the altar and the [4]sanctuary: yea, I say unto you, it shall be required of this generation. 52 ʰWoe unto you lawyers! for ye took away the key of knowledge: ye entered not in yourselves, and them that were entering in ye hindered.

ERV. mg.:   [1] Gr. *breakfast.*   [2] Or, *ye can*   [3] *Teacher*   [4] Gr. *house.*

ARV. txt.:   [1] bathed himself   [2] Now ye the Pharisees   [3] But   [4] justice   [5] Teacher   [6] load

ᵃ Matt. 23:25, 26.   Woe unto you, scribes and Pharisees, hypocrites! for ye cleanse the outside of the cup and of the platter, but within they are full from extortion and excess. 26 Thou blind Pharisee, cleanse first the inside of the cup and of the platter, that the outside thereof may become clean also. (§127)

ᵇ Matt. 23:23.   Woe unto you, scribes and Pharisees, hypocrites! for ye tithe mint and anise and cummin, and have left undone the weightier matters of the law, judgement, and mercy, and faith: but these ye ought to have done, and not to have left the other undone. (§127)

ᶜ Matt. 23:6, 7.   And love the chief place at feasts, and the chief seats in the synagogues,   7 and the salutations in the marketplaces, and to be called of men, Rabbi. (§127)

ᶜ Mark 12:38, 39.   Beware of the scribes, which desire to walk in long robes, and *to have* salutations in the marketplaces,   39 and chief seats in the synagogues, and chief places at feasts. (§127)

ᶜ Luke 20:46.   Beware of the scribes, which desire to walk in long robes, and love salutations in the marketplaces, and chief seats in the synagogues, and chief places at feasts. (§127)

ᵈ Matt. 23:27.   Woe unto you, scribes and Pharisees, hypocrites! for ye are like unto whited sepulchres, which outwardly appear beautiful, but inwardly are full of dead men's bones, and of all uncleanness. (§127)

ᵉ Matt. 23:4.   Yea, they bind heavy burdens and grievous to be borne, and lay them on men's shoulders; but they themselves will not move them with their finger. (§127)

ᶠ Matt. 23:29, 31.   Woe unto you, scribes and Pharisees, hypocrites! for ye build the sepulchres of the prophets, and garnish the tombs of the righteous, . . . 31 Wherefore ye witness to yourselves, that ye are sons of them that slew the prophets. (§127)

ᵍ Matt. 23:34-36.   Therefore, behold, I send unto you prophets, and wise men, and scribes: some of them shall ye kill and crucify; and some of them shall ye scourge in your synagogues, and persecute from city to city: 35 that upon you may come all the righteous blood shed on the earth, from the blood of Abel the righteous unto the blood of Zachariah son of Barachiah, whom ye slew between the sanctuary and the altar. 36 Verily I say unto you, All these things shall come upon this generation. (§127)

ʰ Matt. 23:13.   But woe unto you, scribes and Pharisees, hypocrites! because ye shut the kingdom of heaven against men: for ye enter not in yourselves, neither suffer ye them that are entering in to enter. (§127)

LUKE **11.**

53 And when he was come out from thence, the scribes and the Pharisees began to [1]press upon *him* vehemently, and to provoke him to speak of [2]many things; 54 laying wait for him, to catch something out of his mouth.

§95. TEACHINGS CONCERNING TRUST IN GOD AND COMING JUDGMENT.

LUKE, CHAP. **12.**

1 In the mean time, when [3]the many thousands of the multitude were gathered together, insomuch that they trode[1] one upon another, he began to [4]say unto his disciples first of all, [a]Beware ye of the leaven of the Pharisees, which is hypocrisy. 2 [b]But there is nothing covered up, that shall not be revealed: and hid, that shall not be known. 3 [c]Wherefore whatsoever ye have said in the darkness shall be heard in the light; and what ye have spoken in the ear in the inner chambers shall be proclaimed upon the housetops. 4 And I say unto you my friends, Be not afraid of them which[2] kill the body, and after that have no more that they can do. 5 But I will warn you whom ye shall fear: Fear him, which[3] after he hath killed hath [5]power to cast into [6]hell; yea, I say unto you, Fear him. 6 Are not five sparrows sold for two farthings[4]? and not one of them is forgotten in the sight of God. 7 [d]But the very hairs of your head are all numbered. Fear not: ye are of more value than many sparrows. 8 And I say unto you, Every one who shall confess [7]me before men, [8]him shall the Son of man also confess before the angels of God: 9 [e]but he that denieth me in the presence of men shall be denied in the presence of the angels of God. 10 [f]And every one

---

ERV. mg.: [1] Or, *set themselves vehemently against* him   [2] Or, *more*   [3] Gr. *the myriads of.*   [4] Or, *say unto his disciples, Firs of all beware ye*   [5] Or, *authority*   [6] Gr. Gehenna.   [7] Gr. *in me.*   [8] Gr. *in him.*

ARV. txt.: [1] trod   [2] that   [3] who   [4] pence

---

[a] Matt. 16:6. Take heed and beware of the leaven of the Pharisees and Sadducees. (§73)
[a] Matt. 16:11. But beware of the leaven of the Pharisees and Sadducees. (§73)
[a] Mark 8:15. Take heed, beware of the leaven of the Pharisees and the leaven of Herod. (§73)
[b] Matt. 10:26. For there is nothing covered that shall not be revealed; and hid, that shall not be known. (§64)
[b] Mark 4:22. For there is nothing hid, save that it should be manifested; neither was *anything* made secret, but that it should come to light. (§57)
[b] Luke 8:17. For nothing is hid, that shall not be made manifest; nor *anything* secret that shall not be known and come to light. (§57)
[c] Matt. 10:27-32. What I tell you in the darkness, speak ye in the light: and what ye hear in the ear, proclaim upon the housetops. 28 And be not afraid of them which kill the body, but are not able to kill the soul: but rather fear him which is able to destroy both soul and body in hell. 29 Are not two sparrows sold for a farthing? and not one of them shall fall on the ground without your Father: 30 but the very hairs of your head are all numbered. 31 Fear not therefore; ye are of more value than many sparrows. 32 Every one therefore who shall confess me before men, him will I also confess before my Father which is in heaven. (§64)
[d] Luke 21:18. And not a hair of your head shall perish. (§131)
[e] Matt. 10:33. But whosoever shall deny me before men, him will I also deny before my Father which is in heaven. (§64)
[e] Mark 8:38. For whosoever shall be ashamed of me and of my words in this adulterous and sinful generation, the Son of man also shall be ashamed of him, when he cometh in the glory of his Father with the holy angels. (§76)
[e] Luke 9:26. For whosoever shall be ashamed of me and of my words, of him shall the Son of man be ashamed, when he cometh in his own glory, and *the glory* of the Father, and of the holy angels. (§76)
[f] Matt. 12:31, 32. Therefore I say unto you, Every sin and blasphemy shall be forgiven unto men; but the blasphemy against the Spirit shall not be forgiven. 32 And whosoever shall speak a word against the Son of man, it shall be forgiven him; but whosoever shall speak against the Holy Spirit, it shall not be forgiven him, neither in this world, nor in that which is to come. (§55)
[f] Mark 3:28, 29. Verily I say unto you, All their sins shall be forgiven unto the sons of men, and their blasphemies wherewith soever they shall blaspheme: 29 but whosoever shall blaspheme against the Holy Spirit hath never forgiveness, but is guilty of an eternal sin. (§55)

LUKE 12.

who shall speak a word against the Son of man, it shall be forgiven him: but unto him that blasphemeth against the Holy Spirit it shall not be forgiven. 11 ᵃAnd when they bring you before the synagogues, and the rulers, and the authorities, be not anxious how or what ye shall answer, or what ye shall say: 12 for the Holy Spirit shall teach you in that very hour what ye ought to say.

13 And one out of the multitude said unto him, ¹Master¹, bid my brother divide the inheritance with me. 14 But he said unto him, Man, who made me a judge or a divider over you? 15 And he said unto them, Take heed, and keep yourselves from all covetousness: ²for a man's life consisteth not in the abundance of the things which he possesseth. 16 And he spake a parable unto them, saying, The ground of a certain rich man brought forth plentifully: 17 and he reasoned with himself, saying, What shall I do, because I have not where to bestow my fruits? 18 And he said, This will I do: I will pull down my barns, and build greater; and there will I bestow all my corn² and my goods. 19 And I will say to my ³soul, ³Soul, thou hast much goods laid up for many years; take thine ease, eat, drink, be merry. 20 But God said unto him, Thou foolish one, this night ⁴is thy ³soul required of thee; and the things which thou hast prepared, whose shall they be? 21 So is he that layeth up treasure for himself and is not rich toward God.

22 ᵇAnd he said unto his disciples, Therefore I say unto you, Be not anxious for *your* ⁵life, what ye shall eat; nor yet for your body, what ye shall put on. 23 For the ⁵life is more than the food, and the body than the raiment. 24 Consider the ravens, that they sow not, neither reap; which have no store-chamber nor barn; and God feedeth them: of how much more value are ye than the birds! 25 And which of you by being anxious can add a cubit unto his ⁶stature³? 26 If then ye are not able to do even that which is least, why are ye anxious concerning the rest? 27 Consider the lilies, how they grow: they toil not, neither do they spin; yet I say unto you, Even Solomon in all his glory was not arrayed like one of these. 28 But if God doth so clothe the grass in the field, which to-day is, and to-morrow is cast into the oven; how much more *shall he clothe* you, O ye of little faith? 29 And seek not

---

ERV. mg.. ¹ Or, *Teacher* ² Gr. *for not in a man's abundance consisteth his life, from the things which he possesseth.* ³ Or, *life* ⁴ Gr. *they require thy soul.* ⁵ Or, *soul* ⁶ Or, *age*

ARV. txt.: ¹ Teacher ² grain ³ the measure of his life

ᵃ Matt. 10:19, 20. But when they deliver you up, be not anxious how or what ye shall speak: for it shall be given you in that hour what ye shall speak. 20 For it is not ye that speak, but the Spirit of your Father that speaketh in you. (§ 64)

ᵃ Mark 13:11. And when they lead you *to judgement*, and deliver you up, be not anxious beforehand what ye shall speak: but whatsoever shall be given you in that hour, that speak ye: for it is not ye that speak, but the Holy Ghost. (§ 131)

ᵃ Luke 21:14, 15. Settle it therefore in your hearts, not to meditate beforehand how to answer: 15 for I will give you a mouth and wisdom, which all your adversaries shall not be able to withstand or to gainsay. (§ 131)

ᵇ Matt. 6:25–33. Therefore I say unto you, Be not anxious for your life, what ye shall eat, or what ye shall drink; nor yet for your body, what ye shall put on. Is not the life more than the food, and the body than the raiment? 26 Behold the birds of the heaven, that they sow not, neither do they reap, nor gather into barns; and your heavenly Father feedeth them. Are not ye of much more value than they? 27 And which of you by being anxious can add one cubit unto his stature? 28 And why are ye anxious concerning raiment? Consider the lilies of the field, how they grow; they toil not, neither do they spin: 29 yet I say unto you, that even Solomon in all his glory was not arrayed like one of these. 30 But if God doth so clothe the grass of the field, which to-day is, and to-morrow is cast into the oven, *shall he* not much more *clothe* you, O ye of little faith? 31 Be not therefore anxious, saying, What shall we eat? or, What shall we drink? or, Wherewithal shall we be clothed? 32 For after all these things do the Gentiles seek; for your heavenly Father knoweth that ye have need of all these things. 33 But seek ye first his kingdom, and his righteousness; and all these things shall be added unto you. (§ 49)

LUKE **12.**

ye what ye shall eat, and what ye shall drink, neither be ye of doubtful mind. 30 ᵃFor all these things do the nations of the world seek after: but your Father knoweth that ye have need of these things. 31 Howbeit¹ seek ye ¹his kingdom, and these things shall be added unto you. 32 Fear not, little flock; for it is your Father's good pleasure to give you the kingdom. 33 ᵇSell that² ye have, and give alms; make for yourselves purses which wax not old, a treasure in the heavens that faileth not, where no thief draweth near, neither moth destroyeth. 34 For where your treasure is, there will your heart be also.

35 Let your loins be girded about, and your lamps burning; 36 and be ye yourselves like unto men looking for their lord, when he shall return from the marriage feast; that, when he cometh and knocketh, they may straightway open unto him. 37 Blessed are those ²servants, whom the lord when he cometh shall find watching: verily I say unto you, that he shall gird himself, and make them sit down to meat, and shall come and serve them. 38 And if he shall come in the second watch, and if in the third, and find *them* so, blessed are those *servants.* 39 ᶜ³But know this, that if the master of the house had known in what hour the thief was coming, he would have watched, and not have left his house to be ⁴broken through. 40 Be ye also ready: for in an hour that ye think not the Son of man cometh.

41 And Peter said, Lord, speakest thou this parable unto us, or even unto all? 42 And the Lord said, ᵈWho then is ⁵the faithful and wise steward, whom his lord shall set over his household, to give them their portion of food in due season? 43 Blessed is that ⁶servant, whom his lord when he cometh shall find so doing. 44 Of a truth I say unto you, that he will set him over all that he hath. 45 But if that ⁶servant shall say in his heart, My lord delayeth his coming; and shall begin to beat the menservants and the maidservants, and to eat and drink, and to be drunken; 46 the lord of that ⁶servant shall come in a day when he expecteth not, and in an hour when he knoweth not, and shall ⁷cut him asunder, and appoint his portion with the unfaithful. 47 And that ⁶servant, which³ knew his lord's will, and made not ready, nor did according to his will, shall be beaten with many *stripes;* 48 but he that knew not, and did things worthy of stripes, shall be beaten with few *stripes.* And to whomsoever much is given, of him shall much be required: and to whom they commit much, of him will they ask the more.

ERV. mg.: ¹ Many ancient authorities read *the kingdom of God.* ² Gr. *bondservants.* ³ Or, *But this ye know* ⁴ Gr. *digged through.* ⁵ Or, *the faithful steward, the wise* man *whom &c.* ⁶ Gr. *bondservant.* ⁷ Or, *severely scourge him*

ARV, txt.: ¹ Yet ² that which ³ who

ᵃ Matt. 6:8. Be not therefore like unto them: for your Father knoweth what things ye have need of, before ye ask him. (§ 49)

ᵃ Matt. 6:32. For after all these things do the Gentiles seek; for your heavenly Father knoweth that ye have need of all these things. (§ 49)

ᵇ Matt. 6:19-21. Lay not up for yourselves treasures upon the earth, where moth and rust doth consume, and where thieves break through and steal: 20 but lay up for yourselves treasures in heaven, where neither moth nor rust doth consume, and where thieves do not break through nor steal: 21 for where thy treasure is, there will thy heart be also. (§ 49)

ᶜ Matt. 24:43, 44. But know this, that if the master of the house had known in what watch the thief was coming, he would have watched, and would not have suffered his house to be broken through. 44 Therefore be ye also ready: for in an hour that ye think not the Son of man cometh. (§ 131)

ᵈ Matt. 24:45-51. Who then is the faithful and wise servant, whom his lord hath set over his household, to give them their food in due season? 46 Blessed is that servant, whom his lord when he cometh shall find so doing. 47 Verily I say unto you, that he will set him over all that he hath. 48 But if that evil servant shall say in his heart, My lord tarrieth; 49 and shall begin to beat his fellow-servants, and shall eat and drink with the drunken; 50 the lord of that servant shall come in a day when he expecteth not, and in an hour when he knoweth not, 51 and shall cut him asunder, and appoint his portion with the hypocrites: there shall be the weeping and gnashing of teeth. (§ 131)

LUKE 12.

49 I came to cast fire upon the earth ; and what will I[1] if it is already kindled? 50 [a]But I have a baptism to be baptized with; and how am I straitened till it be accomplished! 51 [b]Think ye that I am come to give peace in the earth? I tell you, Nay; but rather division : 52 for there shall be from henceforth five in one house divided, three against two, and two against three. 53 They shall be divided, father against son, and son against father; mother against daughter, and daughter against her mother; mother in law against her daughter in law, and daughter in law against her mother in law.

54 [c]And he said to the multitudes also, When ye see a cloud rising in the west, straightway ye say, There cometh a shower; and so it cometh to pass. 55 And when *ye see* a south wind blowing, ye say, There will be a [1]scorching heat; and it cometh to pass. 56 Ye hypocrites, ye know how to [2]interpret the face of the earth and the heaven; but how is it that ye know not how to [2]interpret this time? 57 And why even of yourselves judge ye not what is right? 58 [d]For as thou art going with thine adversary before the magistrate, on the way give diligence to be quit of him; lest haply he hale[2] thee unto the judge, and the judge shall deliver thee to the [3]officer, and the [3]officer shall cast thee into prison. 59 I say unto thee, Thou shalt by no means come out thence, till thou have paid the very last mite.

§ 96. THE GALILEANS SLAIN BY PILATE.

LUKE 13 : 1-9.

1 Now there were some present at that very season which[3] told him of the Galilæans, whose blood Pilate had mingled with their sacrifices. 2 And he answered and said unto them, Think ye that these Galilæans were sinners above all the Galilæans, because they have suffered these things? 3 I tell you, Nay: but, except ye repent, ye shall all in like manner perish. 4 Or those eighteen, upon whom the tower in Siloam fell, and killed them, think ye that they were [4]offenders above all the men that dwell in Jerusalem? 5 I tell you, Nay : but, except ye repent, ye shall all likewise perish.

6 And he spake this parable; A certain man had a fig tree planted in his vineyard ; and he came seeking fruit thereon, and found none. 7 And he said unto the vinedresser, Behold, these three years I come seeking fruit on this fig tree, and find none : cut it down ; why doth it also cumber the ground? 8 And he answering saith unto him, Lord, let it alone this year also, till I shall dig about it, and dung it : 9 and if it bear fruit thenceforth, *well*; but if not, thou shalt cut it down.

§ 97. THE WOMAN HEALED ON A SABBATH.

LUKE 13 : 10-21.

10 And he was teaching in one of the synagogues on the sabbath day. 11 And behold, a woman which[4] had a spirit of infirmity eighteen years; and she was bowed together, and

---

ERV. mg.   [1] Or, *hot wind*   [2] Gr. *prove.*   [3] Gr. *exactor*   [4] Gr. *debtors*

ARV. txt.:   [1] do I desire   [2] drag   [3] who   [4] that

---

[a] Mark 10: 38.   With the baptism that I am baptized withal shall ye be baptized. (§ 114)

[b] Matt. 10: 34-36.   Think not that I came to send peace on the earth: I came not to send peace, but a sword. 35 For I came to set a man at variance against his father, and the daughter against her mother, and the daughter in law against her mother in law: 36 and a man's foes *shall be* they of his own household. (§ 64)

[c] Matt. 16: 2, 3.   But he answered and said unto them, When it is evening, ye say, *It will be* fair weather: for the heaven is red. 3 And in the morning, *It will be* foul weather to-day: for the heaven is red and lowring. Ye know how to discern the face of the heaven; but ye cannot *discern* the signs of the times. (§ 73)

[d] Matt. 5: 25, 26.   Agree with thine adversary quickly, whiles thou art with him in the way; lest haply the adversary deliver thee to the judge, and the judge deliver thee to the officer, and thou be cast into prison. 26 Verily I say unto thee, Thou shalt by no means come out thence, till thou have paid the last farthing. (§ 49)

LUKE 13.

could in no wise lift herself up. 12 And when Jesus saw her, he called her, and said to her, Woman, thou art loosed from thine infirmity. 13 And he laid his hands upon her: and immediately she was made straight, and glorified God. 14 And the ruler of the synagogue, being moved with indignation because Jesus had healed on the sabbath, answered and said to the multitude, There are six days in which men ought to work: in them therefore come and be healed, and not on the day of the sabbath. 15 But the Lord answered him, and said, Ye hypocrites, doth not each one of you on the sabbath loose his ox or his ass from the [1]stall, and lead him away to watering? 16 And ought not this woman, being a daughter of Abraham, whom Satan had bound, lo, *these* eighteen years, to have been loosed from this bond on the day of the sabbath? 17 And as he said these things, all his adversaries were put to shame: and all the multitude rejoiced for all the glorious things that were done by him.

18 [a] He said therefore, Unto what is the kingdom of God like? and whereunto shall I liken it? 19 It is like unto a grain of mustard seed, which a man took, and cast into his own garden; and it grew, and became a tree; and the birds of the heaven lodged in the branches thereof. 20 [b] And again he said, Whereunto shall I liken the kingdom of God? 21 It is like unto leaven, which a woman took and hid in three [2] measures of meal, till it was all leavened.

§ 98. THE QUESTION WHETHER FEW ARE SAVED.

LUKE 13 : 22–30.

22 And he went on his way through cities and villages, teaching, and journeying on unto Jerusalem. 23 And one said unto him, Lord, are they few that be[1] saved? And he said unto them, 24 [c] Strive to enter in by the narrow door: for many, I say unto you, shall seek to enter in, and shall not be [3] able. 25 When once the master of the house is risen up, and hath shut to the door, and ye begin to stand without, and to knock at the door, saying, [d] Lord, open to us; and he shall answer and say to you, I know not whence ye are; 26 then shall ye begin to say, We did eat and drink in thy presence, and thou didst teach in our streets; 27 [e] and he shall say, I tell you, I know not whence ye are; depart

---

ERV. mg.: [1] Gr. *manger* [2] See marginal note on Matt. xiii. 33. [3] Or, *able, when once*

ARV. txt.: [1] are

---

[a] Matt. 13:31, 32. Another parable set he before them, saying, The kingdom of heaven is like unto a grain of mustard seed, which a man took, and sowed in his field: 32 which indeed is less than all seeds; but when it is grown, it is greater than the herbs, and becometh a tree, so that the birds of the heaven come and lodge in the branches thereof. (§ 57)

[a] Mark 4:30-32. And he said, How shall we liken the kingdom of God? or in what parable shall we set it forth? 31 It is like a grain of mustard seed, which, when it is sown upon the earth, though it be less than all the seeds that are upon the earth, 32 yet when it is sown, groweth up, and becometh greater than all the herbs, and putteth out great branches; so that the birds of the heaven can lodge under the shadow thereof. (§ 57)

[b] Matt. 13:33. Another parable spake he unto them; The kingdom of heaven is like unto leaven, which a woman took, and hid in three measures of meal, till it was all leavened. (§ 57)

[c] Matt. 7:13, 14. Enter ye in by the narrow gate: for wide is the gate, and broad is the way, that leadeth to destruction, and many be they that enter in thereby. 14 For narrow is the gate, and straitened the way, that leadeth unto life, and few be they that find it. (§ 49)

[d] Matt. 25:11, 12. Lord, Lord, open to us. 12 But he answered and said, Verily I say unto you, I know you not. (§ 131)

[e] Matt. 7:23. And then will I profess unto them, I never knew you: depart from me, ye that work iniquity. (§ 49)

LUKE 13.

from me, all ye workers of iniquity. 28 [a]There shall be the weeping and gnashing[1] of teeth, when ye shall see Abraham, and Isaac, and Jacob, and all the prophets, in the kingdom of God, and yourselves cast forth without. 29 And they shall come from the east and west, and from the north and south, and shall [1]sit down in the kingdom of God. 30 [b]And behold, there are last which[2] shall be first, and there are first which[2] shall be last.

§ 99. REPLY TO THE WARNING AGAINST HEROD.

LUKE 13:31-35.

31 In that very hour there came certain Pharisees, saying to him, Get thee out, and go hence: for Herod would fain kill thee. 32 And he said unto them, Go and say to that fox, Behold, I cast out [2]devils[3] and perform cures to-day and to-morrow, and the third *day* I am perfected. 33 Howbeit[4] I must go on my way to-day and to-morrow and the *day* following: for it cannot be that a prophet perish out of Jerusalem. 34 [c]O Jerusalem, Jerusalem, which[5] killeth the prophets, and stoneth them that are sent unto her! how often would I have gathered thy children together, even as a hen *gathereth* her own brood under her wings, and ye would n**o**t! 35 Behold, your house is left unto you *desolate*: and I say unto you, Ye shall not see me, until ye shall say, Blessed *is* he that cometh in the name of the Lord.

§ 100. DISCOURSE AT A CHIEF PHARISEE'S TABLE.

LUKE 14:1-24.

1 And it came to pass, when he went into the house of one of the rulers of the Pharisees on a sabbath to eat bread, that they were watching him. 2 And behold, there was before him a certain man which[5] had the dropsy. 3 And Jesus answering spake unto the lawyers and Pharisees, saying, Is it lawful to heal on the sabbath, or not? 4 But they held their peace. And he took him, and healed him, and let him go. 5 And he said unto them, [d]Which of you shall have [3]an ass or an ox fallen into a well, and will not straightway draw him up on a sabbath day? 6 And they could not answer again unto these things.

7 And he spake a parable unto those which[5] were bidden, when he marked how they chose out the chief seats; saying unto them, 8 When thou art bidden of any man to a mar-

---

ERV. mg.: [1]Gr. *recline.* [2]Gr. *demons.* [3]Many ancient authorities read *a son.* See ch. xiii. 15.

ARV. txt.: [1]*the gnashing* [2]who [3]demons [4]Nevertheless [5]that

[a]Matt. 8:11, 12. Many shall come from the east and the west, and shall sit down with Abraham, and Isaac, and Jacob, in the kingdom of heaven: 12 but the sons of the kingdom shall be cast forth into the outer darkness: there shall be the weeping and gnashing of teeth. (§57)

[a]Matt. 13:42. And shall cast them into the furnace of fire; there shall be the weeping and gnashing of teeth. (§57)

[a]Matt. 13:50. And shall cast them into the furnace of fire: there shall be the weeping and gnashing of teeth. (§57)

[a]Matt. 22:13. And cast him out into the outer darkness; there shall be the weeping and gnashing of teeth. (§124)

[a]Matt. 24:51. And shall cut him asunder and appoint his portion with the hypocrites: there shall be the weeping and gnashing of teeth. (§131)

[a]Matt. 25:30. And cast ye out the unprofitable servant into the outer darkness: there shall be the weeping and gnashing of teeth. (§131)

[b]Matt. 19:30. But many shall be last *that are* first; and first *that are* last. (§112)

[b]Matt. 20:16. So the last shall be first, and the first last. (§112)

[b]Mark 10:31. But many *that are* first shall be last; and the last first. (§112)

[c]Matt. 23:37-39. O Jerusalem, Jerusalem, which killeth the prophets, and stoneth them that are sent unto her! how often would I have gathered thy children together, even as a hen gathereth her chickens under her wings, and ye would not! 38 Behold, your house is left unto you desolate. 39 For I say unto you, Ye shall not see me henceforth, till ye shall say, Blessed *is* he that cometh in the name of the Lord. (§127)

[d]Matt. 12:11. What man shall there be of you, that shall have one sheep, and if this fall into a pit on the sabbath day, will he not lay hold on it, and lift it out? (§46)

riage feast, [1] sit not down in the chief seat; lest haply a more honourable man than thou be bidden of him, 9 and he that bade thee and him shall come and say to thee, Give this man place; and then thou shalt begin with shame to take the lowest place. 10 But when thou art bidden, go and sit down in the lowest place; that when he that hath bidden thee cometh, he may say to thee, Friend, go up higher: then shalt thou have glory in the presence of all that sit at meat with thee. 11 [a] For every one that exalteth himself shall be humbled; and he that humbleth himself shall be exalted.

12 And he said to him also that had bidden him, When thou makest a dinner or a supper, call not thy friends, nor thy brethren, nor thy kinsmen, nor rich neighbours; lest haply they also bid thee again, and a recompense be made thee. 13 But when thou makest a feast, bid the poor, the maimed, the lame, the blind: 14 and thou shalt be blessed; because they have not *wherewith* to recompense thee: for thou shalt be recompensed in the resurrection of the just.

15 [b] And when one of them that sat at meat with him heard these things, he said unto him, Blessed is he that shall eat bread in the kingdom of God. 16 But he said unto him, A certain man made a great supper; and he bade many: 17 and he sent forth his [2] servant at supper time to say to them that were bidden, Come; for *all* things are now ready. 18 And they all with one *consent* began to make excuse. The first said unto him, I have bought a field, and I must needs go out and see it: I pray thee have me excused. 19 And another said, I have bought five yoke of oxen, and I go to prove them: I pray thee have me excused. 20 And another said, I have married a wife, and therefore I cannot come. 21 And the [2] servant came, and told his lord these things. Then the master of the house being angry said to his [2] servant, Go out quickly into the streets and lanes of the city, and bring in hither the poor and maimed and blind and lame. 22 And the [2] servant said, Lord, what thou didst command is done, and yet there is room. 23 And the lord said unto the [2] servant, Go out into the highways and hedges, and constrain *them* to come in, that my house may be filled. 24 For I say unto you, that none of those men which [1] were bidden shall taste of my supper.

§ 101. DISCOURSE ON COUNTING THE COST.

LUKE 14: 25–35.

25 Now there went with him great multitudes: and he turned, and said unto them, 26 [c] If any man cometh unto me, and hateth not his own father, and mother, and wife, and

[a] Matt. 23:12. And whosoever shall exalt himself shall be humbled; and whosoever shall humble himself shall be exalted. (§ 127)

[a] Luke 18:14. For every one that exalteth himself shall be humbled; but he that humbleth himself shall be exalted. (§ 109)

[b] Matt. 22:1–10. And Jesus answered and spake again in parables unto them, saying, 2 The kingdom of heaven is likened unto a certain king, which made a marriage feast for his son, 3 and sent forth his servants to call them that were bidden to the marriage feast: and they would not come. 4 Again he sent forth other servants, saying, Tell them that are bidden, Behold, I have made ready my dinner: my oxen and my fatlings are killed, and all things are ready: come to the marriage feast. 5 But they made light of it, and went their ways, one to his own farm, another to his merchandise: 6 and the rest laid hold on his servants, and entreated them shamefully, and killed them. 7 But the king was wroth; and he sent his armies, and destroyed those murderers, and burned their city. 8 Then saith he to his servants, The wedding is ready, but they that were bidden were not worthy. 9 Go ye therefore unto the partings of the highways, and as many as ye shall find, bid to the marriage feast. 10 And those servants went out into the highways, and gathered together all as many as they found, both bad and good: and the wedding was filled with guests. (§ 124)

[c] Matt. 10:37. He that loveth father or mother more than me is not worthy of me; and he that loveth son or daughter more than me is not worthy of me. (§ 64)

children, and brethren, and sisters, yea, and his own life also, he cannot be my disciple. 27 ᵃ Whosoever doth not bear his own cross, and come after me, cannot be my disciple. 28 For which of you, desiring to build a tower, doth not first sit down and count the cost, whether he have *wherewith* to complete it ? 29 Lest haply, when he hath laid a foundation, and is not able to finish, all that behold begin to mock him, 30 saying, This man began to build, and was not able to finish. 31 Or, what king, as he goeth to encounter another king in war, will not sit down first and take counsel whether he is able with ten thousand to meet him that cometh against him with twenty thousand ? 32 Or else, while the other is yet a great way off, he sendeth an ambassage, and asketh conditions of peace. 33 So therefore whosoever he be of you that renounceth not all that he hath, he cannot be my disciple. 34 ᵇ Salt therefore is good : but if even the salt have lost its savour, wherewith shall it be seasoned ? 35 It is fit neither for the land nor for the dunghill : *men* cast it out. ᶜ He that hath ears to hear, let him hear.

§102. THREE PARABLES OF GRACE.

Luke, chap. 15.

1 Now all the publicans and sinners were drawing near unto him for¹ to hear him. 2 And both the Pharisees and the scribes murmured, saying, This man receiveth sinners, and eateth with them.

3 And he spake unto them this parable, saying, 4 ᵈ What man of you, having a hundred sheep, and having lost one of them, doth not leave the ninety and nine in the wilderness, and go after that which is lost, until he find it ? 5 And when he hath found it, he layeth it on his shoulders, rejoicing. 6 And when he cometh home, he calleth together his friends and his neighbours, saying unto them, Rejoice with me, for I have found my sheep which was lost. 7 I say unto you, that even so there shall be joy in heaven over one sinner that repenteth, *more* than over ninety and nine righteous persons, which² need no repentance.

8 Or what woman having ten ¹ pieces of silver, if she lose one piece, doth not light a lamp, and sweep the house, and seek diligently until she find it ? 9 And when she hath found it,

---

ERV. mg.:   ¹ Gr. *drachma*, a coin worth about eight pence.

ARV. txt.:   ¹ *Omit* for   ² who

ᵃ Matt. 10:38. And he that doth not take his cross and follow after me, is not worthy of me. (§64)

ᵃ Matt. 16:24. If any man would come after me, let him deny himself, and take up his cross, and follow me. (§ 76)

ᵃ Mark 8:34. If any man would come after me, let him deny himself, and take up his cross, and follow me. (§ 76)

ᵃ Luke 9:23. If any man would come after me, let him deny himself, and take up his cross daily, and follow me. (§ 76)

ᵇ Matt. 5:13. Ye are the salt of the earth: but if the salt have lost its savour, wherewith shall it be salted? it is thenceforth good for nothing, but to be cast out and trodden under foot of men. (§ 49)

ᵇ Mark 9:50. Salt is good: but if the salt have lost its saltness, wherewith will ye season it? Have salt in yourselves, and be at peace one with another. (§ 81)

ᶜ Matt. 11:15. He that have ears to hear, let him hear. (§ 52)

ᶜ Matt. 13:9. He that hath ears, let him hear. (§ 57)

ᶜ Matt. 13:43. He that hath ears, let him hear. (§ 57)

ᶜ Mark 4:9. Who hath ears to hear, let him hear. (§ 57)

ᶜ Mark 4:23. If any man hath ears to hear, let him hear. (§ 57)

ᶜ Luke 8:8. He that hath ears to hear, let him hear. (§ 57)

ᵈ Matt. 18:12-14. How think ye? if any man have a hundred sheep, and one of them be gone astray, doth he not leave the ninety and nine, and go unto the mountains, and seek that which goeth astray? 13 And if so be that he find it, verily I say unto you, he rejoiceth over it more than over the ninety and nine which have not gone astray. 14 Even so it is not the will of your Father which is in heaven, that one of these little ones should perish. (§ 81)

LUKE 15.

she calleth together her friends and neighbours, saying, Rejoice with me, for I have found the piece which I had lost. 10 Even so, I say unto you, there is joy in the presence of the angels of God over one sinner that repenteth.

11 And he said, A certain man had two sons : 12 and the younger of them said to his father, Father, give me the portion of [1]*thy* substance that falleth to me. And he divided unto them his living. 13 And not many days after the younger son gathered all together, and took his journey into a far country; and there he wasted his substance with riotous living. 14 And when he had spent all, there arose a mighty famine in that country; and he began to be in want. 15 And he went and joined himself to one of the citizens of that country; and he sent him into his fields to feed swine. 16 And he would fain have been filled[1] with [2]the husks that the swine did eat : and no man gave unto him. 17 But when he came to himself he said, How many hired servants of my father's have bread enough and to spare, and I perish here with hunger! 18 I will arise and go to my father, and will say unto him, Father, I have sinned against heaven, and in thy sight : 19 I am no more worthy to be called thy son : make me as one of thy hired servants. 20 And he arose, and came to his father. But while he was yet afar off, his father saw him, and was moved with compassion, and ran, and fell on his neck, and [3]kissed him. 21 And the son said unto him, Father, I have sinned against heaven, and in thy sight : I am no more worthy to be called thy [4]son. 22 But the father said to his [5]servants, Bring forth quickly the best robe, and put it on him; and put a ring on his hand, and shoes on his feet : 23 and bring the fatted calf, *and* kill it, and let us eat, and make merry : 24 for this my son was dead, and is alive again; he was lost, and is found. And they began to be merry. 25 Now his elder son was in the field : and as he came and drew nigh to the house, he heard music and dancing. 26 And he called to him one of the [5]servants, and inquired what these things might be. 27 And he said unto him, Thy brother is come; and thy father hath killed the fatted calf, because he hath received him safe and sound. 28 But he was angry, and would not go in : and his father came out and intreated him. 29 But he answered and said to his father, Lo, these many years do I serve thee, and I never transgressed a commandment of thine : and *yet* thou never gavest me a kid, that I might make merry with my friends : 30 but when this thy son came, which[2] hath devoured thy living with harlots, thou killedst for him the fatted calf. 31 And he said unto him, [6]Son, thou art ever with me, and all that is mine is thine. 32 But it was meet to make merry and be glad : for this thy brother was dead, and is alive *again*; and *was* lost, and is found.

§103. TWO PARABLES OF WARNING.

LUKE, CHAP. 16.

1 And he said also unto his disciples, There was a certain rich man, which[2] had a steward; and the same was accused unto him that he was wasting his goods. 2 And he called him, and said unto him, What is this that I hear of thee? render the account of thy stewardship; for thou canst be no longer steward. 3 And the steward said within himself, What shall I do, seeing that my lord taketh away the stewardship from me? I have not strength to dig; to beg I am ashamed. 4 I am resolved what to do, that, when I am put out of the stewardship, they may receive me into their houses. 5 And calling to him each one of his lord's debtors, he said to the first, How much owest thou unto my lord? 6 And he said, A hundred [7]meas-

---

ERV. mg.: [1] Gr. *the.* [2] Gr. *the pods of the carob tree.* [3] Gr. *kissed him much.* [4] Some ancient authorities add *make me as one of thy hired servants.* See ver. 19. [5] Gr. *bondservants.* [6] Gr. *Child.* [7] Gr. *baths*, the bath being a Hebrew measure. See Ezek. xlv. 10, 11, 14.

ARV. txt.: [1] have filled his belly. [2] who

LUKE 16.

ures of oil. And he said unto him, Take thy [1]bond, and sit down quickly and write fifty. 7 Then said he to another, And how much owest thou? And he said, A hundred [2]measures of wheat. He saith unto him, Take thy [1]bond, and write fourscore. 8 And his lord commended [3]the unrighteous steward because he had done wisely: for the sons of this [4]world are for their own generation wiser than the sons of the light. 9 And I say unto you, Make to yourselves friends [5]by means of the mammon of unrighteousness; that, when it shall fail, they may receive you into the eternal tabernacles. 10 He that is faithful in a very little is faithful also in much: and he that is unrighteous in a very little is unrighteous also in much. 11 If therefore ye have not been faithful in the unrighteous mammon, who will commit to your trust the true *riches*? 12 And if ye have not been faithful in that which is another's, who will give you that which is [6]your own? 13 [a]No [7]servant can serve two masters: for either he will hate the one, and love the other; or else he will hold to one, and despise the other. Ye cannot serve God and mammon.

14 And the Pharisees, who were lovers of money, heard all these things; and they scoffed at him. 15 And he said unto them, Ye are they that justify yourselves in the sight of men; but God knoweth your hearts: for that which is exalted among men is an abomination in the sight of God. 16 [b]The law and the prophets *were* until John: from that time the gospel of the kingdom of God is preached, and every man entereth violently into it. 17 [c]But it is easier for heaven and earth to pass away, than for one tittle of the law to fall. 18 [d]Every one that putteth away his wife, and marrieth another, committeth adultery: and he that marrieth one that is put away from a husband committeth adultery.

19 Now there was a certain rich man, and he was clothed in purple and fine linen, [8]faring sumptuously every day: 20 and a certain beggar named Lazarus was laid at his gate, full of sores, 21 and desiring to be fed with the *crumbs* that fell from the rich man's table; yea, even the dogs came and licked his sores. 22 And it came to pass, that the beggar died, and that he was carried away by the angels into Abraham's bosom: and the rich man also died, and was buried. 23 And in Hades he lifted up his eyes, being in torments, and seeth Abraham afar off, and Lazarus in his bosom. 24 And he cried and said, Father Abraham, have mercy on me, and send Lazarus, that he may dip the tip of his finger in water, and cool my tongue; for I am in anguish in this flame. 25 But Abraham said, [9]Son, remember that thou in thy lifetime receivedst thy good things, and Lazarus in like manner evil things: but now here he is comforted, and thou art in anguish. 26 And [10]beside[1] all this, between us and you there is a great gulf fixed, that they which [2] would pass

---

ERV. mg.: [1] Gr. *writings*. [2] Gr. *cors*, the cor being a Hebrew measure. See Ezek. xlv. 14. [3] Gr. *the steward of unrighteousness*. [4] Or, *age* [5] Gr. *out of*. [6] Some ancient authorities read *our own*. [7] Gr. *household-servant*. [8] Or, *living in mirth and splendour every day* [9] Gr. *Child*. [10] Or, *in all these things*

ARV. txt.: [1] besides [2] that

---

[a] Matt. 6:24. No man can serve two masters: for either he will hate the one, and love the other; or else he will hold to one, and despise the other. Ye cannot serve God and mammon. (§49)

[b] Matt. 11:12, 13. And from the days of John the Baptist until now the kingdom of heaven suffereth violence, and men of violence take it by force. 13 For all the prophets and the law prophesied until John. (§52)

[c] Matt. 5:18. For verily I say unto you, Till heaven and earth pass away, one jot or one tittle shall in no wise pass away from the law, till all things be accomplished. (§49)

[d] Matt. 5:32. But I say unto you, that every one that putteth away his wife, saving for the cause of fornication, maketh her an adulteress: and whosoever shall marry her when she is put away committeth adultery. (§49)

[d] Matt. 19:9. And I say unto you, Whosoever shall put away his wife, except for fornication, and shall marry another, committeth adultery: and he that marrieth her when she is put away committeth adultery. (§110)

[d] Mark 10:11. Whosoever shall put away his wife, and marry another, committeth adultery against her. (§110)

LUKE 16.

from hence to you may not be able, and that none may cross over from thence to us. 27 And he said, I pray thee therefore, father, that thou wouldest send him to my father's house; 28 for I have five brethren; that he may testify unto them, lest they also come into this place of torment. 29 But Abraham saith, They have Moses and the prophets; let them hear them. 30 And he said, Nay, father Abraham: but if one go to them from the dead, they will repent. 31 And he said unto him, If they hear not Moses and the prophets, neither will they be persuaded, if one rise from the dead.

§ 104. CONCERNING FORGIVENESS AND FAITH.

LUKE 17: 1–10.

1 And he said unto his disciples, ᵃ It is impossible but that occasions of stumbling should come: but woe unto him, through whom they come! 2 ᵇ It were well for him if a millstone were hanged about his neck, and he were thrown into the sea, rather than that he should cause one of these little ones to stumble. 3 ᶜTake heed to yourselves: if thy brother sin, rebuke him; and if he repent, forgive him. 4 ᵈAnd if he sin against thee seven times in the day, and seven times turn again to thee, saying, I repent; thou shalt forgive him.

5 And the apostles said unto the Lord, Increase our faith. 6 ᵉAnd the Lord said, If ye have ¹ faith as a grain of mustard seed, ye would say unto this sycamine tree, Be thou rooted up, and be thou planted in the sea; and it would have obeyed² you. 7 But who is there of you, having a ¹servant plowing or keeping sheep, that will say unto him, when he is come in from the field, Come straightway and sit down to meat; 8 and will not rather say unto him, Make ready wherewith I may sup, and gird thyself, and serve me, till I have eaten and drunken; and afterward thou shalt eat and drink? 9 Doth he thank the ¹servant because he did the things that were commanded? 10 Even so ye also, when ye shall have done all the things that are commanded you, say, We are unprofitable ²servants; we have done that which it was our duty to do.

ERV. mg.: ¹ Gr. *bondservant.* ² Gr. *bondservants.*

ARV. txt.: ¹ had ² would obey

ᵃ Matt. 18:7. Woe unto the world because of occasions of stumbling! for it must needs be that the occasions come; but woe to that man through whom the occasion cometh! (§ 81)

ᵇ Matt. 18:6. But whoso shall cause one of these little ones which believe on me to stumble, it is profitable for him that a great millstone should be hanged about his neck, and *that* he should be sunk in the depth of the sea. (§ 81)

ᵇ Mark 9:42. And whosoever shall cause one of these little ones that believe on me to stumble, it were better for him if a great millstone were hanged about his neck, and he were cast into the sea. (§ 81)

ᶜ Matt. 18:15. And if thy brother sin against thee, go, shew him his fault between thee and him alone: if he hear thee, thou hast gained thy brother. (§ 81)

ᵈ Matt. 18:21, 22. Then came Peter, and said to him, Lord, how oft shall my brother sin against me, and I forgive him? until seven times? 22 Jesus saith unto him, I say not unto thee, Until seven times; but, Until seventy times seven. (§ 81)

ᵉ Matt. 17:20. For verily I say to you, If ye have faith as a grain of mustard seed, ye shall say unto this mountain, Remove hence to yonder place; and it shall remove; (§ 78)

ᵉ Matt. 21:21. Verily I say unto you, If ye have faith, and doubt not, ye shall not only do what is done to the fig tree, but even if ye shall say unto this mountain, Be thou taken up and cast into the sea, it shall be done. (§ 122)

ᵉ Mark 11:22, 23. Have faith in God. 23 Verily I say unto you, Whosoever shall say unto this mountain, Be thou taken up and cast into the sea; and shall not doubt in his heart, but shall believe that what he saith cometh to pass; he shall have it. (§ 122)

§ 105. THE RAISING OF LAZARUS.

JOHN 11 : 1–46.

1 Now a certain man was sick, Lazarus of Bethany, of the village of Mary and her sister Martha. 2 And it was that Mary which[1] anointed the Lord with ointment, and wiped his feet with her hair, whose brother Lazarus was sick. 3 The sisters therefore sent unto him, saying, Lord, behold, he whom thou lovest is sick. 4 But when Jesus heard it, he said, This sickness is not unto death, but for the glory of God, that the Son of God may be glorified thereby. 5 Now Jesus loved Martha, and her sister, and Lazarus. 6 When therefore he heard that he was sick, he abode at that time two days in the place where he was. 7 Then after this he saith to the disciples, Let us go into Judæa again. 8 The disciples say unto him, Rabbi, the Jews were but now seeking to stone thee ; and goest thou thither again? 9 Jesus answered, Are there not twelve hours in the day? If a man walk in the day, he stumbleth not, because he seeth the light of this world. 10 But if a man walk in the night, he stumbleth, because the light is not in him. 11 These things spake he : and after this he saith unto them, Our friend Lazarus is fallen asleep ; but I go, that I may awake him out of sleep. 12 The disciples therefore said unto him, Lord, if he is fallen asleep, he will[1] recover. 13 Now Jesus had spoken of his death : but they thought that he spake of taking rest in sleep. 14 Then Jesus therefore said unto them plainly, Lazarus is dead. 15 And I am glad for your sakes that I was not there, to the intent ye may believe ; nevertheless let us go unto him. 16 Thomas therefore, who is called [2]Didymus, said unto his fellow-disciples, Let us also go, that we may die with him.

17 So when Jesus came, he found that he had been in the tomb four days already. 18 Now Bethany was nigh unto Jerusalem, about fifteen furlongs off ; 19 and many of the Jews had come to Martha and Mary, to console them concerning their brother. 20 Martha therefore, when she heard that Jesus was coming, went and met him : but Mary still sat in the house. 21 Martha therefore said unto Jesus, Lord, if thou hadst been here, my brother had not died. 22 And even now I know that, whatsoever thou shalt ask of God, God will give thee. 23 Jesus saith unto her, Thy brother shall rise again. 24 Martha saith unto him, I know that he shall rise again in the resurrection at the last day. 25 Jesus said unto her, I am the resurrection, and the life : he that believeth on me, though he die, yet shall he live : 26 and whosoever liveth and believeth on me shall never die. Believest thou this? 27 She saith unto him, Yea, Lord : I have believed that thou art the Christ, the Son of God, *even* he that cometh into the world. 28 And when she had said this, she went away, and called Mary [3]her sister secretly, saying, The [4]Master[2] is here, and calleth thee. 29 And she, when she heard it, arose quickly, and went unto him. 30 (Now Jesus was not yet come into the village, but was still in the place where Martha met him.) 31 The Jews then which[1] were with her in the house, and were comforting[3] her, when they saw Mary, that she rose up quickly and went out, followed her, supposing that she was going unto the tomb to [5]weep there. 32 Mary therefore, when she came where Jesus was, and saw him, fell down at his feet, saying unto him, Lord, if thou hadst been here, my brother had not died. 33 When Jesus therefore saw her [6]weeping, and the Jews *also* [6]weeping which[1] came with her, he [7]groaned in the spirit, and [8]was troubled,   34 and said, Where have ye laid him? They say unto him, Lord, come and see. 35 Jesus wept. 36 The Jews therefore said, Behold how he loved him ! 37 But some of them said, Could not this man, which[1] opened the eyes of him

---

ERV. mg.: [1] Gr. *be saved.* [2] That is, *Twin.* [3] Or, *her sister, saying secretly.* [4] Or, *Teacher* [5] Gr. *wail.* [6] Gr. *wailing.* [7] Gr. *was moved with indignation in the spirit* [8] Gr. *troubled himself.*

ARV. txt.: [1] who [2] Teacher [3] consoling

JOHN 11.

that was blind, have caused that this man also should not die? 38 Jesus therefore again [1]groaning in himself cometh to the tomb. Now it was a cave, and a stone lay [2]against it. 39 Jesus saith, Take ye away the stone. Martha, the sister of him that was dead, saith unto him, Lord, by this time he stinketh[1]: for he hath been *dead* four days. 40 Jesus saith unto her, Said I not unto thee, that, if thou believedst, thou shouldest see the glory of God? 41 So they took away the stone. And Jesus lifted up his eyes, and said, Father, I thank thee that thou heardest me. 42 And I knew that thou hearest me always: but because of the multitude which[2] standeth around I said it, that they may believe that thou didst send me. 43 And when he had thus spoken, he cried with a loud voice, Lazarus, come forth. 44 He that was dead came forth, bound hand and foot with [3]grave-clothes; and his face was bound about with a napkin. Jesus saith unto them, Loose him, and let him go.

45 Many therefore of the Jews, which[3] came to Mary and beheld [4]that which he did, believed on him. 46 But some of them went away to the Pharisees, and told them the things which Jesus had done.

§ 106. THE WITHDRAWAL TO EPHRAIM

JOHN 11:47–54.

The chief priests therefore and the Pharisees gathered a council, and said, What do we? for this man doeth many signs. 48 If we let him thus alone, all men will believe on him: and the Romans will come and take away both our place and our nation. 49 But a certain one of them, Caiaphas, being high priest that year, said unto them, Ye know nothing at all, 50 nor do ye take account that it is expedient for you that one man should die for the people, and that the whole nation perish not. 51 Now this he said not of himself: but being high priest that year, he prophesied that Jesus should die for the nation; 52 and not for the nation only, but that he might also gather together into one the children of God that are scattered abroad. 53 So from that day forth they took counsel that they might put him to death.

54 Jesus therefore walked no more openly among the Jews, but departed thence into the country near to the wilderness, into a city called Ephraim; and there he tarried with the disciples.

§ 107. THE TEN LEPERS.

LUKE 17:11–19.

11 And it came to pass, [5]as they were on their way to Jerusalem, that he was passing [6]through the midst[4] of Samaria and Galilee. 12 And as he entered into a certain village, there met him ten men that were lepers, which[3] stood afar off: 13 and they lifted up their voices, saying, Jesus, Master, have mercy on us. 14 And when he saw them, he said unto them, Go and shew yourselves unto the priests. And it came to pass, as they went, they were cleansed. 15 And one of them, when he saw that he was healed, turned back, with a loud voice glorifying God; 16 and he fell upon his face at his feet, giving him thanks: and he was a Samaritan. 17 And Jesus answering said, Were not the ten cleansed? but where are the nine? 18 [7]Were there none found that returned to give glory to God, save this [8]stranger? 19 And he said unto him, Arise, and go thy way: thy faith hath [9]made thee whole.

ERV. mg.: [1] Or, *being moved with indignation in himself* [2] Or, *upon* [3] Jr, *grave-bands* [4] Many ancient authorities read *the things which he did.* [5] Or, *as he was* [6] Or, *between* [7] Or, *There were none found . . . save this stranger.* [8] Or, *alien* [9] Or, *saved thee*

ARV. txt.: [1] the body decayeth [2] that [3] who [4] along the border

§ 108. THE COMING OF THE KINGDOM.

Luke 17 : 20—18 : 8.

20 And being asked by the Pharisees, when the kingdom of God cometh, he answered them and said, The kingdom of God cometh not with observation : 21 neither shall they say, Lo, here! or, There! for lo, the kingdom of God is ¹within you.

22 And he said unto the disciples, The days will come, when ye shall desire to see one of the days of the Son of man, and ye shall not see it. 23 ªAnd they shall say to you, Lo, there! Lo, here! go not away, nor follow after *them* : 24 for as the lightning, when it lighteneth out of the one part under the heaven, shineth unto the other part under heaven ; so shall the Son of man be ²in his day. 25 ᵇBut first must he suffer many things and be rejected of this generation. 26 ᶜAnd as it came to pass in the days of Noah, even so shall it be also in the days of the Son of man. 27 They ate, they drank, they married, they were given in marriage, until the day that Noah entered into the ark, and the flood came, and destroyed them all. 28 Likewise even as it came to pass in the days of Lot ; they ate, they drank, they bought, they sold, they planted, they builded ; 29 but in the day that Lot went out from Sodom it rained fire and brimstone from heaven, and destroyed them all : 30 after the same manner shall it be in the day that the Son of man is revealed. 31 In that day, he which¹ shall be on the housetop, and his goods in the house, let him not go down to take them away : and let him that is in the field likewise not return back. 32 Remember Lot's wife. 33 ᵈWhosoever shall seek to gain his ³life shall lose it : but whosoever shall lose *his* ³life shall ⁴preserve it. 34 I say unto you, ᵉIn that night there shall be two men on one bed ; the one shall be taken, and the other shall be left. 35 There shall be two women grinding together ; the one shall be taken, and the other shall be ⁵left.   37 And they answering say unto him,

---

ERV. mg. : ¹ Or, *in the midst of you*   ² Some ancient authorities omit *in his day.*   ³ Or, *soul*   ⁴ Gr. *save it alive.*   ⁵ Some ancient authorities add ver. 36 *There shall be two men in the field ; the one shall be taken, and the other shall be left.*

ARV. txt. : ¹ that

ªMatt. 24 : 26, 27. If therefore they shall say unto you, Behold, he is in the wilderness ; go not forth : Behold, he is in the inner chambers ; believe *it* not. 27 For as the lightning cometh forth from the east, and is seen even unto the west ; so shall be the coming of the Son of man. (§ 131)

ᵇMatt. 16 : 21. From that time began Jesus to shew unto his disciples, how that he must go unto Jerusalem, and suffer many things of the elders and chief priests and scribes. (§ 76)

ᵇMark 8 : 31. And he began to teach them, that the Son of man must suffer many things, and be rejected by the elders, and the chief priests, and the scribes. (§ 76)

ᵇLuke 9 : 22. The Son of man must suffer many things, and be rejected of the elders and chief priests and scribes. (§ 76) Cf. also Matt. 17 : 22 ; Mark 9 : 31 ; Luke 9 : 44 (§ 79) ; and Matt. 20 : 18 ; Mark 10 : 33 ; Luke 18 : 31. (§ 113)

ᶜMatt. 24 : 37-39. And as *were* the days of Noah, so shall be the coming of the Son of man. 38 For as in those days which were before the flood they were eating and drinking, marrying and giving in marriage, until the day that Noah entered into the ark, 39 and they knew not until the flood came, and took them all away ; so shall be the coming of the Son of man. (§ 131)

ᵈMatt. 10 : 39. He that findeth his life shall lose it ; and he that loseth his life for my sake shall find it. (§ 64)

ᵈMatt. 16 : 25. For whosoever would save his life shall lose it ; and whosoever shall lose his life for my sake shall find it. (§ 76)

ᵈMark 8 : 35. For whosoever would save his life shall lose it ; and whosoever shall lose his life for my sake and the gospel's shall save it. (§ 76)

ᵈLuke 9 : 24. For whosoever would save his life shall lose it ; but whosoever shall lose his life for my sake, the same shall save it. (§ 76)

ᵈJohn 12 : 25. He that loveth his life loseth it ; and he that hateth his life in this world shall keep it unto life eternal. (§ 129)

ᵉMatt. 24 : 40, 41. Then shall two men be in the field ; one is taken, and one is left : 41 two women *shall be* grinding at the mill ; one is taken, and one is left. (§ 131)

LUKE 17.

Where, Lord ? And he said unto them, ᵃ Where the body *is*, thither will the ¹eagles also be gathered together.

18:1 And he spake a parable unto them to the end that they ought always to pray, and not to faint; 2 saying, There was in a city a judge, which¹ feared not God, and regarded not man : 3 and there was a widow in that city ; and she came oft unto him, saying, ²Avenge me of mine adversary. 4 And he would not for a while : but afterward he said within himself, Though I fear not God, nor regard man ; 5 yet because this widow troubleth me, I will avenge her, lest she ³wear me out by her continual coming. 6 And the Lord said, Hear what ⁴the unrighteous judge saith. 7 And shall not God avenge his elect, which² cry to him day and night, and³ he is longsuffering over them ? 8 I say unto you, that he will avenge them speedily. Howbeit⁴ when the Son of man cometh, shall he find ⁵faith on the earth ?

§109. THE PHARISEE AND THE PUBLICAN.

LUKE 18 : 9–14.

9 And he spake also this parable unto certain which¹ trusted in themselves that they were righteous, and set ⁶all others at nought : 10 Two men went up into the temple to pray ; the one a Pharisee, and the other a publican. 11 The Pharisee stood and prayed thus with himself, God, I thank thee, that I am not as the rest of men, extortioners, unjust, adulterers, or even as this publican. 12 I fast twice in the week ; I give tithes of all that I get. 13 But the publican, standing afar off, would not lift up so much as his eyes unto heaven, but smote his breast, saying, God, ⁷be⁵ merciful to me ⁸a sinner. 14 I say unto you, This man went down to his house justified rather than the other : ᵇ for every one that exalteth himself shall be humbled ; but he that humbleth himself shall be exalted.

§110. CONCERNING DIVORCE.

MATT. 19 : 3–12.	MARK 10 : 2–12.
3 And there came unto him Pharisees, tempting⁶ him, and saying, Is it lawful *for a man* to put away his wife for every cause ? 4 And he answered and said, Have ye not read, that he which¹ ¹⁰made *them* from the beginning made them male and female, 5 and said, For this cause shall a	2 And there came unto him Pharisees, and asked him, Is it lawful for a man to put away *his* wife? tempting him. 3 And he answered and said unto them, What did Moses command you ? 4 And they said, Moses suffered to write a bill of divorcement, and to put her away. 5 But Jesus said

ERV. mg.: ¹ Or, *vultures* ² Or, *Do me justice of*: and so in ver. 5, 7, 8. ³ Gr. *bruise*. ⁴ Gr. *the judge of unrighteousness*. ⁵ Or, *the faith* ⁶ Gr. *the rest*. ⁷ Or, *be propitiated* ⁸ Or, *the sinner* ⁹ Many authorities, some ancient, insert *the*. ¹⁰ Some ancient authorities read *created*.

ARV. txt.: ¹ who ² that ³ and *yet* ⁴ Nevertheless, ⁵ be thou ⁶ trying

ᵃ Matt. 24 : 28. Wheresoever the carcase is, there will the eagles be gathered together. (§ 131)
ᵇ Matt. 23 : 12. And whosoever shall exalt himself shall be humbled ; and whosoever shall humble himself shall be exalted. (§ 127)
ᵇ Luke 14 : 11. For every one that exalteth himself shall be humbled ; and he that humbleth himself shall be exalted. (§ 100)

MATT. **19.**

man leave his father and mother, and shall cleave to his wife; and the twain[1] shall become one flesh? 6 So that they are no more twain[1], but one flesh. What therefore God hath joined together, let not man put asunder. 7 They say unto him, Why then did Moses command to give a bill of divorcement, and to put *her* away? 8 He saith unto them, Moses for your hardness of heart suffered you to put away your wives: but from the beginning it hath not been so. 9 ªAnd I say unto you, Whosoever shall put away his wife, [1]except for fornication, and shall marry another, committeth adultery: [2]and he that marrieth her when she is put away committeth adultery. 10 The disciples say unto him, If the case of the man is so with his wife, it is not expedient to marry. 11 But he said unto them, All men cannot[2] receive this saying, but they to whom it is given. 12 For there are eunuchs, which[3] were so born from their mother's womb: and there are eunuchs, which[3] were made eunuchs by men: and there are eunuchs, which[3] made themselves eunuchs for the kingdom of heaven's sake. He that is able to receive it, let him receive it.

MARK **10.**

unto them, For your hardness of heart he wrote you this commandment. 6 But from the beginning of the creation, Male and female made he them. 7 For this cause shall a man leave his father and mother, [3]and shall cleave to his wife; 8 and the twain[1] shall become one flesh: so that they are no more twain[1], but one flesh. 9 What therefore God hath joined together, let not man put asunder. 10 And in the house the disciples asked him again of this matter. 11 And he saith unto them, ªWhosoever shall put away his wife, and marry another, committeth adultery against her: 12 and if she herself shall put away her husband, and marry another, she committeth adultery.

ERV. mg.: [1] Some ancient authorities read *saving for the cause of fornication, maketh her an adulteress;* as in chap. v. 32. [2] The following words, to the end of the verse, are omitted by some ancient authorities. [3] Some ancient authorities omit *and shall cleave to his wife.*

ARV. txt.: [1] two [2] Not all men can [3] that

ªMatt. 5:32. But I say unto you, that every one that putteth away his wife, saving for the cause of fornication, maketh her an adulteress: and whosoever shall marry her when she is put away committeth adultery. (§ 49)

ªLuke 16:18. Every one that putteth away his wife, and marrieth another, committeth adultery: and he that marrieth one that is put away from a husband committeth adultery. (§ 103)

§111. CHRIST BLESSING LITTLE CHILDREN.

MATT. 19:13-15.

13 Then were there brought unto him little children, that he should lay his hands on them, and pray: and the disciples rebuked them. 14 But Jesus said, Suffer the little children, and forbid them not, to come unto me: for of such is[1] the kingdom of heaven. 15 And he laid his hands on them, and departed thence.

MARK 10:13-16.

13 And they brought[2] unto him little children, that he should touch them: and the disciples rebuked them. 14 But when Jesus saw it, he was moved with indignation, and said unto them, Suffer the little children to come unto me; forbid them not: for of such is[1] the kingdom of God. 15 [a]Verily I say unto you, Whosoever shall not receive the kingdom of God as a little child, he shall in no wise enter therein. 16 And he took them in his arms, and blessed them, laying his hands upon them.

LUKE 18:15-17.

15 And they brought[2] unto him also their babes, that he should touch them: but when the disciples saw it, they rebuked them. 16 But Jesus called them unto him, saying, Suffer the little children to come unto me, and forbid them not: for of such is[1] the kingdom of God. 17 [a]Verily I say unto you, Whosoever shall not receive the kingdom of God as a little child, he shall in no wise enter therein.

§112. THE RICH YOUNG RULER.

MATT. 19:16—20:16

16 And behold, one came to him and said, [1,2]Master[3], what good thing shall I do, that I may have eternal life? 17 And he said unto him, [3]Why askest thou me concerning that which is good? One there is who is good: but if thou wouldest enter into life, keep the commandments. 18 He saith unto him, Which? And Jesus said, Thou shalt not kill, Thou shalt not commit adultery, Thou shalt not steal, Thou shalt not bear false witness, 19 Honour thy father and thy mother: and, Thou shalt love thy neigh-

MARK 10:17-31.

17 And as he was going forth [4]into the way, there ran one to him, and kneeled to him, and asked him, Good [1]Master[3], what shall I do that I may inherit eternal life? 18 And Jesus said unto him, Why callest thou me good? none is good save one, *even* God. 19 Thou knowest the commandments, Do not kill, Do not commit adultery, Do not steal, Do not bear false witness, Do not defraud, Honour thy father and mother. 20 And he said unto him, [1]Master[3], all these things have I observed from my youth.

LUKE 18:18-30.

18 And a certain ruler asked him, saying, Good [1]Master[3], what shall I do to inherit eternal life? 19 And Jesus said unto him, Why callest thou me good? none is good, save one, *even* God. 20 Thou knowest the commandments, Do not commit adultery, Do not kill, Do not steal, Do not bear false witness, Honour thy father and mother. 21 And he said, All these things have I observed from my youth up. 22 And when Jesus heard it, he said unto him, One thing thou lackest yet: sell all that thou hast, and distribute unto

---

ERV. mg.: [1] Or, *Teacher* [2] Some ancient authorities read *Good Master.* See Mark x. 17; Luke xviii. 18. [3] Some ancient authorities read *Why callest thou me good? None is good save one,* even *God.* See Mark x. 18; Luke xviii. 19. [4] Or, *on his way*

ARV. txt.: [1] to such belongeth [2] were bringing [3] Teacher

[a] Matt. 18:3. Verily I say unto you, Except ye turn, and become as little children, ye shall in no wise enter into the kingdom of heaven. (§81)

MATT. 19.	MARK 10.	LUKE 18.
bour as thyself. 20 The young man saith unto him, All these things have I observed: what lack I yet? 21 Jesus said unto him, If thou wouldest be perfect, go, sell that[1] thou hast, and give to the poor, and thou shalt have treasure in heaven: and come, follow me. 22 But when the young man heard the saying, he went away sorrowful: for he was one that had great possessions.	21 And Jesus looking upon him loved him, and said unto him, One thing thou lackest: go, sell whatsoever thou hast, and give to the poor, and thou shalt have treasure in heaven: and come, follow me. 22 But his countenance fell at the saying, and he went away sorrowful: for he was one that had great possessions.	the poor, and thou shalt have treasure in heaven: and come, follow me. 23 But when he heard these things, he became exceeding sorrowful; for he was very rich.
23 And Jesus said unto his disciples, Verily I say unto you, It is hard for a rich man to enter into the kingdom of heaven. 24 And again I say unto you, It is easier for a camel to go through a needle's eye, than for a rich man to enter into the kingdom of God. 25 And when the disciples heard it, they were astonished exceedingly, saying, Who then can be saved? 26 And Jesus looking upon *them* said to them, With men this is impossible; but with God all things are possible. 27 Then answered Peter and said unto him, Lo, we have left all, and followed thee; what then shall we have? 28 And Jesus said unto them, Verily I say unto you, that ye which[2] have followed me, in the regeneration when the Son of man shall sit on the throne of his glory, [a]ye also shall sit upon twelve thrones, judging the twelve tribes of	23 And Jesus looked round about, and saith unto his disciples, How hardly shall they that have riches enter into the kingdom of God! 24 And the disciples were amazed at his words. But Jesus answereth again, and saith unto them, Children, how hard is it [1]for them that trust in riches to enter into the kingdom of God! 25 It is easier for a camel to go through a needle's eye, than for a rich man to enter into the kingdom of God. 26 And they were astonished exceedingly, saying [2]unto him, Then who can be saved? 27 Jesus looking upon them saith, With men it is impossible, but not with God: for all things are possible with God. 28 Peter began to say unto him, Lo, we have left all, and have followed thee. 29 Jesus said, Verily I say unto you, There is no man that hath left house, or brethren, or sisters, or mother, or	24 And Jesus seeing him said, How hardly shall they that have riches enter into the kingdom of God! 25 For it is easier for a camel to enter in through a needle's eye, than for a rich man to enter into the kingdom of God. 26 And they that heard it said, Then who can be saved? 27 But he said, The things which are impossible with men are possible with God. 28 And Peter said, Lo, we have left [3]our own, and followed thee. 29 And he said unto them, Verily I say unto you, There is no man that hath left house, or wife, or brethren, or parents, or children, for the kingdom of God's sake, 30 who shall not receive manifold more in this time, and in the [4]world to come eternal life.

ERV. mg.:   [1] Some ancient authorities omit *for them that trust in riches.*   [2] Many ancient authorities read *among themselves.*   [3] Or, *our own* homes   [4] Or, *age*

ARV. txt.:   [1] that which   [2] who

---

[a] Luke 22:30. And ye shall sit on thrones judging the twelve tribes of Israel. (§ 133)

MATT. 19.	MARK 10.
Israel. 29 And every one that hath left houses, or brethren, or sisters, or father, or ¹mother, or children, or lands, for my name's sake, shall receive ²a hundredfold, and shall inherit eternal life. 30 ªBut many shall be last *that are* first; and first *that are* last. **20**:1 For the kingdom of heaven is like unto a man that is¹ a householder, which² went out early in the morning to hire labourers into his vineyard. 2 And when he had agreed with the labourers for a ³penny³ a day, he sent them into his vineyard. 3 And he went out about the third hour, and saw others standing in the marketplace idle; 4 and to them he said, Go ye also into the vineyard, and whatsoever is right I will give you. And they went their way. 5 Again he went out about the sixth and the ninth hour, and did likewise. 6 And about the eleventh *hour* he went out, and found others standing; and he saith unto them, Why stand ye here all the day idle? 7 They say unto him, Because no man hath hired us. He saith unto them, Go ye also into the vineyard. 8 And when even was come, the lord of the vineyard saith unto his steward, Call the labourers, and pay them their hire, beginning from the last unto	father, or children, or lands, for my sake, and for the gospel's sake, 30 but he shall receive a hundredfold now in this time, houses, and brethren, and sisters, and mothers, and children, and lands, with persecutions; and in the ⁴world to come eternal life. 31 ªBut many *that are* first shall be last; and the last first.

ERV. mg.: ¹ Many ancient authorities add [after *mother*] *or wife*: as in Luke xviii. 29. ² Some ancient authorities read *mani'old*. ³ See marginal note on ch. xviii. 28. ⁴ Or, *age*

ARV. txt.: ¹ was ² who ³ shilling

ª Cf. Matt. 20:16 (p. 162).
ª Luke 13:30. And behold, there are last which shall be first, and there are first which shall be last. (§ 98)

MATT. 20.

the first. 9 And when they came that *were hired* about the eleventh hour, they received every man a [1]penny[1]. 10 And when the first came, they supposed that they would receive more ; and they likewise received every man a [1]penny[1]. 11 And when they received it, they murmured against the householder, 12 saying, These last have spent *but* one hour, and thou hast made them equal unto us, which[2] have borne the burden of the day and the [2]scorching heat. 13 But he answered and said to one of them, Friend, I do thee no wrong : didst not thou agree with me for a [1]penny[1]? 14 Take up that which is thine, and go thy way ; it is my will to give unto this last, even as unto thee. 15 Is it not lawful for me to do what I will with mine own? or is thine eye evil, because I am good? 16 [a]So the last shall be first, and the first last.

§113. CHRIST FORETELLS HIS CRUCIFIXION.

MATT. 20 : 17-19.	MARK 10 : 32-34.	LUKE 18 : 31-34.
17 And as Jesus was going up to Jerusalem, he took the twelve disciples apart, and in[3] the way he said unto them, 18 [b]Behold, we go up to Jerusalem ; and the Son of man shall be delivered unto the chief priests and scribes ; and they shall condemn him to death, 19 and shall deliver	32 And they were in[3] the way, going up to Jerusalem ; and Jesus was going before them : and they were amazed ; [3]and they that followed were afraid. And he took again the twelve, and began to tell them the things that were to happen unto him, 33 *saying,* [b]Behold, we go up to Jerusa-	31 And he took unto him the twelve, and said unto them, [b]Behold, we go up to Jerusalem, and all the things that are written [4]by[4] the prophets shall be accomplished unto the Son of man. 32 For he shall be delivered up unto the Gentiles, and shall bemocked, and shamefully

ERV. mg. :   [1] See marginal note on ch. xviii. 28.   [2] Or, *hot wind*   [3] Or, *but some as they followed were afraid*   [4] Or, *through*

ARV. txt. :   [1] shilling   [2] who   [3] on   [4] through

[a] Cf. Matt. 19 : 30 (p. 161), and reference there.
[b] Cf. Matt. 16 : 21 ; Mark 8 : 31 ; Luke 9 : 22 (§ 76), and references there.

MATT. 20.	MARK 10.	LUKE 18.
him unto the Gentiles to mock, and to scourge, and to crucify: and the third day he shall be raised up.	lem; and the Son of man shall be delivered unto the chief priests and the scribes; and they shall condemn him to death, and shall deliver him unto the Gentiles: 34 and they shall mock him, and shall spit upon him, and shall scourge him, and shall kill him; and after three days he shall rise again.	entreated[1], and spit upon: 33 and they shall scourge and kill him: and the third day he shall rise again. 34 And they understood none of these things; and this saying was hid from them, and they perceived not the things that were said.

§ 114. AMBITION OF JAMES AND JOHN.

MATT. 20:20-28.	MARK 10:35-45.
20 Then came to him the mother of the sons of Zebedee with her sons, worshipping *him*, and asking a certain thing of him. 21 And he said unto her, What wouldest thou? She saith unto him, Command that these my two sons may sit, one on thy right hand, and one on thy left hand, in thy kingdom. 22 But Jesus answered and said, Ye know not what ye ask. Are ye able to drink the cup that I am about to drink? They say unto him, We are able. 23 He saith unto them, My cup indeed ye shall drink: but to sit on my right hand, and on *my* left hand, is not mine to give, but *it is for them* for whom it hath been prepared of my Father. 24 And when the ten heard it, they were moved with indignation concerning the two brethren. 25 But Jesus called them unto him, and said,	35 And there come near unto him James and John, the sons of Zebedee, saying unto him, [1]Master[2], we would that thou shouldest do for us whatsoever we shall ask of thee. 36 And he said unto them, What would ye that I should do for you? 37 And they said unto him, Grant unto us that we may sit, one on thy right hand, and one on *thy* left hand, in thy glory. 38 But Jesus said unto them, Ye know not what ye ask. Are ye able to drink the cup that I drink? or to be baptized with the baptism that I am baptized with? 39 And they said unto him, We are able. And Jesus said unto them, The cup that I drink ye shall drink; and [a]with the baptism that I am baptized withal shall ye be baptized: 40 but to sit on my right hand or on *my* left hand is not mine to give: but *it is for them* for

ERV. mg.: [1] Or, *Teacher*

ARV. txt.: [1] treated [2] Teacher

[a] Luke 12:50. But I have a baptism to be baptized with. (§ 95)

MATT. 20.

a Ye know that the rulers of the Gentiles lord it over them, and their great ones exercise authority over them. 26 Not so shall it be among you: b but whosoever would become great among you shall be your ¹minister; 27 and whosoever would be first among you shall be your ²servant: 28 even as the Son of man came not to be ministered unto, but to minister, and to give his life a ransom for many.

MARK 10.

whom it hath been prepared. 41 And when the ten heard it, they began to be moved with indignation concerning James and John. 42 And Jesus called them to him, and saith unto them, a Ye know that they which¹ are accounted to rule over the Gentiles lord it over them; and their great ones exercise authority over them. 43 But it is not so among you: b but whosoever would become great among you, shall be your ¹minister: 44 and whosoever would be first among you, shall be ²servant of all. 45 For verily the Son of man² came not to be ministered unto, but to minister, and to give his life a ransom for many.

§115. THE BLIND MEN NEAR JERICHO.

MATT. 20: 29-34.

29 And as they went out from Jericho, a great multitude followed him. 30 And behold, two blind men sitting by the way side, when they heard that Jesus was passing by, cried out, saying, Lord, have mercy on us, thou son of David. 31 And the multitude rebuked them, that they should hold their peace: but they cried out the more, saying, Lord, have mercy on us,

MARK 10: 46-52.

46 And they come to Jericho: and as he went out from Jericho, with his disciples and a great multitude, the son of Timæus, Bartimæus, a blind beggar, was sitting by the way side. 47 And when he heard that it was Jesus of Nazareth³, he began to cry out, and say, Jesus, thou son of David, have mercy on me. 48 And many rebuked him, that he should hold his peace:

LUKE 18: 35-43.

35 And it came to pass, as he drew nigh unto Jericho, a certain blind man sat by the way side begging: 36 and hearing a multitude going by, he inquired what this meant. 37 And they told him, that Jesus of Nazareth passeth by. 38 And he cried, saying, Jesus, thou son of David, have mercy on me. 39 And they that went before rebuked him, that he should hold his

---

ERV. mg.: ¹ Or, *servant* ² Gr. *bondservant.*

ARV. txt.: ¹ who ² For the Son of man also ³ the Nazarene

---

a Luke 22:25, 26. The kings of the Gentiles have lordship over them; and they that have authority over them are called Benefactors. 26 But ye *shall* not *be* so: but he that is the greater among you, let him become as the younger; and he that is chief, as he that doth serve. (§ 133)

b Matt. 23:11. But he that is greatest among you shall be your servant. (§ 127)

b Mark 9:35. If any man would be first, he shall be last of all, and minister of all. (§ 81)

b Luke 9: 48. For he that is least among you all, the same is great. (§ 81)

MATT. 20.	MARK 10.	LUKE 18.
thou son of David. 32 And Jesus stood still, and called them, and said, What will ye that I should do unto you? 33 They say unto him, Lord, that our eyes may be opened. 34 And Jesus, being moved with compassion, touched their eyes: and straightway they received their sight, and followed him. (+ § 119)	but he cried out the more a great deal, Thou son of David, have mercy on me. 49 And Jesus stood still, and said, Call ye him. And they call the blind man, saying unto him, Be of good cheer: rise, he calleth thee. 50 And he, casting away his garment, sprang up, and came to Jesus. 51 And Jesus answered him, and said, What wilt thou that I should do unto thee? And the blind man said unto him, [1]Rabboni, that I may receive my sight. 52 And Jesus said unto him, Go thy way; thy faith hath [2]made thee whole. And straightway he received his sight, and followed him in the way. (+ § 119)	peace: but he cried out the more a great deal, Thou son of David, have mercy on me. 40 And Jesus stood, and commanded him to be brought unto him: and when he was come near, he asked him, 41 What wilt thou that I should do unto thee? And he said, Lord, that I may receive my sight. 42 And Jesus said unto him, Receive thy sight: thy faith hath [2]made thee whole. 43 And immediately he received his sight, and followed him, glorifying God: and all the people, when they saw it, gave praise unto God.

§ 116. VISIT TO ZACCHÆUS.

LUKE 19: 1–10.

1 And he entered and was passing through Jericho. 2 And behold, a man called by name Zacchæus; and he was a chief publican, and he was rich. 3 And he sought to see Jesus who he was; and could not for the crowd, because he was little of stature. 4 And he ran on before, and climbed up into a sycomore tree to see him: for he was to pass that way. 5 And when Jesus came to the place, he looked up, and said unto him, Zacchæus, make haste, and come down; for to-day I must abide at thy house. 6 And he made haste, and came down, and received him joyfully. 7 And when they saw it, they all murmured, saying, He is gone in to lodge with a man that is a sinner. 8 And Zacchæus stood, and said unto the Lord, Behold, Lord, the half of my goods I give to the poor; and if I have wrongfully exacted aught of any man, I restore fourfold. 9 And Jesus said unto him, To-day is salvation come to this house, forasmuch as he also is a son of Abraham. 10 For the Son of man came to seek and to save that which was lost.

§ 117. PARABLE OF THE MINÆ.

LUKE 19: 11–28.

11 [a]And as they heard these things, he added and spake a parable, because he was nigh to Jerusalem, and *because* they supposed that the kingdom of God was immediately to appear. 12 He said therefore, A certain nobleman went into a far country, to receive for himself a kingdom, and to return. 13 And he called ten [3]servants of his, and gave them ten

---

ERV. mg.: [1] See John xx. 16. [2] Or, *saved thee* [3] Gr. *bondservants.*

[a] Cf. Matt. 25:14–30 (§ 131).

LUKE 19.

[1] pounds, and said unto them, Trade ye *herewith* till I come. 14 But his citizens hated him, and sent an ambassage after him, saying, We will not that this man reign over us. 15 And it came to pass, when he was come back again, having received the kingdom, that he commanded these [2] servants, unto whom he had given the money, to be called to him, that he might know what they had gained by trading. 16 And the first came before him, saying, Lord, thy pound hath made ten pounds more. 17 And he said unto him, Well done, thou good [3] servant: because thou wast found faithful in a very little, have thou authority over ten cities. 18 And the second came, saying, Thy pound, Lord, hath made five pounds. 19 And he said unto him also, Be thou also over five cities. 20 And [4] another came, saying, Lord, behold, *here is* thy pound, which I kept laid up in a napkin: 21 for I feared thee, because thou art an austere man: thou takest up that[1] thou layedst not down, and reapest that[1] thou didst not sow. 22 He saith unto him, Out of thine own mouth will I judge thee, thou wicked [3] servant. Thou knewest that I am an austere man, taking up that[1] I laid not down, and reaping that[1] I did not sow; 23 then wherefore gavest thou not my money into the bank, and [5] I at my coming should have required it with interest? 24 And he said unto them that stood by, Take away from him the pound, and give it unto him that hath the ten pounds. 25 And they said unto him, Lord, he hath ten pounds. 26 [a] I say unto you, that unto every one that hath shall be given; but from him that hath not, even that which he hath shall be taken away from him. 27 Howbeit[2] these mine enemies, which[3] would not that I should reign over them, bring hither, and slay them before me.

28 And when he had thus spoken, he went on before, going up to Jerusalem.

§ 118. ANOINTING OF JESUS BY MARY OF BETHANY.

MATT. 26:6–13.	MARK 14:3–9.		JOHN 11:55—12:11.
			55 Now the passover of the Jews was at hand: and many went up to Jerusalem out of the country before the passover, to purify themselves. 56 They sought therefore for Jesus, and spake one with another, as they stood in the temple, What

ERV. mg.:   [1] *Mina*, here translated a pound, is equal to one hundred drachmas. See ch. xv. 8.   [2] Gr. *bondservants*.   [3] Gr. *bond-servant*.   [4] Gr. *the other*.   [5] Or, *I should have gone and required*

ARV. txt.:   [1] that which   [2] But   [3] that

[a] Matt. 13:12. For whosoever hath, to him shall be given, and he shall have abundance: but whosoever hath not, from him shall be taken away even that which he hath. (§ 57)

[a] Matt. 25:29. For unto every one that hath shall be given, and he shall have abundance: but from him that hath not, even that which he hath shall be taken away. (§ 131)

[a] Mark 4:25. For he that hath, to him shall be given: and he that hath not, from him shall be taken away even that which he hath. (§ 57)

[a] Luke 8:18. For whosoever hath, to him shall be given; and whosoever hath not, from him shall be taken away even that which he thinketh he hath. (§ 57)

MATT. 26.	MARK 14.		JOHN 11.
			think ye? That he will not come to the feast? 57 Now the chief priests and the Pharisees had given commandment, that, if any man knew where he was, he should shew it, that they might take him.
6 Now when Jesus was in Bethany, in the house of Simon the leper, 7 there came unto him a woman having ¹an alabaster cruse of exceeding precious ointment, and she poured it upon his head, as he sat at meat. 8 But when the disciples saw it, they had indignation, saying, To what purpose is this waste? 9 For this *ointment* might have been sold for much, and given to the poor. 10 But Jesus perceiving it said unto them, Why trouble ye the woman? for she hath wrought a good work upon me. 11 For ye have the poor always with you; but me ye have not always. 12 For in that she ⁴poured this ointment upon my body, she did it to prepare me for burial. 13 Verily I say unto you, Where-	3 And while he was in Bethany in the house of Simon the leper, as he sat at meat, there came a woman having ¹an alabaster cruse of ointment of ²spikenard¹, very costly; *and* she brake the cruse, and poured it over his head. 4 But there were some that had indignation among themselves, *saying*, To what purpose hath this waste of the ointment been made? 5 For this ointment might have been sold for above three hundred ³pence², and given to the poor. And they murmured against her. 6 But Jesus said, Let her alone; why trouble ye her? she hath wrought a good work on me. 7 For ye have the poor always with you, and whensoever ye will ye can do them good:		12:1 Jesus therefore six days before the passover came to Bethany, where Lazarus was, whom Jesus raised from the dead. 2 So they made him a supper there: and Martha served; but Lazarus was one of them that sat at meat with him. 3 Mary therefore took a pound of ointment of ²spikenard¹, very precious, and anointed the feet of Jesus, and wiped his feet with her hair: and the house was filled with the odour of the ointment. 4 But Judas Iscariot, one of his disciples, which³ should betray him, saith, 5 Why was not this ointment sold for three hundred ³pence², and given to the poor? 6 Now this he said, not because he cared for the poor; but because he was a thief, and having the

ERV. mg.: ¹ Or, *a flask.* ² Gr. *pistic nard*, pistic being perhaps a local name. Others take it to mean *genuine*; others, *liquid.* ³ See marginal note on Matt. xviii. 28. ⁴ Gr. *cast.*

ARV. txt.: ¹ pure nard ² shillings ³ that

MATT. 26.	MARK 14.		JOHN 12.
soever [1] this gospel shall be preached in the whole world, that also which this woman hath done shall be spoken of for a memorial of her. (+ § 132)	but me ye have not always. 8 She hath done what she could: she hath anointed my body aforehand[1] for the burying. 9 And verily I say unto you, Wheresoever the gospel shall be preached throughout the whole world, that also which this woman hath done shall be spoken of for a memorial of her. (+ § 132)		[2] bag [3] took away what was put therein. 7 Jesus therefore said [4] Suffer her to keep it against the day of my burying. 8 For the poor ye have always with you; but me ye have not always.
			9 The common people therefore of the Jews learned that he was there: and they came, not for Jesus' sake only, but that they might see Lazarus also, whom he had raised from the dead. 10 But the chief priests took counsel that they might put Lazarus also to death; 11 because that by reason of him many of the Jews went away, and believed on Jesus.

ERV. mg.:   [1] Or, *these good tidings*   [2] Or, *box*   [3] Or, *carried what was put therein*   [4] Or, *Let her alone:* it was *that she might keep it*

ARV. txt.:   [1] beforehand

PART VIII.

THE PASSION WEEK.

FROM THE FINAL ARRIVAL IN JERUSALEM UNTIL THE RESURRECTION.

SUNDAY. §119.

§ 119. THE TRIUMPHAL ENTRY.

MATT. 21 : 1–11.

1 And when they drew nigh unto Jerusalem, and came unto Bethphage, unto the mount of Olives, then Jesus sent two disciples, 2 saying unto them, Go into the village that is over against you, and straightway ye shall find an ass tied, and a colt with her: loose *them,* and bring *them* unto me. 3 And if any one say aught unto you, ye shall say, The Lord hath need of them; and straightway he will send them. 4 Now this is come to pass, that it might be fulfilled which was spoken [1] by [1] the prophet, saying, 5 Tell ye the daughter of Zion,
Behold, thy King cometh unto thee, Meek, and riding upon an ass,

MARK 11 : 1–11.

1 And when they draw nigh unto Jerusalem, unto Bethphage and Bethany, at the mount of Olives, he sendeth two of his disciples, 2 and saith unto them, Go your way into the village that is over against you: and straightway as ye enter into it, ye shall find a colt tied, whereon no man ever yet sat; loose him, and bring him. 3 And if any one say unto you, Why do ye this? say ye, The Lord hath need of him; and straightway he [2] will send him [3] back hither. 4 And they went away, and found a colt tied at the door without in the open street; and they loose him. 5 And certain of them that stood there said unto them,

LUKE 19 : 29–44.

29 And it came to pass, when he drew nigh unto Bethphage and Bethany, at the mount that is called *the mount* of Olives [2], he sent two of the disciples, 30 saying, Go your way into the village over against *you;* in the [3] which as ye enter ye shall find a colt tied, whereon no man ever yet sat: loose him, and bring him. 31 And if any one ask you, Why do ye loose him? thus shall ye say, The Lord hath need of him. 32 And they that were sent went away, and found even as he had said unto them. 33 And as they were loosing the colt, the owners thereof said unto them, Why loose ye the colt? 34 And they said, The Lord

JOHN 12 : 12–19.

12 On the morrow [4] a great multitude that had come to the feast, when they heard that Jesus was coming to Jerusalem, 13 took the branches of the palm trees, and went forth to meet him, and cried out, Hosanna: Blessed *is* he that cometh in the name of the Lord, even the King of Israel. 14 And Jesus, having found a young ass, sat thereon; as it is written, 15 Fear not, daughter of Zion: behold, thy King cometh, sitting on an ass's colt. 16 These things understood not his disciples at the first: but when Jesus was glorified, then remembered they that these things were written of him, and that they had done these things unto

---

ERV. mg.: [1] Or, *through* [2] Gr. *sendeth.* [3] Or, *again* [4] Some ancient authorities read *the common people.*

ARV. txt.: [1] through [2] called Olivet [3] *Omit* the

MATT. 21.	MARK 11.	LUKE 19.	JOHN 12.
And upon a colt the foal of an ass. 6 And the disciples went, and did even as Jesus appointed them, 7 and brought the ass, and the colt, and put on them their garments; and he sat thereon. 8 And the most part of the multitude spread their garments in the way; and others cut branches from the trees, and spread them in the way. 9 And the multitudes that went before him, and that followed, cried, saying, Hosanna to the son of David: Blessed *is* he that cometh in the name of the Lord; Hosanna in the highest.	What do ye, loosing the colt? 6 And they said unto them even as Jesus had said: and they let them go. 7 And they bring the colt unto Jesus, and cast on him their garments; and he sat upon him. 8 And many spread their garments upon the way; and others [1]branches, which they had cut from the fields. 9 And they that went before, and they that followed, cried, Hosanna; Blessed *is* he that cometh in the name of the Lord: 10 Blessed *is* the kingdom that cometh, *the kingdom* of our father David: Hosanna in the highest.	hath need of him. 35 And they brought him to Jesus: and they threw their garments upon the colt, and set Jesus thereon. 36 And as he went, they spread their garments in the way. 37 And as he was now drawing nigh, *even* at the descent of the mount of Olives, the whole multitude of the disciples began to rejoice and praise God with a loud voice for all the [2]mighty works which they had seen; 38 saying, Blessed *is* the King that cometh in the name of the Lord: peace in heaven, and glory in the highest. 39 And some of the Pharisees from the multitude said unto him, [3]Master[1], rebuke thy disciples. 40 And he answered and said, I tell you that, if these shall hold their peace, the stones will cry out. 41 And when he drew nigh, he saw the city and wept over it, 42 saying, [4]If thou hadst known in this day, even thou, the things which belong unto peace! but now they are hid from thine eyes. 43 For the days shall come	him. 17 The multitude therefore that was with him when he called Lazarus out of the tomb, and raised him from the dead, bare witness. 18 For this cause also the multitude went and met him, for that they heard that he had done this sign. 19 The Pharisees therefore said among themselves, [5]Behold how ye prevail nothing: lo, the world is gone after him.

ERV. mg.: [1] Gr. *layers of leaves.* [2] Gr. *powers.* [3] Or, *Teacher* [4] Or, *O that thou hadst known* [5] Or, *Ye behold*

ARV. txt.: [1] Teacher

MATT. 21.	MARK 11.	LUKE 19.
		upon thee, when thine enemies shall cast up a [1]bank about thee, and compass thee round, and keep thee in on every side, 44 and shall dash thee to the ground, and thy children within thee; and they shall not leave in thee one stone upon another: because thou knewest not the time of thy visitation.
10 And when he was come into Jerusalem, all the city was stirred, saying, Who is this? 11 And the multitudes said, This is the prophet, Jesus, from Nazareth of Galilee. (+§ 121)	11 And he entered into Jerusalem, into the temple; and when he had looked round about upon all things, it being now eventide, he went out unto Bethany with the twelve.	

MONDAY. §§ 120, 121.

§ 120.   THE CURSING OF THE FIG TREE.

MATT. 21 : 18, 19 [20-22].	MARK 11 : 12-14.
18 Now in the morning as he returned to the city, he hungered. 19 And seeing [2]a fig tree by the way side, he came to it, and found nothing thereon, but leaves only; and he saith unto it, Let there be no fruit from thee henceforward for ever. And immediately the fig tree withered away. [20 And when the disciples saw it, they marvelled, saying, How did the fig tree immediately wither away? 21 And Jesus answered and said unto them, Verily I say unto you, If ye have faith,	12 And on the morrow, when they were come out from Bethany, he hungered. 13 And seeing a fig tree afar off having leaves, he came, if haply he might find anything thereon: and when he came to it, he found nothing but leaves; for it was not the season of figs. 14 And he answered and said unto it, No man eat fruit from thee henceforward for ever. And his disciples heard it.

ERV. mg.: [1] Gr. *palisade.* [2] Or, *a single*

MATT. 21.

and doubt not, ye shall not only do what is done to the fig tree, but even if ye shall say unto this mountain, Be thou taken up and cast into the sea, it shall be done. 22 And all things, whatsoever ye shall ask in prayer, believing, ye shall receive.] (+ § 123)

§ 121. SECOND CLEANSING OF THE TEMPLE.

MATT. 21:12-17.	MARK 11:15-19.	LUKE 19:45-48.	[JOHN 2:13-22.]
12 And Jesus entered into the temple ¹of God, and cast out all them that sold and bought in the temple, and overthrew the tables of the money-changers, and the seats of them that sold the doves; 13 and he saith unto them, It is written, My house shall be called a house of prayer: but ye make it a den of robbers.	15 And they come to Jerusalem: and he entered into the temple, and began to cast out them that sold and them that bought in the temple, and overthrew the tables of the money-changers, and the seats of them that sold the doves; 16 and he would not suffer that any man should carry a vessel through the temple. 17 And he taught, and said unto them, Is it not written, My house shall be called a house of prayer for all the nations? but ye have made it it a den of robbers.	45 And he entered into the temple, and began to cast out them that sold, 46 saying unto them, It is written, And my house shall be a house of prayer: but ye have made it a den of robbers.	[John 2:13-22. And the passover of the Jews was at hand, and Jesus went up to Jerusalem. 14 And he found in the temple those that sold oxen and sheep and doves, and the changers of money sitting: 15 and he made a scourge of cords, and cast all out of the temple, both the sheep and the oxen; and he poured out the changers' money, and overthrew their tables; 16 and to them that sold the doves he said, Take these things hence; make not my Father's house a house of merchandise. 17 His disciples remembered
14 And the blind and the lame came to him in the temple: and he healed them. 15 But when the chief priests and the scribes saw the wonderful things that he did, and the children that were	18 And the chief priests and the scribes heard it, and sought how they might destroy him: for they feared him, for all the multitude was astonished at his teaching.	47 And he was teaching daily in the temple. But the chief priests and the scribes and the principal men of the people sought to destroy him: 48 and they could not find what they might	that it was written, The zeal of thine¹ house shall eat me up. 18 The Jews therefore answered and said unto him, What sign shewest thou unto us, seeing that thou doest these things? 19 Jesus answered and said unto

ERV. mg.: ¹ Many ancient authorities omit *of God*

ARV. txt.: ¹ Zeal for thy

MATT. 21.	MARK 11.	LUKE 19.	[JOHN 2.]
crying in the temple and saying, Hosanna to the son of David; they were moved with indignation, 16 and said unto him, Hearest thou what these are saying? And Jesus saith unto them, Yea: did ye never read, Out of the mouth of babes and sucklings thou hast perfected praise? 17 And he left them, and went forth out of the city to Bethany, and lodged there. (+ § 120)	19 And ¹every evening ²he went forth out of the city.	do; for the people all hung upon him, listening. [Cf. Luke 21:37, p. 195.]	them, Destroy this ³temple, and in three days I will raise it up. 20 The Jews therefore said, Forty and six years was this ³temple in building, and wilt thou raise it up in three days? 21 But he spake of the ³temple of his body. 22 When therefore he was raised from the dead, his disciples remembered that he spake this; and they believed the scripture, and the word which Jesus had said.] (§ 27)

TUESDAY. §§ 122-132.

§ 122. THE FIG TREE WITHERED AWAY.

⌈MATT. 21: 20-22.⌉	MARK 11: 20-25.
⌈20 And when the disciples saw it, they marvelled, saying, How did the fig tree immediately wither away? 21 And Jesus answered and said unto them, ªVerily I say unto you, If ye have faith, and doubt not, ye shall not only do what is done to the fig tree, but even if ye shall say unto this mountain, Be thou taken up and cast into the sea, it shall be done. 22 And all things, whatsoever ye shall ask in prayer, believing, ye shall receive.⌉ (§ 120)	20 And as they passed by in the morning, they saw the fig tree withered away from the roots. 21 And Peter calling to remembrance saith unto him, Rabbi, behold, the fig tree which thou cursedst is withered away. 22 And Jesus answering saith unto them, ªHave faith in God. 23 Verily I say unto you, Whosoever shall say unto this mountain, Be thou taken up and cast into the sea; and shall not doubt in his heart, but shall believe that what

---

ERV. mg.: ¹ Gr. *whenever evening came*   ² Some ancient authorities read *they*   ³ Or, *sanctuary*

ª Matt. 17:20. Because of your little faith: for verily I say unto you, If ye have faith as a grain of mustard seed, ye shall say unto this mountain, Remove hence to yonder place; and it shall remove. (§ 78)

ª Luke 17:6. If ye have faith as a grain of mustard seed, ye would say unto this sycamine tree, Be thou rooted up, and be thou planted in the sea; and it would have obeyed you. (§ 104)

MARK 11.

he saith cometh to pass; he shall have it. 24 Therefore I say unto you, All things whatsoever ye pray and ask for, believe that ye have received[1] them, and ye shall have them. 25 [a]And whensoever ye stand praying, forgive, if ye have aught against any one; that your Father also which[2] is in heaven may forgive you your [1]trespasses.

§ 123. CHRIST'S AUTHORITY CHALLENGED.

MATT. 21 : 23–27.

23 And when he was come into the temple, the chief priests and the elders of the people came unto him as he was teaching, and said, By what authority doest thou these things? and who gave thee this authority? 24 And Jesus answered and said unto them, I also will ask you one [2]question, which if ye tell me, I likewise will tell you by what authority I do these things. 25 The baptism of John, whence was it? from heaven or from men? And they reasoned with themselves, saying, If we shall say, From heaven; he will say unto us, Why then did ye not believe him? 26 But if we shall say, From men; we fear the multitude; for all hold John as a prophet. 27 And

MARK 11 : 27–33.

27 And they come again to Jerusalem: and as he was walking in the temple, there come to him the chief priests, and the scribes, and the elders; 28 and they said unto him, By what authority doest thou these things? or who gave thee this authority to do these things? 29 And Jesus said unto them, I will ask of you one [2]question, and answer me, and I will tell you by what authority I do these things. 30 The baptism of John, was it from heaven, or from men? answer me. 31 And they reasoned with themselves, saying, If we shall say, From heaven; he will say, Why then did ye not believe him? 32 [3]But should we say, From men—they feared the people: [4]for all verily held

LUKE 20 : 1–8.

1 And it came to pass, on one of the days, as he was teaching the people in the temple, and preaching the gospel, there came upon him the chief priests and the scribes with the elders; 2 and they spake, saying unto him, Tell us: By what authority doest thou these things? or who is he that gave thee this authority? 3 And he answered and said unto them, I also will ask you a [2]question; and tell me: 4 The baptism of John, was it from heaven, or from men? 5 And they reasoned with themselves, saying, If we shall say, From heaven; he will say, Why did ye not believe him? 6 But if we shall say, From men; all the people will stone us: for they be[3] persuaded

---

ERV. mg.: [1] Many ancient authorities add ver. 26 *But if ye do not forgive, neither will your Father which is in heaven forgive your trespasses.* [2] Gr. *word.* [3] Or, *But shall we say, From men?* [4] Or, *for all held John to be a prophet indeed.*

ARV. txt.: [1] ye receive [2] who [3] are

[a] Matt. 6: 14, 15. For if ye forgive men their trespasses, your heavenly Father will also forgive you. 15 But if ye forgive not men their trespasses, neither will your Father forgive your trespasses. (§ 49)

[a] Matt. 18: 35. So shall also my heavenly Father do unto you, if ye forgive not every one his brother from your hearts. (§ 81)

MATT. 21.	MARK 11.	LUKE 20.
they answered Jesus and said, We know not. He also said unto them, Neither tell I you by what authority I do these things.	John to be a prophet. 33 And they answered Jesus and say, We know not. And Jesus saith unto them, Neither tell I you by what authority I do these things.	that John was a prophet. 7 And they answered, that they knew not whence *it was*. 8 And Jesus said unto them, Neither tell I you by what authority I do these things.

§ 124.   THREE PARABLES OF WARNING.

MATT. 21 : 28—22 : 14.	MARK 12 : 1-12.	LUKE 20 : 9-19.
28 But what think ye? A man had two sons; and he came to the first, and said, [1]Son, go work to-day in the vineyard. 29 And he answered and said, I will not : but afterward he repented himself, and went. 30 And he came to the second, and said likewise. And he answered and said, I *go*, sir : and went not. 31 Whether[1] of the twain[2] did the will of his father? They say, The first. Jesus saith unto them, Verily I say unto you, that the publicans and the harlots go into the kingdom of God before you. 32 For John came unto you in the way of righteousness, and ye believed him not : but the publicans and the harlots believed him : and ye, when ye saw it, did not even repent yourselves afterward, that ye might believe him.		
33 Hear another parable : There was a man that was a householder, which[3] planted a vineyard, and set a hedge about it, and digged a winepress in it, and built a tower, and let it out to husbandmen, and went into another coun-	1 And he began to speak unto them in parables. A man planted a vineyard, and set a hedge about it, and digged a pit for the winepress, and built a tower, and let it out to husbandmen, and went into another country. 2 And at	9 And he began to speak unto the people this parable : A man planted a vineyard, and let it out to husbandmen, and went into another country for a long time. 10 And at the season he sent unto the husbandmen a [2]servant, that

ERV. mg. : [1] Gr. *Child*.   [2] Gr. *bondservant*.

ARV. txt. : [1] Which   [2] two   [3] who

MATT. 21.

try. 34 And when the season of the fruits drew near, he sent his [1] servants to the husbandmen, to receive [2] his fruits. 35 And the husbandmen took his [1] servants, and beat one, and killed another, and stoned another. 36 Again, he sent other [1] servants more than the first: and they did unto them in like manner. 37 But afterward he sent unto them his son, saying, They will reverence my son. 38 But the husbandmen, when they saw the son, said among themselves, This is the heir; come, let us kill him, and take his inheritance. 39 And they took him, and cast him forth out of the vineyard, and killed him. 40 When therefore the lord of the vineyard shall come, what will he do unto those husbandmen? 41 They say unto him, He will miserably destroy those miserable men, and will let out the vineyard unto other husbandmen, which [1] shall render him the fruits in their seasons. 42 Jesus saith unto them, Did ye never read in the scriptures,

The stone which the builders rejected,
The same was made the head of the corner:
This was from the Lord,
And it is marvellous in our eyes?

43 Therefore say I unto you, The kingdom of God shall be taken away from you, and shall be given to a nation bringing

MARK 12.

the season he sent to the husbandmen a [3] servant, that he might receive from the husbandmen of the fruits of the vineyard. 3 And they took him, and beat him, and sent him away empty. 4 And again he sent unto them another [3] servant; and him they wounded in the head, and handled shamefully. 5 And he sent another; and him they killed: and many others; beating some, and killing some. 6 He had yet one, a beloved son: he sent him last unto them, saying, They will reverence my son. 7 But those husbandmen said among themselves, This is the heir; come, let us kill him, and the inheritance shall be ours. 8 And they took him, and killed him, and cast him forth out of the vineyard. 9 What therefore will the lord of the vineyard do? he will come and destroy the husbandmen, and will give the vineyard unto others. 10 Have ye not read even this scripture;

The stone which the builders rejected,
The same was made the head of the corner:

11 This was from the Lord,
And it is marvellous in our eyes?

LUKE 20.

they should give him of the fruit of the vineyard: but the husbandmen beat him, and sent him away empty. 11 And he sent yet another [3] servant: and him also they beat, and handled him shamefully, and sent him away empty. 12 And he sent yet a third: and him also they wounded, and cast him forth. 13 And the lord of the vineyard said, What shall I do? I will send my beloved son: it may be they will reverence him. 14 But when the husbandmen saw him, they reasoned one with another, saying, This is the heir: let us kill him, that the inheritance may be ours. 15 And they cast him forth out of the vineyard, and killed him. What therefore will the lord of the vineyard do unto them? 16 He will come and destroy these husbandmen, and will give the vineyard unto others. And when they heard it, they said, [4] God forbid. 17 But he looked upon them, and said, What then is this that is written,

The stone which the builders rejected,
The same was made the head of the corner?

18 Every one that falleth on that stone shall be broken to pieces; but on whomsoever it shall fall, it will scatter him as dust.

ERV. mg.:   [1] Gr. *bondservants*.   [2] Or, *the fruits of it*   [3] Gr. *bondservant*   [4] Gr. *Be it not so.*

ARV. txt.:   [1] who

MATT. 21.	MARK 12.	LUKE 20.
forth the fruits thereof. 44 [1]And he that falleth on this stone shall be broken to pieces: but on whomsoever it shall fall, it will scatter him as dust. 45 And when the chief priests and the Pharisees heard his parables, they perceived that he spake of them.		
46 And when they sought to lay hold on him, they feared the multitudes, because they took him for a prophet.	12 And they sought to lay hold on him; and they feared the multitude; for they perceived that he spake the parable against them: and they left him, and went away.	19 And the scribes and the chief priests sought to lay hands on him in that very hour; and they feared the people: for they perceived that he spake this parable against them.
22:1 [a]And Jesus answered and spake again in parables unto them, saying, 2 The kingdom of heaven is likened unto a certain king, which[1] made a marriage feast for his son, 3 and sent forth his [2]servants to call them that were bidden to the marriage feast: and they would not come. 4 Again he sent forth other [2]servants, saying, Tell them that are bidden, Behold, I have made ready my dinner: my oxen and my fatlings are killed, and all things are ready: come to the marriage feast. 5 But they made light of it, and went their ways, one to his own farm, another to his merchandise: 6 and the rest laid hold on his [2]servants, and entreated[2] them shamefully, and killed them. 7 But the king was wroth; and he sent his armies, and destroyed those murderers, and burned		[a]Luke 14:15-24. And when one of them that sat at meat with him heard these things, he said unto him, Blessed is he that shall eat bread in the kingdom of God. 16 But he said unto him, A certain man made a great supper; and he bade many: 17 and he sent forth his servant at supper time to say to them that were bidden, Come; for *all* things are now ready. 18 And they all with one *consent* began to make excuse. The first said unto him, I have bought a field, and I must needs go out and see it: I pray thee have me excused. 19 And another said, I have bought five yoke of oxen, and I go to prove them: I pray thee have me excused. 20 And another said, I have married a wife, and therefore I cannot come. 21 And the [3]servant came, and told his lord these things. Then the master of the house being angry said to his [3]servant, Go out quickly

ERV. mg.: [1] Some ancient authorities omit ver. 44. [2] Gr. *bondservants*. [3]Gr. *bondservant*.

ARV. txt.: [1] who [2] treated

[a]Luke 14:15-24. (§ 100) See above.

MATT. 22.

their city. 8 Then saith he to his [1]servants, The wedding is ready, but they that were bidden were not worthy. 9 Go ye therefore unto the partings of the highways, and as many as ye shall find, bid to the marriage feast. 10 And those [1]servants went out into the highways, and gathered together all as many as they found, both bad and good : and the wedding was filled with guests. 11 But when the king came in to behold the guests, he saw there a man which[1] had not on a wedding-garment : 12 and he saith unto him, Friend, how camest thou in hither not having a wedding-garment? And he was speechless. 13 Then the king said to the [2]servants, Bind him hand and foot, [a]and cast him out into the outer darkness ; there shall be the weeping and gnashing[2] of teeth. 14 For many are called, but few chosen.

[LUKE 14.]

into the streets and lanes of the city, and bring in hither the poor and maimed and blind and lame. 22 And the [3]servant said, Lord, what thou didst command is done, and yet there is room. 23 And the lord said unto the [3]servant, Go out into the highways and hedges, and constrain *them* to come in, that my house may be filled. 24 For I say unto you, that none of those men which[3] were bidden shall taste of my supper.] (§ 100)

§ 125. THREE QUESTIONS BY THE JEWISH RULERS.

MATT. 22 : 15–40.	MARK 12 : 13–34.	LUKE 20 : 20–40.
15 Then went the Pharisees, and took counsel how	13 And they send unto him certain of the Pharisees and	20 And they watched him, and sent forth spies, which[1]

ERV. mg.:   [1] Gr. *bondservants*.   [2] Or, *ministers*   [3] Gr. *bondservant*.

ARV. txt.:   [1] who   [2] the gnashing   [3] that

[a] Matt. 8 : 12. But the sons of the kingdom shall be cast forth into the outer darkness: there shall be the weeping and gnashing of teeth. (§ 50)

[a] Matt. 13 : 42. And shall cast them into the furnace of fire: there shall be the weeping and gnashing of teeth. (§ 57)

[a] Matt. 13 : 50. And shall cast them into the furnace of fire: there shall be the weeping and gnashing of teeth. (§ 57)

[a] Matt. 24 : 51. And shall cut him asunder, and appoint his portion with the hypocrites: there shall be the weeping and gnashing of teeth. (§ 131)

[a] Matt. 25 : 30. And cast ye out the unprofitable servant into the outer darkness: there shall be the weeping and gnashing of teeth. (§ 131)

[a] Luke 13 : 28. There shall be the weeping and gnashing of teeth, when ye shall see Abraham, and Isaac, and Jacob, and all the prophets, in the kingdom of God, and yourselves cast forth without. (§ 98)

MATT. 22.

they might ensnare·him in *his* talk. 16 And they send to him their disciples, with the Herodians, saying, [1]Master[1], we know that thou art true, and teachest the way of God in truth, and carest not for any one : for thou regardest not the person of men. 17 Tell us therefore, What think-est thou? Is it lawful to give tribute unto Cæsar, or not? 18 But Jesus perceived their wickedness, and said, Why tempt ye[2] me, ye hypocrites? 19 Shew me the tribute money. And they brought unto him a [2]penny[3]. 20 And he saith unto them, Whose is this image and superscrip-tion? 21 They say unto him, Cæsar's. Then saith he unto them, Render therefore unto Cæsar the things that are Cæsar's; and unto God the things that are God's. 22 And when they heard it, they marvelled, and left him, and went their way[4].

23 On that day there came to him Sadducees, [3]which[5] say that there is no resurrec-tion : and they asked him, 24 saying, [1]Master[1], Moses said, If a man die, having no children, his brother [4]shall marry his wife, and raise up seed unto his brother. 25 Now there were with us seven brethren : and the first mar-ried and deceased, and having no seed left his wife unto his brother ; 26 in like manner the second also, and the third,

MARK 12.

of the Herodians, that they might catch him in talk. 14 And when they were come, they say unto him, [1]Master[1], we know that thou art true, and carest not for any one : for thou regardest not the person of men, but of a truth teachest the way of God : Is it lawful to give tribute unto Cæsar, or not? 15 Shall we give, or shall we not give? But he, knowing their hypoc-risy, said unto them, Why tempt ye[2] me? bring me a [2]penny[3], that I may see it. 16 And they brought it. And he saith unto them, Whose is this image and superscrip-tion? And they said unto him, Cæsar's. 17 And Jesus said unto them, Render unto Cæsar the things that are Cæsar's, and unto God the things that are God's. And they marvelled greatly at him.

18 And there come unto him Sadducees, which[6] say that there is no resurrection ; and they asked him, saying, 19 [1]Master[1], Moses wrote unto unto us, If a man's brother die, and leave a wife behind him, and leave no child, that his brother should take his wife, and raise up seed unto his brother. 20 There were seven brethren : and the first took a wife, and dying left no seed ; 21 and the second took her, and died, leaving no seed

LUKE 20.

feigned themselves to be righteous, that they might take hold of his speech, so as to deliver him up to the rule and to the authority of the governor. 21 And they asked him, saying, [1]Master[1], we know that thou sayest and teachest rightly, and accept-est not the person *of any*, but of a truth teachest the way of God : 22 Is it lawful for us to give tribute unto Cæsar, or not? 23 But he perceived their craftiness, and said unto them, 24 Shew me a [2]penny[3]. Whose image and superscrip-tion hath it? And they said, Cæsar's. 25 And he said unto them, Then render unto Cæsar the things that are Cæsar's, and unto God the things that are God's. 26 And they were not able to take hold of the saying before the people : and they marvelled at his answer, and held their peace.

27 And there came to him certain of the Sadducees, they which[5] say that there is no resurrection ; and they asked him, 28 saying, [1]Master[1], Moses wrote unto us, that if a man's brother die, having a wife, and he be childless, his brother should take the wife, and raise up seed unto his brother. 29 There were there-fore seven brethren : and the first took a wife, and died childless ; 30 and the second ; 31 and the third took her ;

ERV. mg.: [1] Or, *Teacher* [2] See marginal note on Matt. xviii. 28. [3] Gr. *saying.* [4] Gr. *shall perform the duty of a husband's brother to his wife.* Compare Deut. xxv. 5.

ARV. txt.: [1] Teacher [2] make ye trial of [3] denarius [4] went away [5] they that [6] who

MATT. 22.

into the [1]seventh. 27 And after them all the woman died. 28 In the resurrection therefore whose wife shall she be of the seven? for they all had her. 29 But Jesus answered and said unto them, Ye do err, not knowing the scriptures, nor the power of God. 30 For in the resurrection they neither marry, nor are given in marriage, but are as [2]angels in heaven. 31 But as touching the resurrection of the dead, have ye not read that which was spoken unto you by God, saying, 32 I am the God of Abraham, and the God of Isaac, and the God of Jacob? God is not *the God* of the dead, but of the living. 33 And when the multitudes heard it, they were astonished at his teaching.

34 But the Pharisees, when they heard that he had put the Sadducees to silence, gathered themselves together. 35 And one of them, a lawyer, asked him a question, tempting[1] him, 36 [3]Master[2], which is the great commandment in the law? 37 And he said unto him, Thou shalt love the Lord thy God with all thy heart, and with all thy soul, and with all thy mind. 38 This is the great and first commandment. 39 [4]And a

MARK 12.

behind him; and the third likewise: 22 and the seven left no seed. Last of all the woman also died. 23 In the resurrection whose wife shall she be of them? for the seven had her to wife. 24 Jesus said unto them, Is it not for this cause that ye err, that ye know not the scriptures, nor the power of God? 25 For when they shall rise from the dead, they neither marry, nor are given in marriage; but are as angels in heaven. 26 But as touching the dead, that they are raised; have ye not read in the book of Moses, in *the place concerning* the Bush, how God spake unto him, saying, I *am* the God of Abraham, and the God of Isaac, and the God of Jacob? 27 He is not the God of the dead, but of the living: ye do greatly err.

28 And one of the scribes came, and heard them questioning together, and knowing that he had answered them well, asked him, What commandment is the first of all? 29 Jesus answered, The first is, Hear, O Israel; [5]The Lord our God, the Lord is one: 30 and thou shalt love the Lord thy God [6]with all thy heart, and [6]with all thy soul, and [6]with all thy mind, and [6]with all thy strength. 31 The second is this, Thou shalt

LUKE 20.

and likewise the seven also left no children, and died. 32 Afterward the woman also died. 33 In the resurrection therefore whose wife of them shall she be? for the seven had her to wife. 34 And Jesus said unto them, The sons of this [7]world marry, and are given in marriage: 35 but they that are accounted worthy to attain to that [7]world, and the resurrection from the dead, neither marry, nor are given in marriage: 36 for neither can they die any more: for they are equal unto the angels; and are sons of God, being sons of the resurrection. 37 But that the dead are raised, even Moses shewed, in *the place concerning* the Bush, when he calleth the Lord the God of Abraham, and the God of Isaac, and the God of Jacob. 38 Now he is not the God of the dead, but of the living: for all live unto him. 39 And certain of the scribes answering said, [3]Master[2], thou hast well said. 40 For they durst not any more ask him any question.

ERV. mg.:   [1] Gr. *seven*.   [2] Many ancient authorities add [after *angels*] *of God.*   [3] Or, *Teacher*   [4] Or, *And a second is like unto it, Thou shalt love &c.*   [5] Or, *The Lord is our God; the Lord is one*   [6] Gr. *from*   [7] Or, *age*

ARV. txt.:   [1] trying   [2] Teacher

MATT. 22.	MARK 12.
second like *unto it* is this, Thou shalt love thy neighbour as thyself. 40 [a]On these two commandments hangeth the whole law[1], and the prophets. [Cf. vs. 45, § 126]	love thy neighbour as thyself. There is none other commandment greater than these. 32 And the scribe said unto him, Of a truth, [1]Master[2], thou hast well said that he is one ; and there is none other but he : 33 and to love him with all the heart, and with all the understanding, and with all the strength, and to love his neighbour as himself, is much more than all whole burnt offerings and sacrifices. 34 And when Jesus saw that he answered discreetly, he said unto him, Thou art not far from the kingdom of God. And no man after that durst ask him any question.

§ 126. CHRIST'S UNANSWERABLE QUESTION.

MATT. 22:41–46.	MARK 12:35–37.	LUKE 20:41–44.
41 Now while the Pharisees were gathered together, Jesus asked them a question, 42 saying, What think ye of the Christ? whose son is he? They say unto him, *The son* of David. 43 He saith unto them, How then doth David in the Spirit call him Lord, saying, 44 The Lord said unto my Lord, Sit thou on my right hand, Till I put thine enemies underneath thy feet? 45 If David then calleth him Lord, how is he his son? 46 And no one was able to answer him a word, neither durst any man from that day forth ask him any more questions.	35 And Jesus answered and said, as he taught in the temple, How say the scribes that the Christ is the son of David? 36 David himself said in the Holy Spirit, The Lord said unto my Lord, Sit thou on my right hand, Till I make thine enemies [2] the footstool of thy feet. 37 David himself calleth him Lord ; and whence is he his son? And [3]the common people heard him gladly. [Cf. vs. 34, § 125.]	41 And he said unto them, How say they that the Christ is David's son? 42 For David himself saith in the book of Psalms, The Lord said unto my Lord, Sit thou on my right hand, 43 Till I make thine enemies the footstool of thy feet. 44 David therefore calleth him Lord, and how is he his son? [Cf. vs. 40, p. 180.]

ERV. mg.: [1] Or, *Teacher* [2] Some ancient authorities read *underneath thy feet*. [3] Or, *the great multitude*

ARV. txt.: [1] the whole law hangeth [2] Teacher

[a] Matt. 7:12. For this is the law and the prophets. (§ 49)

§ 127. WOES AGAINST THE SCRIBES AND PHARISEES.

MATT., CHAP. 23.	MARK 12:38-40.	LUKE 20:45-47.

1 Then spake Jesus to the multitudes and to his disciples, 2 saying, The scribes and the Pharisees sit on Moses' seat: 3 all things therefore whatsoever they bid you, *these* do and observe: but do not ye after their works; for they say, and do not. 4 ᵃYea, they bind heavy burdens ¹and grievous to be borne, and lay them on men's shoulders; but they themselves will not move them with their finger. 5 But all their works they do for¹ to be seen of men: for they make broad their phylacteries, and enlarge the borders *of their garments,* 6 ᵇand love the chief place at feasts, and the chief seats in the synagogues, 7 and the salutations in the marketplaces, and to be called of men, Rabbi. 8 But be not ye called Rabbi: for one is your teacher, and all ye are brethren. 9 And call no man your father on the earth: for one is your Father, ²which³ is in heaven. 10 Neither be ye called masters: for one is your master, *even* the Christ. 11 ᶜBut he that is ³greatest among you shall

38 And in his teaching he said, Beware of the scribes, which⁴ desire to walk in long robes, and *to have* ᵇsalutations in the marketplaces, 39 and chief seats in the synagogues, and chief places at feasts: 40 they which³ devour widows' houses, ⁴and for a pretence make long prayers: these shall receive greater condemnation.

45 And in the hearing of all the people he said unto his disciples, 46 Beware of the scribes, which⁴ desire to walk in long robes, and ᵇlove salutations in the marketplaces, and chief seats in the synagogues, and chief places at feasts; 47 which⁴ devour widows' houses, and for a pretence make long prayers: these shall receive **greater** condemnation.

ERV. mg.: ¹ Many ancient authorities omit *and grievous to be borne.* ² Gr. *the heavenly.* ³ Gr. *greater.* ⁴ Or, *even while for a pretence they make*

ARV. txt.: ¹ *Omit* for ² *even* he who ³ that ⁴ who

ᵃ Luke 11:46. For ye lade men with burdens grievous to be borne, and ye yourselves touch not the burdens with one of your fingers. (§ 94)

ᵇ Luke 11:43. For ye love the chief seats in the synagogues, and the salutations in the marketplaces. (§94)

ᶜ Matt. 20:26, 27. But whosoever would become great among you shall be your minister; 27 and whosoever would be first among you shall be your servant. (§ 114)

ᶜ Mark 9:35. If any man would be first, he shall be last of all, and minister of all. (§ 81)

ᶜ Mark 10:43, 44. But whosoever would become great among you, shall be your minister: 44 and whosoever would be first among you, shall be servant of all. (§ 114)

ᶜ Luke 9:48. For he that is least among you all, the same is great. (§ 81)

ᶜ Luke 22:26. But he that is the greater among you, let him become as the younger; and he that is chief, as he that doth serve. (§ 133)

MATT. **23.**

be your [1]servant. 12 [a]And whosoever shall exalt himself shall be humbled; and whosoever shall humble himself shall be exalted.

13 [b]But woe unto you, scribes and Pharisees, hypocrites! because ye shut the kingdom of heaven [2]against men: for ye enter not in yourselves, neither suffer ye them that are entering in to [3]enter.

15 Woe unto you, scribes and Pharisees, hypocrites! for ye compass sea and land to make one proselyte; and when he is become so, ye make him twofold more a son of [4]hell than yourselves.

16 Woe unto you, ye blind guides, which[1] say, Whosoever shall swear by the [5]temple, it is nothing; but whosoever shall swear by the gold of the [5]temple, he is [6]a debtor. 17 Ye fools and blind: for whether[2] is greater, the gold, or the [5]temple that hath sanctified the gold? 18 And, Whosoever shall swear by the altar, it is nothing; but whosoever shall swear by the gift that is upon it, he is [6]a debtor. 19 Ye blind: for whether[2] is greater, the gift, or the altar that sanctifieth the gift? 20 He therefore that sweareth by the altar, sweareth by it, and by all things thereon. 21 And he that sweareth by the [5]temple, sweareth by it, and by him that dwelleth therein. 22 And he that sweareth by the heaven, sweareth by the throne of God, and by him that sitteth thereon.

23 [c]Woe unto you, scribes and Pharisees, hypocrites! for ye tithe mint and [7]anise and cummin, and have left undone the weightier matters of the law, judgement[3], and mercy, and faith: but these ye ought to have done, and not to have left the other undone. 24 Ye blind guides, which[1] strain out the gnat, and swallow the camel.

25 [d]Woe unto you, scribes and Pharisees, hypocrites! for ye cleanse the outside of the cup and of the platter, but within they are full from extortion and excess. 26 Thou blind Pharisee, cleanse first the inside of the cup and of the platter, that the outside thereof may become clean also.

27 [e]Woe unto you, scribes and Pharisees, hypocrites! for ye are like unto whited sepulchres, which outwardly appear beautiful, but inwardly are full of dead men's bones, and of all uncleanness. 28 Even so ye also outwardly appear righteous unto men, but inwardly ye are full of hypocrisy and iniquity.

29 [f]Woe unto you, scribes and Pharisees, hypocrites! for ye build the sepulchres of the prophets, and garnish the tombs of the righteous, 30 and say, If we had been in the days of our fathers, we should not have been partakers with them in the blood of the prophets.

ERV. mg.: [1] Or, *minister* [2] Gr. *before* [3] Some authorities insert here [after ver. 13], or after ver. 12, ver. 14 *Woe unto you, scribes and Pharisees, hypocrites! for ye devour widows' houses, even while for a pretence ye make long prayers: therefore ye shall receive greater condemnation.* See Mark xii. 40; Luke xx. 47. [4] Gr. *Gehenna.* [5] Or, *sanctuary*: as in ver. 35. [6] Or, *bound* by his oath [7] Or, *dill*

ARV. txt.: [1] that [2] which [3] justice

---

[a] Luke 14:11. For every one that exalteth himself shall be humbled; and he that humbleth himself shall be exalted. (§100)

[a] Luke 18:14. For every one that exalteth himself shall be humbled; but he that humbleth himself shall be exalted. (§109)

[b] Luke 11:52. Woe unto you lawyers! for ye took away the key of knowledge: ye entered not in yourselves, and them that were entering in ye hindered. (§94)

[c] Luke 11:42. But woe unto you Pharisees! for ye tithe mint and rue and every herb, and pass over judgement and the love of God: but these ought ye to have done, and not to leave the other undone. (§94)

[d] Luke 11:39-41. Now do ye Pharisees cleanse the outside of the cup and of the platter; but your inward part is full of extortion and wickedness. 40 Ye foolish ones, did not he that made the outside make the inside also? 41 Howbeit give for alms those things that are within; and behold all things are clean unto you. (§94)

[e] Luke 11:44. Woe unto you! for ye are as the tombs which appear not, and the men that walk over *them* know it not. (§94)

[f] Luke 11 47. Woe unto you! for ye build the tombs of the prophets, and your fathers killed them. (§94)

MATT. 23.

31 [a]Wherefore ye witness to yourselves, that ye are sons of them that slew the prophets. 32 Fill ye up then the measure of your fathers. 33 Ye serpents, ye offspring of vipers, how shall ye escape the judgement of [1]hell? 34 [b]Therefore, behold, I send unto you prophets, and wise men, and scribes: some of them shall ye kill and crucify; and some of them shall ye scourge in your synagogues, and persecute from city to city: 35 that upon you may come all the righteous blood shed on the earth, from the blood of Abel the righteous unto the blood of Zachariah son of Barachiah, whom ye slew between the sanctuary and the altar. 36 Verily I say unto you, All these things shall come upon this generation.

37 [c]O Jerusalem, Jerusalem, which[1] killeth the prophets, and stoneth them that are sent unto her! how often would I have gathered thy children together, even as a hen gathereth her chickens under her wings, and ye would not! 38 Behold, your house is left unto you [2]desolate. 39 For I say unto you, Ye shall not see me henceforth, till ye shall say, Blessed *is* he that cometh in the name of the Lord.

§ 128. THE WIDOW'S TWO MITES.

MARK 12: 41-44.	LUKE 21: 1-4.
41 And he sat down over against the treasury, and beheld how the multitude cast [3]money into the treasury: and many that were rich cast in much. 42 And there came [4]a poor widow, and she cast in two mites, which make a farthing. 43 And he called unto him his disciples, and said unto them, Verily I say unto you, This poor widow cast in more than all they which[1] are casting into the treasury: 44 for they all did cast in of their superfluity; but she of her want did cast in all that she had, *even* all her living.	1 And he looked up, [5]and saw the rich men that were casting their gifts into the treasury. 2 And he saw a certain poor widow casting in thither two mites. 3 And he said, Of a truth I say unto you, This poor widow cast in more than they all: 4 for all these did of their superfluity cast in unto the gifts: but she of her want did cast in all the living that she had.

ERV. mg.: [1] Gr. *Gehenna.* [2] Some ancient authorities omit *desolate.* [3] Gr. *brass.* [4] Gr. *one.* [5] Or, *and saw them that . . . treasury, and they were rich.*

ARV. txt.: [1] that

[a] Luke 11 : 48. So ye are witnesses and consent unto the works of your fathers: for they killed them, and ye build *their tombs.* (§ 94)

[b] Luke 11 : 49-51. Therefore also said the wisdom of God, I will send unto them prophets and apostles; and *some* of them they shall kill and persecute; 50 that the blood of all the prophets, which was shed from the foundation of the world, may be required of this generation; 51 from the blood of Abel unto the blood of Zachariah, who perished between the altar and the sanctuary: yea, I say unto you, it shall be required of this generation. (§ 94)

[c] Luke 13 : 34, 35. O Jerusalem, Jerusalem, which killeth the prophets, and stoneth them that are sent unto her! how often would I have gathered thy children together, even as a hen *gathereth* her own brood under her wings, and ye would not! 35 Behold, your house is left unto you *desolate:* and I say unto you, Ye shall not see me, until ye shall say, Blessed *is* he that cometh in the name of the Lord. (§ 99)

§ 129. GENTILES SEEKING JESUS.

JOHN 12 : 20-36.

20 Now there were certain Greeks among those that went up to worship at the feast. 21 these therefore came to Philip, which[1] was of Bethsaida of Galilee, and asked him, saying, Sir, we would see Jesus. 22 Philip cometh and telleth Andrew : Andrew cometh, and Philip, and they tell Jesus. 23 And Jesus answereth them, saying, The hour is come, that the Son of man should be glorified. 24 Verily, verily, I say unto you, Except a grain of wheat fall into the earth and die, it abideth by itself alone ; but if it die, it beareth much fruit. 25 [a]He that loveth his [1]life loseth it ; and he that hateth his [1]life in this world shall keep it unto life eternal. 26 If any man serve me, let him follow me ; and where I am, there shall also my servant be : if any man serve me, him will the Father honour. 27 [b]Now is my soul troubled ; and what shall I say ? [c]Father, save me from this [2]hour. But for this cause came I unto this hour. 28 Father, glorify thy name. There came therefore a voice out of heaven, *saying*, I have both glorified it, and will glorify it again. 29 The multitude therefore, that stood by, and heard it, said that it had thundered : others said, An angel hath spoken to him. 30 Jesus answered and said, This voice hath not come for my sake, but for your sakes. 31 Now is [3]the judgement of this world : now shall the prince of this world be cast out. 32 And I, if I be lifted up [4]from the earth, will draw all men unto myself. 33 But this he said, signifying by what manner of death he should die. 34 The multitude therefore answered him, We have heard out of the law that the Christ abideth for ever : and how sayest thou, The Son of man must be lifted up ? who is this Son of man ? 35 Jesus therefore said unto them, Yet a little while is the light [5]among you. Walk while ye have the light, that darkness overtake you not : and he that walketh in the darkness knoweth not whither he goeth. 36 While ye have the light, believe on the light, that ye may become sons of light.

These things spake Jesus, and he departed and [6]hid himself from them.

ERV. mg.:   [1] Or, *soul*   [2] Or, *hour?*   [3] Or, *a judgement*   [4] Or, *out of*   [5] Or, *in*   [6] Or, *was hidden from them*

ARV. txt.:   [1] who

[a] Matt. 10 : 39. He that findeth his life shall lose it ; and he that loseth his life for my sake shall find it. (§ 64)

[a] Matt. 16 : 25. For whosoever would save his life shall lose it ; and whosoever shall lose his life for my sake shall save it. (§ 73)

[a] Mark 8 : 35. For whosoever would save his life shall lose it ; and whosoever shall lose his life for my sake and the gospel's shall save it. (§ 76)

[a] Luke 9 : 24. For whosoever would save his life shall lose it ; but whosoever shall lose his life for my sake, the same shall save it. (§ 76)

[a] Luke 17 : 33. Whosoever shall seek to gain his life shall lose it ; but whosoever shall lose *his life* shall preserve it. (§ 108)

[b] Matt. 26 : 38. My soul is exceeding sorrowful, even unto death. (§ 136)

[b] Mark 14 : 34. My soul is exceeding sorrowful, even unto death. (§ 136)

[c] Matt. 26 : 39. O my Father, if it be possible, let this cup pass away from me : nevertheless, not as I will but as thou wilt. (§ 136)

[c] Mark 14 : 36. Abba, Father, all things are possible unto thee ; remove this cup from me : howbeit not what I will, but what thou wilt. (§ 136)

[c] Luke 22 : 42. Father, if thou be willing, remove this cup from me : nevertheless not my will, but thine, be done. (§ 136)

§ 130. THE JEWS' REJECTION OF CHRIST.

JOHN 12: 37-50.

37 But though he had done so many signs before them, yet they believed not on him:
38 that the word of Isaiah the prophet might be fulfilled, which he spake,

> Lord, who hath believed our report?
> And to whom hath the arm of the Lord been revealed?

39 For this cause they could not believe, for that Isaiah said again,

> 40 He hath blinded their eyes, and he hardened their heart;
> Lest they should see with their eyes, and perceive with their heart,
> And should turn,
> And I should heal them.

41 These things said Isaiah, because he saw his glory; and he spake of him. 42 Nevertheless even of the rulers many believed on him; but because of the Pharisees they did not confess ¹it, lest they should be put out of the synagogue: 43 for they loved the glory of¹ men more than the glory of¹ God.

44 And Jesus cried and said, He that believeth on me, believeth not on me, but on him that sent me. 45 And he that beholdeth me beholdeth him that sent me. 46 I am come a light into the world, that whosoever believeth on me may not abide in the darkness. 47 And if any man hear my sayings, and keep them not, I judge him not: for I came not to judge the world, but to save the world. 48 He that rejecteth me, and receiveth not my sayings, hath one that judgeth him: the word that I spake, the same shall judge him in the last day. 49 For I spake not from myself; but the Father which² sent me, he hath given me a commandment, what I should say, and what I should speak. 50 And I know that his commandment is life eternal: the things therefore which I speak, even as the Father hath said unto me, so I speak.

§ 131. DISCOURSE CONCERNING THE DESTRUCTION OF JERUSALEM AND THE END OF THE WORLD.

MATT., CHAPS. 24, 25, ⌈26: 1, 2.⌉	MARK, CHAP. 13.	LUKE 21: 5-38.
1 And Jesus went out from the temple, and was going on his way; and his disciples came to him to shew him the buildings of the temple. 2 But he answered and said unto them, See ye not all these things? verily I say unto you, There shall not be left here one stone upon another, that shall not be thrown down.	1 And as he went forth out of the temple, one of his disciples saith unto him, ²Master³, behold, what manner of stones and what manner of buildings! 2 And Jesus said unto him, Seest thou these great buildings? there shall not be left here one stone upon another, which shall not be thrown down.	5 And as some spake of the temple, how it was adorned with goodly stones and offerings, he said, 6 As for these things which ye behold, the days will come, in which there shall not be left here one stone upon another, that shall not be thrown down.
3 And as he sat on the mount of Olives, the disciples	3 And as he sat on the mount of Olives over against	[Paragraph continued on p. 187.]

ERV. mg.: ¹ Or, him ² Or, *Teacher*

ARV. txt.: ¹ *that is* of ² that ³ Teacher

186

MATT. 24.

came unto him privately, saying, Tell us, when shall these things be? and what *shall be* the sign of thy [1]coming, and of [2]the end of the world? 4 And Jesus answered and said unto them, Take heed that no man lead you astray. 5 For many shall come in my name, saying, I am the Christ; and shall lead many astray. 6 And ye shall hear of wars and rumours of wars : see that ye be not troubled : for *these things* must needs come to pass; but the end is not yet. 7 For nation shall rise against nation, and kingdom against kingdom : and there shall be famines and earthquakes in divers places. 8 But all these things are the beginning of travail. 9 [a]Then shall they deliver you up unto tribulation, and shall kill you : [b]and ye shall be hated of all the nations for my name's sake. 10 And then shall many stumble, and shall deliver up one another, and shall hate one another. 11 And many false prophets shall arise, and shall lead many astray. 12 And because iniquity shall be multiplied, the love of the many shall wax cold.

MARK 13.

the temple, Peter and James and John and Andrew asked him privately, 4 Tell us, when shall these things be? and what *shall be* the sign when these things are all about to be accomplished? 5 And Jesus began to say unto them, Take heed that no man lead you astray. 6 Many shall come in my name, saying, I am *he*; and shall lead many astray. 7 And when ye shall hear of wars and rumours of wars, be not troubled : *these things* must needs come to pass; but the end is not yet. 8 For nation shall rise against nation, and kingdom against kingdom : there shall be earthquakes in divers places; there shall be famines : these things are the beginning of travail. 9 [a]But take ye heed to yourselves : for they shall deliver you up to councils; and in synagogues shall ye be beaten; and before governors and kings shall ye stand for my sake, for a testimony unto them. 10 And the gospel must first be preached unto all the nations. 11 [c]And when they lead you *to judgement*, and deliver you up, be not anxious beforehand what

LUKE 21.

7 And they asked him, saying, [3]Master[1], when therefore shall these things be? and what *shall be* the sign when these things are about to come to pass? 8 And he said, Take heed that ye be not led astray : for many shall come in my name, saying, I am *he*; and, The time is at hand : go ye not after them. 9 And when ye shall hear of wars and tumults, be not terrified : for these things must needs come to pass first; but the end is not immediately.

10 Then said he unto them, Nation shall rise against nation, and kingdom against kingdom : 11 and there shall be great earthquakes, and in divers places famines and pestilences; and there shall be terrors and great signs from heaven. 12 [a]But before all these things, they shall lay their hands on you, and shall persecute you, delivering you up to the synagogues and prisons, [4]bringing you before kings and governors for my name's sake. 13 It shall turn[2] unto you for a testimony. 14 [c]Settle it therefore in your hearts, not to meditate beforehand how to an-

---

ERV. mg.: [1]Gr. *presence.* [2]Or, *the consummation of the age* [3]Or, *Teacher.* [4]Gr. *you being brought.*

ARV. txt.: [1]Teacher [2]turn out

[a]Matt. 10:17, 18. But beware of men: for they will deliver you up to councils, and in their synagogues they will scourge you; 18 yea and before governors and kings shall ye be brought for my sake, for a testimony to them and to the Gentiles. (§ 64)

[b]See note [c] on page 188.

[c]Matt. 10:19, 20. But when they deliver you up, be not anxious how or what ye shall speak: for it shall be given you in that hour what ye shall speak. 20 For it is not ye that speak, but the Spirit of your Father that speaketh in you. (§ 64)

[c]Luke 12:11, 12. And when they bring you before the synagogues, and the rulers, and the authorities, be not anxious how or what ye shall answer, or what ye shall say: 12 for the Holy Spirit shall teach you in that very hour what ye ought to say. (§ 95)

MATT. 24.	MARK 13.	LUKE 21.

13 [a]But he that endureth to the end, the same shall be saved. 14 And [1]this gospel of the kingdom shall be preached in the whole [2]world for a testimony unto all the nations; and then shall the end come.

15 When therefore ye see the abomination of desolation, which was spoken of [3]by[1] Daniel the prophet, standing in [4]the holy place (let him that readeth understand), 16 then let them that are in Judæa flee unto the mountains: 17 [e]let him that is on the housetop not go down to take out the things that are in his house: 18 and let him that is in the field not return back to take his cloke. 19 But woe unto them that are with child and to them that give suck in those days! 20 And pray ye that your flight be not in the winter, neither on a sabbath: 21 for then shall be great tribulation, such as hath not been from the be-

ye shall speak: but whatsoever shall be given you in that hour, that speak ye: for it is not ye that speak, but the Holy Ghost[2]. 12 [b]And brother shall deliver up brother to death, and the father his child; and children shall rise up against parents, and [5]cause them to be put to death. 13 [c]And ye shall be hated of all men for my name's sake: [a]but he that endureth to the end, the same shall be saved.

14 But when ye see the abomination of desolation standing where he ought not (let him that readeth understand), then let them that are in Judæa flee unto the mountains: 15 [e]and let him that is on the housetop not go down, nor enter in, to take anything out of his house: 16 and let him that is in the field not return back to take his cloke. 17 But woe unto them that are with child and to them that give suck in those days! 18 And pray ye that it be not in the winter. 19 For those days shall be tribulation, such as there hath not been the like from the beginning of the creation which God created until now, and never shall be.

swer: 15 for I will give you a mouth and wisdom, which all your adversaries shall not be able to withstand or to gainsay. 16 [b]But ye shall be delivered up even by parents, and brethren, and kinsfolk, and friends; and *some* of you [6]shall they cause to be put to death. 17 [c]And ye shall be hated of all men for my name's sake. 18 [d]And not a hair of your head shall perish. 19 [a]In your patience ye shall win your [7]souls.

20 But when ye see Jerusalem compassed with armies, then know that her desolation is at hand. 21 Then let them that are in Judæa flee unto the mountains; and let them that are in the midst of her depart out; and let not them that are in the country enter therein. 22 For these are days of vengeance, that all things which are written may be fulfilled. 23 Woe unto them that are with child and to them that give suck in those days! for there shall be great distress upon the [8]land, and wrath unto this people. 24 And they shall fall by the edge of the sword, and shall be led captive into all the nations: and Jerusalem shall be trodden down

---

ERV. mg.: [1] Or, *these good tidings*　[2] Gr. *inhabited earth.*　[3] Or, *through*　[4] Or, *a holy place*　[5] Or, *put them to death*　[6] Or, *shall they put to death*　[7] Or, *lives*　[8] Or, *earth*

ARV. txt.: [1] through　[2] Holy Spirit

[c]Matt. 10:22b.　But he that endureth to the end, the same shall be saved.　(§ 64)

[b]Matt. 10:21.　And brother shall deliver up brother to death, and the father his child: and children shall rise up against parents, and cause them to be put to death.　(§64)

[b]John 16:2.　They shall put you out of the synagogues: yea, the hour cometh, that whosoever killeth you shall think that he offereth service unto God.　(§134)

[c]Matt. 10:22a.　And ye shall be hated of all men for my name's sake.　(§ 64)　Cf. John 15:21 (§134)

[d]Matt. 10:30.　But the very hairs of your head are all numbered.　(§ 64) = [d]Luke 12:7 (§ 95)

[e]Luke 17:31.　In that day, he which shall be on the housetop, and his goods in the house, let him not go down to take them away: and let him that is in the field likewise not return back.　(§108)

MATT. 24.	MARK 13.	LUKE 21.
ginning of the world until now, no, nor ever shall be. 22 And except those days had been shortened, no flesh would have been saved : but for the elect's sake those days shall be shortened. 23 ªThen if any man shall say unto you, Lo, here is the Christ, or, Here; believe ¹*it* not. 24 For there shall arise false Christs, and false prophets, and shall shew great signs and wonders; so as to lead astray, if possible, even the elect. 25 Behold, I have told you beforehand. 26 ªIf therefore they shall say unto you, Behold, he is in the wilderness; go not forth : Behold, he is in the inner chambers; believe ²*it* not. 27 ᵇFor as the lightning cometh forth from the east, and is seen even unto the west; so shall be the ³coming of the Son of man. 28 ᶜWheresoever the carcase is, there will the ⁴eagles be gathered together.	20 And except the Lord had shortened the days, no flesh would have been saved : but for the elect's sake, whom he chose, he shortened the days. 21 ªAnd then if any man shall say unto you, Lo, here is the Christ; or, Lo, there; believe ¹*it* not : 22 for there shall arise false Christs and false prophets, and shall shew signs and wonders, that they may lead astray, if possible, the elect. 23 But take ye heed : behold, I have told you all things beforehand.	of the Gentiles, until the times of the Gentiles be fulfilled.
29 But immediately, after the tribulation of those days, the sun shall be darkened, and the moon shall not give her light, and the stars shall fall from heaven, and the powers of the heavens shall be shaken: 30 and then shall appear the sign of the Son of man in heaven : and then shall all the tribes of the earth mourn, and they shall see the Son of man coming on the clouds of	24 But in those days, after that tribulation, the sun shall be darkened, and the moon shall not give her light, 25 and the stars shall be falling from heaven, and the powers that are in the heavens shall be shaken. 26 And then shall they see the Son of man coming in clouds with great power and glory. 27 And then shall he send forth the angels, and shall gather together his elect	25 And there shall be signs in sun and moon and stars; and upon the earth distress of nations, in perplexity for the roaring of the sea and the billows; 26 men ⁵fainting for fear, and for expectation of the things which are coming on ⁶the world : for the powers of the heavens shall be shaken. 27 And then shall they see the Son of man coming in a cloud with power and

ERV. mg.: ¹ Or, him   ² Or, them   ³ Gr. *presence.*   ⁴ Or, *vultures*   ⁵ Or, *expiring*   ⁶ Gr. *the inhabited earth.*

ᵃ Luke 17:23.   And they shall say to you, Lo, there! Lo, here! go not away, nor follow after *them.*   (§ 108)
ᵇ Luke 17:24.   For as the lightning, when it lighteneth out of the one part under the heaven, shineth unto the other part under heaven; so shall the Son of man be in his day.   (§ 108)
ᶜ Luke 17:37.   Where the body *is,* thither will the eagles also be gathered together.   (§ 108)

MATT. 24.	MARK 13.	LUKE 21.
heaven with power and great glory. 31 And he shall send forth his angels ¹with ²a great sound of a trumpet, and they shall gather together his elect from the four winds, from one end of heaven to the other.	from the four winds, from the uttermost part of the earth to the uttermost part of heaven.	great glory. 28 But when these things begin to come to pass, look up, and lift up your heads; because your redemption draweth nigh.
32 Now from the fig tree learn her parable : when her branch is now become tender, and putteth forth its leaves, ye know that the summer is nigh; 33 even so ye also, when ye see all these things, know ye that ³he is nigh, *even* at the doors. 34 Verily I say unto you, This generation shall not pass away, till all these things be accomplished. 35 Heaven and earth shall pass away, but my words shall not pass away. 36 But of that day and hour knoweth no one, not even the angels of heaven, ⁴neither the Son, but the Father only. 37 ªAnd as *were* the days of Noah, so shall be the ⁵coming of the Son of man. 38 For as in those days which were before the flood they were eating and drinking, marrying and giving in marriage, until the day that Noah entered into the ark, 39 and they knew not until the flood came, and took them all away ; so shall be the ⁵coming of the Son of man. 40 ᵇThen shall two men be in the field ; one is	28 Now from the fig tree learn her parable : when her branch is now become tender, and putteth forth its leaves, ye know that the summer is nigh; 29 even so ye also, when ye see these things coming to pass, know ye that ³he is nigh, *even* at the doors. 30 Verily I say unto you, This generation shall not pass away, until all these things be accomplished. 31 Heaven and earth shall pass away: but my words shall not pass away. 32 But of that day or that hour knoweth no one, not even the angels in heaven, neither the Son, but the Father. [Paragraph continued on p. 191.]	29 And he spake to them a parable : Behold the fig tree, and all the trees: 30 when they now shoot forth, ye see it and know of your own selves that the summer is now nigh. 31 Even so ye also, when ye see these things coming to pass, know ye that the kingdom of God is nigh. 32 Verily I say unto you, This generation shall not pass away, till all things be accomplished. 33 Heaven and earth shall pass away: but my words shall not pass away.

ERV. mg.: ¹ Many ancient authorities read *with a great trumpet, and they shall gather, &c.* ² Or, *a trumpet of great sound* ³ Or, *it* ⁴ Many authorities, some ancient, omit *neither the Son.* ⁵ Gr. *presence.*

ª Luke 17 : 26, 27. And as it came to pass in the days of Noah, even so shall it be also in the days of the Son of man. 27 They ate, they drank, they married, they were given in marriage, until the day that Noah entered into the ark, and the flood came, and destroyed them all. (§ 108)

ᵇ Luke 17 : 34, 35. In that night there shall be two men on one bed ; the one shall be taken, and the other shall be left. 35 There shall be two women grinding together ; the one shall be taken, and the other shall be left. (§ 108)

MATT. 24.	MARK 13.	LUKE 21.
taken, and one is left: 41 two women *shall be* grinding at the mill; one is taken, and one is left. 42 ª Watch therefore: for ye know not on what day your Lord cometh. 43 ᵇ¹ But know this, that if the master of the house had known in what watch the thief was coming, he would have watched, and would not have suffered his house to be ² broken through. 44 Therefore be ye also ready: for in an hour that ye think not the Son of man cometh.	33 ª Take ye heed, watch ⁴ and pray: for ye know not when the time is. 34 *It is* as *when* a man, sojourning in another country, having left his house, and given authority to his ⁵ servants, to each one his work, commanded also the porter to watch. 35 ª Watch therefore: for ye know not when the lord of the house cometh, whether at even, or at midnight, or at cock-crowing, or in the morning; 36 lest coming suddenly he find you sleeping. 37 And what I say unto you I say unto all, Watch.	34 But take heed to yourselves, lest haply your hearts be overcharged with surfeiting, and drunkenness, and cares of this life, and that day come on you suddenly 35 as a snare: for *so* shall it come upon all them that dwell on the face of all the earth. 36 ª But watch ye at every season, making supplication, that ye may prevail to escape all these things that shall come to pass, and to stand before the Son of man.
45 ᶜ Who then is the faithful and wise ² servant, whom his lord hath set over his household, to give them their food in due season? 46 Blessed is that ³ servant, whom his lord when he cometh shall find so doing. 47 Verily I say unto you, that he will set him over all that he hath. 48 But if that evil ³ servant shall say in his heart, My lord tarrieth; 49 and shall begin to beat his fellow-servants, and shall eat and drink with the drunken; 50 the lord of that ³ servant shall come in a day when he expecteth not, and in an		[Luke 12:42–46. And the Lord said, Who then is ⁶ the faithful and wise steward, whom his lord shall set over his household, to give them their portion of food in due season? 43 Blessed is that ³ servant, whom his lord when he cometh shall find so doing. 44 Of a truth I say unto you, that he will set him over all that he hath. 45 But if that ³ servant shall say in his heart, My lord delayeth his coming; and shall begin to beat the menservants and the maidservants, and to eat and drink, and to be drunken; 46 the lord of that ³ servant shall come in a day when he expecteth not, and in an hour when he knoweth not,

ERV. mg.: ¹ Or, *But this ye know* ² Gr. *digged through.* ³ Gr. *bondservant.* ⁴ Some ancient authorities omit *and pray.* ⁵ Gr. *bondservants.* ⁶ Or, *the faithful steward, the wise man whom &c.*

ª Cf. Matt. 25:13 (p. 193).

ᵇ Luke 12:39, 40. But know this, that if the master of the house had known in what hour the thief was coming, he would have watched, and not have left his house to be broken through. 40 Be ye also ready: for in an hour that ye think not the Son of man cometh. (§95)

ᶜ Luke 12:42–46. (§95) See above.

MATT. 24.

hour when he knoweth not, 51 [a] and shall [1] cut him asunder, and appoint his portion with the hypocrites: there shall be the weeping and gnashing[1] of teeth.

25:1 Then shall the kingdom of heaven be likened unto ten virgins, which[2] took their [2] lamps, and went forth to meet the bridegroom. 2 And five of them were foolish, and five were wise. 3 For the foolish, when they took their [2] lamps, took no oil with them: 4 but the wise took oil in their vessels with their [2] lamps. 5 Now while the bridegroom tarried, they all slumbered and slept. 6 But at midnight there is a cry, Behold, the bridegroom! Come ye forth to meet him. 7 Then all those virgins arose, and trimmed their [2] lamps. 8 And the foolish said unto the wise, Give us of your oil; for our [2] lamps are going out. 9 But the wise answered, saying, Peradventure there will not be enough for us and you: go ye rather to them that sell, and buy for yourselves. 10 And while they

LUKE [12].

and shall [1] cut him asunder, and appoint his portion with the unfaithful.] (§ 95)

ERV. mg.: [1] Or, *severely scourge him*   [2] Or, *torches*

ARV. txt.: [1] the gnashing   [2] who

[a] Matt. 8:12. But the sons of the kingdom shall be cast forth into the outer darkness: there shall be the weeping and gnashing of teeth. (§ 50)

[a] Matt. 13:42. And shall cast them into the furnace of fire: there shall be the weeping and gnashing of teeth. (§ 57)

[a] Matt. 13:50. And shall cast them into the furnace of fire: there shall be the weeping and gnashing of teeth. (§ 57)

[a] Matt. 22:13. And cast him out into the outer darkness; there shall be the weeping and gnashing of teeth. (§ 124)

[a] Cf. Matt. 25:30 (p. 193).

[a] Luke 12:46 (§ 95). See above.

[a] Luke 13:28. There shall be the weeping and gnashing of teeth, when ye shall see Abraham, and Isaac and Jacob, and all the prophets, in the kingdom of God, and yourselves cast forth without. (§ 98)

MATT. 25.

went away to buy, the bridegroom came; and they that were ready went in with him to the marriage feast: and the door was shut. 11 Afterward come also the other virgins, saying, ª Lord, Lord, open to us. 12 But he answered and said, Verily I say unto you, I know you not. 13 ᵇ Watch therefore, for ye know not the day nor the hour.

14 ᶜ For *it is* as *when* a man, going into another country, called his own ¹servants, and delivered unto them his goods. 15 And unto one he gave five talents, to another two, to another one; to each according to his several ability; and he went on his journey. 16 Straightway he that received the five talents went and traded with them, and made other five talents. 17 In like manner he also that *received* the two gained other two. 18 But he that received the one went away and digged in the earth, and hid his lord's money. 19 Now after a long time the lord of those ¹servants cometh, and maketh a reckoning with them. 20 And he that received the five talents came and brought other five talents, saying, Lord, thou deliveredst unto me five talents: lo, I have gained other five talents. 21 His lord said unto him, Well done, good and faithful ²servant: thou hast been faithful over a few things, I will set thee over many things: enter thou into the joy of thy lord. 22 And he also that *received* the two talents came and said, Lord, thou deliveredst unto me two talents: lo, I have gained other two talents. 23 His lord said unto him, Well done, good and faithful ²servant: thou hast been faithful over a few things, I will set thee over many things: enter thou into the joy of thy lord. 24 And he also that had received the one talent came and said, Lord, I knew thee that thou art a hard man, reaping where thou didst not sow, and gathering where thou didst not scatter: 25 and I was afraid, and went away and hid thy talent in the earth: lo, thou hast thine own. 26 But his lord answered and said unto him, Thou wicked and slothful ²servant, thou knewest that I reap where I sowed not, and gather where I did not scatter; 27 thou oughtest therefore to have put my money to the bankers, and at my coming I should have received back mine own with interest. 28 Take ye away therefore the talent from him, and give it unto him that hath the ten talents. 29 ᵈ For unto every one that hath shall be given, and he shall have abundance: but from him that hath not, even that which he hath shall be taken away. 30 ᵉ And cast ye out the unprofitable ²servant into the outer darkness: there shall be the weeping and gnashing¹ of teeth.

31 But when the Son of man shall come in his glory, and all the angels with him,

---

ERV. mg.: ¹ Gr. *bondservants.* ² Gr. *bondservant.*

ARV. txt.: ¹ the gnashing

ª Luke 13:25. Lord, open to us; and he shall answer and say to you, I know you not whence ye are. (§ 98)

ᵇ Cf. Matt. 24:42; Mark 13:33, 35; Luke 21:36 (p. 191).

ᶜ Cf. Luke 19:11-27. (§ 117)

ᵈ Matt. 13:12. For whosoever hath to him shall be given, and he shall have abundance: but whosoever hath not, from him shall be taken away even that which he hath. (§ 57)

ᵈ Mark 4:25. For he that hath, to him shall be given: and he that hath not, from him shall be taken away even that which he hath. (§ 57)

ᵈ Luke 8:18. For whosoever hath, to him shall be given; and whosoever hath not, from him shall be taken away even that which he thinketh he hath. (§ 57)

ᵈ Luke 19:26. I say unto you, that unto every one that hath shall be given; but from him that hath not even that which he hath shall be taken away from him. (§ 117)

ᵉ Cf. Matt. 24:51 (p. 192), and references there.

MATT. 25.		LUKE 21.
then shall he sit on the throne of his glory: 32 and before him shall be gathered all the nations : and he shall separate them one from another, as the shepherd separateth the sheep from the ¹goats : 33 and he shall set the sheep on his right hand, but the ¹goats on the left. 34 Then shall the King say unto them on his right hand, Come, ye blessed of my Father, inherit the kingdom prepared for you from the foundation of the world : 35 for I was an hungred¹, and ye gave me meat²: I was thirsty, and ye gave me drink : I was a stranger, and ye took me in; 36 naked, and ye clothed me : I was sick, and ye visited me : I was in prison, and ye came unto me. 37 Then shall the righteous answer him, saying, Lord, when saw we thee an hungred³, and fed thee? or athirst, and gave thee drink? 38 And when saw we thee a stranger, and took thee in? or naked, and clothed thee? 39 And when saw we thee sick, or in prison, and came unto thee? 40 And the King shall answer and say unto them, Verily I say unto you, Inasmuch as ye did it unto one of these my brethren, *even* these least, ye did it unto me. 41 Then shall he say also unto them on the left hand, ²Depart from me, ye cursed, into the eternal fire which is prepared for the devil and his angels: 42 for I was an hungred¹, and ye gave me no meat⁴: I was		

ERV. mg.:   ¹ Gr. *kids.*   ² Or, *Depart from me under a curse*

ARV. txt.:   ¹ was hungry   ² to eat   ³ thee hungry   ⁴ did not give me to eat

MATT. 25.

thirsty, and ye gave me no drink: 43 I was a stranger, and ye took me not in; naked, and ye clothed me not; sick, and in prison, and ye visited me not. 44 Then shall they also answer, saying, Lord, when saw we thee an hungred[1], or athirst, or a stranger, or naked, or sick, or in prison, and did not minister unto thee? 45 Then shall he answer them, saying, Verily I say unto you, Inasmuch as ye did it not unto one of these least, ye did it not unto me. 46 And these shall go away into eternal punishment: but the righteous into eternal life. ⌈26:1 And it came to pass, when Jesus had finished all these words, he said unto his disciples, 2 Ye know that after two days the passover cometh, and the Son of man is delivered up to be crucified.⌉ (§ 132)

[Cf. Mark 11:19, p. 173.]

LUKE 21.

37 And every day he was teaching in the temple; and every night he went out, and lodged in the mount that is called *the mount* of Olives[2]. 38 And all the people came early in the morning to him in the temple, to hear him.

§ 132. THE CONSPIRACY BETWEEN THE CHIEF PRIESTS AND JUDAS.

MATT. 26:1-5, 14-16.

1 And it came to pass, when Jesus had finished all these words, he said unto his disciples, 2 Ye know that after two days the passover cometh, and the Son of man is delivered up to be crucified. 3

MARK 14:1, 2, 10, 11.

1 Now after two days was *the feast of* the passover and the unleavened bread: and the chief priests and the scribes sought how they might take him with subtilty, and kill him: 2 for they said, Not

LUKE 22:1-6.

1 Now the feast of unleavened bread drew nigh, which is called the Passover. 2 And the chief priests and the scribes sought how they might put him to death; for they feared the people.

ARV. txt.: 1 thee hungry 2 called Olivet

MATT. 26.	MARK 14.	LUKE 22.
Then were gathered together the chief priests, and the elders of the people, unto the court of the high priest, who was called Caiaphas ; 4 and they took counsel together that they might take Jesus by subtilty, and kill him. 5 But they said, Not during the feast, lest a tumult arise among the people. (+ § 118)	during the feast, lest haply there shall be a tumult of the people. (+ § 118)	
14 Then one of the twelve, who was called Judas Iscariot, went unto the chief priests, 15 and said, What are ye willing to give me, and I will deliver him unto you? And they weighed unto him thirty pieces of silver. 16 And from that time he sought opportunity to deliver him *unto them.*	10 And Judas Iscariot, [1] he that was one of the twelve, went away unto the chief priests, that he might deliver him unto them. 11 And they, when they heard it, were glad, and promised to give him money. And he sought how he might conveniently deliver him *unto them.*	3 And Satan entered into Judas who was called Iscariot, being of the number of the twelve. 4 And he went away, and communed with the chief priests and captains, how he might deliver him unto them. 5 And they were glad, and covenanted to give him money. 6 And he consented, and sought opportunity to deliver him unto them [2] in the absence of the multitude.

WEDNESDAY. [No record.]

THURSDAY. §§ 133-135.

§ 133. THE LAST SUPPER.

MATT. 26 : 17-30.	MARK 14 : 12-26.	LUKE 22 : 7-30.	JOHN 13 : 1-30.
17 Now on the first *day* of unleavened bread the disciples came to Jesus, saying, Where wilt thou that we make ready for thee to eat the passover? 18 And he said, Go into the city to such a man, and say unto him, The [3] Master [1] saith, My time is at hand; I keep the pass-	12 And on the first day of unleavened bread, when they sacrificed the passover, his disciples say unto him, Where wilt thou that we go and make ready that thou mayest eat the passover? 13 And he sendeth two of his disciples, and saith unto them, Go into the city, and	7 And the day of unleavened bread came, on which the passover must be sacrificed. 8 And he sent Peter and John, saying, Go and make ready for us the passover, that we may eat. 9 And they said unto him, Where wilt thou that we make ready? 10 And he said unto them, Be-	

ERV. mg. :   1 Gr. *the one of the twelve.*   2 Or, *without tumult*   3 Or, *Teacher*

ARV. txt. :   1 Teacher

MATT. 26.	MARK 14.	LUKE 22.	JOHN 13.
over at thy house with my disciples. 19 And the disciples did as Jesus appointed them; and they made ready the passover.	there shall meet you a man bearing a pitcher of water: follow him; 14 and wheresoever he shall enter in, say to the goodman[1] of the house, The [2]Master[2] saith, Where is my guest-chamber, where I shall eat the passover with my disciples? 15 And he will himself shew you a large upper room furnished *and* ready: and there make ready for us. 16 And the disciples went forth, and came into the city, and found as he had said unto them: and they made ready the passover.	hold, when ye are entered into the city, there shall meet you a man bearing a pitcher of water; follow him into the house where-into he goeth. 11 And ye shall say unto the goodman[1] of the house, The [2]Master[2] saith unto thee, Where is the guest-chamber, where I shall eat the passover with my disciples? 12 And he will shew you a large upper room furnished: there make ready. 13 And they went, and found as he had said unto them: and they made ready the passover.	
20 Now when even was come, he was sitting at meat with the twelve [1]disciples;	17 And when it was evening he cometh with the twelve.	14 And when the hour was come, he sat down, and the apostles with him. 15 And he said unto them, With desire I have desired to eat this passover with you before I suffer: 16 for I say unto you, I will[3] not eat it, until it be fulfilled in the kingdom of God. 17 And he received a cup, and when he had given thanks, he said, Take this, and divide it among yourselves: 18 for I say unto you, I will[3] not drink from henceforth of the fruit of the vine, until the kingdom of God shall come.	
[Paragraph continued on p. 200.]	.[Paragraph continued on p. 200.]		
[Cf. ver. 29, p. 203.]	[Cf. ver. 25, p. 203.]	[Paragraph continued on p. 202.]	

ERV. mg.: [1] Many authorities, some ancient, omit *disciples*. [2] Or, *Teacher*

ARV. txt.: [1] master [2] Teacher [3] shall

MATT. 26.	MARK 14.	LUKE 22.	JOHN 13.
			1 Now before the feast of the passover, Jesus knowing that his hour was come that he should depart out of this world unto the Father, having loved his own which [1] were in the world, he loved them [1] unto the end. 2 And during supper, the devil having already put into the heart of Judas Iscariot, Simon's *son*, to betray him, 3 *Jesus*, knowing that the Father had given all things into his hands, and that he came forth from God, and goeth unto God, 4 riseth from supper, and layeth aside his garments; and he took a towel, and girded himself. 5 Then he poureth water into the bason, and began to wash the disciples' feet, and to wipe them with the towel wherewith he was girded. 6 So he cometh to Simon Peter. He saith unto him, Lord, dost thou wash my feet? 7 Jesus answered and said unto him, What I do thou knowest not now; but thou shalt understand hereafter. 8 Peter saith unto him, Thou shalt never wash my feet. Jesus

ERV. mg.: [1] Or, *to the uttermost*

ARV. txt.: [1] that

MATT. 26.	MARK 14.	LUKE 22.	JOHN 13.
			answered him, If I wash thee not, thou hast no part with me. 9 Simon Peter saith unto him, Lord, not my feet only, but also my hands and my head. 10 Jesus saith to him, He that is bathed needeth not [1] save to wash his feet, but is clean every whit: and ye are clean, but not all. 11 For he knew him that should betray him; therefore said he, Ye are not all clean. 12 So when he had washed their feet, and taken his garments, and [2] sat down again, he said unto them, Know ye what I have done to you? 13 Ye call me, [3] Master[1], and, Lord: and ye say well; for so I am. 14 If I then, the Lord and the [3] Master[1], have washed your feet, ye also ought to wash one another's feet. 15 For I have given you an example, that ye also should do as I have done to you. 16 [a] Verily, verily, I say unto you, A [4] servant is not greater than his lord; neither [5] one that

ERV. mg.: [1] Some ancient authorities omit *save*, and *his feet*. [2] Gr. *reclined*. [3] Or, *Teacher* [4] Gr. *bondservant*. [5] Gr. *an apostle*.

ARV. txt.: [1] Teacher

[a] Matt. 10:24. A disciple is not above his master, nor a servant above his lord. (§64)

[a] Luke 6:40. The disciple is not above his master: but every one when he is perfected shall be as his master. (§49)

[a] John 15:20. Remember the word that I said unto you, A servant is not greater than his lord. (§134)

Matt. 26.	Mark 14.	Luke 22.	John 13.
			is sent greater than he that sent him. 17 If ye know these things, blessed are ye if ye do them. 18 I speak not of you all: I know whom I ²have chosen: but that the scripture may be fulfilled, He that eateth ³my bread lifted up his heel against me. 19 From henceforth I tell you before it come to pass, that, when it is come to pass, ye may believe that ⁴I am *he*. 20 ᵃVerily, verily, I say unto you, He that receiveth whomsoever I send receiveth me; and he that receiveth me receiveth him that sent me.
21 and as they were eating, he said, Verily I say unto you, that one of you shall betray me. 22 And they were exceeding sorrowful, and began to say unto him every one, Is it I, Lord? 23 And he answered and said, He that dipped his hand with me in the dish, the same shall betray me. 24 The Son of	18 And as they ¹sat and were eating, Jesus said, Verily I say unto you, One of you shall betray me, *even* he that eateth with me. 19 They began to be sorrowful, and to say unto him one by one, Is it I? 20 And he said unto them, *It is* one of the twelve, he that dippeth with me in the dish. 21 For the	21 But behold, the hand of him that betrayeth me is with me on the table. 22 For the Son of man indeed goeth, as it hath been determined: but woe unto that man through whom he is betrayed! 23 And they began to question among themselves, which of them it was that should do this thing.	21 When Jesus had thus said, he was troubled in the spirit, and testified, and said, Verily, verily, I say unto you, that one of you shall betray me. 22 The disciples looked one on another, doubting of whom he spake. 23 There was at the table reclining in Jesus' bosom one of his disciples, whom Jesus loved. 24 Si-

ER.V. mg.: ¹ Gr. *reclined*.   ² Or, *chose*   ³ Many ancient authorities read *his bread with me*.   ⁴ Or, *I am*

ᵃ Matt. 10:40. He that receiveth you receiveth me, and he that receiveth me receiveth him that sent me. (§ 64)

ᵃ Matt. 18:5. And whoso shall receive one such little child in my name, receiveth me. (§ 81)

ᵃ Mark 9:37. Whosoever shall receive one of such little children in my name, receiveth me: and whosoever receiveth me, receiveth not me, but him that sent me. (§ 81)

ᵃ Luke 9:48. Whosoever shall receive this little child in my name receiveth me: and whosoever receiveth me receiveth him that sent me. (§ 81)

ᵃ Luke 10:16. He that heareth you heareth me; and he that rejecteth you rejecteth me; and he that rejecteth me rejecteth him that sent me. (§ 87)

MATT. 26.	MARK 14.	LUKE 22.	JOHN 13.
man goeth, even as it is written of him: but woe unto that man through whom the Son of man is betrayed! good were it [1]for that man if he had not been born. 25 And Judas, which[1] betrayed him, answered and said, Is it I, Rabbi? He saith unto him, Thou hast said.	Son of man goeth, even as it is written of him: but woe unto that man through whom the Son of man is betrayed! good were it [1]for that man if he had not been born.		mon Peter therefore beckoneth to him, and saith unto him, Tell *us* who it is of whom he speaketh. 25 He leaning back, as he was, on Jesus' breast saith unto him, Lord, who is it? 26 Jesus therefore answereth, He it is, for whom I shall dip the sop, and give it him. So when he had dipped the sop, he taketh and giveth it to Judas, *the son* of Simon Iscariot. 27 And after the sop, then entered Satan into him. Jesus therefore saith unto him, That[3] thou doest, do quickly. 28 Now no man at the table knew for what intent he spake this unto him. 29 For some thought, because Judas had the [3]bag, that Jesus said unto him, Buy what things we have need of for the feast; or, that he should give something to the poor. 30 He then having received the sop went out straightway: and it was night.
		24 And there arose also a contention among them, which of them is[2] accounted to be [2]greatest, 25 And he said unto them,	

ERV. mg.: [1] Gr. *for him if that man.* [2] Gr. *greater.* [3] Or, *box*

ARV. txt.: [1] who [2] was [3] What

MATT. 26.	MARK 14.	LUKE 22.
		ᵃ The kings of the Gentiles have lordship over them; and they that have authority over them are called Benefactors. 26 But ye *shall* not *be* so: ᵇ but he that is the greater among you, let him become as the younger; and he that is chief, as he that doth serve. 27 For whether¹ is greater, he that ²sitteth at meat, or he that serveth? is not he that ²sitteth at meat? but I am in the midst of you as he that serveth. 28 But ye are they which² have continued with me in my temptations; 29 and ³ I appoint unto you a kingdom, even as my Father appointed unto me, 30 that ye may eat and drink at my table in my kingdom; ᶜ and ye shall sit on thrones judging the twelve tribes of Israel.
		[Paragraph continued in § 134.]
26 And as they were eating, Jesus took	22 And as they were eating, he took ¹bread,	19 And he took ¹bread, and when he

ERV. mg.: ¹ Or, *a loaf* ² Gr. *reclineth.* ³ Or, *I appoint unto you, even as my Father appointed unto me a kingdom, that ye may eat and drink, &c.*

ARV. txt.: ¹ which ² that

ᵃ Matt. 20:25-27. Ye know that the rulers of the Gentiles lord it over them, and their great ones exercise authority over them. 26 Not so shall it be among you: but whosoever would become great among you shall be your minister; 27 and whosoever would be first among you shall be your servant. (§ 114)

ᵃ Mark 10:42-44. Ye know that they which are accounted to rule over the Gentiles lord it over them; and their great ones exercise authority over them. 43 But it is not so among you: but whosoever would become great among you, shall be your minister: 44 and whosoever would be first among you, shall be servant of all. (§ 114)

ᵇ Matt. 23:11. But he that is greatest among you shall be your servant. (§ 127)

ᵇ Mark 9:35. If any man would be first, he shall be last of all, and minister of all. (§ 81)

ᵇ Luke 9:48. For he that is least among you all, the same is great. (§ 81)

ᶜ Matt. 19:28. Ye also shall sit on thrones, judging the twelve tribes of Israel. (§ 112)

Matt. 26.	Mark 14.	Luke 22.
[1]bread, and blessed, and brake it; and he gave to the disciples, and said, Take, eat; this is my body. 27 And he took [2]a cup, and gave thanks, and gave to them, saying, Drink ye all of it; 28 for this is my blood of [3]the [4]covenant, which is shed[1] for many unto remission of sins. 29 But I say unto you, I will[2] not drink henceforth of this fruit of the vine, until that day when I drink it new with you in my Father's kingdom. 30 And when they had sung a hymn, they went out unto the mount of Olives.	and when he had blessed, he brake it, and gave to them, and said, Take ye: this is my body. 23 And he took a cup, and when he had given thanks, he gave to them: and they all drank of it. 24 And he said unto them, This is my blood of [3]the [4]covenant, which is shed[1] for many. 25 Verily I say unto you, I will[2] no more drink of the fruit of the vine, until that day when I drink it new in the kingdom of God. 26 And when they had sung a hymn, they went out unto the mount of Olives.	had given thanks, he brake it, and gave to them, saying, This is my body [5]which is given for you: this do in remembrance of me. 20 And the cup in like manner after supper, saying, This cup is the new [6]covenant in my blood, *even* that which is poured out for you. [Remainder of paragraph on p. 200.] [Cf. ver. 18, p. 197.]

§ 134. CHRIST'S FAREWELL DISCOURSES.

Matt. 26: 31-35.	Mark 14: 27-31.	Luke 22: 31-38.	John 13: 31—16: 33.
			31 When therefore he was gone out, Jesus saith, Now [7]is the Son of man glorified, and God [7]is glorified in him; 32 and God shall glorify him in himself, and straightway shall he glorify him. 33 Little children, yet a little while I am with you. Ye shall seek me: and as I said unto the Jews, Whither I go, ye cannot come; so now I say unto you.

ERV. mg.: [1] Or, *a loaf* [2] Some ancient authorities read *the cup.* [3] Or, *the testament* [4] Many ancient authorities insert *new.* [5] Some ancient authorities omit *which is given for you . . . which is poured out for you.* [6] Or, *testament* [7] Or, *was*

ARV. txt.: [1] poured out [2] shall

MATT. 26.	MARK 14.	LUKE 22.	JOHN 13.
			34 A new commandment I give unto you, that ye love one another; [3] even as I have loved you, that ye also love one another. 35 By this shall all men know that ye are my disciples, if ye have love one to another.
31 Then saith Jesus unto them, All ye shall be [1] offended in me this night: for it is written, I will smite the shepherd, and the sheep of the flock shall be scattered abroad. 32 But after I am raised up, I will go before you into Galilee. 33 But Peter answered and said unto him, If all shall be [1] offended in thee, I will never be [1] offended. 34 Jesus said unto him, Verily I say unto thee, that this night, before the cock crow, thou shalt deny me thrice. 35 Peter saith unto him, Even if I must die with thee, *yet* will I not deny thee. Likewise also said all the disciples.	27 And Jesus saith unto them, All ye shall be [1] offended: for it is written, I will smite the shepherd, and the sheep shall be scattered abroad. 28 Howbeit, after I am raised up, I will go before you into Galilee. 29 But Peter said unto him, Although all shall be [1] offended, yet will not I. 30 And Jesus saith unto him, Verily I say unto thee, that thou to-day, *even* this night, before the cock crow twice, shalt deny me thrice. 31 But he spake exceeding vehemently, If I must die with thee, I will not deny thee. And in like manner also said they all.	31 Simon, Simon, behold, Satan [2] asked to have you, that he might sift you as wheat: 32 but I made supplication for thee, that thy faith fail not: and do thou, when once thou hast turned again, stablish [1] thy brethren. 33 And he said unto him, Lord, with thee I am ready to go both to prison and to death. 34 And he said, I tell thee, Peter, the cock shall not crow this day, until thou shalt thrice deny that thou knowest me. 35 And he said unto them, When I sent you forth without purse, and wallet, and shoes, lacked ye anything? And they said, Nothing. 36 And he	36 Simon Peter saith unto him, Lord, whither goest thou? Jesus answered, Whither I go, thou canst not follow me now; but thou shalt follow afterwards. 37 Peter saith unto him, Lord, why cannot I follow thee even now? I will lay down my life for thee. 38 Jesus answereth, Wilt thou lay down thy life for me? Verily, verily, I say unto thee, The cock shall not crow, till thou hast denied me thrice.

ERV. mg.:   [1] Gr. *caused to stumble.*   [2] Or, *obtained you by asking*   [3] Or, *even as I loved you, that ye may also love one another*

ARV. txt.:   [1] establish

LUKE **22.**

JOHN **14.**

said unto them, But now, he that hath a purse, let him take it, and likewise a wallet: ¹ and he that hath none, let him sell his cloke, and buy a sword. 37 For I say unto you, that this which is written must be fulfilled in me, And he was reckoned with transgressors: for that which concerneth me hath ² fulfilment. 38 And they said, Lord, behold, here are two swords. And he said unto them, It is enough.

14:1 Let not your heart be troubled: ³ye¹ believe in God, believe also in me. 2 In my Father's house are many ⁴ mansions; if it were not so, I would have told you; for I go to prepare a place for you. 3 And if I go and prepare a place for you, I come again, and will receive you unto myself; that where I am, *there* ye may be also. 4 ⁵ And whither I go, ye know the way. 5 Thomas saith unto him, Lord, we know not whither thou goest; how know we the way? 6 Jesus saith unto him, I am the way, and the truth,

JOHN **14.**

and the life: no one cometh unto the Father, but [1]by me. 7 If ye had known me, ye would have known my Father also: from henceforth ye know him, and have seen him. 8 Philip saith unto him, Lord, shew us the Father, and it sufficeth us. 9 Jesus saith unto him, Have I been so long time with you, and dost thou not know me, Philip? he that hath seen me hath seen the Father; how sayest thou, Shew us the Father? 10 Believest thou not that I am in the Father, and the Father in me? the words that I say unto you I speak not from myself: but the Father abiding in me doeth his works. 11 Believe me that I am in the Father, and the Father in me: or else believe me for the very works' sake. 12 Verily, verily, I say unto you, He that believeth on me, the works that I do shall he do also; and greater *works* than these shall he do; because I go unto the Father. 13 And whatsoever ye shall ask in my name, that will I do, that the Father may be glorified in the Son. 14 If ye shall ask [2]me[1] anything in my name, that will I do. 15 If ye love me, ye will keep my commandments. 16 And I will [3]pray the Father, and he shall give you another [4]Comforter, that he may be with you for ever, 17 *even* the Spirit of truth: whom the world cannot receive; for it beholdeth him not, neither knoweth him: ye know him; for he abideth with you, and shall be in you. 18 I will not leave you [5]desolate: I come unto you. 19 Yet a little while, and the world beholdeth me no more; but ye behold me: because I live, [6]ye shall live also. 20 In that day ye shall know that I am in my Father, and ye in me, and I in you. 21 He that hath my commandments, and keepeth them, he it is that loveth me: and he that loveth me shall be loved of my Father, and I will love him, and will manifest myself unto him. 22 Judas (not Iscariot) saith unto him, Lord, what is come to pass that thou wilt manifest thyself unto us, and not unto the world? 23 Jesus answered and said unto him, If a man love me, he will keep my word: and my Father will love him, and we will come unto him, and make our abode with him. 24 He that loveth me not keepeth not my words: and the word which ye hear is not mine, but the Father's who sent me.

25 These things have I spoken unto you, while *yet* abiding with you. 26 But the [4]Comforter, *even* the Holy Spirit, whom the Father will send in my name, he shall teach you all things, and bring to your remembrance all that I said unto you. 27 Peace I leave with you; my peace I give unto you: not as the world giveth, give I unto you. Let not your heart be troubled, neither let it be fearful. 28 Ye heard how I said to you, I go away, and I come unto you. If ye loved me, ye would have rejoiced, because I go unto the Father: for the Father is greater than I. 29 And now I have told you before it come to pass, that, when it is come to pass, ye may believe. 30 I will no more speak much with you, for the prince of the world cometh: and he hath nothing in me; 31 but that the world may know that I love the Father, and as the Father gave me commandment, even so I do. Arise, let us go hence.

15: 1 I am the true vine, and my Father is the husbandman. 2 Every branch in me that beareth not fruit, he taketh it away: and every *branch* that beareth fruit, he cleanseth it, that it may bear more fruit. 3 Already ye are clean because of the word which I have spoken unto you. 4 Abide in me, and I in you. As the branch cannot bear fruit of itself, except it abide in the vine; so neither can ye, except ye abide in me. 5 I am the vine, ye are the branches: He that abideth in me, and I in him, the same beareth much fruit: for apart from me ye can do nothing. 6 If a man abide not in me, he is cast forth as a branch, and is withered; and they gather them, and cast them into the fire, and they are burned.

ERV. mg.:　[1] Or, *through*　[2] Many ancient authorities omit *me.*　[3] Gr. *make request of.*　[4] Or, *Advocate* Or, *Helper* Gr. *Paraclete.*
[5] Or, *orphans*　[6] Or, *and ye shall live*

ARV. txt.:　[1] *Omit* mo

JOHN **15.**

7 If ye abide in me, and my words abide in you, ask whatsoever ye will, and it shall be done unto you. 8 Herein [1] is my Father glorified, [2] that ye bear much fruit; and *so* shall ye be my disciples. 9 Even as the Father hath loved me, I also have loved you: abide ye in my love. 10 If ye keep my commandments, ye shall abide in my love; even as I have kept my Father's commandments, and abide in his love. 11 These things have I spoken unto you, that my joy may be in you, and *that* your joy may be fulfilled[1]. 12 This is my command-ment, that ye love one another, even as I have loved you. 13 Greater love hath no man than this, that a man lay down his life for his friends. 14 Ye are my friends, if ye do the things which I command you. 15 No longer do I call you [3]servants; for the [4]servant knoweth not what his lord doeth: but I have called you friends; for all things that I heard from my Father I have made known unto you. 16 Ye did not choose me, but I chose you, and appointed you, that ye should go and bear fruit, and *that* your fruit should abide: that whatsoever ye shall ask of the Father in my name, he may give it you. 17 These things I command you, that ye may love one another. 18 If the world hateth you, [5]ye know that it hath hated me before *it hated* you. 19 If ye were of the world, the world would love its own: but because ye are not of the world, but I chose you out of the world, therefore the world hateth you. 20 Remember the word that I said unto you, ᵃA [4]servant is not greater than his lord. If they persecuted me, they will also persecute you; if they kept my word, they will keep yours also. 21 ᵇBut all these things will they do unto you for my name's sake, because they know not him that sent me. 22 If I had not come and spoken unto them, they had not had sin: but now they have no excuse for their sin. 23 He that hateth me hateth my Father also. 24 If I had not done among them the works which none other did, they had not had sin: but now have they both seen and hated both me and my Father. 25 But *this cometh to pass*, that the word may be fulfilled that is written in their law, They hated me without a cause. 26 But when the [6]Comforter is come, whom I will send unto you from the Father, *even* the Spirit of truth, which [7]proceedeth from the Father, he shall bear wit-ness of me: 27 [8]and ye also bear witness, because ye have been with me from the beginning.

16:1 These things have I spoken unto you, that ye should not be made[2] to stumble. 2 ᶜThey shall put you out of the synagogues: yea, the hour cometh, that whosoever killeth you shall think that he offereth service unto God. 3 And these things will they do, because they have not known the Father, nor me. 4 But these things have I spoken unto you, that when their hour is come, ye may remember them, how that I told you. And these things I

ERV. mg.: ¹ Or, *was* ² Many ancient authorities read *that ye bear much fruit, and be my disciples* ³ Gr. *bondservants*. ⁴ Gr. *bondservant*. ⁵ Or, *know ye* ⁶ Or, *Advocate* Or, *Helper* Gr. *Paraclete*. ⁷ Or, *goeth forth from* ⁸ Or, *and bear ye also witness*

ARV. txt.: ¹ made full ² caused

ᵃ Matt. 10:24. A disciple is not above his master, nor a servant above his lord. (§ 64)

ᵃ Luke 6:40. The disciple is not above his master; but every one when he is perfected shall be as his master. (§ 49)

ᵃ John 13:16. Verily, verily, I say unto you, A servant is not greater than his lord; neither one that is sent greater than he that sent him. (§ 133)

ᵇ Matt. 10:22. And ye shall be hated of all men for my name's sake. (§ 64)

ᵇ Matt. 24:9. And ye shall be hated of all the nations for my name's sake. (§ 131)

ᵇ Mark 13:13. And ye shall be hated of all men for my name's sake. (§ 131)

ᵇ Luke 21:17. And ye shall be hated of all men for my name's sake. (§ 131)

ᶜ Matt. 10:21. And brother shall deliver up brother to death, and the father his child: and children shall rise up against parents, and cause them to be put to death. (§ 64)

ᶜ Mark 13:12. And brother shall deliver up brother to death, and the father his child; and children shall rise up against parents, and cause them to be put to death. (§ 131)

ᶜ Luke 21:16. But ye shall be delivered up even by parents, and brethren, and kinsfolk, and friends; and *some* of you shall they cause to be put to death. (§ 131)

John 16.

said not unto you from the beginning, because I was with you. 5 But now I go unto him that sent me; and none of you asketh me, Whither goest thou? 6 But because I have spoken these things unto you, sorrow hath filled your heart. 7 Nevertheless I tell you the truth; It is expedient for you that I go away: for if I go not away, the ¹Comforter will not come unto you; but if I go, I will send him unto you. 8 And he, when he is come, will convict the world in respect of sin, and of righteousness, and of judgement: 9 of sin, because they believe not on me; 10 of righteousness, because I go to the Father, and ye behold me no more; 11 of judgement, because the prince of this world hath been judged. 12 I have yet many things to say unto you, but ye cannot bear them now. 13 Howbeit when he, the Spirit of truth, is come, he shall guide you into all the truth: for he shall not speak from himself; but what things soever he shall hear, *these* shall he speak: and he shall declare unto you the things that are to come. 14 He shall glorify me: for he shall take of mine, and shall declare *it* unto you. 15 All things whatsoever the Father hath are mine: therefore said I, that he taketh of mine, and shall declare *it* unto you. 16 A little while, and ye behold me no more; and again a little while, and ye shall see me. 17 *Some* of his disciples therefore said one to another, What is this that he saith unto us, A little while, and ye behold me not; and again a little while, and ye shall see me: and, Because I go to the Father? 18 They said therefore, What is this that he saith, A little while? We know not what he saith. 19 Jesus perceived that they were desirous to ask him, and he said unto them, Do ye inquire among yourselves concerning this, that I said, A little while, and ye behold me not, and again a little while, and ye shall see me? 20 Verily, verily, I say unto you, that ye shall weep and lament, but the world shall rejoice: ye shall be sorrowful, but your sorrow shall be turned into joy. 21 A woman when she is in travail hath sorrow, because her hour is come: but when she is delivered of the child, she remembereth no more the anguish, for the joy that a man is born into the world. 22 And ye therefore now have sorrow: but I will see you again, and your heart shall rejoice, and your joy no one taketh away from you. 23 And in that day ye shall ²ask me nothing¹. Verily, verily, I say unto you, if ye shall ask anything of the Father, he will give it you in my name. 24 Hitherto have ye asked nothing in my name: ask, and ye shall receive, that your joy may be fulfilled².

25 These things have I spoken unto you in ³proverbs³: the hour cometh, when I shall no more speak unto you in ³proverbs³, but shall tell you plainly of the Father. 26 In that day ye shall ask in my name: and I say not unto you, that I will ⁴pray the Father for you; 27 for the Father himself loveth you, because ye have loved me, and have believed that I came forth from the Father. 28 I came out from the Father, and am come into the world: again, I leave the world, and go unto the Father. 29 His disciples say, Lo, now speakest thou plainly, and speakest no ⁵proverb⁴. 30 Now know we that thou knowest all things, and needest not that any man should ask thee: by this we believe that thou camest forth from God. 31 Jesus answered them, Do ye now believe? 32 Behold, the hour cometh, yea, is come, that ye shall be scattered, every man to his own, and shall leave me alone: and *yet* I am not alone, because the Father is with me. 33 These things have I spoken unto you, that in me ye may have peace. In the world ye have tribulation: but be of good cheer; I have overcome the world.

ERV. mg.: ¹ Or, *Advocate* Or, *Helper* Gr. *Paraclete.*   ² Or, *ask me no question*   ³ Or, *parables*   ⁴ Gr. *make request of.*   ⁵ Or, *parable*

ARV. txt.: ¹ ask me no question   ² made full   ³ dark sayings   ⁴ dark saying

§135. THE INTERCESSORY PRAYER.

JOHN, CHAP. **17.**

1 These things spake Jesus; and lifting up his eyes to heaven, he said, Father, the hour is come ; glorify thy Son, that the Son may glorify thee : 2 even as thou gavest him authority over all flesh, that whatsoever thou hast given him, to them[1] he should give eternal life. 3 And this is life eternal, that they should know thee the only true God, and him whom thou didst send, *even* Jesus Christ. 4 I glorified thee on the earth, having accomplished the work which thou hast given me to do. 5 And now, O[2] Father, glorify thou me with thine own self with the glory which I had with thee before the world was. 6 I manifested thy name unto the men whom thou gavest me out of the world : thine they were, and thou gavest them to me ; and they have kept thy word. 7 Now they know that all things whatsoever thou hast given me are from thee : 8 for the words which thou gavest me I have given unto them ; and they received *them*, and knew of a truth that I came forth from thee, and they believed that thou didst send me. 9 I [1]pray for them : I [1]pray not for the world, but for those whom thou hast given me ; for they are thine : 10 and all things that are mine are thine, and thine are mine : and I am glorified in them. 11 And I am no more in the world, and these are in the world, and I come to thee. Holy Father, keep them in thy name which thou hast given me, that they may be one, even as we *are*. 12 While I was with them, I kept them in thy name which thou hast given me : and I guarded them, and not one of them perished, but the son of perdition ; that the scripture might be fulfilled. 13 But now I come to thee ; and these things I speak in the world, that they may have my joy fulfilled[3] in themselves. 14 I have given them thy word ; and the world hated them, because they are not of the world, even as I am not of the world. 15 I [1]pray not that thou shouldest take them [2]from the world, but that thou shouldest keep them [2]from [3]the evil *one*. 16 They are not of the world, even as I am not of the world. 17 [4]Sanctify them in the truth : thy word is truth. 18 As thou didst send me into the world, even so sent I them into the world. 19 And for their sakes I [4]sanctify myself, that they themselves also may be sanctified in truth. 20 Neither for these only do I [1]pray, but for them also that believe on me through their word ; 21 that they may all be one ; even as thou, Father, *art* in me, and I in thee, that they also may be in us : that the world may believe that thou didst send me. 22 And the glory which thou hast given me I have given unto them ; that they may be one, even as we *are* one ; 23 I in them, and thou in me, that they may be perfected into one ; that the world may know that thou didst send me, and lovedst them, even as thou lovedst me. 24 Father, [5]that which thou hast given me, I will that, where I am, they also may be with me ;[4] that they may behold my glory, which thou hast given me : for thou lovedst me before the foundation of the world. 25 O righteous Father, the world knew thee not, but I knew thee ; and these knew that thou didst send me ; 26 and I made known unto them thy name, and will make it known ; that the love wherewith thou lovedst me may be in them, and I in them.

ERV. mg.: [1] Gr. *make request*. [2] Gr. *out of*. [3] Or, *evil* [4] Or, *Consecrate* [5] Many ancient authorities read *those whom*.

ARV. txt.: [1] that to all whom thou hast given him, [2] *Omit* O [3] made full [4] Father, I desire that they also whom thou hast given me be with me where I am,

FRIDAY. §§ 136-141.

§ 136. THE AGONY IN GETHSEMANE.

MATT. 26 : ⌐30⌐ 36–46.	MARK 14 : ⌐26⌐ 32–42.	LUKE 22 : 39–46.	⌐JOHN 18 : 1.⌐
⌐30 And when they had sung a hymn, they went out unto the mount of Olives.⌐ (§ 133)	⌐26 And when they had sung a hymn, they went out unto the mount of Olives.⌐ (§ 133)	39 And he came out, and went, as his custom was, unto the mount of Olives ; and the disciples also followed him. 40 And when he was at the the place, he said unto them, Pray that ye enter not into temptation. 41 And he was parted from them about a stone's cast ; and he kneeled down and prayed, 42 saying, ᵇ Father, if thou be willing, remove this cup from me : nevertheless not my will, but thine, be done. 43 ²And there appeared unto him an angel from heaven, strengthening him. 44 And being in an agony he prayed more earnestly : and his sweat became as it were great drops of blood falling down upon the ground. 45 And when he rose up from his prayer, he came unto the disciples, and found them sleeping for sorrow, 46 and	⌐1 When Jesus had spoken these words, he went forth with his disciples over the ³ brook ⁴ Kidron, where was a garden, into the² which he entered, himself and his disciples.⌐ (§ 137)
36 Then cometh Jesus with them unto ¹a place called Gethsemane, and saith unto his disciples, Sit ye here, while I go yonder and pray. 37 And he took with him Peter and the two sons of Zebedee, and began to be sorrowful and sore troubled. 38 Then saith he unto them, ᵃMy soul is exceeding sorrowful, even unto death : abide ye here, and watch with me. 39 And he went forward a little and fell on his face, and prayed, saying, ᵇO¹ my Father, if it be possible, let this cup pass away from me : nevertheless, not as I will, but as thou wilt. 40 And he cometh unto the disciples, and findeth them sleeping, and saith unto Peter, What, could	32 And they come unto ¹a place which was named Gethsemane ; and he saith unto his disciples, Sit ye here, while I pray. 33 And he taketh with him Peter and James and John, and began to be greatly amazed, and sore troubled. 34 And he saith unto them, ᵃMy soul is exceeding sorrowful even unto death : abide ye here, and watch. 35 And he went forward a little, and fell on the ground, and prayed that, if it were possible, the hour might pass away from him. 36 And he said, ᵇAbba, Father, all things are possible unto thee ; remove this cup from me : howbeit not what I will, but what thou wilt. 37 And he cometh, and findeth them		

ERV. mg.: ¹ Gr. *an enclosed piece of ground*. ² Many ancient authorities omit ver. 43, 44. ³ Or, *ravine* Gr. *winter-torrent*. ⁴ Or, *of the Cedars*

ARV. txt.: ¹ *Omit* O ² *Omit* the

ᵃ John 12 : 27. Now is my soul troubled ; and what shall I say? (§ 129)

ᵇ John 12 : 27, 28. Father, save me from this hour. But for this cause came I unto this hour. 28 Father, glorify thy name. (§ 129)

MATT. 26.	MARK 14.	LUKE 22.	
ye not watch with me one hour? 41 [1]Watch and pray, that ye enter not into temptation: the spirit indeed is willing, but the flesh is weak. 42 Again a second time he went away, and prayed, saying, O[1] my Father, if this cannot pass away, except I drink it, thy will be done. 43 And he came again and found them sleeping, for their eyes were heavy. 44 And he left them again, and went away, and prayed a third time, saying again the same words. 45 Then cometh he to the disciples, and saith unto them, Sleep on now, and take your rest: behold, the hour is at hand, and the Son of man is betrayed unto[2] the hands of sinners. 46 Arise, let us be going: behold, he is at hand that betrayeth me.	sleeping, and saith unto Peter, Simon, sleepest thou? couldest thou not watch one hour? 38 [1]Watch and pray, that ye enter not into temptation: the spirit indeed is willing, but the flesh is weak. 39 And again he went away, and prayed, saying the same words. 40 And again he came, and found them sleeping, for their eyes were very heavy; and they wist[3] not what to answer him. 41 And he cometh the third time, and saith unto them, Sleep on now, and take your rest: it is enough; the hour is come; behold, the Son of man is betrayed into the hands of sinners. 42 Arise, let us be going: behold, he that betrayeth me is at hand.	said unto them, Why sleep ye? rise and pray, that ye enter not into temptation.	

§ 137. THE BETRAYAL AND ARREST.

MATT. 26: 47-56.	MARK 14: 43-52.	LUKE 22: 47-53.	JOHN 18: 1-11 ⌜12⌝.
47 And while he yet spake, lo, Judas, one of the twelve, came, and with him a great multitude with swords and staves, from the chief priests and elders of the peo-	43 And straightway, while he yet spake, cometh Judas, one of the twelve, and with him a multitude with swords and staves, from the chief priests and the scribes and	47 While he yet spake, behold, a multitude, and he that was called Judas, one of the twelve, went before them; and he drew near unto Jesus to kiss him. 48 But	1 When Jesus had spoken these words, he went forth with his disciples over the [2]brook [3]Kidron, where was a garden, into the[4] which he entered, himself and his disci-

ERV. mg.: [1] Or, *Watch ye, and pray that ye enter not* [2] Or, *ravine* Gr. *winter-torrent*. [3] Or, *of the Cedars*

ARV. txt.: [1] *Omit* O [2] into [3] knew [4] *Omit* the

MATT. 26.	MARK 14.	LUKE 22.	JOHN 18.
ple. 48 Now he that betrayed him gave them a sign, saying, Whomsoever I shall kiss, that is he: take him. 49 And straightway he came to Jesus, and said, Hail, Rabbi; and [1] kissed him. 50 And Jesus said unto him, Friend, *do* that for which thou art come. Then they came and laid hands on Jesus, and took him. 51 And behold, one of them that were with Jesus stretched out his hand, and drew his sword, and smote the [2] servant of the high priest, and struck off his ear. 52 Then saith Jesus unto him, Put up again thy sword into its place: for all they that take the sword shall perish with the sword. 53 Or thinkest thou that I cannot beseech my Father, and he shall even now send me more than twelve legions of angels? 54 How then should the scriptures be fulfilled, that thus it must be? 55 In that hour said Jesus to the multitudes, Are ye come out as against a robber with swords and staves to seize me? I sat daily in the tem-	the elders. 44 Now he that betrayed him had given them a token, saying, Whomsoever I shall kiss, that is he; take him, and lead him away safely. 45 And when he was come, straightway he came to him, and saith, Rabbi; and [1] kissed him. 46 And they laid hands on him, and took him. 47 But a certain one of them that stood by drew his sword, and smote the [2] servant of the high priest, and struck off his ear. 48 And Jesus answered and said unto them, Are ye come out, as against a robber, with swords and staves to seize me? 49 I was daily with you in the temple teaching, and ye took me not: but *this is done* that the scriptures might be fulfilled. 50 And they all left him, and fled.	Jesus said unto him, Judas, betrayest thou the Son of man with a kiss? 49 And when they that were about him saw what would follow, they said, Lord, shall we smite with the sword? 50 And a certain one of them smote the [2] servant of the high priest, and struck off his right ear. 51 But Jesus answered and said, Suffer ye [1] thus far. And he touched his ear, and healed him. 52 And Jesus said unto the chief priests, and captains of the temple, and elders, which [2] were come against him, Are ye come out, as against a robber, with swords and staves? 53 When I was daily with you in the temple, ye stretched not forth your hands against me: but this is 'your hour, and the power of darkness.	ples. 2 Now Judas also, which [3] betrayed him, knew the place: for Jesus ofttimes resorted thither with his disciples. 3 Judas then, having received the [3] band *of soldiers*, and officers from the chief priests and the Pharisees, cometh thither with lanterns and torches and weapons. 4 Jesus therefore, knowing all the things that were coming upon him, went forth, and saith unto them, Whom seek ye? [5] They answered him, Jesus of Nazareth. Jesus saith unto them, I am *he.* And Judas also, which [3] betrayed him, was standing with them. 6 When therefore he said unto them, I am *he,* they went backward, and fell to the ground. 7 Again therefore he asked them, Whom seek ye? And they said, Jesus of Nazareth. 8 Jesus answered, I told you that I am *he*: if therefore ye seek me, let these go their way: 9 that the word might be fulfilled which he spake, Of those whom thou hast given me I lost not one. 10 Simon Peter therefore

ERV. mg.: [1] Gr. *kissed him much.*   [2] Gr. *bondservant.*   [3] Or, *cohort*

ARV. txt.: [1] ye *them*   [2] that   [3] who

MATT. 26.	MARK 14.		JOHN 18.
ple teaching, and ye took me not. 56 But all this is come to pass, that the scriptures of the prophets might be fulfilled. Then all the disciples left him, and fled.			having a sword drew it, and struck the high priest's [1]servant, and cut off his right ear. Now the [1]servant's name was Malchus. 11 Jesus therefore said unto Peter, Put up the sword into the sheath: the cup which the Father hath given me, shall I not drink it?
	51 And a certain young man followed with him, having a linen cloth cast about him, over *his* naked *body*: and they lay hold on him; 52 but he left the linen cloth, and fled naked.		
			⌐12 So the [2]band and the [3]chief captain, and the officers of the Jews, seized Jesus and bound him,¬ (§ 138)

§138. THE TRIAL BEFORE THE JEWISH AUTHORITIES.

MATT. 26:57—27:10.	MARK 14:53–72 ⌐15:1a¬.	LUKE 22:54–71.	JOHN 18:12–27.
[Cf. ver. 57, p. 215.]	[Cf. ver. 53, p. 215.]	[Cf. ver. 54, p. 215.]	12 So the [2]band and the [3]chief captain, and the officers of the Jews, seized Jesus and bound him, 13 and led him to Annas first; for he was father in law to Caiaphas, which[1] was high priest that year. 14 Now Caiaphas was he which[2] gave counsel to the Jews, that it was expedient that

ERV. mg.: [1] Gr. *bondservant.* [2] Or, *cohort* [3] Or, *military tribune* Gr. *chiliarch.*

ARV. txt.: [1] who [2] that

MATT. 26.	MARK 14.	LUKE 22.	JOHN 18.
[Cf. vss. 69, 70, p. 217.]	[Cf. vss. 66–68, p. 217.]	[Cf. vss. 55–57, p. 217.]	one man should die for the people. 15 And Simon Peter followed Jesus, and *so did* another disciple. Now that disciple was known unto the high priest, and entered in with Jesus into the court of the high priest; 16 but Peter was standing at the door without. So the other disciple, which[1] was known unto the high priest, went out and spake unto her that kept the door, and brought in Peter. 17 The maid therefore that kept the door saith unto Peter, Art thou also *one* of this man's disciples? He saith, I am not. 18 Now the [1] servants and the officers were standing *there*, having made [2] a fire of coals; for it was cold; and they were warming themselves: and Peter also was with them, standing and warming himself. 19 The high priest therefore asked Jesus of his disciples, and of his teaching. 20 Jesus answered him, I have spoken openly to the world; I ever taught in [3] synagogues, and in the temple, where

ERV. mg.:   [1] Gr. *bondservants.*   [2] Gr. *a fire of charcoal.*   [3] Gr, *synagogue.*

ARV. txt.:   [1] who

MATT. 26.	MARK 14.	LUKE 22.	JOHN 18.
			all the Jews come together; and in secret spake I nothing. 21 Why askest thou me? ask them that have heard *me*, what I spake unto them: behold, these know the things which I said. 22 And when he had said this, one of the officers standing by struck Jesus [1] with his hand, saying, Answerest thou the high priest so? 23 Jesus answered him, If I have spoken evil, bear witness of the evil: but if well, why smitest thou me? 24 Annas therefore sent him bound unto Caiaphas the high priest.
57 And they that had taken Jesus led him away to *the house of* Caiaphas the high priest, where the scribes and the elders were gathered together. 58 But Peter followed him afar off, unto the court of the high priest, and entered in, and sat with the officers, to see the end. 59 Now the chief priests and the whole council sought false witness against Jesus, that they might put him to death; 60 and they found it not, though many false witnesses came. But	53 And they led Jesus away to the high priest: and there come together with him all the chief priests and the elders and the scribes. 54 And Peter had followed him afar off, even within, into the court of the high priest; and he was sitting with the officers, and warming himself in the light *of the fire*. 55 Now the chief priests and the whole council sought witness against Jesus to put him to death; and found it not. 56 For many bare false witness against him,	54 And they seized him, and led him *away*, and brought him into the high priest's house. But Peter followed afar off. ⌜55 And when they had kindled a fire in the midst of the court, and had sat down together, Peter sat in the midst of them. 56 And a certain maid seeing him as he sat in the light *of the fire*,—⌝ [Paragraph continued on p. 217.]	

ERV. mg.: [1] Or, *with a rod*

MATT. 26.	MARK 14.	LUKE 22.	JOHN 18.
afterward came two, 61 and said, This man said, I am able to destroy the [1] temple of God, and to build it in three days. 62 And the high priest stood up, and said unto him, Answerest thou nothing? what is it which these witness against thee? 63 But Jesus held his peace. And the high priest said unto him, I adjure thee by the living God, that thou tell us whether thou be[1] the Christ, the Son of God. 64 Jesus saith unto him, Thou hast said: nevertheless I say unto you, Henceforth ye shall see the Son of man sitting at the right hand of power[2], and coming on the clouds of heaven. 65 Then the high priest rent his garments, saying, He hath spoken blasphemy: what further need have we of witnesses? behold, now ye have heard the blasphemy: 66 what think ye? They answered and said, He is [2]worthy of death.	and their witness agreed not together. 57 And there stood up certain, and bare false witness against him, saying, 58 We heard him say, I will destroy this [1]temple that is made with hands, and in three days I will build another made without hands. 59 And not even so did their witness agree together. 60 And the high priest stood up in the midst, and asked Jesus, saying, Answerest thou nothing? what is it which these witness against thee? 61 But he held his peace, and answered nothing. Again the high priest asked him, and saith unto him, Art thou the Christ, the Son of the Blessed? 62 And Jesus said, I am: and ye shall see the Son of man sitting at the right hand of power[2], and coming with the clouds of heaven. 63 And the high priest rent his clothes, and saith, What further need have we of witnesses? 64 Ye have heard the blasphemy: what think ye? And they all condemned him to be [2]worthy of death.		

ERV. mg.: [1] Or, *sanctuary*: as in Matt. xxiii. 35; xxvii. 5. [2] Gr. *liable to.*

ARV. txt.: [1] art [2] Power

MATT. 26.	MARK 14.	LUKE 22.	JOHN 18.
67 Then did they spit in his face and buffet him : and some smote him ¹with the palms of their hands, 68 saying, Prophesy unto us, thou Christ : who is he that struck thee ?	65 And some began to spit on him, and to cover his face, and to buffet him, and to say unto him, Prophesy : and the officers received him with ²blows of their hands.	63 And the men that held ⁶*Jesus* mocked him, and beat him. 64 And they blindfolded him, and asked him, saying, Prophesy : who is he that struck thee ? 65 And many other things spake they against him, reviling him. [Ver. 66 ff., p. 218.]	
69 Now Peter was sitting without in the court : and a maid came unto him, saying, Thou also wast with Jesus the Galilæan. 70 But he denied before them all, saying, I know not what thou sayest. 71 And when he was gone out into the porch, another *maid* saw him, and saith unto them that were there, This man also was with Jesus the Nazarene¹. 72 And again he denied with an oath, I know not the man. 73 And after a little while they that stood by came and said to Peter, Of a truth thou also art *one* of them ; for thy speech bewrayeth thee². 74 Then began he to curse and to swear, I know not the man. And straightway the cock crew. 75 And Peter remem-	66 And as Peter was beneath in the court, there cometh one of the maids of the high priest ; 67 and seeing Peter warming himself, she looked upon him, and saith, Thou also wast with the Nazarene, *even* Jesus. 68 But he denied, saying, ³I neither know, nor understand what thou sayest : and he went out into the ⁴porch ; ⁵and the cock crew. 69 And the maid saw him, and began again to say to them that stood by, This is *one* of them. 70 But he again denied it. And after a little while again they that stood by said to Peter, Of a truth thou art *one* of them ; for thou art a Galilæan. 71 But he began to curse, and to swear, I know not this man of whom ye speak. 72 And	55 And when they had kindled a fire in the midst of the court, and had sat down together, Peter sat in the midst of them. 56 And a certain maid seeing him as he sat in the light *of the fire*, and looking stedfastly upon him, said, This man also was with him. 57 But he denied, saying, Woman, I know him not. 58 And after a little while another saw him, and said, Thou also art *one* of them. But Peter said, Man, I am not. 59 And after the space of about one hour another confidently affirmed, saying, Of a truth this man also was with him : for he is a Galilæan. 60 But Peter said, Man, I know not what thou sayest. And immediately, while he yet spake, the cock crew. 61 And the	[Cf. ver. 15-18, p. 214.] 25 Now Simon Peter was standing and warming himself. They said therefore unto him, Art thou also *one* of his disciples? He denied, and said, I am not. 26 One of the ⁷servants of the high priest, being a kinsman of him whose ear Peter cut off, saith, Did not I see thee in the garden with him? 27 Peter therefore denied again : and straightway the cock crew.

ERV. mg.: ¹ ¹ Or, *with rods*   ² Or, *strokes of rods*   ³ Or, *I neither know, nor understand: thou, what sayest thou?*   ⁴ Gr. *fore-court.*   ⁵ Many ancient authorities omit *and the cock crew.*   ⁶ Gr. *him.*   ⁷ Gr. *bondservants.*

ARV. txt.: ¹ Jesus of Nazareth   ² maketh thee known

MATT. 26.	MARK 14.	LUKE 22.
bered the word which Jesus had said, Before the cock crow, thou shalt deny me thrice. And he went out, and wept bitterly.	straightway the second time the cock crew. And Peter called to mind the word, how that Jesus said unto him, Before the cock crow twice, thou shalt deny me thrice. ¹And when he thought thereon, he wept.	Lord turned, and looked upon Peter. And Peter remembered the word of the Lord, how that he said unto him, Before the cock crow this day, thou shalt deny me thrice. 62 And he went out, and wept bitterly.
		[Ver. 63 ff., p. 217.]
.27:1 Now when morning was come, all the chief priests and the elders of the people took counsel against Jesus to put him to death: [2 and they bound him, and led him away, and delivered him up to Pilate the governor.] (§ 139)	⌐15:1 And straightway in the morning the chief priests with the elders and scribes, and the whole council, held a consultation,—⌐ (§ 139)	66 And as soon as it was day, the assembly of the elders of the people was gathered together, both chief priests and scribes; and they led him away into their council, saying, 67 If thou art the Christ, tell us. But he said unto them, If I tell you, ye will not believe: 68 and if I ask you, ye will not answer. 69 But from henceforth shall the Son of man be seated at the right hand of the power of God. 70 And they all said, Art thou then the Son of God? And he said unto them, ²Ye say that I am. 71 And they said, What further need have we of witness? for we ourselves have heard from his own mouth.
3 Then Judas, which¹ betrayed him, when he saw that he was		

ERV. mg.: ¹ Or, *And he began to weep.* ² Or, *Ye say it, because I am*

ARV. txt.: ¹ who

MATT. **27.**

condemned, repented himself, and brought back the thirty pieces of silver to the chief priests and elders, 4 saying, I have sinned in that I betrayed [1] innocent blood. But they said, What is that to us? see thou *to it.* 5 And he cast down the pieces of silver into the sanctuary, and departed; and he went away and hanged himself. 6 And the chief priests took the pieces of silver, and said, It is not lawful to put them into the [2] treasury, since it is the price of blood. 7 And they took counsel, and bought with them the potter's field, to bury strangers in. 8 Wherefore that field was called, The field of blood, unto this day. 9 Then was fulfilled that which was spoken [3] by [1] Jeremiah the prophet, saying, And [4] they took the thirty pieces of silver, the price of him that was priced, [5] whom *certain* of the children of Israel did price; 10 and [6] they gave them for the potter's field, as the Lord appointed me.

ERV. mg.: **1** Many ancient authorities read *righteous.* **2** Gr. *corbanas,* that is, *sacred treasury.* Compare Mark vii. 11. **3** Or, *through* **4** Or, *I took* **5** Or, *whom they priced on the part of the sons of Israel* **6** Some ancient authorities read *I gave.*

ARV. txt.: **1** through

§ 139. THE TRIAL BEFORE PILATE.

MATT. 27: ⌜2⌝ 11–31.	MARK 15: 1–20.	LUKE 23: 1–25.	JOHN 18: 28—19: 16a.
⌜2⌝ and they bound him, and led him away, and delivered him up to Pilate the governor.⌝ (§ 138)	1 And straightway in the morning the chief priests with the elders and scribes, and the whole council, held a consultation, and bound Jesus, and carried him away, and delivered him up to Pilate.	1 And the whole company of them rose up, and brought him before Pilate. 2 And they began to accuse him, saying, We found this man perverting our nation, and forbidding to give tribute to Cæsar, and saying that he himself is ¹Christ a king.	28 They lead Jesus therefore from Caiaphas into the ²palace¹: and it was early; and they themselves entered not into the ²palace¹, that they might not be defiled, but might eat the passover. 29 Pilate therefore went out unto them, and saith, What accusation bring ye against this man? 30 They answered and said unto him, If this man were not an evildoer, we should not have delivered him up unto thee. 31 Pilate therefore said unto them, Take him yourselves, and judge him according to your law. The Jews said unto him, It is not lawful for us to put any man to death: 32 that the word of Jesus might be fulfilled, which he spake, signifying by what manner of death he should die.
	[Paragraph continued below.]	Paragraph continued below.]	
11 Now Jesus stood before the governor: and the govervor asked him, saying, Art thou the King of the Jews? And Jesus said unto him, Thou sayest. 12 And when he was accused by the	2 And Pilate asked him, Art thou the King of the Jews? And he answering, saith unto him, Thou sayest. 3 And the chief priests accused him of many things. 4 And Pilate again	3 And Pilate asked him, saying, Art thou the King of the Jews? And he answered and said, Thou sayest. [Paragraph continued on p. 221.]	33 Pilate therefore entered again into the ²palace¹, and called Jesus, and said unto him, Art thou the King of the Jews? 34 Jesus answered, Sayest thou this of thyself, or did others tell

ERV. mg.: ¹ Or, *an anointed king* ² Gr. *Prætorium*.

ARV. txt.: ¹ Prætorium

MATT. 27.	MARK 15.	LUKE 23.	JOHN 18.
chief priests and elders, he answered nothing. 13 Then saith Pilate unto him, Hearest thou not how many things they witness against thee? 14 And he gave him no answer, not even to one word: insomuch that the governor marvelled greatly.	asked him, saying, answerest thou nothing? behold how many things they accuse thee of. 5 But Jesus no more answered anything; insomuch that Pilate marvelled.		it thee concerning me? 35 Pilate answered, Am I a Jew? Thine own nation and the chief priests delivered thee unto me: what hast thou done? 36 Jesus answered, My kingdom is not of this world: if my kingdom were of this world, then would my ¹servants fight, that I should not be delivered to the Jews: but now is my kingdom not from hence. 37 Pilate therefore said unto him, Art thou a king then? Jesus answered ²Thou sayest that I am a king. To this end have I been born, and to this end am I come into the world, that I should bear witness unto the truth. Every one that is of the truth heareth my voice. 38 Pilate saith unto him, What is truth?
		4 And Pilate said unto the chief priests and the multitudes, I find no fault in this man. But they were the more urgent, saying, He stirreth up the people, teaching throughout all Judæa, and beginning from Galilee even unto this place. 6 But when Pilate heard it, he asked whether the	And when he had said this, he went out again unto the Jews, and saith unto them, I find no crime in him. [Paragraph continued on p. 223.]

ERV. mg.: ¹ Or, *officers*: as in ver. 3, 12, 18, 22. ² Or, *Thou sayest* it, *because I am a king.*

MATT. 27.	MARK 15.	LUKE 23.	JOHN 18.
		man were a Galilæan. 7 And when he knew that he was of Herod's jurisdiction, he sent him unto Herod, who himself also was at Jerusalem in these days. 8 Now when Herod saw Jesus, he was exceeding glad: for he was of a long time desirous to see him, because he had heard concerning him; and he hoped to see some [1] miracle done by him. 9 And he questioned him in many words; but he answered him nothing. 10 And the chief priests and the scribes stood, vehemently accusing him. 11 And Herod with his soldiers set him at nought, and mocked him, and arraying him in gorgeous apparel sent him back to Pilate. 12 And Herod and Pilate became friends with each other that very day: for before they were at enmity between themselves. 13 And Pilate called together the chief priests and the rulers and the people, 14 and said unto them, Ye brought unto me this man, as one that perverteth the people: and behold, I, having examined him before you, found no fault in	

R.V. mg.: [1] Gr. *sign*.

MATT. 27.	MARK 15.	LUKE 23.	JOHN 18.
		this man touching those things whereof ye accuse him: 15 no, nor yet Herod: for he sent him back unto us; and behold, nothing worthy of death hath been done by him. 16 I will therefore chastise him, and release ²him.	
15 Now at ¹the feast the governor was wont to release unto the multitude one prisoner, whom they would. 16 And they had then a notable prisoner, called Barabbas. 17 When therefore they were gathered together, Pilate said unto them, Whom will ye that I release unto you? Barabbas, or Jesus which¹ is called Christ? 18 For he knew that for envy they had delivered him up. 19 And while he was sitting on the judgement-seat, his wife sent unto him, saying, Have thou nothing to do with that righteous man: for I have suffered many things this day in a dream because of him. 20 Now the chief priests and the elders persuaded the multitudes that they should ask for Barabbas, and destroy Jesus.	6 Now at ¹the feast he used to release unto them one prisoner, whom they asked of him. 7 And there was one called Barabbas, *lying* bound with them that had made insurrection, men who in the insurrection had committed murder. 8 And the multitude went up and began to ask him *to do* as he was wont to do unto them. 9 And Pilate answered them, saying, Will ye that I release unto you the King of the Jews? 10 For he perceived that for envy the chief priests had delivered him up. 11 But the chief priests stirred up the multitude, that he should rather release Barabbas unto them. 12 And Pilate again answered and said unto them, What then shall I do unto him whom ye call the King of the	[Paragraph continued below.]

18 But they cried out all together, saying, Away with this man, and release unto us Barabbas: 19 one who for a certain insurrection made in the city, and for murder, was cast into prison. 20 And Pilate spake unto them again, desiring | 39 But ye have a custom, that I should release unto you one at the passover: will ye therefore that I release unto you the King of the Jews? 40 They cried out therefore again, saying, Not this man, but Barabbas. Now Barabbas was a robber. |

ERV. mg.: ¹ Or, *a feast* ² Many ancient authorities insert ver. 17 *Now he must needs release unto them at the feast one* prisoner. Others add the same words after ver. 19.

ARV. txt.: ¹ who

Matt. 27.	Mark 15.	Luke 23.	John 19.
21 But the governor answered and said unto them, Whether[1] of the twain[2] will ye that I release unto you? And they said, Barabbas. 22 Pilate saith unto them, What then shall I do unto Jesus which[3] is called Christ? They all say, Let him be crucified. 23 And he said, Why, what evil hath he done? But they cried out exceedingly, saying, Let him be crucified. 24 So when Pilate saw that he prevailed nothing, but rather that a tumult was arising, he took water, and washed his hands before the multitude, saying, I am innocent[1] of the blood of this righteous man: see ye *to it*. 25 And all the people answered and said, His blood *be* on us, and on our children. 26 Then released he unto them Barabbas: but Jesus he scourged and delivered to be crucified.	Jews? 13 And they cried out again, Crucify him. 14 And Pilate said unto them, Why, what evil hath he done? But they cried out exceedingly, Crucify him. 15 And Pilate, wishing to content the multitude, released unto them Barabbas, and delivered Jesus, when he had scourged him, to be crucified.	to release Jesus; 21 but they shouted, saying, Crucify, crucify him. 22 And he said unto them the third time, Why, what evil hath this man done? I have found no cause of death in him: I will therefore chastise him and release him. 23 But they were instant[7] with loud voices, asking that he might be crucified. And their voices prevailed. 24 And Pilate gave sentence that what they asked for should be done. 25 And he released him that for insurrection and murder had been cast into prison, whom they asked for; but Jesus he delivered up to their will.	[Cf. 19:1.]
27 Then the soldiers of the governor took Jesus into the [2]palace[4], and gathered unto him the whole [3]band. 28 And they [4]stripped him, and put on him a scarlet robe. 29 And they plaited[5] a crown	16 And the soldiers led him away within the court, which is the [5]Prætorium; and they call together the whole [3]band. 17 And they clothe him with purple, and plaiting[6] a crown of thorns,		19:1 Then Pilate therefore took Jesus, and scourged him. 2 And the soldiers plaited[5] a crown of thorns, and put it on his head, and arrayed him in a purple garment; 3 and they came unto

ERV. mg.: 1 Some ancient authorities read *of this blood: see ye &c.* 2 Gr. *Prætorium.* See Mark xv. 16. 3 Or, *cohort* 4 Some ancient authorities read *clothed.* 5 Or, *palace*

ARV. txt.: 1 Which 2 two 3 who 4 Prætorium 5 platted 6 platting 7 urgent

224

MATT. 27.	MARK 15.		JOHN 19.
of thorns and put it upon his head, and a reed in his right hand; and they kneeled down before him, and mocked him, saying, Hail, King of the Jews! 30 And they spat upon him, and took the reed and smote him on the head. [Paragraph continued on p. 227.]	they put it on him; 18 and they began to salute him, Hail, King of the Jews! 19 And they smote his head with a reed, and did spit[1] upon him, and bowing their knees worshipped him. [Paragraph continued on p. 227.		him, and said, Hail, King of the Jews! and they struck him [1] with their hands. 4 And Pilate went out again, and saith unto them, Behold, I bring him out to you, that ye may know that I find no crime in him. 5 Jesus therefore came out, wearing the crown of thorns and the purple garment. And *Pilate* saith unto them, Behold, the man! 6 When therefore the chief priests and the officers saw him, they cried out, saying, Crucify *him*, crucify *him*. Pilate saith unto them, Take him yourselves, and crucify him: for I find no crime in him. 7 The Jews answered him, We have a law, and by that law he ought to die, because he made himself the Son of God. 8 When Pilate therefore heard this saying, he was the more afraid; 9 and he entered into

ERV. mg.: [1] Or, *with rods*

ARV. txt.: [1] and spat

JOHN **19.**

the [1]palace[1] again, and saith unto Jesus, Whence art thou? But Jesus gave him no answer. 10 Pilate therefore saith unto him, Speakest thou not unto me? knowest thou not that I have [2]power to release thee, and have [2]power to crucify thee? 11 Jesus answered him, Thou wouldest have no [2]power against me, except it were given thee from above: therefore he that delivered me unto thee hath greater sin. 12 Upon this Pilate sought to release him: but the Jews cried out, saying, If thou release this man, thou art not Cæsar's friend: every one that maketh himself a king [3]speaketh against Cæsar. 13 When Pilate therefore heard these words, he brought Jesus out, and sat down on the judgement-seat at a place called The Pavement, but in Hebrew, Gabbatha. 14 Now it was the Preparation of the passover: it was about the sixth hour. And he saith unto the Jews, Behold, your King! 15 They therefore cried out, Away with *him*, away with *him*, crucify him.

BRV. mg.: [1] Gr. *Prætorium.*   [2] Or, *authority*   [3] Or, *opposeth Cæsar*

ARV. txt.: [1] Prætorium

MATT. 27.	MARK 15.		JOHN 19.
			Pilate saith unto them, Shall I crucify your King? The chief priests answered, We have no king but Cæsar. 16 Then therefore he delivered him unto them to be crucified.
31 And when they had mocked him, they took off from him the robe, and put on him his garments, and led him away to crucify him.	20 And when they had mocked him, they took off from him the purple, and put on him his garments. And they lead him out to crucify him.		

§ 140. THE CRUCIFIXION.

MATT. 27 : 32–56.	MARK 15 : 21–41.	LUKE 23 : 26–49.	JOHN 19 : 16b–37.
32 And as they came out, they found a man of Cyrene, Simon by name : him they [1]compelled to go *with them*, that he might bear his cross. [Paragraph continued on p. 228.]	21 And they [2]compel one passing by, Simon of Cyrene, coming from the country, the father of Alexander and Rufus, to go *with them*, that he might bear his cross. [Paragraph continued on p. 228.]	26 And when they led him away, they laid hold upon one Simon of Cyrene, coming from the country, and laid on him the cross, to bear it after Jesus. 27 And there followed him a great multitude of the people, and of women who bewailed and lamented him. 28 But Jesus turning unto them said, Daughters of Jerusalem, weep not for me, but weep for yourselves, and for your children. 29 For behold, the days are coming, in which they shall say, Blessed are the barren, and the wombs that never bare, and the breasts that never gave suck.	[Cf. ver. 17, page 228.]

ERV. mg.: [1] Gr. *impressed*. [2] Gr. *impress*.

MATT. 27.	MARK 15.	LUKE 23.	JOHN 19.
		30 Then shall they begin to say to the mountains, Fall on us ; and to the hills, Cover us. 31 For if they do these things in the green tree, what shall be done in the dry? 32 And there were also two others, malefactors, led with him to be put to death.	
33 And when they were come unto a place called Golgotha, that is to say, The place of a skull, 34 they gave him wine to drink mingled with gall : and when he had tasted it, he would not drink. 35 And when they had crucified him, they parted his garments among them, casting lots : 36 and they sat and watched him there. 37 And they set up over his head his accusation written, THIS IS JESUS THE KING OF THE JEWS. 38 Then are there crucified with him two robbers, one on the right hand, and one on the left.	22 And they bring him unto the place Golgotha, which is, being interpreted, The place of a skull. 23 And they offered him wine mingled with myrrh : but he received it not. 24 And they crucify him, and part his garments among them, casting lots upon them, what each should take. 25 And it was the third hour, and they crucified him. 26 And the superscription of his accusation was written over, THE KING OF THE JEWS. 27 And with him they crucify two robbers ; one on his right hand, and one on his ¹ left.	33 And when they came unto the place which is called ²The skull, there they crucified him, and the malefactors, one on the right hand and the other on the left. 34 ³And Jesus said, Father, forgive them ; for they know not what they do. And parting his garments among them, they cast lots. [Paragraph continued on p. 229.] [Cf. also ver. 38, p. 230.]	16*b* They took Jesus therefore:* 17 and he went out, bearing the cross for himself, unto the place called The place of a skull, which is called ﹐in Hebrew Golgotha: 18 where they crucified him, and with him two others, on either side one, and Jesus in the midst. 19 And Pilate wrote a title also, and put it on the cross. And there was written, JESUS OF NAZARETH, THE KING OF THE JEWS. 20 This title therefore read many of the Jews: ⁴for the place where Jesus was crucified was nigh to the city: and it was written in Hebrew, *and* in Latin, *and* in Greek. 21 The chief priests of the Jews therefore said to Pilate, Write not, The King of the Jews; but, that he
[Paragraph continued on p. 229.]	[Paragraph continued on p. 229.]		

ERV. mg.﹒ ¹ Many ancient authorities insert ver. 28 *And the scripture was fulfilled, which saith, And he was reckoned with transgressors.* See Luke xxii. 37. ² According to the Latin, *Calvary,* which has the same meaning. ³ Some ancient authorities omit *And Jesus said, Father, forgive them; for they know not what they do.* ⁴ Or, *for the place of the city where Jesus was crucified was nigh at hand*

*ARV. *includes* They . . . therefore: *in ver. 17.*

MATT. 27.	MARK 15.	LUKE 23.	JOHN 19.
			said, I am King of the Jews. 22 Pilate answered, What I have written I have written.
[Cf. ver. 35, p. 228.]	[Cf. ver. 24, p. 228.]	[Cf. ver. 34, p. 228.]	23 The soldiers therefore, when they had crucified Jesus, took his garments, and made four parts, to every soldier a part; and also the ³coat: now the ³coat was without seam, woven from the top throughout. 24 They said therefore one to another, Let us not rend it, but cast lots for it, whose it shall be: that the scripture might be fulfilled, which saith,
			They parted my garments among them, And upon my vesture did they cast lots.
			These things therefore the soldiers did.
39 And they that passed by railed on him, wagging their heads, 40 and saying, Thou that destroyest the ¹temple, and buildest it in three days, save thyself: if thou art the Son of God, come down from the cross. 41 In like manner also the chief priests mocking *him*, with the scribes and elders, said, 42 He saved	29 And they that passed by railed on him, wagging their heads, and saying, Ha! thou that destroyest the ¹temple, and buildest it in three days, 30 save thyself, and come down from the cross. 31 In like manner also the chief priests mocking *him* among themselves with the scribes said, He saved others; ²himself he cannot	35 And the people stood beholding. And the rulers also scoffed at him, saying, He saved others; let him save himself, if this is the Christ of God, his chosen. 36 And the soldiers also mocked him, coming to him, offering him vinegar, 37 and saying, If thou art the King of the Jews, save thyself. 38 And there was also	

ERV.: mg.: ¹ Or. *sanctuary* ² Or, *can he not save himself*? ³ Or, *tunic*

229

MATT. 27.	MARK 15.	LUKE 23.	JOHN 19.
others; [1] himself he cannot save. He is the King of Israel; let him now come down from the cross, and we will believe on him. 43 He trusteth on God; let him deliver him now, if he desireth him: for he said, I am the Son of God. 44 And the robbers also that were crucified with him cast upon him the same reproach.	save. 32 Let the Christ, the King of Israel, now come down from the cross, that we may see and believe. And they that were crucified with him reproached him.	a superscription over him, THIS IS THE KING OF THE JEWS. 39 And one of the malefactors which [1] were hanged railed on him, saying, Art not thou the Christ? save thyself and us. 40 But the other answered, and rebuking him said, Dost thou not even fear God, seeing thou art in the same condemnation? 41 And we indeed justly; for we receive the due reward of our deeds: but this man hath done nothing amiss. 42 And he said, Jesus, remember me when thou comest [2] in thy kingdom. 43 And he said unto him, Verily I say unto thee, To-day shalt thou be with me in Paradise.	[Cf. ver. 19, p. 228, and parallels there.] 25 But there were standing by the cross of Jesus his mother, and his mother's sister, Mary the *wife* of Clopas, and Mary Magdalene. 26 When Jesus therefore saw his mother, and the
[Cf. ver. 55, 56, p. 232.]	[Cf. ver. 40, 41, p. 232.]	[Cf. ver. 49, page 232.]	

ERV. mg.:   [1] Or, *can he not save himself?*   [2] Some ancient authorities read *into thy kingdom*

ARV. txt.:   [1] that

MATT. 27.	MARK 15.	LUKE 23.	JOHN 19.
			disciple standing by, whom he loved, he saith unto his mother, Woman, behold, thy son! 27 Then saith he to the disciple, Behold, thy mother! And from that hour the disciple took her unto his own *home.*
45 Now from the sixth hour there was darkness over all the ¹land until the ninth hour. 46 And about the ninth hour Jesus cried with a loud voice, saying, Eli, Eli, lama sabachthani? that is, My God, my God, ²why hast thou forsaken me? 47 And some of them that stood there, when they heard it, said, This man calleth Elijah. 48 And straightway one of them ran, and took a sponge, and filled it with vinegar, and put it on a reed, and gave him to drink. 49 And the rest said, Let be; let us see whether Elijah cometh to save ³him. 50 And Jesus cried again with a loud voice, and yielded up his spirit.	33 And when the sixth hour was come, there was darkness over the whole ¹land until the ninth hour. 34 And at the ninth hour Jesus cried with a loud voice, Eloi, Eloi, lama sabachthani? which is, being interpreted, My God, my God, ²why hast thou forsaken me? 35 And some of them that stood by, when they heard it, said, Behold, he calleth Elijah. 36 And one ran, and filling a sponge full of vinegar, put it on a reed, and gave him to drink, saying, Let be; let us see whether Elijah cometh to take him down. 37 And Jesus uttered a loud voice, and gave up the ghost.	44 And it was now about the sixth hour, and a darkness came over the whole ¹land until the ninth hour, 45 ⁵the sun's light failing: and the veil of the ⁴temple was rent in the midst. 46 ⁶And when Jesus had cried with a loud voice, he said², Father, into thy hands I commend my spirit: and having said this, he gave up the ghost. [Paragraph continued on p. 232.]	28 After this Jesus, knowing that all things are now finished, that the scripture might be accomplished, saith, I thirst, 29 There was set there a vessel full of vinegar: so they put a sponge full of the vinegar upon hyssop, and brought it to his mouth. 30 When Jesus therefore had received the vinegar, he said, It is finished: and he bowed his head, and gave up his spirit.
51 And behold, the veil of the ⁴temple was rent in twain¹ from the top to the	38 And the veil of the ⁴temple was rent in twain¹ from the top to the bottom.		

ERV. mg.: ¹ Or, *earth* ² Or, *why didst thou forsake me?* ³ Many ancient authorities add *And another took a spear and pierced his side, and there came out water and blood.* See John xix. 34. ⁴ Or, *sanctuary* ⁵ Gr. *the sun failing.* ⁶ Or, *And Jesus, crying with a loud voice, said*

ARV. txt.: ¹ *two* ² And Jesus, crying with a loud voice, said,

MATT. 27.	MARK 15.	LUKE 23.	JOHN 19.
bottom; and the earth did quake; and the rocks were rent; 52 and the tombs were opened; and many bodies of the saints that had fallen asleep were raised; 53 and coming forth out of the tombs after his resurrection they entered into the holy city and appeared unto many. 54 Now the centurion, and they that were with him watching Jesus, when they saw the earthquake, and the things that were done, feared exceedingly, saying, Truly this was [1]the Son of God. 55 And many women were there beholding from afar, which[1] had followed Jesus from Galilee, ministering unto him: 56 among whom was Mary Magdalene, and Mary the mother of James and Joses, and the mother of the sons of Zebedee.	39 And when the centurion, which[1] stood by over against him, saw that he [2]so gave up the ghost, he said, Truly this man was [1]the Son of God. 40 And there were also women beholding from afar: among whom *were* both Mary Magdalene, and Mary the mother of James the [3]less and of Joses, and Salome; 41 who, when he was in Galilee, followed him, and ministered unto him; and many other women which[2] came up with him unto Jerusalem.	47 And when the centurion saw what was done, he glorified God, saying, Certainly this was a righteous man. 48 And all the multitudes that came together to this sight, when they beheld the things that were done, returned smiting their breasts. 49 And all his acquaintance, and the women that followed with him from Galilee, stood afar off, seeing these things.	[Cf. ver. 25, p. 230. 31 The Jews therefore, because it was the Preparation, that the bodies should not remain on the cross upon the sabbath (for the day of that sabbath was a high *day*), asked of Pilate that their legs might be

ERV. mg.:   [1] Or, *a son of God*   [2] Many ancient authorities read *so cried out, and gave up the ghost.*   [3] Gr. *little*

ARV. txt.:   [1] who   [2] that

JOHN 19.

broken, and *that* they might be taken away. 32 The soldiers therefore came, and brake the legs of the first, and of the other which[1] was crucified with him: 33 but when they came to Jesus, and saw that he was dead already, they brake not his legs: 34 howbeit one of the soldiers with a spear pierced his side, and straightway there came out blood and water. 35 And he that hath seen hath borne witness, and his witness is true: and he knoweth that he saith true, that ye also may believe. 36 For these things came to pass, that the scripture might be fulfilled, A bone of him shall not be [1]broken. 37 And again another scripture saith, They shall look on him whom they pierced.

§ 141. THE BURIAL.

MATT. 27:57-61.	MARK 15:42-47.	LUKE 23:50-56a.	JOHN 19:38-42.
57 And when even was come, there came a rich man from Arimathæa, named Joseph, who also himself was Jesus' disciple: 58 this man went to Pilate, and	42 And when even was now come, because it was the Preparation, that is, the day before the sabbath, 43 there came Joseph of Arimathæa, a councillor of hon-	50 And behold, a man named Joseph, who was a councillor, a good man and a righteous[2] 51 (he had not consented to their counsel and deed), *a man* of Arimathæa, a	38 And after these things Joseph of Arimathæa, being a disciple of Jesus, but secretly for fear of the Jews, asked of Pilate that he might take away the body of

MATT. 27.	MARK 15.	LUKE 23.	JOHN 19.
asked for the body of Jesus. Then Pilate commanded it to be given up. 59 And Joseph took the body, and wrapped it in a clean linen cloth, 60 and laid it in his own new tomb, which he had hewn out in the rock: and he rolled a great stone to the door of the tomb, and departed. 61 And Mary Magdalene was there, and the other Mary, sitting over against the sepulchre.	ourable estate, who also himself was looking for the kingdom of God; and he boldly went in unto Pilate, and asked for the body of Jesus. 44 And Pilate marvelled if he were already dead: and calling unto him the centurion, he asked him whether he ¹had been any while dead. 45 And when he learned it of the centurion, he granted the corpse to Joseph. 46 And he bought a linen cloth and taking him down, wound him in the linen cloth, and laid him in a tomb which had been hewn out of a rock; and he rolled a stone against the door of the tomb. 47 And Mary Magdalene and Mary the *mother* of Joses beheld where he was laid.	city of the Jews, who was looking for the kingdom of God: 52 this man went to Pilate, and asked for the body of Jesus. 53 And he took it down, and wrapped it in a linen cloth, and laid him in a tomb that was hewn in stone, where never man had yet lain. 54 And it was the day of the Preparation, and the sabbath ²drew on. 55 And the women, which¹ had come with him out of Galilee, followed after, and beheld the tomb, and how his body was laid. 56 And they returned, and prepared spices and ointments.	Jesus: and Pilate gave *him* leave. He came therefore, and took away his body. 39 And there came also Nicodemus, he who at the first came to him by night, bringing a ³mixture of myrrh and aloes, about a hundred pound *weight*². 40 So they took the body of Jesus, and bound it in linen cloths with the spices, as the custom of the Jews is to bury. 41 Now in the place where he was crucified there was a garden; and in the garden a new tomb wherein was never man yet laid. 42 There then because of the Jews' Preparation (for the tomb was nigh at hand) they laid Jesus.

SATURDAY. § 142.

§ 142. THE WATCH AT THE SEPULCHRE.

MATT. 27: 62–66.

62 Now on the morrow, which is *the day* after the Preparation, the chief priests and the Pharisees were gathered together unto Pilate, 63 saying, Sir, we remember that that deceiver said, while he was yet alive, After three days I rise again. 64 Command therefore that the sepulchre be made sure until the third day, lest haply his disciples come and steal him away, and say unto the people, He is risen from the dead: and the last error will be worse than the first. 65 Pilate said unto them, ⁴Ye have a guard: go your way³, ⁵make it *as* sure as ye can. 66 So they went, and made the sepulchre sure, sealing the stone, the guard being with them.

ERV. mg.: ¹ Many ancient authorities read *were already dead.* ² Gr. *began to dawn.* ³ Some ancient authorities read *roll.* ⁴ Or, *Take a guard* ⁵ Gr. *make it sure, as ye know.*

ARV. txt,: ¹ who ² a hundred pounds ³ *Omit* your way

PART IX.

THE FORTY DAYS.

FROM THE RESURRECTION UNTIL THE ASCENSION.

---

§143. THE RESURRECTION MORNING.

MATT. 28:1–10.

1 Now late on the sabbath day, as it began to dawn toward the first *day* of the week, came Mary Magdalene and the other Mary to see the sepulchre. 2 And behold, there was a great earthquake; for an angel of the Lord descended from heaven, and came and rolled away the stone, and sat upon it. 3 His appearance was as lightning, and his raiment white as snow: 4 and for fear of him the watchers did quake, and became as dead men. 5 And the angel answered and said unto the women, Fear not ye: for I know that ye seek Jesus, which[1] hath been crucified. 6 He is not here; for he is risen, even as he said. Come, see the place [1]where the Lord lay.

MARK 16:1–8, 9–11.

1 And when the sabbath was past, Mary Magdalene, and Mary the *mother* of James and Salome, bought spices, that they might come and anoint him. 2 And very early on the first day of the week, they come to the tomb when the sun was risen. 3 And they were saying among themselves, Who shall roll us away the stone from the door of the tomb? 4 and looking up, they see that the stone is rolled back: for it was exceeding great. 5 And entering into the tomb, they saw a young man sitting on the right side, arrayed in a white robe; and they were amazed. 6 And he saith unto them, Be not amazed: ye seek Jesus, the Nazarene, which[1] hath been cru-

LUKE 23:56b—24:12.

56b And on the sabbath they rested according to the commandment. 24:1 But on the first day of the week, at early dawn, they came unto the tomb, bringing the spices which they had prepared. 2 And they found the stone rolled away from the tomb.

3 And they entered in, and found not the body [2]of the Lord Jesus. 4 And it came to pass, while they were perplexed thereabout, behold, two men stood by them in dazzling apparel: 5 and as they were affrighted, and bowed down their

JOHN 20:1–18.

1 Now on the first *day* of the week cometh Mary Magdalene early, while it was yet dark, unto the tomb, and seeth the stone taken away from the tomb.

[Paragraph continued on p. 236.]

ERV. mg.: [1] **Many ancient authorities read** *where he lay.*   [2] Some ancient authorities omit *of the Lord Jesus.*

ARV. txt.: [1] who

MATT. 28	MARK 16.	LUKE 24.	JOHN 20.
7 And go quickly, and tell his disciples, He is risen from the dead; and lo, he goeth before you into Galilee; there shall ye see him: lo, I have told you. 8 And they departed quickly from the tomb with fear and great joy, and ran to bring his disciples word. [Paragraph continued on p. 237.]	cified: he is risen; he is not here: behold, the place where they laid him! 7 But go, tell his disciples and Peter, He goeth before you into Galilee: there shall ye see him, as he said unto you. 8 And they went out, and fled from the tomb; for trembling and astonishment had come upon them: and they said nothing to any one; for they were afraid.	faces to the earth, they said unto them, Why seek ye ¹the living among the dead? 6 ²He is not here, but is risen: remember how he spake unto you when he was yet in Galilee, 7 saying that the Son of man must be delivered up into the hands of sinful men, and be crucified, and the third day rise again. 8 And they remembered his words, 9 and returned ³from the tomb, and told all these things to the eleven, and to all the rest. 10 Now they were Mary Magdalene, and Joanna, and Mary the *mother* of James: and the other women with them told these things unto the apostles. 11 And these words appeared in their sight as idle talk; and they disbelieved them. 12 ⁴But Peter arose, and ran unto the tomb; and stooping and looking in, he seeth the linen cloths by themselves; and he ⁵departed to his home, wondering at that which was come to pass.	2 She runneth therefore, and cometh to Simon Peter, and to the other disciple, whom Jesus loved, and saith unto them, They have taken away the Lord out of the tomb, and we know not where they have laid him. 3 Peter therefore went forth, and the other disciple, and they went toward the tomb. 4 And they ran both together: and the other disciple outran Peter, and came first to the tomb; 5 and stooping and looking in, he seeth the linen cloths lying; yet entered he not in. 6 Simon Peter therefore also cometh, fol-

ERV. mg.: ¹ Gr. *him that liveth*   ² Some ancient authorities omit *He is not here, but is risen.*   ³ Some ancient authorities omit *from the tomb.*   ⁴ Some ancient authorities omit ver. 12.   ⁵ Or, *departed, wondering with himself*

Matt. 28.	*Mark 16.*		*John 20.*
			lowing him, and entered into the tomb; and he beholdeth the linen cloths lying, 7 and the napkin, that was upon his head, not lying with the linen cloths, but rolled up in a place by itself. 8 Then entered in therefore the other disciple also, which[1] came first to the tomb, and he saw, and believed. 9 For as yet they knew not the scripture, that he must rise again from the dead. 10 So the disciples went away again unto their own home.
9 And behold, Jesus met them, saying, All hail. And they came and took hold of his feet, and worshipped him. 10 Then saith Jesus unto them, Fear not: go tell my brethren that they depart into Galilee, and there shall they see me.	9 [1]Now when he was risen early on the first day of the week, he appeared first to Mary Magdalene, from whom he had cast out seven [2]devils. 10 She went and told them that had been with him, as they mourned and wept. 11 And they, when they heard that he was alive, and had been seen of her, disbelieved.		11 But Mary was standing without at the tomb weeping: so, as she wept, she stooped and looked into the tomb; 12 and she beholdeth two angels in white sitting, one at the head, and one at the feet, where the body of Jesus had lain. 13 And they say unto her, Woman, why weepest thou? She saith unto them, Because they have taken away my Lord, and I know not where they have laid him. 14 When she had thus said, she

ERV. mg.: [1] The two oldest Greek manuscripts, and some other authorities, omit from ver. 9 to the end. Some other authorities have a different ending to the Gospel. [2] Gr. *demons.*

ARV. txt.: [1] who

*See Appendix I, p. 252.

JOHN 20.
turned herself back, and beholdeth Jesus standing, and knew not that it was Jesus. 15 Jesus saith unto her, Woman, why weepest thou? whom seekest thou? She, supposing him to be the gardener, saith unto him, Sir, if thou hast borne him hence, tell me where thou hast laid him, and I will take him away. 16 Jesus saith unto her, Mary. She turneth herself, and saith unto him in Hebrew, Rabboni; which is to say, [1]Master[1]. 17 Jesus saith to her, [2]Touch me not; for I am not yet ascended unto the Father: but go unto my brethren, and say to them, I ascend unto my Father and your Father, and my God and your God. 18 Mary Magdalene cometh and telleth the disciples, I have seen the Lord; and *how*[2] *that* he had said these things unto her.

§ 144. THE REPORT OF THE WATCH.

MATT. 28:11–15.

11 Now while they were going, behold, some of the guard came into the city, and told unto the chief priests all the things that were come to pass. 12 And when they were assembled with the elders, and had taken counsel, they gave large[3] money unto the soldiers, 13 saying, Say ye, His disciples came by night, and stole him away while we slept. 14 And if this [3]come to the governor's ears, we will persuade him, and rid you of care. 15 So they took the money, and did as they were taught: and this saying was spread abroad among the Jews, *and continueth* until this day.

ERV. mg.:   [1] Or, *Teacher*   [2] Or, *Take not hold on me*   [3] Or, *come to a hearing before the governor*

ARV. txt.:   [1] Teacher   [2] *Omit how*   [3] much

§ 145. THE WALK TO EMMAUS.

MARK 16 : 12, 13.	LUKE 24 : 13–35.
12 And after these things he was manifested in another form unto two of them, as they walked, on their way into the country. 13 And they went away and told it unto the rest : neither believed they them.	13 And behold, two of them were going that very day to a village named Emmaus, which was threescore furlongs from Jerusalem. 14 And they communed with each other of all these things which had happened. 15 And it came to pass, while they communed and questioned together, that Jesus himself drew near, and went with them. 16 But their eyes were holden that they should not know him. 17 And he said unto them, [1] What communications are these that ye have one with another, as ye walk ? And they stood still, looking sad. 18 And one of them, named Cleopas, answering said unto him, [2] Dost thou alone sojourn in Jerusalem and not know the things which are come to pass there in these days ? 19 And he said unto them, What things? And they said unto him, The things concerning Jesus of Nazareth[1], which[2] was a prophet mighty in deed and word before God and all the people : 20 and how the chief priests and our rulers delivered him up to be condemned to death, and crucified him. 21 But we hoped that it was he which[2] should redeem Israel. Yea and beside[3] all this, it is now the third day since these things came to pass. 22 Moreover certain women of our company amazed us, having been early

ERV. mg.: [1] Gr. *What words are these that ye exchange one with another.* [2] Or, *Dost thou sojourn alone in Jerusalem, and knowest thou not the things*

ARV. txt.: [1] Jesus the Nazarene [2] who [3] besides

LUKE **24.**

at the tomb; 23 and when they found not his body, they came, saying, that they had also seen a vision of angels, which [1] said that he was alive. 24 And certain of them that were with us went to the tomb, and found it even so as the women had said: but him they saw not. 25 And he said unto them, O foolish men, and slow of heart to believe [1] in all that the prophets have spoken! 26 Behoved it not the Christ to suffer these things, and to enter into his glory? 27 And beginning from Moses and from all the prophets, he interpreted to them in all the scriptures the things concerning himself. 28 And they drew nigh unto the village, whither they were going: and he made as though he would go further. 29 And they constrained him, saying, Abide with us: for it is toward evening, and the day is now far spent. And he went in to abide with them. 30 And it came to pass, when he had sat down with them to meat, he took the [2]bread, and blessed it, and brake, and gave[2] to them. 31 And their eyes were opened, and they knew him; and he vanished out of their sight. 32 And they said one to another, Was not our heart burning within us, while he spake to us in the way, while he opened to us the scriptures? 33 And they rose up that very hour, and returned to Jerusalem, and found the

ERV. mg.:   [1] Or, *after*   [2] Or, *loaf*

ARV. txt.:   [1] who   [2] and blessed; and breaking *it* he gave

LUKE 24.

eleven gathered together, and them that were with them, 34 saying, The Lord is risen indeed, and hath appeared to Simon. 35 And they rehearsed the things *that happened* in the way, and how he was known of them in the breaking of the bread.

§ 146. THE APPEARANCE TO THE DISCIPLES IN JERUSALEM, THOMAS BEING ABSENT.

MARK 16:14.	LUKE 24:36–43.	JOHN 20:19–25.
14 And afterward he was manifested unto the eleven themselves as they sat at meat; and he upbraided them with their unbelief and hardness of heart, because they believed not them which [1] had seen him after he was risen.	36 And as they spake these things, he himself stood in the midst of them, [1] and saith unto them, Peace *be* unto you. 37 But they were terrified and affrighted, and supposed that they beheld a spirit. 38 And he said unto them, Why are ye troubled? and wherefore do reasonings [2] arise in your heart? 39 See my hands and my feet, that it is I myself: handle me, and see; for a spirit hath not flesh and bones, as ye behold me having. 40 [2] And when he had said this, he shewed them his hands and his feet. 41 And while they still disbelieved for joy, and wondered, he said	19 When therefore it was evening, on that day, the first *day* of the week, and when the doors were shut where the disciples were, for fear of the Jews, Jesus came and stood in the midst, and saith unto them, Peace *be* unto you. 20 And when he had said this, he shewed unto them his hands and his side. The disciples therefore were glad, when they saw the Lord. 21 Jesus therefore said to them again, Peace *be* unto you: as the Father has sent me, even so send I you. 22 And when he had said this, he breathed on them, and saith unto them, Receive ye the [3] Holy Ghost [3]: 23 [a] whose soever sins ye

ERV. mg.: [1] Some ancient authorities omit *and saith unto them, Peace* be *unto you.* [2] Some ancient authorities omit ver. 40. [3] Or, *Holy Spirit*

ARV. txt.: [1] that [2] questionings [3] Holy Spirit

[a] Matt. 16:19. I will give unto thee the keys of the kingdom of heaven: and whatsoever thou shalt bind on earth shall be bound in heaven: and whatsoever thou shalt loose on earth shall be loosed in heaven. (§ 75)

[a] Matt. 18:18. Verily I say unto you, What things soever ye shall bind on earth shall be bound in heaven: and what things soever ye shall loose on earth shall be loosed in heaven. (§ 81)

LUKE 24.	JOHN 20.
unto them, Have ye here anything to eat? 42 And they gave him a piece of broiled [1]fish. 43 And he took it, and did eat[1] before them.	forgive, they are forgiven unto them; whose soever *sins* ye retain, they are retained. 24 But Thomas, one of the twelve, called [2]Didymus, was not with them when Jesus came. 25 The other disciples therefore said unto him, We have seen the Lord. But he said unto them, Except I shall see in his hands the print of the nails, and put my finger into the print of the nails, and put my hand into his side, I will not believe.

§ 147. THE APPEARANCE TO THOMAS WITH THE OTHER DISCIPLES.

JOHN 20: 26-29.

26 And after eight days again his disciples were within, and Thomas with them. Jesus cometh, the doors being shut, and stood in the midst, and said, Peace *be* unto you. 27 Then saith he to Thomas, Reach hither thy finger, and see my hands; and reach *hither* thy hand, and put it into my side: and be not faithless, but believing. 28 Thomas answered and said unto him, My Lord and my God. 29 Jesus saith unto him, Because thou hast seen me, [3]thou hast believed: blessed *are* they that have not seen, and *yet* have believed. (+§ 151)

§ 148. THE APPEARANCE TO SEVEN DISCIPLES BY THE SEA OF GALILEE.

JOHN 21: 1-24.

1 After these things Jesus manifested himself again to the disciples at the sea of Tiberias; and he manifested *himself* on this wise. 2 There were together Simon Peter, and Thomas called [2]Didymus, and Nathanael of Cana in Galilee, and the *sons* of Zebedee, and two other of his disciples. 3 Simon Peter saith unto them, I go a fishing. They say unto him, We also come with thee. They went forth, and entered into the boat; and that night they took nothing. 4 But when day was now breaking, Jesus stood on the beach: howbeit[2] the disciples knew not that it was Jesus. 5 Jesus therefore saith unto them, Children, have ye aught to eat? They answered him, No. 6 And he said unto them, Cast the net on the right side of the boat, and ye shall find. They cast therefore, and now they were not able to draw it for the multitude of fishes. 7 That disciple therefore whom Jesus loved saith unto Peter,

---

ERV. mg.:   [1] Many ancient authorities add *and a honeycomb.*   [2] That is, *Twin.*   [3] Or, *hast thou believed?*

ARV. txt.:   [1] and ate   [2] yet

JOHN 21.

It is the Lord. So when Simon Peter heard that it was the Lord, he girt his coat about him (for he was naked), and cast himself into the sea. 8 But the other disciples came in the little boat (for they were not far from the land, but about two hundred cubits off), dragging the net *full* of fishes. 9 So when they got out upon the land, they see [1] a fire of coals there, and [2] fish laid thereon, and [3] bread. 10 Jesus saith unto them, Bring of the fish which ye have now taken. 11 Simon Peter therefore went [4] up, and drew the net to land, full of great fishes, a hundred and fifty and three: and for all there were so many, the net was not rent. 12 Jesus saith unto them, Come *and* break your fast. And none of the disciples durst inquire of him, Who art thou? knowing that it was the Lord. 13 Jesus cometh, and taketh the [3] bread, and giveth them, and the fish likewise. 14 This is now the third time that Jesus was manifested to the disciples, after that he was risen from the dead.

15 So when they had broken their fast, Jesus saith to Simon Peter, Simon, *son* of [5] John, [6] lovest thou me more than these? He saith unto him, Yea, Lord; thou knowest that I [7] love thee. He saith unto him, Feed my lambs. 16 He saith to him again a second time, Simon, *son* of [5] John, [7] lovest thou me? He saith unto him, Yea, Lord; thou knowest that I [7] love thee. He saith unto him, Tend my sheep. 17 He saith unto him the third time, Simon, *son* of [5] John, [7] lovest thou me? Peter was grieved because he said unto him the third time, [7] Lovest thou me? And he said unto him, Lord, thou knowest all things; thou [8] knowest that I [7] love thee. Jesus saith unto him, Feed my sheep. 18 Verily, verily, I say unto thee, When thou wast young, thou girdedst thyself, and walkedst whither thou wouldest: but when thou shalt be old, thou shalt stretch forth thy hands, and another shall gird thee, and carry thee whither thou wouldest not. 19 Now this he spake, signifying by what manner of death he should glorify God. And when he had spoken this, he saith unto him, Follow me. 20 Peter, turning about, seeth the disciple whom Jesus loved following; which[1] also leaned back on his breast at the supper, and said, Lord, who is he that betrayeth thee? 21 Peter therefore seeing him saith to Jesus, Lord, [9] and what shall this man do? 22 Jesus saith unto him, If I will that he tarry till I come, what *is that* to thee? follow thou me. 23 This saying therefore went forth among the brethren, that that disciple should not die: yet Jesus said not unto him, that he should not die; but, If I will that he tarry till I come, what *is that* to thee?

24 This is the disciple which[2] beareth witness of these things, and wrote these things: and we know that his witness is true. (+ § 151)

§ 149. THE APPEARANCE TO THE ELEVEN ON A MOUNTAIN IN GALILEE.

MATT. 28 : 16–20.	MARK 16 : 15–18.
16 But the eleven disciples went into Galilee, unto the mountain where Jesus had appointed them. 17 And when they saw him, they worshipped *him*: but some doubted. 18	15 And he said unto them, Go ye into all the world, and preach the gospel to the whole creation. 16 [a] He that believeth and is baptized shall be saved; but he that disbelieveth shall be condemned.

ERV. mg.: [1] Gr. *a fire of charcoal.* [2] Or, *a fish* [3] Or, *a loaf* [4] Or, *aboard* [5] Gr. *Joanes.* See ch. i. 42, margin. [6, 7] *Love* in these places represents two different Greek words. [8] Or, *perceivest* [9] Gr. *and this man, what?*

ARV. txt.: [1] who [2] that

[a] John 3:18. He that believeth on him is not judged: he that believeth not hath been judged already, because he hath not believed on the name of the only begotten Son of God. (§ 23)

Matt. 28.	Mark 16.
And Jesus came to them and spake unto them, saying, a All authority hath been given unto me in heaven and on earth. 19 Go ye therefore, and make disciples of all the nations, baptizing them into the name of the Father and of the Son and of the Holy Ghost[1]: 20 teaching them to observe all things whatsoever I commanded you: and lo, I am with you [1] alway[2], even unto [2] the end of the world.	17 And these signs shall follow[3] them that believe: in my name shall they cast out [3] devils[4]; they shall speak with [4] new tongues; 18 b they shall take up serpents, and if they drink any deadly thing, it shall in no wise hurt them; they shall lay hands on the sick, and they shall recover.

§ 150. CHRIST'S FINAL APPEARANCE, AND HIS ASCENSION.

Mark 16:19, 20.	Luke 24:44–53.
	44 And he said unto them, These are my words which I spake unto you, while I was yet with you, how[5] that all things must needs be fulfilled, which are written in the law of Moses, and the prophets, and the psalms, concerning me. 45 Then opened he their mind, that they might understand the scriptures; 46 and he said unto them, Thus it is written, that the Christ should suffer, and rise again from the dead the third day; 47 and that repentance [5] and remission of sins should be preached in his name unto all the [6] nations, beginning from Jerusalem. 48 Ye are witnesses of these things. 49 And behold, I send forth the promise of my Father upon

ERV. mg.:   [1] Gr. *all the days.*   [2] Or, *the consummation of the age*   [3] Gr. *demons.*   [4] Some ancient authorities omit *new.*   [5] Some ancient authorities read *unto.*   [6] Or, *nations. Beginning from Jerusalem, ye are witnesses*

ARV. txt.:   [1] Holy Spirit   [2] always   [3] accompany   [4] demons   [5] *Omit* how

a Matt. 11:27.   All things have been delivered unto me of my Father.   (§ 87)
a Luke 10:22.   All things have been delivered unto me of my Father.   (§ 87)   Cf. John 17:2.   (§ 135)
b Luke 10:19.   Behold, I have given you authority to tread upon serpents and scorpions, and over all the power of the enemy: and nothing shall in any wise hurt you.   (§ 87)

MARK 16.	LUKE 24.
	you : but tarry ye in the city, until ye be clothed with power from on high.
19 So then the Lord Jesus, after he had spoken unto them, was received up into heaven, and sat down at the right hand of God. 20 And they went forth, and preached everywhere, the Lord working with them, and confirming the word by the signs that followed. Amen.	50 And he led them out until *they were* over against Bethany : and he lifted up his hands, and blessed them. 51 And it came to pass, while he blessed them, he parted from them, [1]and was carried up into heaven. 52 And they [2]worshipped him, and returned to Jerusalem with great joy : 53 and were continually in the temple, blessing God.

§151. THE CONCLUSION OF JOHN'S GOSPEL.

JOHN 20 : 30, 31.

30 Many other signs therefore did Jesus in the presence of the disciples, which are not written in this book : 31 but these are written, that ye may believe that Jesus is the Christ, the Son of God ; and that believing ye may have life in his name.

JOHN 21 : 25.

25 And there are also many other things which Jesus did, the which if they should be written every one, I suppose that even the world itself would not contain the books that should be written.

ERV. mg.: [1] Some ancient authorities omit *and was carried up into heaven.* [2] Some ancient authorities omit *worshipped him, and*

APPENDICES

APPENDIX I.

PRINCIPLES AND METHODS IN ACCORDANCE WITH WHICH THE HARMONY IS CONSTRUCTED.

THE fundamental principle which we have endeavored to follow throughout our work—viz., to exhibit the witness of the several gospels with the utmost fidelity consistent with the parallelism essential to the idea of a harmony—has already been stated in the Preface. It lies in the very nature of a harmony of the gospels, that it should exhibit their parallelism passage by passage. We have endeavored, at the same time, to preserve, as far as is consistent with the exhibiting of this parallelism, the structure and peculiarities of the several gospels.

I. THE PART DIVISIONS.

The whole material of the four gospels is divided into nine main Parts. These nine Parts are intended to correspond to the natural periods of the life and ministry of Jesus, as these are indicated in the gospels themselves. The difference of plan between the several gospels, especially between the fourth and the synoptic gospels, makes it impossible that each main division line of the Harmony should coincide with a main dividing line running through all four of the gospels alike. It is hoped, however, that it will be recognized that the plan here adopted is built solely upon the gospels, and exhibits the natural periods of the history, as these appear from a comparison of the four accounts.

We have deemed it of the first importance to fix attention upon these natural divisions of the history. The table of Principal Divisions, or Parts, is therefore spread upon a separate page, preceding the Analytical Outline. The Analytical Outline also exhibits, in a form convenient for memorizing or reference, a more complete articulation of the whole history. These tables are, therefore, not mere tables of contents for the Harmony that follows. They furnish a conspectus of the history, and are intended to aid the mind in grasping the relation of its several parts to one another.

II.   THE CHAPTER DIVISIONS IN THE OUTLINE.

In the Analytical Outline the Parts are divided into chapters.   The purpose of these chapter divisions is twofold : first, to group together the sections for convenience of study; and, second, to recognize the existence of certain divisions of the material, intermediate between the section and the Part, which in some portions of the narrative seem to have been in the mind of one or another of the gospel writers themselves.   Chapter VII perhaps represents the chapter division at its best : the events of sections 21–26 seem manifestly to constitute in the mind of the evangelist himself a distinct portion of his book.   Chapter XIII furnishes nearly as good an illustration : a careful reader of the synoptists can hardly fail to see that in Mark 2:1—3:6 the evangelist has given a rapid sketch of the development of the hostility of the scribes and Pharisees to Jesus.   The section inserted here from the fourth gospel does not interrupt the course of events, but only presents another stage in the development sketched by the synoptists.   It seems desirable to recognize these facts by grouping these sections into a chapter.   These chapter divisions in general, however, are chiefly useful when the eye can take in at one vision the relation of the chapter on the one hand to the Part, and on the other to the section.   For this reason the chapter titles, though included in the Outline, are omitted from the body of the book.

III.   THE SECTIONS OF THE HARMONY.

The limits of the sections have also been determined in accordance with our general principle.   A detailed explanation of its application to individual cases is neither practicable within reasonable limits, nor necessary.   The sections have been made to begin where there was reason to believe that the gospel writer himself intended to pass to a new division of the subject, and to include the material referred by the evangelist to a single occasion or treated as constituting a single discourse.   A section begins in the midst of a paragraph only when required by a difference of paragraphing in the different gospels.   But two instances of this occur.   It has seemed necessary to run the line separating sections 75 and 76 through what in Luke is but one paragraph, following in this the strongly marked paragraphing of Matthew and Mark.   For similar reasons, a paragraph of Luke has been divided between sections 133 and 134.

1. The Limits of the Sections

The order in which the sections have been placed has been determined by the principle stated in the opening paragraph of this Appendix. The order of

2. Order of Sections the evangelists has been followed except when a difference between two gospels compels a departure from the order of one or the other of them in order to bring into the same section corresponding material occurring in the different gospels.

Only when the parallelism of the gospels affords no criterion have we resorted to any other principle. In the arrangement of the two narratives of the birth and early years of Jesus, for example, and in the placing of certain sections of the Johannine narrative to which there is no parallel in the synoptic gospels, we have been obliged to appeal to other considerations, and have adopted that arrangement which seems to yield the most probable order of events, or which best satisfies the documentary data, however meager these may sometimes be. The succession of events thus obtained can in some instances, notably in the adjustment of the Lucan narrative of the Perean ministry to the fourth gospel, make no high claim to intrinsic probability.

In order to adhere more faithfully to this principle, in the present edition, we have in two instances transferred material from one section to another. Luke 11:14-36, which in the first edition stood in section 55, placed there because of its partial parallelism with Mark 3:19-30, has been incorporated in section 94, the position required by Luke's order. Matt. 11:20-30, which in the first edition stood in section 87, placed there because of the partial parallelism of the material with Luke 10:12-23, has been transferred to section 52, the position required by the order of the first gospel, in which this passage is contained. The parallelism between this passage and Luke 10:12-23, in respect to discourse material (section 87), is shown in the method regularly adopted for the Repeated Sayings.

We have applied to paragraphs within a section the same principle that we have followed in determining the order of sections. The order of the

3. Order of Paragraphs within the Section evangelists has been departed from only when a difference between them has compelled the modification of the order of one of them, in order to bring paragraphs of similar content into parallelism. The only instances of such transposition of paragraphs within a section occur in sections 133 and 138.

In the narrative of the Last Supper, section 133, Luke's account of the strife among the Twelve, 22:24-30, which in the first edition stood before verses 19-23, is in the present edition placed after verse 23, the arrangement being thus more nearly conformed to the order of Luke. Had we conceived it to be our task to arrange the events of this section in what we might reasonably believe to be the probable order of their occurrence, as do most harmonists and writers on the Life of Christ, we should doubtless have adopted a different arrangement. Fidelity to the principles which we have followed constrained us, however, to adopt that arrangement which involves the least disturbance of the order of Luke consistent with the placing of his narrative in parallelism with that of the other gospels.

The same general principle of preserving as far as possible the structure of each gospel, as well as our judgment that it is important that the gospel **4. Paragraphs** history should be read by paragraphs, not by verses, has led us **Retained Intact** to keep paragraphs intact, and to abandon the plan adopted in those harmonies which make it a matter of chief importance that similar sentences or even phrases stand opposite one another on the page. This plan involves indefinite *dissection* of the gospel narratives, and is then only partially successful in exhibiting their parallelism in details. For the purpose of this Harmony, which is planned with a view to the historical study of the gospels, we have thought it wiser to be content in general with placing parallel *paragraphs* opposite one another, leaving it to the student to make the more detailed comparison himself.

This method is the more necessary because there are many different kinds of parallelism, even when sections or paragraphs in the different gospels manifestly refer to the same events or discourses. This arises from the fact that the various writers differ widely in style and in their method of narration. No printed page can adequately exhibit the exact character of the parallelism between paragraphs of dissimilar scope and structure. Sometimes several incidents in a paragraph of one gospel seem to have little relation to those narrated in a paragraph of another, when nevertheless both paragraphs relate what may be called comprehensively one event. For example, Matthew relates that early on the resurrection morning Jesus appeared to Mary Magdalene and to the other Mary, while John speaks only of Mary Magdalene. We have placed these accounts in *general* parallelism, not attempting to draw out the details of those early appearances to the women into a minute chronological arrangement for which the gospels afford no data. The proper function of the harmony is served, if its page exhibits whatever parallelism there is in the accounts themselves. The denials of Peter, which occurred during the progress of Christ's trial, are properly treated in a similar way.

In cases of unequal paragraphing in different gospels—that is, when matter contained in two or more paragraphs in one of the gospels is in another

5. Spacing of Paragraphs within the Section gospel, by reason of different treatment, brought together into one paragraph—it has sometimes been necessary to introduce blank spaces dividing the more condensed account into parts corresponding to the paragraphs of the parallel account; see, for example, section 139. Such spacing has also occasionally been employed to bring clearly marked subdivisions of corresponding paragraphs opposite one another; see, for example, section 143. In all cases where the space thus introduced into a paragraph exceeds a very few lines, attention is called to the continuance of the paragraph further on by the insertion in small type of the words, "Paragraph continued below," or a similar phrase.

In sections 133 and 138 not only spacing but slight transposition of material within the paragraph has been necessary in order to bring evidently parallel

6. Transposition within Paragraphs narratives opposite one another. At each point at which by reason of this transposition a paragraph is interrupted, a note has been inserted showing where the remainder of the paragraph is to be found.

When parallel material could not be brought together without doing violence to the structure of one account or the other, we have left each paragraph

7. Cross-References intact as the evangelist wrote it, but have frequently inserted a reference in the parallel column to indicate where the similar material of the parallel accounts is to be found. This method is illustrated in sections 139 and 140.

IV. REPETITION OF MATERIAL.

An adequate exhibit of the parallelism of the gospels requires the repetition of certain portions of the gospel text, but demands also that the fact of such repetition shall be indicated. This necessity pertains to both *narratives* and *sayings*, but demands in general a different treatment of the two kinds of material.

Narrative material, when repeated, is in general placed in the parallel columns in both instances of its occurrence; its repetition is in every such

1. Narrative Material case indicated by brackets [ ] or half-brackets ⌐ ⌐. The brackets are omitted only in the exceptional cases, mentioned below, in which the repeated material is given the form of a footnote. The narrative passages that are used more than once are of several classes.

253

In the first class of cases, in consequence of condensation in the narrative, a single sentence or paragraph covers two distinct events or historical occasions, separated perhaps by some distance of time. In this class of cases it is necessary that certain portions of the record be repeated in order to bring the paragraph or verse into connection with both the occasions to which it refers. The repeated material is placed in half-brackets in the instance in which it is detached from the paragraph connection given it by the evangelists. The instances of this use of half-brackets occur in sections **9, 15, 19, 31, 40, 47, 48, 80, 121, 131, 136, 138.**

In the second class of cases two gospels containing practically identical accounts of the same event locate this event differently, yet each attaches it by introductory or concluding words to the context in which it stands. In this case it is necessary to repeat the introductory or concluding sentence, in order at the one point to preserve the logical connection—to the extent, that is, of presenting each entire paragraph as we judge the writer conceived it in his own mind—and at the other to show the more probable historical position of the event. The repeated matter is placed in half-brackets in the instance in which it is detached from the paragraph of which it was a part, its insertion at this point representing the historical place of the event as indicated by a comparison of the gospels. In the other instance of its occurrence—namely, when it is retained in the paragraph to which it belongs but is by such retention detached from its more probable historical position—it is placed in full brackets. The pairs of instances falling under this head are in sections 34 and 37, sections 40 and 49, sections 41 and 60, sections 58 and 86, sections 120 and 122, sections 138 and 139. In one instance (Matt. 1:18–25) a paragraph containing material belonging to two different points of the history, yet blended inextricably into a single narrative, has been repeated entire, being placed in half-brackets in the second instance of its occurrence, this being the position called for by the parallelism of a portion of the narrative with the account in Luke.

In a third class of cases, narratives of events which on the authority of the evangelists must be assigned to distinctly different chronological positions are, for purposes of comparison, repeated. In the instance in which the narrative occupies a position other than that given it by the evangelists, it is printed in smaller type and placed between brackets in parallel columns with the narrative with which it is to be compared; the repetition at this point being for purposes of comparison, and involving no pronouncement upon the identity of the two events. The three pairs of instances falling under this head are in sections 27 and 121, sections 36 and 62, sections 55 and 94. The adoption of this expedient in the present edition is an extension to similar narratives of the method applied in the first edition to the Repeated Sayings of Jesus. Theoretically the same principle would apply to the narratives of section 38. But the slight difference in location makes it seem more expedient in this case to avoid repetition by a slight modification of Luke's order.

In a fourth class of cases the event or period to which a section refers is spoken of incidentally or by way of explanation, yet so as to add important data, in a section dealing in the main with an entirely different event. In these cases we have placed this contributory material in the form of a footnote at the bottom of the page. The only instances of this method of treatment are in sections 15 and 34.

The sayings of Christ assigned by the different evangelists to different occasions demand special consideration, furnishing, as they do, one of the most

2. Repeated Sayings difficult, and at the same time one of the most important, problems of the harmony. It should be observed that, in the report of the sayings and discourses of Jesus, there are two kinds of parallelism. The same saying, or series of sayings, may be reported by two evangelists in the same historical connection, as in Matt. 16:25 and Luke 9:24; or it may be reported by both, but assigned to different historical occasions, as in Matt. 16:25 and Luke 17:33; or it may even be reported by the same evangelist in two different connections, as in Matt. 10:39 and 16:25. In the first class of cases we have only the ordinary question of harmony, such as arises in the treatment of narrative material also. The second and third classes, however, present a different problem. It cannot be maintained that every one of these sayings was repeatedly uttered by Jesus; it would be rash to say that in no case were sayings repeated; it would require a keen critic indeed to determine in each case whether the saying was repeated by Jesus on different occasions, or only differently placed by the evangelists; and, if the latter, on which of the two or more occasions to which it is assigned it was really uttered. It has therefore seemed best not to undertake to solve this problem, but rather to exhibit the facts as fully as possible, and with the smallest possible admixture of theory. We have accordingly adopted a method by which every saying of Jesus is retained in the place or places to which each evangelist assigns it, and at the same time all its parallels, if any, even those in the same gospel, are shown on the same page with it, their position in the gospels and their location in the Harmony being also indicated. This method is more fully explained in Appendix II, which also contains a full table of the sayings of Christ assigned by the evangelist to more than one occasion.

V.   USE OF THE REVISED VERSION.

With the consent and approval of the Oxford and Cambridge University Presses of England, courteously granted to us, we have, as in the former editions, employed the text of the English Revision of 1881 in the body of the book. While at many points we should have been glad to modify the text of this version, or its margin, it has seemed best to adopt it without change or comment other than the occasional modification of its paragraphs. These changes in the limits of the paragraphs have been made, not in a harmonistic interest, but on independent grounds. The marginal readings of this version are shown in the margin at the foot of the page immediately below the text. A second margin shows the renderings incorporated by the American Revision Committee in the text of the American Revision of 1901. We have not, however, undertaken to show differences between the English and American editions affecting punctuation and spelling only, or the marginal readings of the American Revision. We acknowledge with appreciation the courtesy of Thomas Nelson & Sons, owners of the copyright (1901) of the American Standard Revised Bible, in thus permitting the use of this edition.

The superior figures prefixed to words in the text refer to the marginal readings of the English Revision; those affixed refer to the readings of the text of the American Revision.

The two passages, John 7:53—8:1 and Mark 16:9–20, which, though contained in the Revised Version, are by the soundest criticism not regarded as belonging properly to the gospels in connection with which they stand, seem to call for special treatment. Both are accordingly set in smaller type than the other portions of the text.

VI.   ARRANGEMENT IN COLUMNS.

In the arrangement of the material on the page the effort has been rather to make a perspicuous and easily intelligible page than to economize space. In sections in which there is but one gospel authority the text is printed in one wide column.   When the authorities are two or more of the synoptists, and there is no account from the fourth gospel, three parallel columns are used, one being left blank if there are but two accounts.   If the account is contained in John and in the synoptists, four columns are used, one for each gospel.   In general the same width of column is maintained throughout the section.   In sections 94, 127, 131, 134, where, for a large portion of the section, there is but one authority, a change from the narrow to the broad column is permitted, to avoid several successive pages containing but one narrow column.

VII.   RECAPITULATION OF TYPOGRAPHICAL FEATURES.

For the practical convenience of the student, it may be desirable to recapitulate briefly the significance of those typographical features of the book which are not obviously self-explanatory.

1. COLUMNS.   When a section is printed in four columns, this indicates that for some portion of that section there is material from the gospel of John and from two or more of the synoptic gospels.

When there are three columns, this indicates that matter for this section is found in two or more of the synoptists, the fourth gospel furnishing no account.

There are no two-column pages.

When there is but one column, there is but one authority for any portion of the section, which may be any one of the four gospels.   But concerning sections 94, 127, 131, 134, see vi, above.

2. BRACKETS.   Two kind of brackets are used, half-brackets and full brackets.   That a passage is inclosed either in half-brackets or in full brackets indicates that it is repeated at some other point on the page of the Harmony.

a) Half-brackets indicate that the words so inclosed are detached from the paragraph of which they form a part, in order to place them in the chronological position indicated by a comparison of the different accounts. But concerning Matt. 1:18–25, see iv, 1, in this Appendix.

b) Full brackets are used for three purposes:

(1) They inclose words necessary to complete a paragraph, but repeated elsewhere in their more probable chronological position.

(2) They inclose narrative passages repeated simply for purposes of comparison.

(3) They inclose certain of the longer Repeated Sayings, printed in parallel columns instead of at the foot of the page for the sake of easier comparison.

To the student who is seeking simply to frame a narrative of the life of Jesus, section by section, the following practical rule may be useful: Use in each section all unbracketed material and all material in half-brackets; omit for this purpose material in full brackets; this is added either to complete a paragraph or for purposes of comparison.

3. FOOTNOTES. There are four kinds of footnotes.

a) Superior figures prefixed to a word or phrase in the text refer to the marginal readings of the Revised Version of 1881. These are reprinted without change, except as required by the arrangement of the figures. They are preceded by the abbreviation: ERV. mg. In the comparatively few instances in which, by the transposition of a reference figure from the end to the beginning of a word (in order to distinguish these readings from those of the American Revision), the meaning of the note is obscured, we have removed the obscurity by the insertion of explanatory words in the note, inclosing them in brackets.

b) Superior figures affixed to a word or phrase in the text refer to the renderings adopted by the American Revision Committee and incorporated in the text of the American Revision of 1901. They are preceded by the abbreviation: ARV. txt.

c) Superior letters in the text refer to the Repeated Sayings of Jesus, that is, to sayings of Christ similar to those standing in the text, but reported in a different connection. The number in parenthesis at the end of the footnote indicates the section in which the passage appears in the body of the text. When the footnote contains only a reference by chapter and verse without text or section number, the passage referred to belongs, not to another section, but to another part of the same section.

d) A few necessary footnotes not included in either of the above classes are indicated by asterisks. See IV, 1, fourth class.

4. SMALLER TYPE IN THE TEXT. Smaller type has been used in the body of the text, in sections 83, 143, 145, 146, 149, 150, for material not regarded as a genuine part of the Gospel under which it is cited. It is also used in sections 27, 36, 55, 62, 94, 121 for narrative matter repeated for the sake of comparison only; and in sections 49, 52, 55, 57, 64, 81, 94, 124, 131 for the Repeated Sayings that are printed in the parallel columns for the sake of easier comparison.

5. SECTION NUMBERS SUBJOINED TO SECTIONS OR SHORTER PASSAGES. Of these there are two kinds:

a) A section number in parenthesis placed at the end of a passage, without preceding sign, refers to the section from which the passage is taken.

b) A section number preceded by the sign +, and inclosed in parenthesis, refers the reader to that section of the Harmony in which will be found the paragraph which, in the gospel itself, immediately follows the passage to which the number is attached.

APPENDIX II.

To the student of the gospels it is a matter of special interest to determine the historical situation of the sayings of Christ. This portion of his task, however, is complicated by the fact that many of these sayings are given by the different gospels in substantially the same form, but in entirely different historical situations. In a few instances the same passage even occurs more than once in the same gospel. In the present state of knowledge respecting the way in which our four gospels were produced it is impossible to determine with certainty in each case on which of two or more occasions a given saying was uttered, or whether on more than one occasion. In the preceding Appendix we have explained our method of dealing with these cases. In no case have we detached a paragraph of Christ's sayings from the historical situation given it by the evangelist, or *dissected* what is given in the gospels as a discourse, in order to bring similar discourse material into the same section. In thus assigning more than one historical situation to similar or practically identical sayings, we by no means maintain that all of them were spoken more than once. We simply maintain that in the present state of New Testament criticism it is impossible to determine to which historical situation each of the parallel sayings belongs, and which of them were actually repeated on more than one occasion.

The following table is designed to exhibit this parallelism in the discourses of Christ. Under each section of the table the figures in bold-face type designate passages which belong to the corresponding section of the Harmony. The figures in lighter-face type designate passages which are assigned by the evangelists to a different historical occasion, yet are closely parallel in thought and language to the passages opposite which they stand in this table. In the case of parallel passages occurring in the same gospel we have placed the citations in the same column connected by a brace. Any passage cited in bold-face type under a given section in the table will be found in the corresponding section of the Harmony, while the passages cited in lighter-face type will be found at the foot of the page under the same section, except that a few of the longer passages of the latter class have been printed in the parallel columns inclosed in brackets.

When a saying occurs at two distinctly different points in the same section, either by being repeated in the same account, or by being placed in different connections in parallel accounts, cross-reference is made in the Harmony from each passage to the other. The footnote in such a case, however, consists of reference only, and does not include the text of the passage referred to. See, for example, pages 64 and 87. These cases do not appear in the table unless the passage is also repeated in a different section.

It will be observed that there are at least forty discourses of Christ, shorter or longer, which contain parallel matter of the kind above described. A typical and interesting instance of discourse parallelism is found in the parables of the sheep gone astray, in section 81, and of the lost sheep, in section 102. Section 64, the mission of the Twelve, illustrates the wide distribution in the other gospels of matter which forms one discourse in Matthew. And, to add one more instance, the often-quoted text, "He that findeth his life shall lose it; and he that loseth his life for my sake shall find it," occurs in slightly varied forms six times, and is assigned by the evangelists to four different historical situations.

This exhibit of the parallelism in Christ's discourses, in the following table as well as on the page of the Harmony, will be serviceable in many ways in the study of the teachings of Christ. Thus it will enable the student to note at a glance the various contexts in which many of the sayings of Jesus are found. It will also serve to throw light upon the difficult problem of the process by which the discourses of Jesus received their present form.

It should be particularly observed that the list does not undertake to include all the sayings of Christ of which there is more than one report in the gospels, but only those which are assigned by the evangelists to more than one historical situation.

TABLE OF REPEATED SAYINGS.

§ 28. Discourse with Nicodemus.

Mark 16:16 . . . . John **3**:**18**

§ 36. First Rejection at Nazareth.

Matt. 13:57 . . . . Mark **6**:4 . . . Luke **4**:**24** . . . Cf. John 4:44

§ 46. The Man with the Withered Hand.

Matt. **12**:**11** . . . . Luke 14:5 . . . .

§ 49. Sermon on the Mount.

Matt. **5**:**13** . . . . Mark 9:50 . . .	Luke 14:34, 35 . . . . . .
Matt. **5**:**15** . . . . Mark 4:21 . . .	{ Luke 8:16 } . . . . . .
	{ 11:33 }
Matt. **5**:**18**	Luke 16:17 . . . . . .
Matt. **5**:**25**, **26**	Luke 12:58, 59 . . . . .
Matt. **5**:**29**, **30** } . . Mark 9:43, 47 . .	
18:8, 9 }	
Matt. **5**:**32** } . . Mark 10:11 . . .	Luke 16:18 . . . . . .
19:9 }	
Matt. **6**:**8**, **32**	Luke 12:30 . . . . . .
Matt. **6**:**9**–**13**	Luke 11:2–4 . . . . . .
Matt. **6**:**14**, **15** . . Mark 11:25	. . . .
Matt. **6**:**15** }	. . . .
18:35 }	
Matt. **6**:**19**–**21**	Luke 12:33, 34 . . . . .
Matt. **6**:**22**, **23**	Luke 11:34–36 . . . . .
Matt. **6**:**24**	Luke 16:13 . . . . . .
Matt. **6**:**25**–**33**	Luke 12:22–31 . . . . .
Matt. **7**:**2***b* . . . Mark 4:24*b* . . .	Luke **6**:**38***b* . . . . .
Matt. 15:14*b*	Luke **6**:**39** . . . . . .
Matt. 10:24, 25*a*	Luke **6**:**40** . . { John 13:16
	{ 15:20*a*
Matt. **7**:**7**–**11**	Luke 11:9–13 . . . . .
Matt. **7**:**12***b* }	. . . .
22:40 }	
Matt. **7**:**13**, **14**	Luke 13:24 . . . . . .
Matt. **7**:**16**–**18**, **20** }	Luke **6**:**43**–**45** . . . .
12:33–35 }	
Matt. **7**:**23**	Luke 13:27 . . . . . .

§ 50. The Centurion's Servant.

Matt. **8 : 11, 12** . . . . Luke 13 : 28, 29 . . . . .

Matt. **8 : 12** ⎫
13 : 42 ⎪
13 : 50 ⎬ . . . .
22 : 13*b* ⎪
24 : 51 ⎪
25 : 30 ⎭

§ 52. John the Baptist's Last Message.

Matt. **11 : 12, 13** . . . . Luke 16 : 16 . . . . .

Matt. **11 : 15** ⎫
13 : 9 ⎬ . . { Mark **4 : 9** ⎫ . . . { Luke **8 : 8***b* ⎫ . . . .
13 : 43*b* ⎭ . . { **4 : 23** ⎭ . . . { 14 : 35*b* ⎭

Matt. **11 : 21-24** . . . . Luke 10 : 12-15 . . . . .

Matt. **11 : 25-27** . . . . Luke 10 : 21, 22 . . . . .

Matt. **11 : 27***a* ⎫
28 : 18 ⎭ . . . . Luke 10 : 22*a* . . . . .

Matt. **11 : 27***b* . . . . Luke 10 : 22*b* . . . John 6 : 46

§ 55. Warnings to the Scribes and Pharisees.

Matt. **12 : 25***b*, **26** . . . Mark **3 : 23***b*-**26** . . . Luke 11 : 17*b*, 18 . . .

Matt. **12 : 27, 28** . . . . Luke 11 : 19, 20 . . .

Matt. **12 : 29** . . . Mark **3 : 27** . . . Luke 11 : 21, 22 . . .

Matt. **12 : 30** . . . . Luke 11 : 23 . . . . .

Matt. **12 : 31, 32** . . . Mark **3 : 28, 29** . . . Luke 12 : 10 . . . . .

Matt. **12 : 33 35** ⎫
7 : 16-18, 20 ⎭ . . . . Luke 6 : 43-45 . . . .

Matt. **12 : 38-42** . . . . Luke 11 : 29-32 . . .

Matt. **12 : 39** ⎫
16 : 4 ⎭ . . Mark **8 : 12** . . . Luke 11 : 29 . . . . .

Matt. **12 : 43-45** . . . . Luke 11 : 24-26 . . . .

§ 57. The Parables by the Sea.

Matt. **13 : 9** ⎫ ⎫ . . { Mark **4 : 9** ⎫ . . . { Luke **8 : 8***b* ⎫
13 : 43*b* ⎬ ⎬ . . { **4 : 23** ⎭ . . . { . . . .
11 : 15 ⎭ . . . . { Luke 14 : 35*b* ⎭

Matt. **5 : 15** . . . . Mark **4 : 21** . . . { Luke **8 : 16** ⎫ . . . .
{ 11 : 33 ⎭

Matt. **10 : 26** . . . Mark **4 : 22** . . . { Luke **8 : 17** ⎫ . . .
{ 12 : 2 ⎭

Matt. **7 : 2***b* . . . Mark **4 : 24***b* . . Luke 6 : 38*b* . . . . .

Matt. **13 : 12** ⎫
25 : 29 ⎭ . . Mark **4 : 25** . . . { Luke **8 : 18***b* ⎫ . . . .
{ 19 : 26 ⎭

Matt. **13 : 16, 17** . . . . Luke 10 : 23, 24 . . . . .

Matt. 13 : 31, 32	. . .	Mark 4 : 30–32	. . .	Luke 13 : 18, 19	. . . .
Matt. 13 : 33 .	. . . . . .			Luke 13 : 20, 21	. . . .
Matt. 13 : 42 } 13 : 50 } 8 : 12 22 : 13b } 24 : 51 25 : 30 }	. . . .			Luke 13 : 28	. . . .

§ 62. SECOND REJECTION AT NAZARETH.

| Matt. 13 : 57 . | . . . | Mark 6 : 4 | . . . | Luke 4 : 24 | . . . | Cf. John 4 : 44 |

§ 64. THE MISSION OF THE TWELVE.

Matt. 9 : 37, 38	. . . .			Luke 10 : 2	. . . .
Matt. 10 : 7–16	. . .	Mark 6 : 8–11	. . .	{ Luke 9 : 3–5 } 10 : 3–12 }	. . .
Matt. 10 : 17, 18 } 24 : 9a }	. .	Mark 13 : 9	. . .	Luke 21 : 12, 13	. . .
Matt. 10 : 19, 20	. . .	Mark 13 : 11	. . .	{ Luke 12 : 11, 12 } 21 : 14, 15 }	. . .
Matt. 10 : 21 .	. .	Mark 13 : 12	. . .	Luke 21 : 16	. . John 16 : 2
Matt. 10 : 22 } 24 : 9b, 13 }	. .	Mark 13 : 13	. . .	Luke 21 : 17, 19	. John 15 : 21
Matt. 10 : 24, 25a .	. . . . .			Luke 6 : 40	. . { John 13 : 16 15 : 20a }
Matt. 10 : 26 .	. . .	Mark 4 : 22	. . .	{ Luke 8 : 17 } 12 : 2 }	. . . .
Matt. 10 : 27–33	. . . . . .			Luke 12 : 3–9	. . . .
Matt. 10 : 30	. . . . . .			Luke 21 : 18	. . . .
Matt. 10 : 33 .	. . .	Mark 8 : 38	. . .	Luke 9 : 26	. . . .
Matt. 10 : 34–36	. . . . . .			Luke 12 : 51–53	. . . .
Matt. 10 : 37 .	. . . . . .			Luke 14 : 26	. . . .
Matt. 10 : 38 } 16 : 24 }	. .	Mark 8 : 34	. . .	{ Luke 14 : 27 } 9 : 23 }	. . .
Matt. 10 : 39 } 16 : 25 }	. .	Mark 8 : 35	. . .	{ Luke 17 : 33 } 9 : 24 }	. . John 12 : 25
Matt. 10 : 40 } 18 : 5 }	. .	Mark 9 : 37	. . .	{ Luke 10 : 16 } 9 : 48 }	. . John 13 : 20
Matt. 10 : 42	. .	Mark 9 : 41	. . . .		

§ 68. DISCOURSE ON THE BREAD OF LIFE.

| Matt. 11 : 27b | . . . . | | | Luke 10 : 22b | . . . John 6 : 46 |

§ 69. DISCOURSE ON EATING WITH UNWASHEN HANDS.

| Matt. 15 : 14b . | . . . . | | | Luke 6 : 39 | . . . . . |

§ 73. The Pharisees and Sadducees Demanding a Sign from Heaven.

Matt. **16 : 2, 3**		Luke 12 : 54–56
Matt. **16 : 4** 12 : 39	Mark **8 : 12**	Luke 11 : 29
Matt. **16 : 6** 16 : 11*b*	Mark **8 : 15**	Luke 12 : 1*b*

§ 75. Peter's Confession.

Matt. **16 : 19***b* 18 : 18	John 20 : 23

§ 76. Christ Foretells His Death and Resurrection.

Matt. **16 : 21**	Mark **8 : 31**	Luke **9 : 22** 17 : 25	
Matt. **16 : 24** 10 : 38	Mark **8 : 34**	Luke **9 : 23** 14 : 27	
Matt. **16 : 25** 10 : 39	Mark **8 : 35**	Luke **9 : 24** 17 : 33	John 12 : 25
Matt. 10 : 33	Mark **8 : 38**	Luke **9 : 26** 12 : 9	

§ 78. The Demoniac Boy.

Matt. **17 : 20** 21 : 21	Mark 11 : 22, 23	Luke 17 : 6

§ 81. Discourse on Humility and Forgiveness.

Matt. **18 : 3**	Mark 10 : 15	Luke 18 : 17	
Matt. 23 : 11 20 : 26, 27	Mark **9 : 35** 10 : 43*b*, 44	Luke **9 : 48***b* 22 : 26*b*	
Matt. **18 : 5** 10 : 40	Mark **9 : 37**	Luke **9 : 48***a* 10 : 16	John 13 : 20
Matt. 10 : 42	Mark **9 : 41**		
Matt. **18 : 6**	Mark **9 : 42**	Luke 17 : 2	
Matt. **18 : 7**		Luke 17 : 1	
Matt. **18 : 8, 9** 5 : 29, 30	Mark **9 : 43–47**		
Matt. 5 : 13*a*	Mark **9 : 50***a*	Luke 14 : 34	
Matt. **18 : 12–14**		Luke 15 : 4–7	
Matt. **18 : 15**		Luke 17 : 3	
Matt. **18 : 18** 16 : 19			John 20 : 23
Matt. **18 : 21, 22**		Luke 17 : 4	
Matt. **18 : 35** 6 : 15			

§ 87. The Mission of the Seventy.

Matt. 9:37, 38		Luke 10:2	
Matt. 10:7–16	Mark 6:8–11	{ Luke 10:3–12 } { 9:3–5 }	
Matt. 11:21–24		Luke 10:12–15	
Matt. 10:40 } 18:5 }	Mark 9:37	{ Luke 10:16 } { 9:48a }	John 13:20
	Mark 16:18	Luke 10:19	
Matt. 11:25–27		Luke 10:21, 22	
Matt. 11:27a } 28:18 }		Luke 10:22a	
Matt. 11:27b		Luke 10:22b	John 6:46
Matt. 13:16, 17		Luke 10:23, 24	

§ 93. Discourse on Prayer.

Matt. 6:9–13	Luke 11:2–4
Matt. 7:7–11	Luke 11:9–13

§ 94. Discourses against the Pharisees.

Matt. 12:25, 26	Mark 3:23–26	Luke 11:17, 18
Matt. 12:27, 28		Luke 11:19, 20
Matt. 12:29	Mark 3:27	Luke 11:21, 22
Matt. 12:30		Luke 11:23
Matt. 12:43–45a		Luke 11:24–26
Matt. 12:38–42		Luke 11:29–32
Matt. 12:39 } 16:4 }	Mark 8:12	Luke 11:29
Matt. 5:15	Mark 4:21	{ Luke 11:33 } { 8:16 }
Matt. 6:22, 23		Luke 11:34–36
Matt. 23:25, 26		Luke 11:39–41
Matt. 23:23		Luke 11:42
Matt. 23:6, 7	Mark 12:38, 39	{ Luke 11:43 } { 20:46 }
Matt. 23:27		Luke 11:44
Matt. 23:4		Luke 11:46b
Matt. 23:29, 31		Luke 11:47, 48
Matt. 23:34–36		Luke 11:49–51
Matt. 23:13		Luke 11:52

§ 95. Teachings concerning Trust in God and Coming Judgment.

Matt. 16:6 16:11*b* } . . .	Mark 8:15 . . .	Luke 12:1 . . . . .
Matt. 10:26*b* . . .	Mark 4:22 . . .	{ Luke 12:2 8:17 } . . . . . .
Matt. 10:27–32		Luke 12:3–8 . . . . .
Matt. 10:30		{ Luke 12:7*a* 21:18 } . . . . . .
Matt. 10:33	Mark 8:38 . .	{ Luke 9:26 12:9 } . . . . . .
Matt. 12:31, 32 . . .	Mark 3:28, 29 . .	Luke 12:10 . . . . . .
Matt. 10:19, 20 . . .	Mark 13:11 . .	{ Luke 12:11, 12 21:14, 15 } . . . . .
Matt. 6:25–33		Luke 12:22–31 . . . . .
Matt. 6:8, 32		Luke 12:30 . . . . . .
Matt. 6:19–21		Luke 12:33, 34 . . . . .
Matt. 24:43, 44		Luke 12:39, 40 . . . . .
Matt. 24:45–51		Luke 12:42–46 . . . . .
. . . . .	Mark 10:39*b* . .	Luke 12:50*a* . . . . .
Matt. 10:34–36		Luke 12:51–53 . . . . .
Matt. 16:2, 3		Luke 12:54–56 . . . . .
Matt. 5:25, 26		Luke 12:58, 59 . . . . .

§ 97. The Woman Healed on a Sabbath.

Matt. 13:31, 32 . . .	Mark 4:30–32 . . .	Luke 13:18, 19 . . . . .
Matt. 13:33		Luke 13:20, 21 . . . . .

§ 98. The Question whether Few are Saved.

Matt. 7:13, 14		Luke 13:24 . . . . . .
Matt. 25:11*b*, 12		Luke 13:25*b* . . . . . .
Matt. 7:23		Luke 13:27 . . . . . .
Matt. 8:11, 12		Luke 13:28, 29 . . . . .
Matt. 13:42 13:50 22:13*b* } 24:51 25:30		Luke 13:28 . . . . . .
Matt. 19:30 20:16 } . . .	Mark 10:31 . . .	Luke 13:30 . . . . . .

§ 99. Reply to the Warning Against Herod.

Matt. 23:37–39		Luke 13:34, 35 . . . . .

§ 100. Discourse at a Chief Pharisee's Table.

Matt. 12:11	. . . .	Luke **14:5**	. . . . .
Matt. 23:12	. . . .	{ Luke **14:11** } { 18:14*b* }	. . . .
Matt. 22:1–10	. . . .	Luke **14:15–24**	. . . . .

§ 101. Discourse on Counting the Cost.

Matt. 10:37	. . . . . .	Luke **14:26**	. . . . .
Matt. 10:38 } 16:24 }	. . Mark **8:34** . .	{ Luke **14:27** } { 9:23 }	. . . . .
Matt. 5:13	. . Mark **9:50** . .	Luke **14:34, 35***a*	. . . .
Matt. 11:15 } 13:9 } 13:43*b* }	. . { Mark **4:9** } { 4:23 }	. . { Luke **14:35***b* } { 8:8*b* }	. . . .

§ 102. Three Parables of Grace.

Matt. 18:12–14	. . . .	Luke **15:4–7**	. . . . .

§ 103. Two Parables of Warning.

Matt. 6:24	. . . .	Luke **16:13**	. . . . .
Matt. 11:12, 13	. . . . . .	Luke **16:16**	. . . . .
Matt. 5:18	. . . .	Luke **16:17**	. . . . .
Matt. 5:32 } 19:9 }	. . Mark **10:11** . .	Luke **16:18**	. . . . .

§ 104. Concerning Forgiveness and Faith.

Matt. 18:7	. . . .	Luke **17:1**	. . . . .
Matt. 18:6	. . Mark **9:42** . .	Luke **17:2**	. . . . .
Matt. 18:15	. . . .	Luke **17:3**	. . . . .
Matt. 18:21, 22	. . . . . .	Luke **17:4**	. . . . .
Matt. 17:20 } 21:21 }	. . Mark **11:22, 23** . .	Luke **17:6**	. . . . .

§ 108. The Coming of the Kingdom.

Matt. 24:26, 27	. . . . . .	Luke **17:23, 24**	. . . .	
Matt. 16:21	. . Mark **8:31** . .	{ Luke **9:22** } { 17:25 }	. . . .	
Matt. 24:37–39	. . . . . .	Luke **17:26, 27**	. . . .	
Matt. 10:39 } 16:25 }	. . Mark **8:35** . .	{ Luke **17:33** } { 9:24 }	-	John 12:25 .
Matt. 24:40, 41	. . . . . .	Luke **17:34, 35**	. . . .	
Matt. 24:28	. . . . . .	Luke **17:37***b*	. . . .	

§ 109. THE PHARISEE AND THE PUBLICAN.

Matt. 23:12 . . . . $\left\{\begin{array}{l}\text{Luke } 14:11\\18:14b\end{array}\right\}$ . . . . . .

§ 110. CONCERNING DIVORCE.

Matt. $\left.\begin{array}{l}19:9\\5:32\end{array}\right\}$ . . . Mark 10:11 . . . Luke 16:18 . . . . . .

§ 111. CHRIST BLESSING LITTLE CHILDREN.

Matt. 18:3 . . . . Mark 10:15 . . . Luke 18:17 . . . . . .

§ 112. THE RICH YOUNG RULER.

Matt. 19:28b . . . . Luke 22:30b . . . . . .

Matt. $\left.\begin{array}{l}19:30\\20:16\end{array}\right\}$ . . . Mark 10:31 . . . Luke 13:30 . . . . .

§ 114. AMBITION OF JAMES AND JOHN.

. . . . . Mark 10:39b . . . Luke 12:50a .

Matt. 20:25–27 . . . Mark 10:42–44 . . . Luke 22:25, 26 . . . . .

Matt. $\left.\begin{array}{l}20:26b, 27\\23:11\end{array}\right\}$. $\left\{\begin{array}{l}\text{Mark } 10:43b, 44\\9:35\end{array}\right\}$ . . $\left\{\begin{array}{l}\text{Luke } 9:48b\\22:26b\end{array}\right\}$ . . . .

§ 117. PARABLE OF THE MINÆ.

Matt. $\left.\begin{array}{l}13:12\\25:29\end{array}\right\}$ . . . Mark 4:25 . . . $\left\{\begin{array}{l}\text{Luke } 19:26\\8:18b\end{array}\right\}$ . . . . .

§ 122. THE FIG TREE WITHERED AWAY.

Matt. $\left.\begin{array}{l}21:21\\17:20\end{array}\right\}$ . . . Mark 11:22, 23 . . Luke 17:6 . . . . . .

Matt. $\left.\begin{array}{l}6:14, 15\\18:35\end{array}\right\}$ . . . Mark 11:25 . . . .

§ 124. THREE PARABLES OF WARNING.

Matt. 22:1–10 . . . . Luke 14:15–24 . . . . . .

Matt. $\left.\begin{array}{l}22:13b\\8:12\\13:42\\13:50\\24:51\\25:30\end{array}\right\}$ . . . . Luke 13:28 . . . . .

§ 125. THREE QUESTIONS BY THE JEWISH RULERS.

Matt. $\left.\begin{array}{l}22:40\\7:12b\end{array}\right\}$ . . . .

§ 127. WOES AGAINST THE SCRIBES AND PHARISEES.

Matt. 23:4 . . . . Luke 11:46b . . . . . .

Matt. 23:6, 7 . . . Mark 12:38, 39 . . $\left\{\begin{array}{l}\text{Luke } 20:46b\\11:43\end{array}\right\}$ . . . . .

Matt. **23:11** 20:26*b*, 27 }	.	{ Mark 9:35 10:43*b*, 44 } . .	{ Luke 9:48*b* } 22:26*b* . . . . . .
Matt. **23:12**			{ Luke 14:11 } 18:14*b* . . . . .
Matt. **23:13**		Luke 11:52 . . . . . .
Matt. **23:23**		Luke 11:42 . . . . . .
Matt. **23:25, 26**		Luke 11:39–41 . . . . .
Matt. **23:27**		Luke 11:44 . . . . . .
Matt. **23:29, 31**		Luke 11:47, 48 . . . . . –
Matt. **23:34–36** . . . . –		Luke 11:49–51 . . . . .
Matt. **23:37–39**		Luke 13:34, 35 . . . . .

§ 129. Gentiles Seeking Jesus.

Matt. 10:39 } 16:25 } . . .	Mark 8:35 . . .	{ Luke 17:33 } 9:24 } . .	. John 12:25 .
Matt. 26:38*a* . . .	Mark 14:34*a*	Luke 22:42 . . .	John 12:27*a* .
Matt. 26:39 . . .	Mark 14:36 . . .	Luke 22:42 . . .	John 12:27*b*,28*a* .

§ 131. Discourse concerning the Destruction of Jerusalem and the End of the World.

Matt. **24:9*a*** } 10:17, 18 } . . .	Mark **13:9** . . .	Luke **21:12, 13** . . .	.
Matt. 10:19, 20 . . .	Mark **13:11** . . .	{ Luke **21:14, 15** } 12:11, 12 } . . .	. .
Matt. 10:21 . . .	Mark **13:12** . . .	Luke **21:16** . . .	John 16:2 . .
Matt. **24:9*b*** } 10:22*a* } . .	Mark **13:13*a*** . . .	Luke **21:17** . . .	John 15:21 .
Matt. 10:30		{ Luke **21:18** } 12:7*a* } . .	.
Matt. **24:13** } 10:22*b* } . .	Mark **13:13*b*** . . .	Luke **21:19** . . .	.
Matt. **24:23** . . .	Mark **13:21** . . .	Luke 17:23 . . .	.
Matt. **24:26, 27**		Luke 17:23, 24 . . .	.
Matt. **24:28**		Luke 17:37*b* . . .	.
Matt. **24:37–39**		Luke 17:26, 27 . . .	.
Matt. **24:40, 41**		Luke 17:34, 35 . . .	.
Matt. **24:43, 44**		Luke 12:39, 40 . . .	.
Matt. **24:45–51**		Luke 12:42–46 . . .	.
Matt. **24:51** } 25:30 } 8:12 } 13:42 } 13:50 } 22:13*b* }		{ Luke 13:28 } 12:46 }	.
Matt. **25:11*b*, 12**		Luke 13:25*b*	.
Matt. 25:29 } 13:12 } . . .	Mark 4:25 . . .	{ Luke 8:18*b* } 19:26 } . . .	. . .

§ 133. The Last Supper.

Matt. 10:24 .	. . . .		Luke 6:40 . . . ⎰ John **13:16** .	⎱ **15:20**
Matt. 10:40 ⎱ 18:5 ⎰	. . . Mark 9:37 . . . ⎰ Luke 10:16 ⎱ ⎱ 9:48*a* ⎰		. . John **13:20** .	
Matt. 20:25–27 .	. . Mark 10:42–44 . . .	Luke 22:25, 26	. . . . .
Matt. 23:11 ⎱ 20:26*b*, 27 ⎰	. ⎰ Mark 9:35 ⎱ ⎱ 10:43*b*, 44 ⎰ . . . ⎰ Luke 22:26*b* ⎱ ⎱ 9:48*b* ⎰		. . . . .	
Matt. 19:28*b* .	. . . .	Luke 22:30*b* .	. . . . .

§ 134. Christ's Farewell Discourses.

Matt. 10:24 .	. . . .		Luke 6:40 . . . ⎰ John **13:16** .	⎱ **15:20**
Matt. 10:22*a* ⎱ 24:9*b* ⎰	. . . Mark 13:13*a* . . .	Luke 21:17	. . John **15:21** .
Matt. 10:21 .	. . . Mark 13:12 . . .	Luke 21:16	. . John **16:2** . .

§ 136. The Agony in Gethsemane.

Matt. **26:38***a*	. . . Mark 14:34*a*	. .	. . John 12:27*a* . .
Matt. **26:39**	. . . Mark 14:36 . . .	Luke **22:42** .	. . John 12:27*b*, 28*a*

§ 146. The Appearance to the Disciples in Jerusalem.

Matt. 16:19 ⎱ 18:18 ⎰	. . . .		. . John **20:23** .

§ 149. The Appearance to the Eleven on a Mountain in Galilee.

Matt. **28:18** ⎱ 11:27*a* ⎰	. . . .	Luke 10:22*a* . . .	. (Cf. John 17:2)
. . . . .	. Mark **16:16** . . .	. . . .	. John 3:18 .
. . . . .	. Mark **16:18** . . .	Luke 10:19 .	. . . . .

APPENDIX III.

OLD TESTAMENT QUOTATIONS AND ALLUSIONS IN THE GOSPELS
IN THE ORDER OF THEIR OCCURRENCE IN THE HARMONY.[1]

SECTION.				
4			e Luke 1:15	Num. 6:3
4			e Luke 1:17	Mal. 4:5, 6
5		[2] Cf. § 112	e Luke 1:37	Gen. 18:14
6	b Matt. 1:23			Isa. 7:14
7			e Luke 1:46, 47	1 Sam. 2:1
7			e Luke 1:48	1 Sam. 1:11
7			e Luke 1:50	Ps. 103:17
7			e Luke 1:51	Ps. 89:10
7			e Luke 1:52	Job 12:19 ⎫
				Job 5:11 ⎬
				1 Sam. 2:7, 8 ⎭
7			e Luke 1:53	Ps. 107:9 ⎫
				1 Sam. 2:5 ⎭
7			e Luke 1:54, 55	Isa. 41:8, 9
7			e Luke 1:55; cf. § 8	Mic. 7:20
8			e Luke 1:68	Ps. 72:18 ⎫
				Ps. 111:9 ⎭
8			e Luke 1:69	1 Sam. 2:10
8			e Luke 1:71	Ps. 106:10
8			e Luke 1:72; cf. § 7	Ps. 105:8, 9 ⎫
				Mic. 7:20 ⎭
8		Cf. § 18	e Luke 1:76	Mal. 3:1
8			e Luke 1:79	Isa. 9:2
12			d Luke 2:22	Lev. 12:6

[1] The significance of the superior letters prefixed to the citations is as follows:

a Express quotations (i. e., quotations introduced by a formula designating them as quotations), occurring in the language of Jesus.

b Express quotations, occurring in the language of the gospel writer.

c Express quotations, occurring in the language of others.

d Allusions to Old Testament events, laws, etc., without definite quotation.

e Employment of Old Testament language without express designation of it as quoted.

[2] This and other cross-references of a similar form indicate that the Old Testament passage opposite which the cross-reference stands is also quoted in the section to which the cross-reference refers.

SECTION.				
12		ᵇ Luke 2:23		Ex. 13:12
12		ᵇ Luke 2:24		Lev. 12:8 ⎫
				Cf. Lev. 5:11 ⎬
12		ᵉ Luke 2:30, 31		Isa. 52:10
12		ᵉ Luke 2:32		Isa. 42:6 ⎫
				Isa. 49:6 ⎬
13	ᶜ Matt. 2:6		Cf. § 82	Mic. 5:2
14	ᵇ Matt. 2:15			Hos. 11:1
14	ᵇ Matt. 2:18			Jer. 31:15
14	ᵇ Matt. 2:23			Isa. 11:1(?)
17		ᵉ Luke 2:52		1 Sam. 2:26
18		ᵇ Mark 1:2	Cf. §§ 8, 52	Mal. 3:1
18	ᵇ Matt. 3:3	ᵇ Mark 1:3	ᵇ Luke 3:4	Cf. § 21	Isa. 40:3
18			ᵇ Luke 3:5, 6	Isa. 40:4, 5
20	ᵃ Matt. 4:4		ᵃ Luke 4:4	Deut. 8:3
20	ᶜ Matt. 4:6		ᶜ Luke 4:10, 11	Ps. 91:11, 12
20	ᵃ Matt. 4:7		ᵃ Luke 4:12	Deut. 6:16
20	ᵃ Matt. 4:10		ᵃ Luke 4:8	Deut. 6:13
21	Cf. § 18		ᶜ John 1:23	Isa. 40:3
24			ᵉ John 1:51	Gen. 28:12
27			ᵇ John 2:17	Ps. 69:9
34	ᵇ Matt. 4:15, 16			Isa. 9:1, 2
36			ᵃ Luke 4:18, 19; cf. vs. 21	Isa. 61:1, 2
36			ᵈ Luke 4:26	1 Kings 17:9
36			ᵈ Luke 4:27	2 Kings 5:1, 14
39	ᵇ Matt. 8:17			Isa. 53:4
40	ᵈ Matt. 8:4	ᵈ Mark 1:44	ᵈ Luke 5:14; cf. § 107	Lev. 13:49
42	ᵃ Matt. 9:13; cf. § 45			Hos. 6:6
45	ᵈ Matt. 12:3, 4	ᵈ Mark 2:25, 26	ᵈ Luke 6:3, 4	1 Sam. 21:6
45	ᵈ Matt. 12:5			Num. 28:9, 10
45	ᵃ Matt. 12:7; cf. § 42			Hos. 6:6
47	ᵇ Matt. 12:18–21			Isa. 42:1–4
49	ᵉ Matt. 5:5			Ps. 37:11
49	ᵃ Matt. 5:21			Ex. 20:13 ⎫
				Deut. 5:17 ⎬
49	ᵃ Matt. 5:27			Ex. 20:14 ⎫
				Deut. 5:18 ⎬
49	ᵃ Matt. 5:31			Deut. 24:1

SECTION.

49	ᵃMatt. 5 : 33			Lev. 19:12 ⎫ Deut. 23:21 ⎬ Num. 30:2 ⎭
49	ᵉMatt. 5 : 34			Isa. 66:1
49	ᵉMatt. 5 : 35			Ps. 48:2
49	ᵃMatt. 5 : 38			Ex. 21:24 ⎫ Deut. 19:21 ⎬
49	ᵃMatt. 5 : 43a	Cf. §§ 88, 112, 125		Lev. 19:18
49	ᵃMatt. 5 : 43b			Deut. 23:6 ⎫ Deut. 25:19 ⎬
49	ᵉMatt. 7 : 23	Cf. § 98		Ps. 6:8
52	ᵉMatt. 11 : 5	ᵉLuke 7 : 22		Isa. 61:1
52	ᵃMatt. 11 : 10	Cf. §§ 8, 18	ᵃLuke 7 : 27;	Mal. 3:1
52	ᵉMatt. 11 : 23a	Cf. § 87		Isa. 14:13, 15
52	ᵈMatt. 11 : 23b		⸴	Gen. 19:24
52	ᵉMatt. 11 : 29			Jer. 6:16
55	ᵈMatt. 12 : 39, 40			Jon. 1:17
55	ᵈMatt. 12 : 41	Cf. § 94		Jon. 3:5, 10
55	ᵈMatt. 12 : 42	Cf. § 94		1 Kings 10:1 ff.
57	ᵉMatt. 13 : 13	ᵉMark 4 : 12 · ᵉLuke 8 : 10 · Cf. § 130		Isa. 6:9, 10
57	ᵃ ᵒʳ ᵇMatt. 13 : 14, 15			Isa. 6:9, 10
57		ᵉMark 4 : 29		Joel 3:13
57	ᵉMatt. 13 : 32	ᵉMark 4 : 32 · Cf. § 97		Dan. 4:12, 21
57	ᵇMatt. 13 : 35			Ps. 78:2
64	ᵉMatt. 9 : 36	Cf. § 66		Num. 27:17 ⎫ Ezek. 34:5 ⎬
64	ᵉMatt. 10 : 35	Cf. § 131 · Cf. § 95		Mic. 7:6
66	Cf. § 64	ᵉMark 6 : 34		Num. 27:17 ⎫ Ezek. 34:5 ⎬
68			ᵈJohn 6 : 31a	Ex. 16:15
68			ᶜJohn 6 : 31b	Ex. 16:4 ⎫ Ps. 78:24, 25 ⎬
68			ᵃJohn 6 : 45	Isa. 54:13
69	ᵃMatt. 15 : 8, 9	ᵃMark 7 : 6, 7		Isa. 29:13
69	ᵃMatt. 15 : 4	ᵃMark 7 : 10 · Cf. § 112		Ex. 20:12 ⎫ Deut. 5:16 ⎬ Ex. 21:17 ⎭
73		ᵉMark 8 : 18		Jer. 5:21
76	ᵉMatt. 16 : 27			Ps. 62:12 ⎫ Prov. 24:12 ⎬

SECTION.					
77	ᵈ Matt. 17:11	ᵈ Mark 9:12			Mal. 4:5, 6
81		ᵉ Mark 9:48			Isa. 66:24
81	ᵉ Matt. 18:16				Deut. 19:15
82				ᵈ John 7:22, 23	Lev. 12:3
82	Cf. § 13			ᵉ John 7:42	Mic. 5:2
86			ᵉ Luke 9:54		2 Kings 1:10
87	Cf. § 52		ᵉ Luke 10:15		Isa. 14:13, 15
88		Cf. § 125	ᶜ Luke 10:27a		Deut. 6:5
88	Cf. §§ 49, 112, 125		ᶜ Luke 10:27b		Lev. 19:18
88			ᵉ Luke 10:28		Lev. 18:5
91				ᵉ John 10:16	Ezek. 37:24 ⎱ Ezek. 34:23 ⎰
92				ᵃ John 10:34	Ps. 82:6
94	Cf. § 55		ᵈ Luke 11:31		1 Kings 10:1 ff.
94	Cf. § 55		ᵈ Luke 11:32		Jon. 3:5, 10
95	Cf. § 64	Cf. § 131	ᵉ Luke 12:53		Mic. 7:6
97	Cf. § 57		ᵉ Luke 13:19		Dan. 4:12, 21
98	Cf. § 49		ᵉ Luke 13:27		Ps. 6:8
99			ᵉ Luke 13:35a		Jer. 22:5 ⎱ Jer. 12:7 ⎰
99	Cf. § 119		ᵉ Luke 13:35b		Ps. 118:26
107	Cf. § 40		ᵈ Luke 17:14		Lev. 13:49
108			ᵈ Luke 17:27		Gen. 7:7
108			ᵈ Luke 17:29		Gen. 19:24
108			ᵈ Luke 17:32		Gen. 19:26
110	ᶜ Matt. 19:7	ᶜ Mark 10:4			Deut. 24:1
110	ᵃ Matt. 19:4	ᵉ Mark 10:6			Gen. 1:27
110	ᵃ ᵒʳ ᵉ Matt. 19:5	ᵉ Mark 10:7, 8			Gen. 2:24
112	ᵃ Matt. 19:18	ᵃ Mark 10:19a	ᵃ Luke 18:20a		Ex. 20:13–16 ⎱ Deut. 5:17–20 ⎰
112	ᵃ Matt. 19:19a	ᵃ Mark 10:19b	ᵃ Luke 18:20b		Ex. 20:12 ⎱ Deut. 5:16 ⎰
112	ᵃ Matt. 19:19b	Cf. §§ 49, 88, 125			Lev. 19:18
112	ᵉ Matt. 19:26	ᵉ Mark 10:27	ᵉ Luke 18:27; cf. § 5		Gen. 18:14 ⎱ Job 42:2 ⎰
116			ᵉ Luke 19:10		Ezek. 34:16
119	ᵇ Matt. 21:5a				Isa. 62:11
119	ᵇ Matt. 21:5b			ᵇ John 12:15	Zech. 9:9
119	ᵉ Matt. 21:9	ᵉ Mark 11:9, 10	ᵉ Luke 19:38; . cf. § 99	ᵉ John 12:13	Ps. 118:25, 26

APPENDIX III

SECTION.				
119			e Luke 19:44	Ps. 137:9
121	a Matt. 21:13a	a Mark 11:17a	a Luke 19:46a	Isa. 56:7
121	e Matt. 21:13b	e Mark 11:17b	e Luke 19:46b	Jer. 7:11
121	a Matt. 21:16			Ps. 8:2
124	e Matt. 21:33	e Mark 12:1	e Luke 20:9	Isa. 5:1, 2
124	a Matt. 21:42	a Mark 12:10, 11	a Luke 20:17	Ps. 118:22, 23
125	c Matt. 22:24	c Mark 12:19	c Luke 20:28	Deut. 25:5
125	a Matt. 22:32	a Mark 12:26	a Luke 20:37	Ex. 3:6
125		a Mark 12:29; cf. vs. 32		Deut. 6:4
125	a Matt. 22:37	a Mark 12:30	Cf. § 88	Deut. 6:5
125	a Matt. 22:39	a Mark 12:31; cf. §§ 49, 88, 112		Lev. 19:18
125		e Mark 12:32a; cf. vs. 29		Deut. 6:4
125		e Mark 12:32b		Deut. 4:35
125		e Mark 12:33a	Cf. § 88	Deut. 6:5
125	Cf. §§ 49, 88, 112	e Mark 12:33b		Lev. 19:18 ⎫ 1 Sam. 15:22 ⎭
126	a Matt. 22:44; cf. §§ 138, 150	a Mark 12:36	a Luke 20:42, 43	Ps. 110:1
127	e Matt. 23:38		Cf. § 99	Jer. 22:5 ⎫ Jer. 12:7 ⎭
127	e Matt. 23:39		Cf. §§ 99, 119	Ps. 118:26
129	Cf. § 136			e John 12:27	Ps. 42:6
130				b John 12:38	Isa. 53:1
130	Cf. § 57			b John 12:40	Isa. 6:10
131	e Matt. 24:7	e Mark 13:8	e Luke 21:10	Isa. 19:2
131	Cf. § 64	e Mark 13:12	Cf. § 95	Mic. 7:6
131	a Matt. 24:15	e Mark 13:14		Dan. 11:31 ⎫ Dan. 12:11 ⎬ 1 Macc. 1:54 ⎭
131	e Matt. 24:21	e Mark 13:19		Dan. 12:1
131	e Matt. 24:24	e Mark 13:22		Deut. 13:1
131	e Matt. 24:29	e Mark 13:24, 25	e Luke 21:26	Isa. 13:10 ⎫ Ezek. 32:7, 8 ⎬ Am. 8:9 ⎭
131	e Matt. 24:30a			Zech. 12:12
131	e Matt. 24:30b	e Mark 13:26	e Luke 21:27; cf. § 138	Dan. 7:13
131	d Matt. 24:38			Gen. 7:7
131	e Matt. 25:31			Zech. 14:5

276

SECTION.					
131	ᵉ Matt. 25:46				Dan. 12:2
132	ᵉ Matt. 26:15				Zech. 11:12
133		ᵉ Mark 14:18		ᵃ John 13:18	Ps. 41:9
133	ᵉ Matt. 26:28a	ᵉ Mark 14:24a	ᵉ Luke 22:20a		Ex. 24:8 ⎫
					Zech. 9:11 ⎬
					Jer. 31:31 ⎭
133	ᵉ Matt. 26:28b	ᵉ Mark 14:24b	ᵉ Luke 22:20b		Lev. 4:18, 20
133	ᵃ Matt. 26:31	ᵃ Mark 14:27			Zech. 13:7
134			ᵃ Luke 22:37		Isa. 53:12
134				ᵃ John 15:25	Ps. 35:19 ⎫
					Ps. 69:4 ⎬
134				ᵉ John 16:22	Isa. 66:14
136	ᵉ Matt. 26:38	ᵉ Mark 14:34		Cf. § 129	Ps. 42:6
138	ᵉ Matt. 26:64	ᵉ Mark 14:62; cf. §§ 126, 150	ᵉ Luke 22:69; cf. § 131		Dan. 7:13 ⎫
					Ps. 110:1 ⎬
138	ᵇ Matt. 27:9				Zech. 11:13
140			ᵉ Luke 23:30		Hos. 10:8
140	ᵉ Matt. 27:34; cf. vs. 48		ᵉ Luke 23:36		Ps. 69:21
140	ᵉ Matt. 27:35	ᵉ Mark 15:24	ᵉ Luke 23:34	ᵇ John 19:24	Ps. 22:18
140	ᵉ Matt 27:39	ᵉ Mark 15:29	ᵉ Luke 23:35		Ps. 22:7
140	ᵉ Matt. 27:43				Ps. 22:8
140	ᵉ Matt. 27:46	ᶜ Mark 15:34			Ps. 22:1
140	ᵉ Matt. 27:48; c . vs. 34	ᵉ Mark 15:36		ᵇ John 19:28, 29	Ps. 69:21
140			ᵉ Luke 23:46		Ps. 31:5
140				ᵇ John 19:36	Ex. 12:46 ⎫
					Num. 9:12 ⎬
					Ps. 34:20 ⎭
140				ᵇ John 19:37	Zech. 12:10
150	Cf. §§ 126, 138	ᵉ Mark 16:19			Ps. 110:1

APPENDIX IV.

SUGGESTIONS TO TEACHERS AND STUDENTS.

THE aim determines the method. The Life of Christ is a chapter of the world's history, and is to be studied first of all historically. The object of the study which the present Harmony is designed to facilitate is to gain a knowledge of the events of the life of Jesus as these are presented to us in the four gospels, and to form a true conception of the historical relations of this life. In other words, it aims to read this life in the true relation of its events to each other, and against the background of the history of the times. To accomplish this:—

1. *Study the historical background.* The gospel writers assume that their readers have some knowledge of the times of which they write. Such knowledge we must acquire, if we would read the gospel history intelligently. In particular:—

a) Become acquainted with the history of the New Testament period, not only of the Roman government and the Gentile world in general, but especially of Jewish life and thought in Palestine. A bare skeleton of the leading events of Jewish history is shown in the table on pp. 281, 282, and the diagram on p. 283. This skeleton should be filled out by further reading.

b) Study the geography of Palestine, becoming familiar with its main physical features, its political divisions, its chief localities.

2. *Memorize the material.* The facts of this history are by reason of their transcendent importance well worthy of all necessary effort to fix them in memory. Moreover, the facts appear in their true relations only to him who has acquired an easy command of them as facts. In particular:—

a) Learn the full title of each of the nine Parts into which the life of Jesus is divided in the Outline. Let this be done at the outset, thus fixing in mind at the beginning the general framework of the whole gospel narrative.

b) As you take up each Part or chapter, learn the order of events in that Part or chapter. Some will perhaps prefer to learn only the chapter-titles, others only the section-titles. Better than either of these is to learn both chapter-titles and section-titles.

c) From the Scripture passages cited under each section, master the historical substance of the section—all the more important facts therein narrated. Where there are two or more accounts it is best to select the narrative of one of the gospels as the basis, and then compare the other accounts with this one. Except in the case of brief passages of special importance it is not necessary to commit the passage to memory verbally. What is important to fix in mind is not the words, but the facts. Of the long discourses only the central thought or general outline can be learned in this study.

3. *Organize the material.* History is not a succession of disconnected events, but an organic unity. It is this unity which we seek to construct. In particular:—

a) Connect the successive events together as far as possible into a continuous narrative.

b) Locate each event geographically, and trace the journeys of Jesus from point to point.

c) Make frequent reviews from the beginning, especially by naming in order the Parts, chapters, and sections, and by tracing the movements of Jesus by means of a map.

d) Endeavor as a result of these various lines of study to acquire a clearly defined conception of the external life of our Lord in its historical setting, in its chronological order, and in its organic unity, and, so far as may be, of the inner life also—his mental and spiritual history.

Observe that this task, though large, has its limits. The interpretation of Christ's discourses as such, the formulation of his doctrines, the application of his principles to questions of personal duty and of modern life, are tasks for which our present study will lay secure foundations, but which are not included in the study of the Life of Christ, as that study is now ordinarily defined.

The table of Sayings of Christ assigned by the evangelists to more than one historical situation, pp. 262–271, will be useful chiefly in this advanced study of the teaching of Christ.

4. Finally, and above all, seek for spiritual sympathy with this unique person, and for spiritual insight into this unique history. The Life of Christ is biography; it is even more truly history—the history of a great spiritual achievement. Alike as biography and as history, it demands for its true understanding sympathy and insight. The life of the poet and the career of the statesman can be understood only by him who brings to the study of them some measure of sympathy with the person whose life is studied, some power of insight into his plan and work. It is not less true respecting Jesus Christ. The life and work of him who spake as never man spake, and lived as never man lived, reveal their true meaning only to him who comes to their study with a mind open to the beauty and power of the life, and to the grandeur of its far-reaching plan for the redemption of our race.

APPENDIX V.

PRINCIPAL DIVISIONS OF THE LIFE OF CHRIST

WITH CALENDAR DATES.

NOTE.—The chronology of the life of Christ cannot be definitely fixed throughout. The date of our Lord's birth cannot be later than the early part of B. C. 4, nor much earlier. With a somewhat less degree of certainty A. D. 30 is fixed as the year of the crucifixion. Respecting the length of the public ministry, especially as between the so-called tripaschal and quadripaschal schemes, there is decided disagreement among authorities. On the tripaschal theory there were but three passovers in the course of the ministry of Christ, and its length was about two and a half years. On the quadripaschal theory there were four passovers, and the ministry was about three and a half years in length.

The Harmony is constructed independently of any chronological theory. For the convenience, however, of students whose study of the Life of Jesus will be facilitated by definitely relating its events to contemporary history, the following table is inserted. It shows the chronological limits of the various periods of the life of Christ on the basis of these three data, namely, the Birth not far from the end of B. C. 5 or the beginning of B. C. 4, the Crucifixion in A. D. 30, the Ministry occupying between three and four years.

PART   I.—**THE THIRTY YEARS OF PRIVATE LIFE:** From the Birth of Jesus until the Coming of John the Baptist. **From B. C. 5 to the Summer of A. D. 26.**

PART   II.—**THE OPENING EVENTS OF CHRIST'S MINISTRY:** From the Coming of John the Baptist until the Public Appearance of Jesus in Jerusalem. **From the Summer of A. D. 26 to the Passover, April 11, A. D. 27.**

PART   III.—**THE EARLY JUDEAN MINISTRY:** From the Public Appearance of Jesus in Jerusalem until his Return to Galilee. **From the Passover, April 11, A. D. 27, to December, A. D. 27.**

PART   IV.—**FIRST PERIOD OF THE GALILEAN MINISTRY:** From the Return to Galilee until the Choosing of the Twelve. **From December, A. D. 27, to early Summer, A. D. 28.**

PART   V.—**SECOND PERIOD OF THE GALILEAN MINISTRY:** From the Choosing of the Twelve until the Withdrawal into Northern Galilee. **From early Summer, A. D. 28, to the Passover, April 18, A. D. 29.**

PART   VI.—**THIRD PERIOD OF THE GALILEAN MINISTRY:** From the Withdrawal into Northern Galilee until the Final Departure for Jerusalem. **From the Passover, April 18, A. D. 29, to November, A. D. 29.**

PART VII.—**THE PEREAN MINISTRY:** From the Final Departure from Galilee until the Final Arrival at Jerusalem. **From November, A. D. 29, to the Sunday before the Passover, April 2, A. D. 30.**

PART VIII.—**THE PASSION WEEK:** From the Final Arrival at Jerusalem until the Resurrection. **From Sunday, April 2, to Sunday, April 9, A. D. 30.**

PART   IX.—**THE FORTY DAYS:** From the Resurrection until the Ascension. **From Sunday, April 9, to Thursday, May 18, A. D. 30.**

APPENDIX VI.

LEADING EVENTS OF JEWISH HISTORY

FROM THE RETURN FROM THE CAPTIVITY TO THE DESTRUCTION OF JERUSALEM BY THE ROMANS.

The Persian Period. 536-333 B. C.

536 B. C.	Return from Babylon under Zerubbabel.
459	Ezra comes to Jerusalem.
445	Nehemiah comes to Jerusalem.

The Greek Period. 333-142 B. C.

333	By Alexander's conquest of Persia, Palestine comes under Greek dominion.
323	In the division of Alexander's empire after his death Palestine falls to Syria, but is soon (320) seized by Ptolemy and added to Egypt.
320–203	Palestine is subject for the most part to Egypt, but frequent efforts are made by Syria to acquire it.
203–198	Antiochus III., the Great, makes an effort, at length successful, to wrest Palestine from Egypt and subject it to Syria.
175–104	Reign of Antiochus Epiphanes; he seeks by cruel persecution of the Jews to compel them to abandon their religion.
167	Mattathias the Asmonean raises a revolt against Antiochus.
166–142	Mattathias dying is succeeded as leader by his son Judas, surnamed the Maccabee, and Judas in turn by his brothers, Jonathan and Simon.
142	Under Simon, Palestine throws off the Syrian yoke.

Independence under the Asmoneans (Maccabees) 142-63 (circa) B. C.

141	The Jews declare Simon high priest and general and ethnarch, and make these offices hereditary.
142–135	Simon.
135–105	John Hyrcanus.
105–104	Aristobulus I., the first Asmonean who was called king.
104–78	Alexander Jannæus.

78–70 B. C. Queen Alexandra.

70 Queen Alexandra dying leaves two sons; Hyrcanus II., conquered by Aristobulus II. in battle, is compelled to surrender to him both the high-priestly and the civil power. Antipater, the Idumean, takes the side of Hyrcanus, and a struggle ensues.

70–63 Aristobulus II.

The Roman Period. 63 B. C.–70 A. D.

63 The Roman general Pompey, being appealed to by both Hyrcanus and Aristobulus, sides with Hyrcanus and Antipater, and captures Jerusalem.

63–40 Hyrcanus II.

47 Julius Cæsar appoints Antipater procurator of Judea, Hyrcanus ethnarch and high priest. Antipater is the real ruler.   He appoints his son Herod governor of Galilee.

40 Herod is appointed by the Roman Senate king of Judea.

37 Herod conquers Antigonus, son of Aristobulus II., captures Jerusalem and becomes king in fact.   Thus the Idumean dynasty supplants the Asmonean.

4 Death of Herod.   His kingdom is divided among his sons.

6 A. D. Archelaus, ethnarch of Judea, is banished; Judea becomes an equestrian province under a procurator.

34 Philip, tetrarch of northeastern Palestine, dies, and his territory is added to the Roman province of Syria.

37 Herod Agrippa I. receives the territories of Philip and Lysanias, and the title of king.

39 Herod Antipas is deposed and banished, and his territory (soon after) added to that of Agrippa.

41 Judea is also given to Agrippa; all Palestine is again under a Herodian prince.

44 Agrippa I. dies, and all Palestine is placed under a Roman procurator.

53 Agrippa II. receives the territories of Philip and Lysanias, and the title of king.   To this territory was afterward added a part of Galilee and Perea.   Southern Palestine remains under a Roman procurator.

66–73 Judeo-Roman War.

70 Destruction of Jerusalem by the Romans.

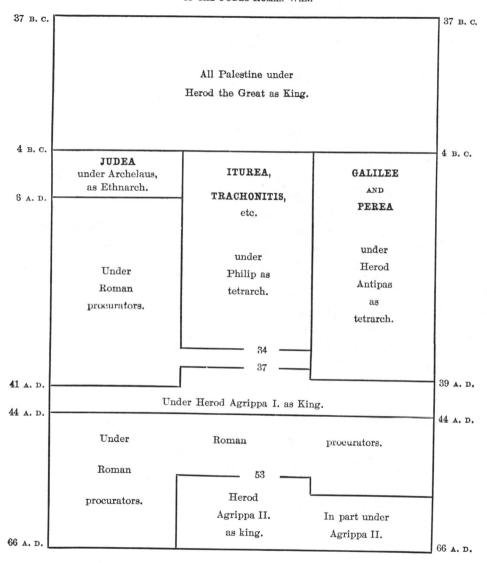